Renaissance Texts, Medieval Subjectivities

Medieval & Renaissance Literary Studies

General Editor

Rebecca Totaro

Editorial Board

Judith H. Anderson	Jonathan Gil Harris
Diana Treviño Benet	Margaret Healy
William C. Carroll	Ken Hiltner
Donald Cheney	Arthur F. Kinney
Ann Baynes Coiro	David Loewenstein
Mary T. Crane	Robert W. Maslen
Stephen B. Dobranski	Thomas P. Roche Jr.
Wendy Furman-Adams	Mary Beth Rose
A. C. Hamilton	Mihoko Suzuki
Hannibal Hamlin	Humphrey Tonkin
Margaret P. Hannay	Susanne Woods

Originally titled the *Duquesne Studies: Philological Series* (and later renamed the *Language & Literature Series*), the **Medieval & Renaissance Literary Studies Series** has been published by Duquesne University Press since 1960. This publishing endeavor seeks to promote the study of late medieval, Renaissance, and seventeenth century English literature by presenting scholarly and critical monographs, collections of essays, editions, and compilations. The series encourages a broad range of interpretation, including the relationship of literature and its cultural contexts, close textual analysis, and the use of contemporary critical methodologies.

Foster Provost	Albert C. Labriola	Richard J. DuRocher
EDITOR, 1960–1984	EDITOR, 1985–2009	EDITOR, 2010

Renaissance Texts, Medieval Subjectivities

Rethinking Petrarchan Desire from Wyatt to Shakespeare

Danila Sokolov

DUQUESNE UNIVERSITY PRESS
Pittsburgh, Pennsylvania

Copyright © 2017 Duquesne University Press
All rights reserved

Published in the United States of America by
DUQUESNE UNIVERSITY PRESS
600 Forbes Avenue
Pittsburgh, Pennsylvania 15282

No part of this book may be used or reproduced,
in any manner or form whatsoever,
without written permission from the publisher,
except in the case of short quotations
in critical articles or reviews.

Library of Congress Cataloging-in-Publication Data

Names: Sokolov, D. A. (Danila Alekseevich), author.
Title: Renaissance texts, medieval subjectivities : rethinking Petrarchan
  desire from Wyatt to Shakespeare / Danila A. Sokolov.
Description: Pittsburgh, Pennsylvania : Duquesne University Press, [2017] |
  Series: Medieval & renaissance literary studies | Includes bibliographical
references and index.
Identifiers: LCCN 2016046672 | ISBN 9780820704975 (cloth : alk. paper)
Subjects: LCSH: English literature—Early modern, 1500–1700—History
and criticism. | Self (Philosophy) in literature. | Subjectivity in
  literature. | Petrarca, Francesco, 1304–1374—Influence. |
  Renaissance—Great Britain.
Classification: LCC PR428.S45 S65 2017 | DDC 820.9/384—dc23
LC record available at https://lccn.loc.gov/2016046672

∞ Printed on acid-free paper.

Contents

Acknowledgments	vii
INTRODUCTION Vernacular Memories of English Petrarchism	1
ONE The Measure of Meed: Symbolic Economies in Langland, Wyatt, and Spenser	25
TWO Chaucerian Melancholy in Renaissance England: Surrey's *Songes and Sonettes* and Sidney's *Astrophil and Stella*	83
THREE Sovereign Love, Medieval and Early Modern: The Arts of Marriage in the Casket Sonnets and *The Kingis Quair*	135
FOUR Petrarchan Afterlives of Erotic Legality: Love and Law in Lydgate, Daniel, and Drayton	175

FIVE
Medieval Pathologies of Affect:
Reading Hoccleve and Henryson
in Shakespeare's *Sonnets* — 221

CONCLUSION
The "English Straine" in Early
Modern Petrarchism: Poetry,
Genealogy, Hermeneutics — 269

Notes — 281

Index — 344

Acknowledgments

In the long process of writing this book, I have incurred many debts, and it is my pleasure to acknowledge them here (although I may never be able to reciprocate). First of all, I thank Sarah Tolmie for her unwavering support and faith in this project from its inception, as well as for her no-nonsense approach to scholarship, brilliant sense of humor, hospitality, and unfailing generosity. I also owe a special debt of gratitude to Kenneth Graham, whose incisive questions, helpful suggestions, and valuable insights, as well as a dose of healthy skepticism combined with genuine enthusiasm, have helped me along the way on more than one occasion. Special thanks to Jonathan Hart, who has always been unselfish with his intellectual and emotional support, even in the darkest and coldest depths of an Edmonton winter. I am also grateful to Elizabeth Sauer for her sympathy, encouragement, and collegial conversations. I would like to acknowledge my debt of gratitude to Irina I. Burova, who first introduced me to English Renaissance poetry all those years ago. For the many years of friendship, collegiality, and encouragement, I am deeply indebted to Heather Dubrow, Arthur Marotti, Paul Marquis, Mary Ellen Lamb, and Roland Greene, all of whom offered invaluable comments on various drafts and versions of the arguments presented here (whether in the form of ideas, conference papers, articles, or chapters) and thus left their indelible imprint on my work. The book is much stronger for your counsel.

The book was conceived at the University of Waterloo, agonized over and thought out at the University of Alberta, and completed at Brock University. All three universities were terrific environments for research and writing. In particular, I thank my fellow early modernists at these places—Katherine Acheson, Diane Jakacki, Joel Rodgers, Jane Wong, Rachel Prusko, Leah Knight, and Mathew Martin—for wonderfully illuminating conversations (and equally enjoyable lunches). Bradin Cormack and Carolyn Sale were instrumental in their help with questions of the law. Jason Powell was an invaluable source of information on Wyatt's manuscripts. Outside of the early modern circles, I thank David Shakespeare, Alexis McQuigge, Fraser Easton, Kevin McGuirk, Murray McArthur, and Jason Hawreliak.

At Duquesne University Press, I am deeply grateful to Rebecca Totaro, editor of the Medieval and Renaissance Literary Studies series, and Susan Wadsworth-Booth, director, for their enthusiasm for this project; and to the two anonymous press readers whose perceptive comments and critiques greatly improved the manuscript. Kathleen Meyer, managing editor, was wonderful to work with.

My research for this book was substantially supported by an Izaak Walton Killam Memorial Postdoctoral Fellowship, which I held at the University of Alberta. I also thank the Social Sciences and Humanities Research Council of Canada and the Banting Postdoctoral Fellowship Program for generously funding my work on this book.

My deepest debt, however, is to my wife Maria and my daughters Sonia and Zoya, whose gifts of love, understanding, and patience have made it all not only possible but worthwhile.

Parts of chapter 2 previously appeared as "'Love gave the wound, which while I breathe doth bleed': Sidney's *Astrophil and Stella* and the Subject of Melancholy," *Sidney Journal* 30, no. 1 (2012): 27–50. Chapter 3 is an extended and revised version of "'Nat being (to my displesure) your wife as she': The Poetics of Sovereign Marriage in the Casket Sonnets," *Modern Philology* 112, no. 3 (2015): 458–78. Finally, some parts of the introduction and chapter 5 were published as "Elizabethan Petrarchism and Medieval Begging in Robert Sidney's Sonnets," *SEL: Studies in English Literature, 1500–1900* 55, no. 1 (Winter 2015): 21–43. I thank the publishers for giving me permission to use these materials here.

Introduction

Vernacular Memories of English Petrarchism

In one of the most recognizable passages from *The Arte of English Poesie* (1589), George Puttenham associates the arrival of Petrarchism on English soil—through the translations and imitations of Petrarch by Thomas Wyatt and Henry Howard, Earl of Surrey—with the onset of a new Renaissance poetry in England. Wyatt and Surrey, Puttenham writes, were "two chieftaines" among "a new company of courtly makers...who hauing trauailed into Italie, and there tasted the sweete and stately measures and stile of the Italian Poesie, as nouices newly crept out of the schooles of *Dante Arioste* and *Petrarch*, they greatly pollished our rude & homely maner of vulgar Poesie, from that it had been before, and for that cause may iustly be sayd the first reformers of our English meetre and stile."[1] In defining Wyatt and Surrey's revolution in English verse against the "rude & homely maner" of what one understands as late medieval poetry and equating the novel qualities of their writings with Italian—specifically Petrarchan—influence, Puttenham makes an argument that is as familiar as it is enduring. It simultaneously couples Petrarch with the emergence of historical, cultural, and literary modernity and associates the dawn of the Renaissance in England with the impact of Petrarchism. Writing 400 years after Puttenham, William Kerrigan and Gordon Braden, for instance, remark, "Petrarchism was in fairly precise ways the distinctive genre of the English Renaissance...the historical record almost compels us to discuss Petrarchism in terms of the period concept."[2] Kerrigan and Braden are not alone: A. C. Spearing equates literary modernity with Petrarch's writings and hails Wyatt's and Surrey's poetic endeavors as unprecedented; Thomas Greene discovers in Wyatt's Petrarchan poems the first instances of genuinely humanist imitation in English.[3] For these critics, as for Puttenham, the Petrarchism of Wyatt and Surrey marks a break from the medieval past and announces the birth of a modern poetic voice.

In our familiarity with this passage, however, we may overlook that, for all Puttenham's enthusiasm for Wyatt and Surrey's Petrarchism, his description of their place in the annals of English poetry forms part of a larger historical discussion in chapter 31 under the heading "Who in any age haue bene most commended writers in our English Poesie." "It will be found," Puttenham writes, "our nation is in nothing inferiour to the French or Italian for copie of language, subtiltie of deuice, good method and proportion in any forme of poeme, but that they may compare with the most, and perchance passe a great many of them" (*Arte* 59). What deserves praise, in Puttenham's view, moreover, stretches back into the past and includes at least some of the poetry that his remarks about Wyatt and Surrey's modernizing effect may appear to denigrate. "I will not reach," he announces, "aboue the time of king *Edward* the third and *Richard* the second for any that wrote in English meeter, because before their times, by reason of the late Normane conquest, which had brought into this Realme much alteration both of our language and lawes...there is litle or nothing worth commendation to be founde written in this arte" (59–60). Having established the temporal limits of praiseworthy poetry, Puttenham proceeds to name "*Chaucer* and *Gower* both of them...Knightes," "*Iohn Lydgate,* the monke of Bury, & that nameless, who wrote the *Satyre* called Piers Plowman," until by way of Skelton "surnamed the Poet *Laureat*" and the "courtly makers" Wyatt and Surrey and the likes of "Lord *Nicholas Vaux*" and "*Thomas Sternehold*," he arrives at the Elizabethan courtiers "Sir *Philip Sidney,* Sir *Walter Rawleigh,* Master *Edward Dyar,* Maister *Fulke Greuell, Gascon, Britton, Turberuille* and a great many other learned Gentlemen" (61). In this fuller sketch of poetic history, Wyatt and Surrey become part of a tradition that goes back to the late fourteenth century, to Chaucer, Gower, Langland, and Lydgate, and also looks to the future of Elizabethan Petrarchism. Puttenham posits Ricardian and Lancastrian poetry as part of the imaginary continuum of poetic intelligibility, and the Henrician poets' "imitating very naturally and studiously their Maister *Francis Petrarcha*" (62) is woven into the fabric of vernacular poetic discourse. English Petrarchism thus finds itself in the cross-fire between Puttenham's rhetoric of rupture and his narrative of continuity. Even as Wyatt and Surrey are cast as instigating a departure from the "rude & homely maner of vulgar Poesie," their work is presented as belonging to the same poetic tradition as English medieval poetry, "rude & homely" though this tradition may be.

Puttenham is not the only Elizabethan writer to complicate the relationship between the new Petrarchan and the old medieval vernacular poetry. In *A Discourse of English Poetrie* (1586), William Webbe also locates the origins of English poetry that deserves to be considered part of the native tradition in the reign of Richard II: "the first of our English

Poets I haue heard of was *Iohn Gower*, about the time of king *Rychard* the seconde...whose workes I could wysh they were all whole and perfect among vs, for no doubt they contained very much deep knowledge and delight." Gower's name is followed by that of "Chawcer...the God of English Poets," Lydgate, and "Pierce Ploughman," before Webbe moves on to the sixteenth century and contemporary court poetry, including Sidney and Spenser.[4] In Webbe's version, the texts of Chaucer and Sidney are governed by the same codes of production and reception, where shared regularities of enunciation make understanding and appreciation of medieval poetic discourse possible for the Elizabethan mind. Similarly, mid-Tudor poetic collections such as Barnabe Googe's *Eglogs, Epytaphes, and Sonettes* (1563), George Turberville's *Epitaphes, Epigrams, Songs and Sonets* (1567, 1570) and Thomas Howell's *Newe Sonets and Pretie Pamphlets* (1570, 1575), despite their use of new forms and genres, insistently invoke in their prefatory matter the medieval poets Chaucer and Gower as legitimizing precedents for the Renaissance articulations of post-Petrarchan erotic sensibilities, displaying what Cathy Shrank characterizes as a "self-consciousness regarding their potential contribution in building a native literary heritage."[5] At the close of the Elizabethan period, in Richard Barnfield's elegiac sonnet "Against the Dispraysers of Poetrie," the famous dead poets whose "liuing fame, no Fortune can confound; / Nor euer shall their Labours be forlorne"—namely, Chaucer, Gower, Surrey, Gascoigne, and Sidney—are purposefully picked from both sides of the temporal divide between the medieval past and the Renaissance present.[6] In all these instances, Petrarchism functions as much as a Renaissance intervention in poetic practice as a continuation of earlier traditions.

This book explores the potential poetic continuum between the medieval period and the Renaissance by rereading a number of early modern Petrarchan texts as discursively linked to medieval English poetry and its poetics of selfhood. My central claim is that in sixteenth and early seventeenth century England, Petrarchan subjectivities were articulated in the vernacular poetic medium that to a tangible degree retained traces of medieval structures of discourse and selfhood, and that vestigial fragments of medieval poetic imaginations can be uncovered in the poetry of English Petrarchans from Wyatt to Shakespeare. In particular, the chapters that follow analyze several instances of the presence of medieval imaginative fragments in early modern Petrarchan discourse: the persistence of William Langland's poetics of meed in Wyatt and Spenser; the role of Chaucer's *Book of the Duchess* in the production of vernacular melancholy that underpins the Petrarchan poems of Henry Howard, Earl of Surrey, and Philip Sidney; the medieval substrate in the figure of sovereign marriage in Mary Stuart's casket sonnets; the afterlives of Lydgate's vision of erotic legality in the sonnets of Samuel Daniel and Michael Drayton; and the medieval genealogies of pathological affect (Thomas Hoccleve, Robert Henryson) in William Shakespeare's sonnets. By identifying and investigating traces of medieval poetry in the Petrarchan texts, this volume questions the familiar narratives of literary history and the history of subjectivity and demonstrates that some of the radical historical changes associated with Petrarchism are anticipated by a rich tradition of medieval vernacular writing. The book further suggests that fragments of medieval discourses and selves persist in English love poetry into the high Renaissance, where they continue to operate as potent imaginative resources.

As a study of vernacular medieval genealogies of English Renaissance Petrarchism, *Renaissance Texts, Medieval Subjectivities* simultaneously belongs to two critical paradigms. One is the intellectual movement dedicated to reasserting "the legitimacy of the Middle Ages" for the culture of modernity. This intellectual project investigates, as Andrew Cole and D. Vance Smith formulate it, how "'the medieval' is never overcome and rarely superseded but rather continuously posited as that necessary anachronism that paradoxically generates 'the modern' as we know it."[7] Literary history has proven to be a fertile ground for probing the relevance of the Middle Ages to the English Renaissance. In recent years, significant scholarly energy has been dedicated to investigating various facets of the claim that "the early modern was constructed through or in negotiation with the medieval."[8] A number of excellent studies have alerted us to the role that late medieval English literature and culture played in formulating a host of ideas about genre, poetic voice, gender, national identity, and political philosophy that continued to hold currency during the early modern period.[9] At the same time, I am interested in further questioning the apparent conventionality and inflexibility of the Petrarchan manner. As we have learned in the past three decades, far from being a stockpile of exhausted figures and attitudes, in early modern England Petrarchism was a vibrant and malleable discursive mode that was adapted to express complex sociocultural issues of the Tudor period. Reserving for its speakers a profusion of subject positions—political, religious, sexual, nationalist, colonial, and social[10]—the language of unrequited desire generated a rich tapestry of intertwined discursive strands that we know as English Petrarchism. This book maps a critical space in which these two analytical paradigms, usually envisaged as incompatible, intersect and forge a productive alliance. It undertakes a diachronic interpretation of English Petrarchism through the lens of medieval poetics of selfhood, seeking to uncover the play of past imaginative structures within the configurations of Petrarchan poetry. Simultaneously engaging issues of periodization and the legitimacy of the medieval *and* looking to expand the boundaries of early modern Petrarchan signification, this study—a project of medievalizing Renaissance Petrarchism, so to speak—seeks to unsettle some of the most enduring scripts of modern literary scholarship.

This dictates the focus, scope, and theoretical commitment of this volume. Concentration on structures of subjectivity is an obvious choice for any study of Petrarchism. As a Latin humanist writer, Petrarch is often credited as the originator of the concept (if not the term) of the Middle Ages as an age of cultural and scholarly darkness, one fundamentally distinct from the modern era.[11] But in the realm of poetry, Petrarch's contribution to the invention of modernity is taken to be the creation in the *Canzoniere* of a new form of poetic selfhood characterized by a heightened sense of inwardness, complexity, and historical isolation from the past.[12] Out of his unrequited love for Laura, the familiar story goes, Petrarch articulates a self inherently fractured by a conflict between desire and language, eroticism and spirituality, transience and impermeability—"a new, post-medieval individualism" that challenges "the radical stasis of the medieval personality."[13] Although the subject of some incisive critiques,[14] this narrative of Petrarch's discovery of modern poetic selfhood continues to govern our approaches to periodization and literary history. Petrarchism's status as a markedly Renaissance form of discourse may explain, for example, why even scholars interested in the medieval/early modern divide in English literature typically have not considered sonnet sequences in their inquiries.

There are, however, some issues with reading Petrarchism as the epitome of modernity. First, at least in England, Petrarchism does not chronologically equal Renaissance. Although a claim that "the first major impact on English poetry of Petrarchanism...comes with Wyatt and Surrey"[15] may sound unproblematic, it is only partially accurate. Already in Chaucer's *Troilus and Criseyde* (c. 1380s), the soliloquy of the lovesick Troilus—"If no love is, O God, what fele I so?" (1.400–20)—is a translation of Petrarch's sonnet 132: "S'amor non è, che dunque è quel ch'io sento" ("If it is not love, what then is it that I feel").[16] In the 21 lines of Chaucer's medieval romance, Petrarchan desire and diction—with the characteristic oxymora, antitheses, and paradoxes that configure the conflicting vicissitudes of Petrarchan erotic selfhood—penetrate English literary discourse roughly 150 years before Wyatt's first forays in the territory of Petrarchan poetics in the 1520s.[17] We might dismiss this first instance of Petrarchism as a non-event, an isolated incident that had almost no bearing on Renaissance Petrarchism.[18] Or one might argue, by contrast, for an overwhelming effect of Chaucer's translation on subsequent English poetic practice, as "a mandate for later poets such as Wyatt and Surrey" that "lays the formal foundations for the English sonnet."[19] Of course, there is always a position somewhere in between these extremes.[20] Whatever our reaction, there is no denying that this makes the history and chronology of English Petrarchan poetry more complicated than is often assumed.

Some Elizabethan Petrarchists in fact acknowledged Chaucer's translation as a legitimate precedent to their own practice. For example, when Thomas Watson in his sonnet sequence Ἑκατομπαθία; or, *Passionate Centurie of Love* (1582) translates sonnet 132 as "If't be not love I feele, what is it then?," he is compelled to account for the relationship between his Renaissance sonnet and Chaucer's medieval version. "All this passion (two verses only excepted) is wholly translated out of *Petrarch*," Watson announces in the subheading, but immediately adds, "And it may be noted, that the Author in his first halfe verse of this translation varieth from that sense, which *Chawcer* vseth in translating the selfe same [poem]."²¹ By the same token, an anonymous poet from the Park-Hill manuscript (BL Add. 36529) in his or her version of sonnet 132 not only replicates a good deal of Chaucer's vocabulary but misreads the first line of the Italian original as "If love be not, what throes do I sustain," which can be put down to the transformative effect of Chaucer's original misreading of Petrarch.²² It is also worth mentioning that in Renaissance England Petrarch was often considered a medieval writer. Roger Ascham in *The Schoolmaster* (1590) counts both Petrarch and Chaucer among the "Gothians," and in Samuel Daniel's chronology of writers in *A Defence of Ryme* (1603) Petrarch is relegated to the darkness of the thirteenth century.²³ Less obviously but still suggestively, Sidney, in his *Apologie for Poetrie* (c. 1580), grants Chaucer and Gower the inaugural role in the development of English poetic discourse by analogy with the great Italians of the Renaissance era: "So in the Italian language the first that made it aspire to be a Treasure-house of Science were the Poets *Dante, Boccace,* and *Petrarch*. So in our English were *Gower* and *Chawcer*."²⁴ But whether in Sidney's version the medieval English writers Gower and Chaucer are equated with the Renaissance poets of Italy, or the Italians "*Dante, Boccace,* and *Petrarch*" are taken to be hopelessly medieval, is impossible to determine.

Another, perhaps more urgent, problem with the received narrative of Petrarch's invention of the modern self is that it often entails a wholesale denial of subjectivity to the pre-Petrarchan Middle Ages. The messy history of English Petrarchism is evidence that what we take to be the pre-eminent form of modern textual subjectivity is possible in English poetry at least 150 years before its official inauguration. However, in focusing on Chaucer's translation, we risk losing sight of the fact that individual selfhood was a medieval phenomenon beyond isolated instances of rudimentary Petrarchism. In a spate of recent arguments, critics have repeatedly demonstrated that medieval literature boasted many of the techniques of subjectivity taken to be essentially modern, with a rich tradition of writing the self in existence in European culture at least since Augustine. As David Aers observes, "there is no reason to think that languages and experiences of inwardness, of interiority, of divided selves, of splits between outer realities and inner forms of being, were unknown before the seventeenth century."[25] Helen Cooper echoes this position from the medieval side of the trenches, noting that an absence in the literature of the Middle Ages of a Petrarch or a Hamlet "does not however mean that a sense of subjectivity, of the uniqueness of individual experience as it is registered inwardly, is necessarily absent in the later Middle Ages" but, rather, that we are put off by the "unfamiliarity of the means of representation."[26] On the Renaissance side, David Schalkwyk concurs: "Human subjectivity does not belong to any one culture or period; it does not arise at any discernable historical moment; it is born with language itself. We should not be misled by the undeniable historical case that techniques for the representation of such speech acts do develop historically, but it is a mistake to believe that this represents the development of human subjectivity itself."[27] While, as Jason Scott-Warren points out, the early modern period did develop a number of new technologies of the self (including self-portrait and Petrarchism), that does not mean that the idea of selfhood itself was born in the early modern period.[28] Quite the contrary, numerous medieval writers and texts display a distinct appreciation of subjective individuality. At least in this respect, the break between the medieval and the Renaissance is just not there.

Understanding historical subjectivity, in other words, defies ordered chronology, for "the various slippages or repetitions that seem to beset the telling of the history of the subject testify to the impossibility of specifying when an epistemic formation is latent or burgeoning or fully achieved, or what its constituent elements are."[29] Frederic Jameson formulates this principle even more bluntly: "The narrative of modernity cannot be organized around categories of subjectivity."[30] In place of a tidy (and culturally imperialist) opposition of post-Petrarchan subjectivity and medieval collectivity (or underdeveloped subjectivity at best), we are then left with a historical muddle—a multitude of forms of textual selfhood that populate poetic texts on both sides of the porous divide. The question of historical subjectivity thus once again reminds us that it is only through an abnegation or denial of the Middle Ages that the *grand récit* of the emergence of modernity can be sustained.[31] Once reintroduced into the equation, the medieval begins to operate as "a powerful mechanism for questioning the traditional schemes of periodization and temporality in the Western tradition."[32] This results in a view of nonlinear historical time haunted by returns and reversions, proleptic pushes and halting pulls—what some (predominantly medievalist) critics have come to call a "queer temporality."[33]

Consequently, it becomes possible to think through the history of Western selfhood in terms other than erasure and supersession, not as a forgetting of medieval nonselfhood and an irreversibly teleological progression toward the complexity and dynamism of modern subjectivity but, rather, as a field of vagaries among prolegomenal or belated, but always equally complex and unstable, forms of selfhood. In this book, I examine a specific segment of this fluid field, by considering continuities and changes within the structures of poetic imagination and textual subjectivity from the medieval to the Petrarchan. I demonstrate that, despite ruptures in political, social, cultural, and literary history, in a number of instances the imaginative vocabularies of self-articulation deployed by early modern English Petrarchans contain traces of the languages of subjectivity practiced by English medieval poets, with the concomitant connotations that attach themselves to poetic discourse and continue to lurk behind configurations of Petrarchan desire and selfhood in the sixteenth and early seventeenth centuries.

Still, reading English Petrarchan poetry—a Renaissance discourse par excellence—with a view to uncover its possible medieval past(s) may justifiably appear counterintuitive, so the question of how one can theorize the elusive relationship between the medieval and the early modern in Petrarchan verse is not an idle one. Few scholars would deny the value of reading Renaissance poetry, to adopt John Watkins's phrase, "in more comparative temporal...contexts,"[34] but the precise practical modes of engaging texts across the medieval/early modern divide remain a matter of contention. A case in point, continuities between medieval and Petrarchan poetics that I seek to trace in this book do not fall under the rubric of conscious medievalism; nor (with the possible exception of Spenser) are they necessarily governed by codes of imitation of archaic styles.[35] In the following chapters, I frame these continuities as a form of discursive memory, a concept I base on Mikhail M. Bakhtin's ideas. In a well-known passage from "The Theory of Speech Genres," Bakhtin describes any literary utterance as "complex and multiplanar," as "a link in the chain of speech communication," which "has clearcut boundaries that are determined by the change of speech subjects (speakers), but within these boundaries the utterance...reflects the speech process, others' utterances, and, above all, preceding links in the chain (sometimes close and sometimes—in areas of cultural communication—very distant)." According to Bakhtin, literary discourse is "furrowed with distant and barely audible echoes of changes of speech subjects and dialogic overtones."[36] It is an accretive institution where the sedimentation of prior forms and meanings, voices and gestures, rather than being lost over the course of time, contributes to the shape of later poetic enunciations. These past discursive fragments coalesce to form, according to Bakhtin, "the objective memory of genre"—a "representative of creative memory in the process of literary development."[37]

From this perspective, reading poetry means being attuned to the pulsation of history. Early modern selfhood, Nancy Selleck argues, is not a form of isolated individuality; rather, it is a configuration involved in a constant Bakhtinian dialogue with other selves. In this sense, she writes, early modern subjectivity is always "an exchange, permeation, borrowing, anticipation."[38] Selleck focuses on the synchronic dimension of this dialogue, on how early modern selves in the process of self-articulation incorporate other early modern selves. Her argument, however, is stimulating because it highlights the instability of early modern selfhood and its openness to other forms of identity. I explore the diachronic potentiality of this receptivity of early modern subjectivity by rethinking Renaissance Petrarchan selves as sites of discursive traffic between the past and the present, between the medieval and the early modern. In the wake of these considerations, I approach Petrarchan discourse as a form of historical continuity haunted by latent but powerful memories of its anterior otherness, as a kaleidoscope of past discursive structures and selves which, when recalled to the surface in an act of interpretation, displace the totality of the textual present and make it nonidentical and nonsynchronic with itself.

With its focus on residual traces of the past in Renaissance artifacts, this book also shares ground with some of the recent studies inspired by Bruno Latour and Michel Serres's theories of polychronicity and multitemporality. Their underlying idea is that human objects and actions always simultaneously belong to multiple temporal registers, that they mix up "periods, ontologies, and genres," and that elements of the past survive in the present where they overlap with fragments of other times.[39] For example, as Alexander Nagel and Christopher S. Wood's brilliantly provocative *Anachronic Renaissance* demonstrates for the sphere of visual arts, a great many so-called Renaissance techniques of and ideas about representation simultaneously belonged to different chronologies as the obstreperously medieval modes of seeing and depicting continued to cling to the revolutionary discoveries of the new art.[40] Developing similar notions for the early modern literary context, Jonathan Gil Harris argues in *Untimely Matter* that in the Renaissance objects of material culture are palimpsests in the sense that they are "often saturated with the unmistakable if frequently faint imprints of many times."[41] The palimpsest metaphor Harris uses is apt. Palimpsests are texts in which earlier writing has been erased in order to create space for a later inscription. But the paradox of the palimpsest, Sarah Dillon argues, is that "although the first writing on the vellum *seemed* to have been eradicated after treatment, it was often imperfectly erased. Its ghostly trace then reappeared in the following centuries," producing an interweaving of layers of textual fabric. The result of palimpsesting is, again, a kind of queer textual temporality in which "the 'present' of the palimpsest is only constituted in and by the 'presence' of texts from the 'past.'"[42]

In the following pages, I also operate on an assumption that there are multiple temporalities compressed in the singularity of a given Petrarchan text. Instead of material objects, however, this book focuses on structures of poetic discourse and subject positions associated with them. For Bakhtin, poetic language is saturated with "tastes of the context and contexts in which it has lived it socially charged life."[43] I am more interested in literary than social memories of poetic language, but by bringing Bakhtin's philological considerations into this conversation, I want to stress that poetic language and poetic imagination are also among the temporally heterogeneous orders insofar as any act of speech or writing unavoidably weaves together words, forms, genres, styles, and images from multiple periods. Historical stratification is a characteristic of poetic languages as much as it is of natural ones. In the latter, Daniel Heller-Roazen writes, "the present invariably contains the stratified residues of a past that, when examined, retreats beyond the memory of the individual who uncovers it."[44] The same can be said about poetic discourse. Rather than being rendered obsolete, residual fragments of poetic anteriority make up part of the fabric of the literary present, forming a kind of "rhetorical and symbolic vocabulary, a storehouse of signifying capacities potentially available to each member of a given culture."[45] Such imaginative continuities between the medieval and the Renaissance may often be, to use Brian Cummings and James Simpson's phrase, "invisible,"[46] but they are no less real and do deserve critical attention.

Material history is nonetheless instructive for a project like this one, for there is ample evidence that medieval poetry was an integral part of the early modern literary landscape. One of the paradoxical consequences of the invention of printing, as Elizabeth L. Eisenstein observes, was that the new medium was often used to reproduce and disseminate old texts, including literary.[47] By highlighting the transience of such material signs of the past as buildings and monuments, the English Reformation shifted emphasis to texts and their immaterial contents as the primary instruments of defining and perpetuating nationhood.[48] The time of most violent destruction of national memory was also the time when the national literary canon—through the work of humanist antiquarian John Leland (1503–52) and radical Protestant writer John Bale (1495–1563)—was inaugurated.[49] During the long sixteenth century, all major medieval writers became available to English readers in Renaissance editions. Starting with Caxton's *The Canterbury Tales* (1476, 1483), reprinted by Wynken de Worde in 1498, the complete works of Geoffrey Chaucer appeared in 1526 (edited by Richard Pynson); in 1532, 1542, and 1550 (edited by William Thynne); in 1561 (edited by John Stow); and in 1598 (edited by Thomas Speght). Lydgate was equally popular: *Temple of Glas* appeared in 1495, 1497, 1500, 1503, 1506, and 1529; *Complaynt of a Loueres Lyfe* in 1508 and 1531; the massive *Troy Book* in 1513 and 1555; *The Fall of Princes* in 1494, 1527, and twice in 1554; and *Siege (Destruction) of Thebes* in 1497 and 1561. Gower's *Confessio Amantis* was printed by Caxton (1483) and by Thomas Berthelette (1532, 1552). Langland's *Piers Plowman* attracted the close attention of the Reformist printer and poet Robert Crowley, who brought out two editions of the medieval poem in 1550.[50] Chaucerian poets such as Hoccleve and Henryson did not warrant separate editions, but their works (for instance, Hoccleve's "L'epistre de Cupide" and Henryson's *Testament of Cresseid*) were routinely printed in the editions of Chaucer as apocrypha. Besides, John Stow (1525–1605), a celebrated Elizabethan antiquarian and editor of the 1561 version of *The Workes of Geffrey Chaucer*, was evidently in possession of several manuscripts of Middle English poetry, including "L'epistre de Cupide," *The Regiment of Princes*, and the *Series* by Hoccleve.[51]

Paying attention to the ineluctable presence of medieval texts in the early modern literary culture can help us "understand literary history as neither progressive nor revolutionary but as a story of influence in which the past is...accessible through the technologies of reproduction that enable the literary imagination," William Kuskin justly notes.[52] However, putting our absolute faith in material history and the "technologies of reproduction" is tricky business. As Anne Coldiron warns us, inferring causality and influence from circulation (of which our picture is incomplete and sketchy at best) is a precarious enterprise.[53] Middle English was increasingly seen as an obsolete language few could understand;[54] many words had changed their form and meaning, at times becoming unrecognizable to Elizabethan readers.[55] In light of these considerations, I do not look for signs of the English Petrarchans' deliberate engagement with the medieval but, rather, seek to capture some of the rich medieval overtones that their vehicle—vernacular poetic discourse—itself carried. As Derrida writes, "a writer cannot not be concerned, interested, anxious about the past, that of literature, history, or philosophy, of culture in general. S/he cannot take account of it in some way and not consider her- or himself a responsible heir, inscribed in a genealogy, whatever ruptures or denials on this subject may be." Yet, he continues, "this historicity or this historical responsibility is not necessarily linked to awareness, knowledge, or even the themes of history."[56] Derrida's explicit acknowledgment of the unconscious pressures that past discursive structures exert upon present writing unpacks Bakhtin's tentative gesturing toward the vastness of distance that accompanies the historical responsibility of literary texts. The preceding verbal, rhetorical, and imaginative structures configure a kind of a text's "unconscious which is history, the play of history beyond its edges, encroaching on those edges."[57]

Avoiding questions of direct borrowing between medieval poetic texts and English Petrarchism, this book focuses instead on larger units: recurring figures of discourse, structures of poetic imagination, and patterns of selfhood which constitute "a structural unconscious...a space from which historical agents can selectively employ and manipulate a determined range of rhetorical possibilities to achieve authentically indeterminate results."[58] These medieval articulations of selfhood did not disappear with the waning of the Middle

Ages but were retained by discursive memory. Surviving into the early modern period, they remained part of the imaginative archive of English poetry, a space of discursive potentialities that can be reactivated in discourse beyond a specific writerly agenda. This book reads early modern texts as sites of collision and intertwining between the medieval and the Petrarchan, unraveling the dense skeins of early modern discourse and bringing to light the importance of fragments of the past to the construction of the present.

I will develop my argument across five case studies. Each chapter takes as its central object a distinct scenario of subjectivity found in English Renaissance Petrarchism, whose medieval prefigurations and prehistories the chapter traces, often in relation to larger cultural discourses and their histories (and with assistance from modern theoretical frameworks). Chapter 1, "The Measure of Meed: Symbolic Economies in Langland, Wyatt, and Spenser," investigates the subtle presence of William Langland's concept of meed—sexual, monetary, spiritual, and poetic reward—in Wyatt's sonnets and Spenser's *Amoretti*. Langland seeks to define meed by interrogating the measure and incommensurability of reward, by testing the relationship between payment and gift and between the secular and the sacred, and by uncovering the investment of life and death into the mechanisms of giving and taking. So when Wyatt's Petrarchan poems not only metaphorize erotic gratification as economic reward but contrast both with the experience of the divine at the point of death, and when Spenser's *Amoretti* seeks to formulate a poetics that would translate both the economic aspirations of laureateship and the erotic allure of courtliness into a salvific textual experience, these early modern texts, I argue, reactivate the Langlandian language of meed. At the close of the chapter, I briefly glance at two marginal Elizabethan sonnet sequences, Barnabe Barnes's *Parthenophil and Parthenophe* and E. C.'s *Emaricdulfe*, both of which further indicate the pervasiveness of Langlandian undertones that hover in Petrarchan discourse around the notion of meed.

Chapter 2, "Chaucerian Melancholy in Renaissance England: Surrey's *Songes and Sonnets* and Sidney's *Astrophil and Stella*," explores the ways in which Chaucerian courtly legacy operates in two sixteenth century Petrarchan sequences: Surrey's section of Richard Tottel's *Songes and Sonettes* and Sidney's *Astrophil and Stella*. Focusing on the medical and cultural language of melancholy, I suggest that the lovesick Sidneian subject is prefigured in English literary discourse by Chaucer's poetics of melancholy, which in turn informs Surrey's anti-Petrarchan experiments in Tottel's volume. In order to adumbrate melancholic subjectivity, I read Chaucer's *Book of the Duchess* in the context of both pre-modern and modern theories of melancholy and identify melancholy as a splintering of identity that dissolves selfhood into a series of quasi-theatrical performances of the "I." Both Surrey and Sidney configure their poetic subjects as captured by an endless proliferation of new forms of selfhood. I further argue that Surrey's and Sidney's relationships with Petrarchism, in both cases entailing an ambivalent form of poetic discourse where the production of amorous verse is carried out alongside its radical critique, replicates the simultaneous disavowal and preservation of the continental legacy articulated in Chaucer's medieval poetics of melancholy.

The next chapter, "Sovereign Love, Medieval and Early Modern: The Arts of Marriage in the Casket Sonnets and *The Kingis Quair*," focuses on the figurations of royal marriage in the casket sonnets, a sequence of 12 Petrarchan poems attributed to Mary Stuart, Queen of Scots. The collection is unique not only in its royal authorship but in that it appropriates the language of Petrarchism in order to articulate a consummated form of matrimonial desire. But the form of subjectivity configured in the casket sonnets—a royal self consumed by conjugal eros—is not without precedent in English poetry. After considering the imagery of sovereign love in Mary's sonnets in the context of Elizabethan matrimonial politics and poetics, including Elizabeth's own Petrarchan poem "On Monsieur's Departure," I turn to a medieval articulation of royal desire in *The Kingis Quair* (c. 1420), a prison love poem attributed to Scots king James I Stewart. As I juxtapose Mary Stuart's treatment of royal marriage in the casket sonnets with the idea of chaste sovereign love in *The Kingis Quair*, I emphasize both the early modern text's disruption of marital bonds, its departure from the typology of sovereign love, and the hermeneutic importance of reading early modern Petrarchan texts in conjunction with their medieval precursors.

Chapter 4, "Petrarchan Afterlives of Erotic Legality: Love and Law in Lydgate, Daniel, and Drayton," investigates intersections between erotic and legal subjectivity in Petrarchan and medieval English verse. The starting point for my argument is the curious phenomenon of the laws of love—an autonomous system of jurisprudence in which the rights and wrongs of desire are debated and arbitrated as a legal matter. The chapter focuses on medieval English poetry that places desire under the sign of the law, primarily on John Lydgate's *Temple of Glas* and *Complaynte of a Louers Lyfe*. As I argue, Elizabethan Petrarchans, such as Samuel Daniel in *Delia* and Michael Drayton in *Idea*, offer their own version of the laws of love by deploying the language of criminal culpability derived from the common law to describe erotic passion. These sonnet sequences register a crucial shift in the status of the laws of love from imagining the latter as a separate jurisdiction toward casting desire in the language of historical positive law, while at the same time they reassert the legitimacy of medieval poetics of erotic legality for our understanding of early modern discursive strategies.

Finally, chapter 5, "Medieval Pathologies of Affect: Reading Hoccleve and Henryson in Shakespeare's *Sonnets*," seeks to reimagine William Shakespeare's Petrarchan sonnets as part of the vernacular poetic tradition and to problematize the institutionally embedded conviction that in his sonnets Shakespeare invents modern subjectivity by voiding the forgoing poetic praxis. Shakespeare's representations of the desiring subject as afflicted with a debilitating disease of love, I argue, have antecedents in medieval English poetry. On the one hand, the chapter traces vernacular genealogies of Shakespeare's articulations of selfhood in the young man sonnets as suffering from financial, medical, and erotic lack and of the object of desire (his patron) as the site of plenitude and wholeness. Here one discovers residual traces of English medieval begging poetry, exemplified most eloquently by Thomas Hoccleve's "La male regle." On the other hand, the dark lady sonnets are involved in their own form of vernacular accountability: the speaker's pathological desire for the disgusting female body in Shakespeare's sequence revisits the scenario of subject formation at work in Henryson's *Testament of Cresseid,* a late medieval poem which constructs its own version of the aesthetics of disgust as it explores the erotic bond between masculine subjectivity and the repulsive feminine object of desire, the leprous body of Cresseid.

The chapters are arranged roughly chronologically (according to an early modern perspective), from the first experiments with Petrarchan legacy in Wyatt's and Surrey's love verse (c. 1530–40s) through the casket sonnets (1571) and the sonnet sequences of the 1590s (Sidney, Daniel, Drayton, Barnes) to what many perceive as the culmination of English Petrarchism, Shakespeare's sonnets (published 1609). But rather than present a chronological narrative, the chapters aim to demonstrate that medieval genealogies permeate a surprisingly wide range of Petrarchan texts—poems that not only belong to different literary periods (Henrician, Elizabethan, Jacobean) but also grow out of diverse social milieus (from the middle-class sensibilities of Drayton and Spenser to Sidney's aristocratic aspirations to the royal desires of Mary Stuart and Elizabeth I), absorb different semantic fields (economy, medicine, politics, law), and enjoy unequal canonical status (from Sidney and Shakespeare to such marginal figures as E. C. and Barnes).

Despite this heterogeneity of form and content, however, a number of things hold these chapters together. First, each considers a classical trope of Petrarchan—and, more broadly, European erotic—poetry: love as service and reward, love as a melancholy wound, love as a form of political subjection, love as a legal trespass, and love as an economic deprivation and a contagious disease. Not unique to Petrarchism, they are nonetheless prominent in the sonnets and sonnet sequences I consider, where they contribute to the configuration of definable poetics of subjectivity, such as the melancholy self in Sidney's *Astrophil and Stella,* the economic self in Spenser's *Amoretti,* the legal self in Daniel's *Delia,* or the pathological self in Shakespeare's sonnets. Second, each chapter locates the traditional rhetoric of amorous poetry in a relation to specific historical moments, such as Protestant attitudes to labor and salvation (chapter 1), early modern concepts of melancholy (chapter 2), the real and symbolic value of royal marriage (chapter 3), English legal history (chapter 4), or the rise of syphilis (chapter 5). At once formalist and historicist in its outlook, the book is based on a conviction that understanding pre-modern subjectivity simultaneously requires grasping its rhetorical nature and understanding its connections with wider sociocultural contexts. As Paul Strohm phrases it, "the medieval (and pre-modern) writer is more likely to deploy the self, not as the ultimate center of interest, but as an imaginative exemplification of broader issues."[59] Every form of poetic selfhood examined here emerges, as it were, in answer to diverse cultural and social pressures (at least in this sense it is thus a *subjectivity*) and articulates itself through the recognizable instruments of sophisticated erotic language. But as each chapter develops its own local narrative, taken together these arguments converge upon the central claim of this book—that a clamor of medieval voices can be heard within Petrarchan discourse in early modern England. Often subdued and distorted, these voices continue to speak in their own language, one that is not necessarily identical with the overt language in which early modern Petrarchan poems were written; once discerned, they have the potential to change our understanding of the texts that harbor them. What follows is an attempt to hear these medieval voices and record their stories.

ONE

The Measure of Meed
Symbolic Economies in Langland, Wyatt, and Spenser

William Langland and English Petrarchists would appear to make strange bedfellows. As is widely recognized, in early modern England, Langland was recruited predominantly as a proto-Protestant satirical writer.[1] For Robert Crowley, the man behind the two 1550 printings of *The Vision of Piers Plowman*, the poem "doth most christianlie enstructe the weake, and sharplye rebuke the obstynate blynde. There is no maner of vice, that reygneth in anye estate of man, whyche thys wryter hath not godly, learnedly, and wittilye, rebuked."[2] George Puttenham, at the other end of the social and cultural spectrum, similarly holds in the *Arte of English Poesie* that *Piers Plowman* is a "Satyr," essentially an anticourt (and equally anticourtly) form, describing its author as one who "bent himselfe wholy to taxe the disorders of that age, and specially the pride of the Romane Clergy, of whose fall he seemeth to be a very true Prophet."[3] Crowley admires Langland while Puttenham finds *Piers Plowman* a slog (as he writes, "his verse is but loose meetre, and his termes hard and obscure, so as in them is litle pleasure to be taken" [*Arte* 62]). Yet both agree that *Piers Plowman* is a polemical text without any connection to courtly culture. Even today one finds a deep critical conviction that Langland is a poet "definitely divorced from [court] environment."[4]

The poem's local textual strategies, however, are not contained by a single genre. Langland assimilates a handful of literary and nonliterary discourses, including courtly writing.[5] James Weldon argues, for instance, that the poem's structure (a series of interconnected dream visions) is analogous to sonnet sequences of the Renaissance.[6] This would suggest that there are certain areas of overlap between Tudor love poetry and Langland's medieval satire. But formal and generic parallels between Langland's text and sixteenth century Petrarchism are largely subsidiary to my argument. Rather, focusing on the Mede passūs (from Latin, "steps") from *Piers Plowman* (II–IV), I argue in this chapter that the episode's central allegorical nodule—the complex and multifaceted notion of "meed" (reward, payment, gift)—inscribes in the vernacular memory of discourse imaginative structures crucial for our understanding of the economies of desire in several English Petrarchan texts, including Thomas Wyatt's sonnets and Edmund Spenser's *Amoretti* (1595), as well as two marginal Elizabethan sonnet sequences—Barnabe Barnes's *Parthenophil and Parthenophe* (1593) and E. C.'s *Emaricdulfe* (1595).

The choice of the Renaissance poets involved in a dialogue with Langland about meed is less whimsical than it might initially appear. Granted, on one level, all Petrarchan poetry, as a discourse of unrequited yearning, is obsessed with the (im)possibility of reward.[7] In this sense, Petrarchan lovers do live the idea that "all sexuality is a matter of economy."[8] However, the persistence and elaboration that Wyatt and Spenser (as well as E. C. and Barnes) demonstrate in their constructions of meed sets them apart from other early modern

Petrarchan hopefuls and opens up channels of discursive association with *Piers Plowman*. Langland in his poem develops a distinct vocabulary for theorizing meed. His text interrogates the measure and incommensurability of reward, tests the relationship between payment and gift and between the secular and the sacred, and uncovers the investment of life and death into the mechanisms of giving and taking. As I demonstrate below, similar to the Mede episode of *Piers Plowman*, Wyatt's sonnets, Spenser's *Amoretti*, Barnes's *Parthenophil and Parthenophe*, and E. C.'s *Emaricdulfe* persistently trace the unfolding of masculine subjectivity in response to a desire for sexual, monetary, spiritual, and poetic reward. Wyatt not only metaphorizes erotic gratification as economic recompense but also contrasts both with the experience of God at the point of death; Spenser seeks to translate both the economic aspirations of laureateship and the eroticism of courtly love into a salvific textual experience; E. C. equates his beloved with divine grace; and, inversely, Barnabe Barnes's lover sacrifices everything for the reward of sexual pleasure. In all these instances, I argue, the early modern poets speak the language of meed. To borrow the terminology that Jacques Derrida proposed for thinking through the persistence of certain philosophical vocabulary across historical periods and schools of thought, this language is not fully arbitrary or conventional but bears a burden of discursive association with the text of Langland's poem.[9] Reflecting the specific conditions of their application, the early modern Petrarchan poems of meed at the same time retain a historical consciousness and acknowledge their medieval provenance.

Defining Meed in *Piers Plowman*

The Mede episode occupies the bulk of *Piers Plowman*'s first dream.[10] In the course of this dream, Will, the dreamer, guided by Holi Chirche, attempts to discover the meaning of the truth and the false. He is shown Mede, a richly adorned lady about to be married to "oon Fals Fikel-tonge, a fendes biyete [i.e., fiend's offspring]" (II.41). The wedding, however, is interrupted by Theology, who claims that this marriage is unlawful because Mede is betrothed to Truth, and the characters move to London where this legal predicament is to be resolved. In passus III, the King's trial of Mede commences: she is accused of choosing the wrong husband ("Unwittily, womman, wroght hastow ofte; / Ac worse wroghtes thow nevere than tho thow Fals toke," the King says [III.106–07]), yet she is promised pardon provided she agrees to marry Conscience, one of the king's courtiers, to which Mede readily assents. But Conscience is averse to the proposal: woe to the realm where the King loves Mede, he exclaims ("Ther she [Mede] is wel with the kyng wo is the reaume" [III.153]). In the next passus, Reason is recruited to persuade him, but the focus of the episode shifts to Peace's complaint against Wrong (IV.47–60), with Mede interfering unsuccessfully on his behalf. After that, she quietly vanishes from the text, presumably leaving the kingdom governed by Reason and Conscience (IV.177–95). The passus ends, and the dreamer awakens, chagrined that he "ne hadde slept sadder [i.e. more soundly] and yseighen moore" (V.4).

On the surface, Mede is an allegory of riches and their insidious power revealed in the "fals" uses of wealth, such as bribery and simony. This has prompted influential characterizations of the episode as a venality satire.[11] However, in Middle English, the word "meed" covered a surprising semantic range. Most commonly, it was used to refer to different kinds of payment and reward, including gifts and wages; sometimes the word denoted wealth in general but could occasionally indicate bribe or graft, and it was also applied to signify such polar notions as punishment for a transgression and spiritual rewards, including salvation.[12] As James Simpson succinctly phrases it, "meed" is "an ambiguity, a word which refuses to be tied down in any fixed way, and which can provoke exclusive and opposed definitions."[13] As such, "meed" is a "complex word"[14] that offers unlimited linguistic potentialities for exploring the relationship between subjectivity and economic desire.

The episode itself provides an arena for a clash between two definitions of "meed." One belongs to Mede herself, who claims,

> It bicometh to a kyng that kepeth a reaume
> To yeve [men mede] that mekly hym serveth—
> To aliens and to alle men, to honouren hem with yiftes;
> Mede maketh hym biloved and for a man holden.
> Emperours and erles and alle manere lordes
> Thorugh yiftes han yomen to yerne and to ryde.
> The Pope and alle prelates presents underfongen
> And medeth men hemselven to mayntene hir lawes,
> Servaunts for hire servyce, we seeth wel the sothe,
> Taken mede of hir maistres, as thei mowe acorde.
> Beggeres for hir biddyinge bidden men mede.
> Mynstrales for hir myrthe mede thei aske.
> The Kyng hath mede of his men to make pees in londe.
> Men that [kenne clerkes] craven of hem mede.
> Preestes that prechen the peple to goode
> Asken mede and massepens and hire mete [alse].
> Alle kynne crafty men craven mede for hir prenties.
> Marchaundise and mede mote need go togideres:
> No wight, as I wene, withouten Mede may libbe! (III.209–27)

According to Mede's fluid vision, she embodies a broad spectrum of relationships of giving and receiving. Her definition covers diverse, even conflicting, types of economic exchange, such as payments rendered for services to retainers, free gifts, tradesmen's wages, payments for merchandise, and even alms given to beggars. Earned for labor, paid or traded for commodities, even received gratis, in this interpretation meed is a protean socioeconomic category that holds society together.

Mede's proposed husband, Conscience, however, smells danger in this semantic elasticity. Speaking against Mede the bride and meed the concept, he offers his own definition of the word, in which he seeks to exclude certain forms of economic relationship altogether and set up a hierarchy of morally acceptable and morally reprehensible forms of meed:

> Ther are two manere of medes, my lord, by youre leve.
> That oon God of his grace graunteth in his blisse
> To tho that wel werchen while thei ben here.
> ....
> Tho that entren of o colour and of one wille,
> And han ywroght werkes with right and with reson,
> And he that useth noght the lyf of usurie
> And enformeth povere men and pursueth truthe:
> *Qui pecuniam suam non dedit ad usuram, et munera super innocentem...*
> And alle that helpen the innocent and holden with the rightfulle,
> Withouten mede doth hem good and the truthe helpeth —
> Swiche manere men, my lord, shul have this firste mede
> Of God at a gret nede, whan thei gon hennes.
> Ther is another mede mesurelees, that maistres desireth:
> To mayntene mysdoers mede thei take,
> And therof seith the Sauter [i.e. Psalter] in a salmes ende —
> *In quorum manibus iniquitates sunt; dextra eorum repleta est muneribus;*
> And he that gripeth hir gold, so me God helpe,
> Shal abien it ful bittre, or the Book lieth!
> Preestes and persons that plesynge desireth,
> That taken mede and moneie for masses that thei syngeth,
> Taken hire mede here as Mathew us techeth:
> *Amen, Amen, receperunt mercedem suam.*
> That laborers and lowe [lewede] folk taken of hire maistres,

It is no manere mede but a mesurable hire.
In marchaundise is no mede, I may it wel avowe:
It is a permutacion apertly—a penyworth for another.
(III.231–33, 238–58)

There are two analytical moves here. One, which comes at the close of the passage, is Conscience's attempt to distinguish between meed and nonmeed. Unlike Mede, for whom "kynne crafty men craven mede for hir prenties" and "marchaundise and mede mote need go togideres," Conscience believes that neither laborers' wages nor payments to merchants for their goods belongs to meed proper. The former is "but a mesurable hire" while the latter is an exchange of identical values, "permutacion apertly—a penyworth for another." Symmetrical exchanges of labor, money, and commodities are not governed by meed. The second distinction Conscience draws is between two morally exclusive kinds of meed: "that oon God of his grace graunteth in his blisse / To tho that wel werchen while thei ben here," and "another mede mesurelees, that maistres desireth." The former belongs to the divine economy and is reserved for those who seek the truth and espouse righteousness by avoiding any sort of unscrupulous economic activity that pays unreasonable, measureless benefits, such as usury. By contrast, measureless meed is associated with immoral and even illegal practices, such as bribery, simony, and corruption ("Mede of mysdoeres maketh manye lordes, / And over lordes lawes [lord]eth the reaumes" [III.297–98])—activities that yield unmeasured and undeserved rewards.

The language of insatiable human desire in Conscience's speech emphasizes the gender aspect of Mede's allegorical representation. With Langland, the genders he chooses for his personifications "are not casual... [but] each choice he makes becomes significant in a way that the compulsory feminines of the classical and continental counterparts are not."[15] It has thus become somewhat of a critical *locus communis* that the Mede episode epitomizes the traffic in women—"the use of women as exchangeable, perhaps symbolic, property for the primary purpose of cementing the bonds of men with men."[16] This makes Mede an object of both pecuniary and erotic appetite, and the notion of measureless meed can be expanded to include economic excess and rampant sexual desire. What matters for Conscience, however, is that "mede mesurelees" forms an antithesis to divine grace. Earlier in the dream, Will's guide Holi Chirche announces that "what man taketh Mede.../...he shal lese for hire love a lappe of *Caritatis*" (II.34–35); Conscience's speech confirms that, positing "firste mede / Of God" and "mede mesurelees" as mutually exclusive.

Conscience's analytical work is founded on the opposition of measurable and *un*measurable ("mesurelees") forms of compensation. As A. G. Mitchell summarizes Conscience's logic, "Where there is an exact relationship between the payment and the goods handed over or the work or service done, the payment is said to be measurable, proportionate, in exact relationship. When there is not this settled, exact relationship the reward is measureless, out of proportion."[17] Where Mede lumped together both measurable (marketplace exchange, fair wages) and measureless (alms, bribes) instances of reward, Conscience strives to keep these apart, using them to oppose meed and nonmeed, although there are potential pitfalls associated with this approach.[18] But Conscience wants the same opposition of measure and *un*measure to account for the contrast of meed proper and meed measureless, which leads to certain confusion. For since measurable exchange (nonmeed) is excluded from the domain of meed, both remaining versions of meed—the "bad" meed of bribery and simony (underserved gift or payment) and the "good" meed of grace (salvation)—open themselves to being thought of as examples of "mede mesurelees."

The point may seem counterintuitive, yet the text of the poem does not foreclose such possibility. It is clear that unethical economic actions yield undeserved—and in this sense "mesurelees"—benefits. But in the quoted passage, divine grace can also appear to operate beyond measure. The "firste mede / Of God," Langland writes, is given to those who "wel werchen while thei ben here" and "han ywroght werkes with right and with reson." This clearly makes heavenly reward contingent upon—"measured" by—worldly deeds. Yet he disrupts this sense of proportionate recompense by saying that this meed "oon God of his grace graunteth in his blisse," which would place salvation solely at God's (unpredictable) discretion outside of the economy of measured exchange. That is, God's grace is as much a payment for good works in this world (heavenly meed) as it is a free gift of divine generosity and thus a form of "mede mesurelees"—measureless in the sense that its status as a unilateral gift undermines the notion of commensurability between a life of Christian virtue and its ultimate reward.

Unsurprisingly, there is disagreement among Langlandian critics about the status of God's meed in this episode. For Robert Adams, God's meed is *meritum de condigne*—a reward proportionate and measured in accord with one's worldly deeds.[19] James Simpson, despite conceding that Langland's divine meed implies God's "gift beyond desert" and "the impossibility of man matching the demands of God's justice," still maintains that this gift is made conditionally, depending upon man's desire to repent. For Simpson, divine gift is not "mesurelees" but, rather, proportionate, even if essentially underserved; it clearly exceeds human endeavor but nonetheless proceeds from it.[20] Samuel A. Overstreet, on the contrary, speculates that divine meed in *Piers Plowman* is in fact "mede mesurelees"—*meritum de congruo* which "lacks any sense of proportion between the work and the reward."[21]

Indeed, despite Conscience's efforts, a certain asymmetry, an incommensurability between man's deed and God's meed haunts the idea of reward granted by God's grace. Conscience's tenacity in clinging to the same term in describing divine meed and meed measureless undermines his analytical rigor. In the lines "And alle that helpen the innocent and holden with the rightfulle, / Withouten *mede* doth hem good and the truthe helpeth— / Swiche manere men, my lord, shul have this firste *mede*" (emphasis added), "mede" is used to denote both worldly, measureless reward and God's grace. Rejecting one meed results in obtaining the other, but how exactly the word "mede" will be divided between the two forms of reward remains unclear. Despite Conscience's frantic attempts at adjectival clarification ("firste mede," "mede mesurelees"), one sense of "mede" is constantly coopted by the other.

Conscience's conflicted taxonomy will become more intelligible if we reformulate it in modern terms. Mede's view of the function of meed in society—as a totality of social and economic exchanges, from alms to commerce, that ensures a workable community—in some sense anticipates Marcel Mauss's idea of the gift.[22] Conscience's distinction between measured exchange and measureless meed, meanwhile, has more in common with Georges Bataille's notions of the general and restricted economy. Bataille envisions the restricted (or limited) economy as underwritten by the ideas of scarcity and calculation, where every investment of money, labor, or energy is expected to yield a return. In contrast, the foundations of the general (or unrestricted) economy are found in surplus, excess, and abundance of resources, which must accordingly be "lost without profit...spent, willingly or not, gloriously or catastrophically" through "that glorious operation, useless consumption...destruction or at least unproductive use without any possible profit."[23] The two extremes of "mede mesurelees"—measureless in both senses of the word, disproportionate and excessive—resonate with Bataille's general economy and expenditure without profit. "Mede mesurelees" is consonant with excessive luxury and rampant sexuality, the inordinate riches and erotic pleasures that exceed rational necessity (and may eventually lead to destruction). But even more poignantly, redemption—the meed that "oon God of his grace graunteth in his blisse" (and its dark obverse in the form of God's punishment of perdition)—constitutes an instance, perhaps the primary instance, of "mede mesurelees" and thus of the general economy of expenditure. "The gift that divinity makes of itself to the faithful soul cannot be paid for," Bataille writes.[24] God's meed of salvation attained through Christ's sacrifice is a gift that cannot be reciprocated by humans; it is the ultimate form of wastefulness.

Indeed, any gift is fundamentally measureless. Granted, for Mauss, gifts represent a continuous practice of exchange; there is no free gift, he writes, and anything given must be reciprocated: "in theory, [gifts] are voluntary, in reality they are given and reciprocated obligatorily."[25] For other theorists of the gift, however, there is a fundamental difference between the economy of gift and the economy of exchange and obligation. Bataille considers gift-giving to be a form of "squandering without reciprocation."[26] That is, a reciprocated gift is no gift, and a truly "free" gift presupposes no return. For there to be a true gift, Derrida writes in his reading of Mauss and Bataille, "there must be no reciprocity, return, exchange, countergift, or debt...the gift not only must not be repayed but must not be kept in memory, retained as symbol of sacrifice...to reduce [the gift] to exchange is quite simply to annul the very possibility of the gift."[27] On the contrary, reciprocation is "an undoing or a reversal of the gift relation."[28] The ultimate example of a gift is, then, the gift of death—giving one's life in order to obviate the very possibility of reciprocation, with death being "the fatality that destines a gift *not to return* to the donor agency."[29] It is only death that guarantees a breach in the circle of reciprocity. God occupies "the same aneconomic—impossible—space as the gift...outside the economic circle of exchange."[30] It is perhaps not accidental that "firste mede / Of God" in Langland's poem is closely entangled with death: it is granted "of God at a gret nede, whan thei [people] gon hennes," which makes this meed essentially irredeemable.

This opposition between the economy of exchange and the unilateral gift—or, as Scott Shershow in his admirable reconsideration of Bataille reformulates it, between the work and the gift[31]—lies at the heart of Conscience's dichotomy of meed and nonmeed. In contrasting the restricted economy of wages and commerce with the general economy of "mede mesurelees" (both economic excess and divine grace), Conscience sets the world of work apart from the world of the gift. Even though at the crucial point Conscience undermines this taxonomy by positing salvation as at once contingent upon worldly work (given to those who "wel werchen while thei ben here") and given by God "of his grace" "in his blisse," thus betraying a "fatal discursive conjunction of work and the gift," a feature of Western thought,[32] the poem still does vital theoretical work. Through an opposition of measure and *un*measure, the Mede episode outlines a complex system of symbolic economies of meed that imagines a whole spectrum of relationships of giving and taking between humans and their God.

Economies of Subjectivity in Will's Dream

The theoretical debate about the scope and nature of meed between Mede and Conscience provides a backdrop for Langland's interrogation of what is involved in an individual subject's encounter with reward. As Will, the primary enunciating "I" of the poem, recounts his experience of Mede at the beginning of the episode,

> I loked on my left half as the lady [i.e., Holi Chirche] me taughte,
> And was war of a womman wonderliche yclothed—
> Purfiled with pelure, the pureste on erthe,
> Ycorouned with a coroune, the Kyng hath noon bettre.
> Fetisliche hire fyngres were fretted with gold wyr,
> And theron rede rubies as rede as any gleede,
> And diamaundes of derrest pris and double manere saphires,
> Orientals and ewages envenymes to destroye.
> Hire robe was ful riche, of reed scarlet engreyned,
> With ribanes of reed gold and of riche stones.
> Hire array me ravysshed; swich richesse saugh I nevere.
> I hadde wonder what she was and whos wif she were.
> (II.7–18)

The very structure of this quasi-cinematic mise-en-scène imposes upon the players the sharply defined roles of a desiring subject-viewer (Will) and an object of sight and desire (Mede).[33] But what kind of desire? On the one hand, by emphasizing the richness of her dress and the cost of the stones that adorn it, the narrator equates Mede with material wealth. On the other hand, the language of Will's response suggests that he also interprets Mede in sexualized terms: "Hire array me ravysshed; swich richesse saugh I nevere," he confesses, conflating economic vocabulary with the language of intercourse. The verb he uses ("to ravysshe") "explicitly combines male sexual desire for women with that for worldly riches."[34] Besides, Will's response to this spectacle is likely to be "coveitise of Mede," against which Holi Chirche warned him earlier in the dream (II.51). Produced through an act of looking, this "coveitise" is an instance of *concupiscentia oculorum* ("covetousness of eyes"). It is not accidental that of the three instances when Will uses the first-person pronoun "I" in the opening passage, two are coupled with predicates of visual perception ("I loked," "saugh I nevere"). Though A. C. Spearing remarks that in medieval culture *concupiscentia oculorum* is normally linked with avarice rather than sexual appetite,[35] it is impossible to ignore the visual eroticism of Mede's description. At her interrupted wedding, Mede is rumored to receive as part of her dowry "the lordshipe of Leccherie.../ As in werkes and in wordes and in waitynges with eighes, / And in wenynges and in wisshynges and with ydel thoughtes" (2.89–91). She is richly endowed with an ability to arouse both economic and erotic desire through ocular perception, to which Will is about to fall prey.

The poetic form of the passage likewise amalgamates sexuality and economy. Even though it has been previously suggested that Mede here resembles a courtly lady,[36] it has not been recognized that Will's description of Mede closely replicates the conventions of blazon. That genre is structured around a male scopophilic gaze that dismembers and then reassembles the female body as "a collection of exquisitely beautiful disassociated objects," assigning both material and sexual value to the fetishistic assemblage of displaced elements.[37] Will here occupies an essentially courtly, even lyric subject position; under his lingering gaze Mede turns into a roster of fragments scattered and rearranged through linguistic parallelism (head, fingers, torso, crown, rings, jewelry, dress). That Langland's blazon focuses on the textiles, furs, and stones rather than Mede's naked body does not diminish the erotic pull of the portrait. On the contrary, the precarious status of nudity in medieval Christian culture rendered the adorning of female bodies with various accoutrements a poetic vehicle equally, if not more, powerful than undressing them has been in later times.[38] Mede's expensive attire also signifies her class, marking her as socially superior to Will, which may translate into his sexual desire as well. As James Shultz suggests, heroes of medieval romances often fall in love with women not because the latter are differentiated morphologically along the lines of sex, but because of the nobility—expressed through dress—of their courtly bodies.[39] Will's description of Mede is indeed sex-neutral; none of the body parts or items of clothing is specifically female. Rather, her dress is suggestive of aristocracy, which likely functions as an aphrodisiac for Will.

During the opening scene of courtly gazing and coveting Will emerges as a subject of erotic and economic desire in response to the irresistibly attractive vision of meed. Although the contours of his subjectivity are nebulous, indicated by Langland by a few offhand uses of the first person scattered across the passage, it still has a degree of urgency that attaches itself to the human experience of meed. The poem lays the groundwork here for poetic examination of what trajectory subjectivity can take when faced with an opportunity to pursue reward, making Will the paradigmatic subject consumed with a desire for meed. The exteriority of visual experience (Mede's description) translates into the interiority of subjectivity (Will's remarks about his desires). What stands out in this construction of subjectivity is that it is articulated in the language of vulnerability—the spectacle unfolding before Will's eyes is overpowering, almost physically unbearable (he is "ravysshed" by it). I would like to connect this danger of violence to the nature of meed as a force of *un*measure. Mede is clearly portrayed in the blazon as a personification of economic excess: the gems and fabrics of her dress and the sexual promise of her body can be read as figures of glorious wastefulness. As Bataille notes, adorned female bodies, "the focal points of luxury and lust, though they present themselves as goods and as values, dissipate a part of human labor in a *useless* splendor" that "prefigures death."[40] But the imagery of Mede's description is also ostensibly apocalyptic, invoking the Whore of Babylon.[41] This connects Mede with the other form of nonproductive expenditure—the eschatological meed of divine wrath and unmeasured retribution. As a result, the blazon places in front of Will "mede mesurelees" in its ambivalence: riches and sexual activity on the one hand and the destruction of bodies and things in the catastrophe of God's judgment on the other.

After this snapshot of "coveitise of Mede," the text of *Piers Plowman* attempts to redefine and reposition the concept of meed in the world of the poem and in relation to Will: as a character, Mede is castigated as sexually promiscuous, lecherous, and villainous and banished from the poem; as a word, *meed* is reduced by Conscience to a narrow and negatively connoted unit and in the end relegated to textual silence. Langland seeks to write meed out of the text, first by limiting the semantic compass of the word from a comprehensive totality of economic exchange to a radically restrictive definition, then by forcing Mede to vanish from the poem altogether. Yet Will's detachment from meed is never quite completed. Despite the opprobrium Mede receives during her trial, the dreamer cannot force himself to abandon her. When he awakens from his dream, he is disappointed that he has not seen more ("Thanne waked I of my wynkyng and wo was withalle / That I ne hadde slept sadder and yseighen moore" [V.3–4]). Insofar as Will confesses that he has not seen enough of (the spectacle of) Mede, the exclamation yet again places him in a position similar to that of a courtly lover whose beloved is agonizingly distant and unattainable. In this last paroxysm of erotic longing, Will's unrequited desire for Mede resurfaces in exacerbated form.

At least in part this is determined by the nature of *Piers Plowman* as a verbal text. Here Derrida is useful again. "The definition of language," he writes, "as well as of the text in general, cannot be formed without a certain relation to gift, to giving-taking and so forth"; and, consequently, "a discourse on the gift...must and can only be part or party in the field it describes, analyzes, defines."[42] That is, language is not only something already given, but it engages its subjects in giving and receiving; any verbal text—especially one about the gift (meed) such as *Piers Plowman*—will engage in a certain relationship with meed. Tellingly, Langland's definition of poetry as "meddling with making" ("thow medlest thee with makynge," Ymaginatif points out to Will [XII.16]) punningly includes "mede." Although the text imposes an embargo of silence on the concept of meed, its linguistic nature renders this desire for a meed-free discourse largely unfeasible. In this sense, writing itself is a form of "mede mesurelees."

This serves as an invitation to consider the poem's own status within the conglomerate of economic relations of meed. Given that Langland's definition of poetry as "meddling with making" entails some idea of labor, writing appears to belong to the restricted realm of work.[43] But as a product of an unsuccessful utterance whose subject is still attached to "mede mesurelees," the text advertises its status as nonproductive wastefulness. If writing is a measureless activity, it puts Langland's own work in a curious relationship with meed. On the one hand, considering that in the Middle Ages human language—and especially writing—was taken to be a sign of the Fall,[44] the ever sprawling, dilating dream resembles the "mede mesurelees" of excessive riches and irrational erotic pleasures. On the other hand, as a form of investment without return, the dream of Mede operates as an analogue of that highest form of "mede mesurelees"—the gift of grace that God "graunteth in his blisse." It is hard to tell whether Langland's own work is intended to be found alongside those "werkes" "ywroght" "with right and with reson" that lead to "firste mede / Of God." But just as this ultimate meed of salvation is "mesurelees" because of the asymmetry between divine gifts and human works, the text's wasteful expenditure—its always coming up short of matching the ultimate form of meed—reiterates, albeit negatively, the *un*measure of God's "firste mede." In the squandering of its verbal resources, the text of Will's dream enacts a negative analogy of divine meed, becoming at once the latter's profane opposite and disturbing equivalent. As I suggest in the following pages, various aspects of Langland's blueprint of selfhood ravished by a desire for meed—the conflation of economy and sexuality in the image of meed, the dangers of measureless meed, the uncertain role of writing in obtaining meed—persist in English poetic discourse into the late sixteenth century and posit critical terms for reading the textual subjectivities in Wyatt, Spenser, E. C., and Barnes.

Thomas Wyatt and the Gift of Death

One thing several generations of Wyatt scholars have held in common is the conviction that his poetry should only be understood in the context of Henry VIII's court. Although new historicism may have replaced the playful images of courtly entertainment painted by earlier critics with a grim snapshot of the horrors of Henrician tyranny, the interpretive framework of courtier service endures in Wyatt criticism.[45] Despite falls from favor, including imprisonments in 1534, 1536, and 1541, Wyatt's life was largely shaped by courtiership, exemplifying the ideal of an early modern servant of the state, with all its splendor and peril.[46] His service to the king thus provides a useful system of coordinates for locating the poet's social and poetic identity. Although it was perhaps accidental that it fell to Wyatt to introduce Petrarchism to early modern English culture and become the "first great English Petrarchan,"[47] the Renaissance rendition of *fin' amor* clearly reverberated with the poet's role at the king's court.

But if the idea of service features prominently in critical analyses of Wyatt's love lyrics, the notion of reward receives significantly less attention. Meanwhile, a number of Wyatt's poems not only place their speaker in a relationship of obligation but also conceive of this relationship in explicitly economic terms. One of them is "What vaileth trouth?":

> What vaileth trouth? or, by it, to take payn?
> To stryve, by stedfastnes, for to attayne,
> To be iuste, and true: and fle from dowblenes:
> Sythens all alike, where rueleth craftines
> Rewarded is boeth fals, and plain.
> Sonest he spedeth, that moost can fain;
> True meanyng hert is had in disdayn.
> Against deceipte and dowblenes
>   What vaileth trouth?
> Decyved is he by crafty trayn
> That meaneth no gile and doeth remayn
> Within the trapp, withoute redresse,
> But, for to love, lo, suche a maisteres,
> Whose crueltie nothing can refrayn,
>   What vaileth trouth?[48]   (II)

This poem is as much about unrequited love as it is about returns on a bad investment, for the speaker appears to be concerned primarily with "attayn[ing]" "redresse" and being "rewarded" for his labors. The refrain ("What vaileth trouth?") likewise explores the ideas of profitability and (economic) gain and of measuring the value of truth, perhaps with a pun on vail/avail/value, given that all three words derive etymologically from the Latin *valere*. But what kind of reward is he after? If much of the poem suggests that the payment the speaker expects should take a pecuniary form, the last lines shift the focus toward sexual gratification. Steven Greenblatt summarizes the poem as "a brooding reflection on career, rule, and reward until the close jars us into connecting the disillusioned perception of power with the disillusioned perception of love."[49] But in contrasting reward with love, Greenblatt misses the crucial point that *fin' amor* is also predicated upon giving and taking—the payment of sexual grace bestowed upon the lover. Rather, the reward Wyatt's speaker is after is at once pecuniary and sexual, a combination we have encountered in the figure of Mede. Granted, the spectacle of exuberance that accompanies Mede's description in *Piers Plowman* is altogether missing from Wyatt's poem; the meticulously inventoried riches that trigger Will's desires give way to bleak fiscal metaphorics. In place of Langland's preoccupation with defining "meed," Wyatt is obsessed with the introspective agonizing of vulnerable subjectivity at the moment of encounter with meed. Despite that, the economic recompense of erotic desire sought by Wyatt also posits sexuality as a question of measure and compensation, replicating the imaginative structure of Langlandian meed.

Further, similar to Will, who is encouraged to abandon Mede, Wyatt's lover, even as he associates the lady with worldly riches and erotic pleasures, himself disdains this reward. As he admits, "where rueleth craftines / Rewarded is boeth fals, and plain." Plainness is a crucial category for Wyatt, representing a major strategy of asserting his speaker's moral identity.[50] If both the "plain" speaker and his "fals" rival(s) are rewarded with the same kind of meed, what is the value of such compensation? Like Will, however, Wyatt's speaker is unable fully to extricate himself from the economic and the erotic (as well as the verbal) allures of meed. At the close of a text driven by formal and thematic recurrence, he remains "within the trapp, withoute redresse," still consumed by his desire.[51] Even writing itself—the product of Wyatt's "craft"—is knitted into the fabric of "craftines" that the lady weaves around her lover(s).[52] A crafty, dissimulating text, Wyatt's poem itself enters the circle of "deceipte and dowblenes," at once rejecting the meed of sexual and economic profit and clinging to the impossibility of its attainment.

The economy of interpersonal attachment in "What vaileth trouth," then, operates simultaneously in the restricted (measured) and the general (measureless) modes. On the one hand, the relationship between the lover and his beloved is governed by the codes of exchange, work (service), and remuneration: the lover "stryve[s]" and "take[s] payn" in the hope of gratification, whereas the lady pays her suitors with the counterfeit money of "deceipte and dowblenes." The exchange may be imperfect (the speaker is clearly being shortchanged), yet it is a relationship of giving and taking, a back-and-forth between an investment of labor ("payn") and subsequent return. On the other hand, in the world of the poem, the repetitiveness of desire and frustration on the part of the lover points toward a different form of economic subjectivity. The speaker is trapped "withoute redresse" and receives no subsistence whatsoever from the lady, which makes his passion a form of unilateral giving of unrequited desire, an instance of the general economy of expenditure. In order to perpetuate this unreciprocated exchange, he has to rely on the resources of his own subjectivity. Unable or unwilling to terminate his involvement in this scenario of libidinal investment without return, Wyatt's speaker makes his own selfhood part of the bargain. The impossibility of *having* (he cannot have a reward from the lady) makes *being* (the speaker's subjectivity) the only resource available. The terse, economical form of Wyatt's poem—a rondeau that parsimoniously repeats its own patterns of discourse without expanding its thematic and verbal repertoire—suggests an inadequacy of resources available to the speaker. Wyatt's poem thus offers a striking illustration of Bataille's idea of poetry as "creation by means of loss."[53] His self is driven by a dangerous sexual and economic generosity that seeks to preserve the relationship by tapping the resources of subjectivity. Behind the verbal façade of measured exchange of passion, Wyatt's poem portrays an unrequited lover in danger of depleting and draining his being in an endless repetition of unquenchable desire.[54]

Accordingly, the meaning of "payn" from the opening line undergoes a subtle but unmistakable shift by the time we reach the end of the poem: originally a metonymy for work and part of the same verbal pool as "stryv[ing]," "attayn[ing]," "reward," and "redresse" (including the visual and aural pun on "pay"), it is gradually transformed into a sign of the lady's cruelty. This cruelty is measureless because "nothing can refrayn" it—that is, nothing can restrain but, additionally, nothing can replicate, echo, match it (as happens in a poetic refrain). In this sense, there is no refrain from her cruelty because her violence against the lover is not commensurate with anything; hers is such a cruelty that it can stop all reciprocity ("refrayn") in the poem (and by extension, to terminate the poem itself) by demanding the lover's absolute sacrifice. The lady's reluctance to grant the lover's suit and recompense him for his labor, which would provide him with a source of emotional sustenance other than his own being, forces him to squander without reciprocation his very life, so that his "payn" of love becomes a sign of ultimate, irrevocable loss, of self-exhausting and eventually self-destructive generosity toward the other. Like Will, who faces destruction in the proximity to Mede's apocalyptic power to ravish him sexually and economically, Wyatt's lover finds himself in grave danger.

It is therefore not altogether surprising that the only occurrence of the word "meed" in all of Wyatt's oeuvre is tainted with death:

> Resound my voyse, ye wodes that here me plain,
> Boeth hilles and vales causing reflexion;

> And Ryvers eke record ye of my pain,
> Which have ye oft forced by compassion
> As Judges to here myn exclamation;
> Emong whome pitie I fynde doeth remayn:
> Where I it seke, Alas, there is disdain.
> ....
> Why then, helas, doeth not she on me rew?
> Or is her hert so herd that no pitie
> May in it synke my Joye for to renew?
> O stony hert, who hath thus joined the
> So cruell that art, cloked with beaultie?
> No grace to me from the there may procede,
> But as rewarded deth for to be my mede.   (XXII.1–7, 15–21)

The theme of this poem—the failure of language to persuade the lady—is common for Wyatt.[55] What makes it interesting is the asymmetry the poet identifies between the verbal work he performs and the meed he receives for it. The lover is engaged in a cyclical repetition of linguistic marks, in the production of endlessly proliferating, dilatory discourse, but its communicative collapse is rendered all the more spectacular by the discrepancy between the energy he has invested in his utterance and the lady's imperturbable resolve not to "rew" on her suitor. His only reward comes under the sign of death: "No grace to me from the there may procede, / But as rewarded deth for to be my mede." And before we hasten to read it as ubiquitous early modern English slang for orgasm, in Wyatt's poem death is in fact the opposite of sexual gratification. The latter is undoubtedly what the lover seeks, but because it is indefinitely deferred, self-depletion in the process of unrequited loving emerges as the lover's only meed. As in "What vaileth trouth," here Wyatt's lover realizes that insisting on his desire—that is, engaging in a nonreciprocal relationship "withoute redresse"—can only result in self-consumption and death. Through squandering his linguistic energies for the sake of unattainable "grace," he comes close to forfeiting his life.

The poem that lends itself most interestingly to a Langlandian reading is "Who so list to hounte," a famous rendition of Petrarch's 190 "Una candida cerva."[56] In this text, Wyatt goes beyond outlining the dangers of wasteful subjectivity and imagines an antithesis to this form of meed in the absolute experience of measureless meed—an encounter with the sacred.

> Who so list to hounte I know where is an hynde;
> But as for me, helas, I may no more:
> The vayne travaill hath weried me so sore,
> I ame of theim that farthest cometh behinde;
> Yet may I by no meanes my weried mynde
> Drawe from the Diere: but as she fleeth afore
> Faynting I folowe; I leve of therefore,
> Sithens in a nett I seke to hold the wynde.
> Who list her hount, I put him owte of dowbte,
> As well as I, may spend his tyme in vain:
> And graven with Diamondes in letters plain
> There is written her faier neck rounde abowte:
> "Noli me tangere for Cesars I ame,
> And wylde for to hold, though I seme tame." (VII)

Once again, the speaker's desire is mediated primarily in economic terms. The courtly context of the poem implies sexual gratification as the ultimate prize for the lover, though the identification of the hind as erotic object also arises out of her characterization as "wild," that is, sexually incontinent.[57] In the context of the instability of early modern English orthography, however, the "dier" the lover and his fellow hunters seek is not just a deer but a "costly" and "expensive" object.[58] Her collar is "graven with Diamondes," Langland's stones "of derrest pris." It is also worth remembering that in Petrarch's original the lover is a "miser" who "seeks treasure" ("l'avaro che 'n cercar tesoro" [7]).

The hind's fiscal desirability is reinforced by the sovereign's words engraved on her collar. The line "Noli me tangere for

Cesars I ame" carries a double biblical allusion. The first halfline appears to quote Jesus's words addressed to Mary Magdalene on the morning after his Resurrection, "touche me not, for I am not yet ascended to my father" (John 20:17), an allusion to which I will return later. The second phrase, "Cesars I ame," echoes Christ's reply to the Pharisees when he was asked whether Jews should pay taxes to Rome: pointing out that the coins in which the taxes are paid bear the images of Caesar, Jesus says, "Geue therfore vnto Cesar, the thinges which are Cesars: and vnto God, those thinges that are Gods" (Matt. 22:21).[59] As Marguerite Waller suggests, the second allusion associates the beloved with coins bearing the royal image.[60] In addition, the inscription that seeks to differentiate between temporal and spiritual authority may imply the jurisdictional battles of Henry's reign so that "Cesars I ame" "may also allude to Henry's making himself the head of the English Church."[61] But the "consolidation of royal power at the expense of the ecclesiastical jurisdiction"[62] in the wake of the Reformation also entailed a transfer of revenues. If the hind is *Anglicana Ecclesia*—whose "only supreme head on earth," according to the 1534 Act of Supremacy, is "the King our sovereign lord"— the title allows him to claim not only the church's "honours, dignities, [and] preeminences" but also her "profits and commodities."[63] In addition, all these riches (diamonds, coins, church revenues) point toward the exorbitant, especially in light of the Great Debasement undertaken by Henry VIII between 1542 and 1549. In order to deal with his expenses the king decided to replace a significant amount of bullion in the coinage with copper, which resulted in a dramatic drop in the value of English money but steep profits for the crown.[64] Although the poem most likely dates from the 1530s, it was still read later in the century, when the disastrous consequences of the government's monetary policies had become palpable.[65] Wyatt's hind, then, is an embodiment of the "mede mesurelees" of excessive riches and inordinate appetites.

By contrast, the masculine world of the poem is predicated on scarcity. The hunt reads less like a pleasant pastime and more like a strenuous exertion of labor. Although the speaker knows where the hind is, he is utterly exhausted by the work of the pursuit ("I may no more: / The vayne travaill hath weried me so sore"). Where Petrarch leaves all labor *in order* to follow the vision of the white doe ("Era sua vista si dolce superba / ch'i'lasciai per seguirla ogni lavoro" [5–6]), for Wyatt's lover the hunt itself is work. Everything is in short supply here: breath, stamina, bodily energy (he is "weried...so sore" and "faynting"), sexual potency, time, hope. Language itself is scarce; the poem abounds in repetitions: lexical ("Who so list to hounte...Who list her hount," "weried...weried," "I ame...I ame," "may...I may" "To hold...to hold"), auricular ("Yet may I by no *m*eanes *m*y weried *m*ynde / *D*rawe from the *D*iere: but as she *f*leeth a*f*ore / *F*aynting I *f*olowe; I *l*eve o*f* there*f*ore"), and visual ("owte...dowbte...abowte," "wynde...wylde"). This generates an iterative pattern that points toward barrenness and dearth.⁶⁶ The hunters all "spend [their] tyme in vain," being involved in a futile pursuit and desiring meed denied them by Caesar's prohibitive edict, which is inscribed, in the imperious Latin, on the hind's collar: "Noli me tangere for Cesars I ame."⁶⁷

As a result, the wildly measureless ("wylde for to hold, though I seme tame") demands of the pursuit place the subject on a threshold of death. It is indeed a poem "full of threats."⁶⁸ Obviously, it is tempting to read the sonnet in the context of Wyatt's conjectural loss of Anne Boleyn to Henry VIII and the peril in which the rivalry with the king put the poet.⁶⁹ Caesar does represent a source of danger for the hunter; since "the beloved wears a collar that marks her as the king's property, desire for her becomes a way of exploring a desire to displace the king himself."⁷⁰ It is also useful to recall that the sonnet is set in a royal forest, a distinct jurisdictional domain, and Henry's reign was one of the most severe forestry regimes in English history.[71] But is this threat of destruction exclusively secular? The line "Noli me tangere for Cesars I ame" is ambivalent: it points "in contradictory directions: the echo of Christ's words in the Garden of Gethsemane associates the lady with his untouchable charisma, while the second reduces her, like the coins, to a sign of wealth, irredeemably of this world, in opposition to the things of God."[72] However, in recent criticism the second biblical allusion—one asserting the preeminence of temporal authority and worldly economy—has been taken to supersede, and in fact annul, the first scriptural reference to Christ's "touche me not." In Greenblatt's paradigmatic reading, "the religious context" of the line "is invoked only to be violated, so that the reader experiences the wrenching transformation of the sacred to the profane."[73] Even nonhistoricist accounts of Wyatt's sonnet deny it any sense of transcendence of temporality.[74]

Yet the phrase "Noli me tangere," by putting Wyatt's speaker in the position of Mary Magdalene vis-à-vis Christ on the morning of his rising from the dead, invokes the problematic of subjectivity in the presence of a divine rather than secular authority. Its foreign language (Latin) already bears a mark of "eternal power, duration, alterity, and exclusiveness."[75] If anything, the collar and the motto imply a longevity way beyond temporal power: according to the legend, hinds wearing collars were still being found long after their imperial owners were dead.[76] Even if the text of the poem seeks to replace echoes of sacrality with the speaker's encounter with temporal power, residual traces of the divine experience still linger in the text, which remains "suspended" between these two frames of reference.[77] Wyatt's sonnet, in other words, is a fleeting record of God's manifestation of his divinity to man.

This experience of God re-emphasizes the Langlandian genealogy traceable in Wyatt's poem. By writing Christ's words into the speaker's experience of frustrated desire of meed, Wyatt constructs a form of subjectivity that in a number of important ways revisits Langland's poetic rumination on the potentialities of "mede mesurelees." On the one hand, the ban "Noli me tangere" implies a denial of materiality; it is something that should not, or may not, be touched. The measureless reward the weary hunter initially sought is material (the hind's flesh, the diamonds on her collar, or the coins she allegorizes), yet he is told to forego his tactile experience, not to touch this reward. It is also worth recalling that like a good Protestant, Wyatt purges Petrarch's Italian poem of all its visual exuberance, replacing it with written words "graven...in letters plain."[78] If all these material riches are "mede mesurelees, that maistres desireth," which constitutes, according to Langland, the primary object of the "coveitise of Mede," the speaker of Wyatt's poem replicates the experience of Will, who desires the material riches of Mede's body yet is exhorted by Holi Chirche to abandon them.

But this movement away from the "mede mesurelees" of economic and erotic desires coincides in Wyatt's sonnet with a step toward what Langland's poem presses Will to embrace but never succeeds in achieving—"first mede / of God." The lover, like Mary Magdalene, finds himself face to face with a God whose glory shines through death and whose terrifying presence-as-disappearance the subject cannot comprehend. The words on the hind's collar suggest the absolute gift of salvation, achieved through Christ's death as a promise of eternal life; and the scene of reading the inscription "Noli me tangere" is transformed into an encounter with God as absolute Other, the gift of life and death. All the threats inscribed in the sonnet are at this point rewritten as a form of being-toward-God, which translates into being-toward-death. The experience of desiring and being warned off the hind becomes, in the words of Jean-Luc Nancy, a matter of "holding oneself in the place of the impossible," which "comes down to holding oneself to where man is at his limit, that of his violence and his death."[79] The impossible, which is God's gift, is suggested as the lover's ultimate meed; the violence that we are tempted to attribute to Henry VIII is rewritten as the divine gift of death, the true measureless meed. The threat of destruction underpinning possession of the hind annuls this investment of labor and puts the reward the lover craves, as true "mede mesurelees," outside of the circle of exchange, into the aneconomic space of the divine. From this perspective, in the poetic time of "Noli me tangere for Cesars I ame," the authority of Caesar, seemingly usurping the divine gift of death, in fact serves as a mechanism for preserving life. Horrified by God's gift, Wyatt's subject withdraws from the chase in order to avoid touching the divine, into the sphere of worldly economy and property relations. The last image of the poem is that of the lover clinging to the profane materiality of the diamond-studded collar as his only link to human existence.

The experience of divine grace, which places the lover dangerously close to receiving the gift of death (so close that he can read the words that promise it), determines the status of poetry in Wyatt's sonnet. In contrast to Will's massive but ultimately wasteful verbal tapestry whose abundant expenditure is intended to emulate "mede mesurelees," "Who so list to hounte" seeks to disintegrate, either into the evanescent immateriality of the "wynde" of words slipping through the lover's fingers (with possible implications of excremental waste), or into the obscurity and even unreadability of the Latin inscribed at the core of an English poem (a poetic equivalent of God as the impossible and the untouchable). If the operations of language are analogous to the exchange of coins,[80] the only chance for a poem to break the economic circle of meed (coins, words, property), to avoid being an economy of exchange, is to dissolve into silence. In an attempt to imagine the ultimate expenditure (God's gift of death), the sonnet stages its own discursive self-erasure.[81] In its self-abortive brevity, its lexical parsimony (repeated phrases, structures, words, sounds), and its delegation of poetic vocality to other speakers (hind, Caesar, God), the sonnet echoes the unbearable intensity of touching the divine—the true "mede mesurelees."

"Greater Meed" of Spenser's *Amoretti*

Although ascribed to a G. W. J., the second commendatory sonnet at the beginning of Edmund Spenser's *Amoretti* occupies a prominent paratextual position, suggesting the terms in which the sequence will be read.

> Ah Colin, whether on the lowly plaine
> pyping to shepherds thy sweete roundelaies:
> or whether singing in some lofty vaine,
> heroick deedes, of past, or present daies:
> Or whether in thy louely mistris praise,
> thou list to exercise thy learned quill,
> thy muse hath got such grace, and power to please,
> with rare inuention bewtified by skill,
> As who therein can euer ioy their fill.
> O therefore let that happy muse proceede
> to clime the height of vertues sacred hill,
> where endles honor shall be made thy meede.
> Because no malice of succeeding daies,
> can rase those records of thy lasting praise.[82]

Its focus is what Heather Dubrow has aptly termed "genre criticism."[83] From the eclogues of *The Shepheardes Calender* and the epic of *The Faerie Queene,* the poem—and Spenser's career—progresses toward the *Amoretti,* a collection of amorous verse ("thy lovely mistris praise"). If the poet can take the next step ("O therefore let that happy muse proceede / to clime the height of vertues sacred hill") and retranslate his earlier achievements into a successful Petrarchan project, he will gain everlasting glory.

The intriguing aspect of the poem is that G. W. J. posits Spenser's ultimate reward as meed ("endles honor shall be made thy meede"), a word that appears ill suited to English Petrarchan sonnets but which Spenser—"the most English of early modern poets"[84]—himself uses in the *Amoretti* four times (in sonnets XXV, XXIX, LII, and LXXXVI).[85] A closer look suggests that several aspects of Langland's medieval "mede" do resonate with the "meede" prefacing Spenser's Petrarchan sequence. G. W. J. envisions it as a product of negotiating several genres, yet in the context of Spenser's career, the epic and the sonnet sequence also presuppose two distinct types of reward. Laureates, according to Richard Helgerson, view poetry as "a means of making a contribution to the order and improvement of the state," which leads them to become official poets.[86] But the office of a laureate also entails a financial benefit; it is not "an *economically* autonomous post" but, rather, "a task that the laureate performs for economic favors."[87] As Richard Rambuss notes, "Given Spenser's social and presumably financial ambitions... Spenser's laureate aspirations were inscribed within an established career track which projected advancement through dual service as a poet/bureaucrat."[88] Thus, 1591 brought Spenser a royal pension of £50 per annum clearly linked to the first three books of *The Faerie Queene*.[89] Spenser himself refers to this form of reward as meed in *Colin Clovts Come Home Againe* (1595): describing Cynthia's—that is, Queen Elizabeth's—generosity, Colin claims that her "euerie gift and euerie goodly meed...demaunds a day" (592–93). Meanwhile, the discourse of Petrarchan love is primarily associated with sexual favor that the lover/poet desires from his lady. Spenser's *Amoretti*, his "lovely mistris praise" and a chronicle of his courtship of Elizabeth Boyle, would thus imply the reward of erotic gratification.[90] The line between these two types of reward is of course not impenetrable. Bearing in mind that the language of passion in English Renaissance sonnet sequences often metaphorized social ambition, the erotic hopes of the Spenserian lover may encode an economic hope.[91] If anything, sales of the printed collection would constitute some financial gain, however paltry. As the unknown author of *Zepheria* (1594) sneered at his fellow Petrarchans,

> And some againe in mercinary writ
> Belch forth desire, making reward their Mistresse:
> And though it chaunce some *Lais* Patron it,
> At least they sell her prayses to the presse.[92]

Conversely, aspects of the erotic cult of Elizabeth found their way into the text of not only *The Faerie Queene* (Belphoebe) but of the *Amoretti* as well, where the lady is at times indistinguishable from the queen.[93]

The double sexual and pecuniary valence encoded in Langland's "mede mesurelees" is thus readable in the "meede" of the *Amoretti*'s commendatory sonnet. But the poem also envisions this meed as going beyond acquisitive desire and sexual appetite. As Patrick Cheney writes, in the *Amoretti*, "private relation with his beloved returns [Spenser] to the divine origin of his art."[94] Echoes of sacrality embedded in Spenser's "meede" ("vertues sacred hill") indeed deserve careful consideration: tying up poetic achievement with divine grace, the dedicatory sonnet places the project of the *Amoretti* at a conjunction of erotic love, economic reward, poetic fame, and divine experience. As a result, the "meede" that Spenser will find at "the height of vertues sacred hill" emerges as a structural equivalent of Langland's other meed—"that oon God of his grace graunteth in his blisse / To tho that wel werchen while thei ben here."

At this point in the *Amoretti* "meede" arguably invokes poetic glory rather than salvific grace, but what appears as a secularization of the Langlandian framework in G. W. J.'s sonnet can also be viewed as an extension of Reformation theology. Critics interested in the Protestantism of the *Amoretti* have focused on its endorsement of marriage as a temporal yet divinely sanctioned equivalent of the Petrarchan ideal of spiritual fulfillment, "a secular means for a sacred end."[95] But Protestant ideas also inflect the relationship between divine grace and the work of writing in Spenser's sequence. The new, Reformed vision of labor destroys the causal relationship between work and salvation and instead takes work as "the necessary means by which divine gifts are developed and employed."[96] Protestantism sees worldly work not as a road to salvation but, rather, as proof thereof. For Luther, "the fulfillment of duty in worldly affairs" became valued as "the highest form which the moral activity could assume," which "inevitably gave every-day worldly activity a religious significance"; and Calvinism added to this "the necessity of proving one's faith in worldly activity."[97] As R. H. Tawney formulates it, in Calvinism, the aim is "not personal salvation but the glorification of God, to be sought, not by prayer only, but by action—the sanctification of the world by strife and labor...Good works are not a way of attaining salvation, but they are indispensable as a proof that salvation has been attained."[98] In G. W. J.'s sonnet, the meed of worldly fame awaits the poet at the end of his work ("endles honor shall be made thy meede"), yet the very same work required of him ("clim[ing] the height of vertues sacred hill") is predicated on—rather than simply leads to—sacrality.

The opening sonnet of the *Amoretti* proper further develops this complex problematic of meed:

> Happy ye leaues when as those lilly hands,
> which hold my life in their dead doing might
> shall handle you and hold in loues soft bands,
> lyke captiues trembling at the victors sight.
> And happy lines, on which with starry light,
> those lamping eyes will deigne sometimes to look
> and reade the sorrowes of my dying spright,
> written with teares in harts close bleeding book.
> And happy rymes bath'd in the sacred brooke,
> of *Helicon* whence she deriued is,
> when ye behold the Angels blessed looke,
> my soules long lacked foode, my heauens blis.
> Leaues, lines, and rymes, seeke her to please alone,
> whom if ye please, I care for other none.

The poem picks up G. W. J.'s idea of several competing economies of desire. Erotic seduction is the lover's obvious goal; he hopes that his "trembling" "lines" (with a possible pun on "loins") will be "handled" by his mistress, "pleasing" her and, conversely, him as well. However, the financial reward for his book qua commodity, as well as aesthetic recognition for his work, should not be discounted. After all, the poet addresses his poems, not the lady. Further, sending his "trembling" verse to plead his case before the mistress is clearly an act of calculable investment on the part of the lover and thus an element of the restricted economy of reciprocity. But this act is performed at the point of death: his mistress's hands hold his life "in their dead doing might," his "spright" is "dying," and what he brings forth is "written with teares in harts close bleeding book." From this angle, the lover's desire of erotic and economic reward is negated by his looming death, turning his investment into a unilateral aneconomical gift. At the same time, the lover's pursuit of the lady whose "Angels blessed looke" is also his "soules long lacked foode, [his] heauens blis" signals a salvific dimension to their relationship. Coupled with the images of his impending death, the lady's love is endowed with redemptive qualities and molded into a form of God's ultimate gift.[99] Heavenly bliss becomes the lover's measureless meed. Furthermore, the sonnet establishes a correlation between the lady's attributes as a form of divine grace and her role as the source of the poet's inspiration. While his "happy rymes" are "bath'd in the sacred brooke," the very same "brooke" is the place of origin of his beloved ("the sacred brooke / of *Helicon* whence she deriued is"). Divine grace here becomes indistinguishable not only from poetic inspiration but also from the latter's product, "leaues, lines, and rymes." The sonnet presents Spenser's secular book simultaneously as an instrument of attaining the divine ("heauens blis") and as a sign of grace, for his own writing originates in a Christianized Helicon. The book is not only a means to a divine end but a sign of election.

That the Spenserian lover's subjectivity is articulated at an intersection of erotic, economic, poetic, and religious desire can, of course, be read as an Englishing of Petrarch: the *Rime sparse* also investigates the constant paronomastic metamorphosis of Laura (erotic object) into *l'aura* (breeze, or speech), *lauro* (laurels, fame), and *l'auro* (gold), even as it longs for a final resolution of the sequence's numerous tensions through a communion with the divine.[100] But the spatial proximity of Spenser's first sonnet to the fourfold vision of "meede" in G. W. J.'s prefatory poem also indicates that in order to conceptualize his subject's intertwined relationships with sexuality, economy, literature, and God, Spenser's sequence, at least in part, speaks the language of Langland's poem. What is remarkable about the *Amoretti* is not that it encodes economic, religious, or poetic concerns in an amatory language, but that it commingles them in one central idea expressed through a pointedly English concept ("meede") burdened with vernacular memory.

However, Spenser's meed is as much a continuation of Langland's meed as it is a radical rewriting of it. The constitutive elements of meed in the *Amoretti* are analogous to Will's, yet the architectonic of their relationship is strikingly different, with Langland's obsession with the singularity of meaning giving way to Spenser's celebration of semantic and conceptual fluidity. The text of *Piers Plowman* is preoccupied with restricting the play of signification offered by meed; it ruthlessly eliminates those aspects and meanings that it deems inadequate. By contrast, where Langland dissects, constricts, and rejects, Spenser builds up connections in order to keep the whole gamut of meed in play. Multiple desires freely roam the space of the opening sonnet, translating into one another and linking diverse forms of meed. Sexuality becomes the driving force behind textual production, which in turn is predicated on divine grace; the latter takes the form of the temporal labor of writing and book production, which is underwritten by a libidinous passion. Instead of Langland's careful semantic calibration, Spenser keeps all possibilities—meed as sexual gratification, as economic reward, as poetic glory, as divine gift—in constant motion and dialogue with one another.

It is also symptomatic that if in Langland and in Wyatt death enters the space of poetry as the *conditio sine qua* of the true gift, in Spenser's opening sonnet death operates as an open process ("dead doing," "dying") rather than finitude. The lady's "dead doing might" threatens but never quite extinguishes the lover's "lyfe." The line between the general economy of excess and expenditure and the restricted economy of scarcity and preservation is blurred; death becomes life, gift becomes exchange. To put it in a historical perspective, as meed moves from feudalism (*Piers Plowman*) to capitalism (*Amoretti*), an assemblage of decoded flows of desire comes to replace the rigid signifier.[101] Abandoning

Langland's dream of a fixed meaning in favor of the unhinged circulation of competing symbolic economies, Spenser seeks to arrive at the ultimate reward this side of life through the gift of poetic work and erotic relationship with the lady. In what follows I develop this argument and read the erotic narrative of the *Amoretti* as a metapoetic journey in search of non-Langlandian meed. The courtship part of the *Amoretti* (sonnets I–LXVI) is driven forward by the poet's struggles to articulate an allegory of reward that would amalgamate the many valences of meed; whereas the postbetrothal stage (sonnets LXVII–LXXXIX) deploys a newly discovered poetics of meed in a series of poems that celebrate the beloved as an answer to the multiplicity of the lover's desires.

Sonnet XV, a paraphrase of a poem by Philippe Desportes (*Diane* I.XXXII),[102] maps out the discursive field upon which the Langlandian and the Spenserian concepts of meed are negotiated:

> Ye tradefull Merchants that with weary toyle,
> do seeke most pretious things to make your gain:
> and both the Indias of their treasures spoile,
> what needeth you to seeke so farre in vaine?
> For loe my loue doth in her selfe containe
> all this worlds riches that may farre be found,
> if Saphyres, loe her eies be Saphyres plaine,
> if Rubies, loe hir lips be Rubies sound;
> If Pearles, hir teeth be pearles both pure and round;
> if Yuorie, her forhead yuory weene;
> if Gold, her locks are finest gold on ground;
> if siluer, her faire hands are siluer sheene,
> But that which fairest is, but few behold,
> her mind adornd with vertues manifold.

Although it is tempting to focus on the verbal parallels between Spenser's sonnet and Langland's mock-blazon, the continuity between the two texts lies more in the subject position they construct. Inviting the merchants to partake of this visual feast ("loe...loe...loe"), Spenser's poem follows the trajectory of Will's gaze that eroticizes and commodifies Mede. Not only is the lady sexually attractive to the masculine eye but her body also represents, and even surpasses, the material wealth so craved by the "tradefull Merchants."[103] The reward his lady promises, in other words, fuses the sexual and the pecuniary. Lisa Jardine singles out this type of admiration, "a mental response in which sensual delight is strenuously linked with an appreciation of the market value of the goods and the urge to acquire," as a specifically Renaissance phenomenon produced by a combination of burgeoning international trade and new developments in visual arts.[104] But the subject position Spenser's Renaissance poem constructs also replicates Will's medieval paralysis at the moment of his optic ravishment by Mede. As Spenser insinuates elsewhere in the *Amoretti,* this ocular desire may well be a form of *concupiscentia oculorum,* a blend of erotic longing with economic aspiration ("My hungry eyes through greedy couetize,.../ with no contentment can themselues suffize / but hauing pine and hauing not complaine" [XXXV.1, 3–4]). Like Langland's medieval "coveitise," this Protestant "couetize" invokes "a certain elision...between the cardinal sins of avarice and lust."[105] The lady is an erotic commodity that promises to fill the lover's eyes *and* warehouses ("Yet are mine eyes so filled with the store / of that faire sight, that nothing else they brooke" [XXXV.9–10]).

Unlike the Mede blazon, however, Spenser's sonnet XV offers more than a vision of "mede mesurelees." The couplet privileges the beloved's mind as a Neoplatonic paragon of intellectual beauty and virtue and even seeks to play down the visual element of his lady's appearance (her mind is what "few behold"). Yet this move is one of integration, not disjunction. Nowhere does the poem reject the erotic and economic pleasures the lady's body promises; rather, those are included in the reward of her virtuous mind, for the speaker "distinguishes himself from the merchants in terms of an economy he ascribes to them."[106] What he seeks, rather, is to recast these disparate aspirations as parts of his larger project of reward where material possessions, sexuality, and writing open onto each other. Roger Kuin may be right to argue that the couplet "seems within the invention of this sonnet quite out of place" and represents a "false" or "fruitless" solution to the poet's problem.[107] It does register, however, an attempt to transcend the "mede mesurelees" of commodified sexuality and attain the all-encompassing—"manifold"—form of meed, even though the poet himself may be unhappy with the result.[108]

One of the challenges of wrestling meed from Langlandian influence is that in the early sonnets Spenser repeatedly imagines the process as "toyle." He applies this term to his erotic wooing (his "restless toile" in sonnet XI.6), economic activity (the merchants' "weary toyle" in sonnet XV), and his own writing (the "tædious toyle" of *The Faerie Queene* and "this one" of the *Amoretti* in sonnet XXXIII). But his meed does not fully subscribe to the principles of the restricted economy of work:

> How long shall this lyke dying lyfe endure,
> And know no end of her owne mysery:
> but wast and weare away in termes vnsure,
> twixt feare and hope depending doubtfully.
> Yet better were attonce to let me die,
> and shew the last ensample of your pride:
> then to torment me thus with cruelty,
> to proue your powre, which I too wel haue tride.
> But yet if in your hardned brest ye hide,
> a close intent at last to shew me grace:
> then all the woes and wrecks which I abide,
> as meanes of blisse I gladly wil embrace.
> And wish that more and greater they might be,
> that greater meede at last may turne to mee.   (XXV)

In this sonnet, the lover faces two outcomes: to perish in a Wyattesque general economy of unrequited passion never to be reciprocated by his Petrarchan mistress; or to survive through the promise of a future erotic reciprocity. But the latter will be merely an intensification of the lover's current condition of "lyke dying lyfe" that "know[s] no end of her owne mysery." The grace his lady will grant him will reveal itself as an increase of "all the woes and wrecks," which he will embrace as a "meanes of blisse" and his "greater meede." Yet his "greater meede" is not a form of compensation for his toil but rather a free gift that chooses its recipient ("that greater meede at last may turne to mee"). Besides, if greater "woes and wrecks" constitute "greater meede," then the "woes and wrecks" he already feels can also be read as a form of meed, which would indicate that his "lyke dying lyfe," a vulnerable form of being at the limit of life and death, is in itself a manifestation of "grace" and "blisse" (with clear religious connotations)—a sign of meed rather than the labor that will bring it.

Not surprising, when the poet appears to reach his erotic and poetic goal, in sonnet LXVII, his possession of meed "presents itself apart from his action."[109] The poem allegorizes the promise of marriage by rewriting Petrarch's *"Una candida cerva"* and Wyatt's "Who so list to hounte" as a story of success. Spenser's hind "sought not to fly, but fearelesse still did bide: / till I in hand her yet halfe trembling tooke, / and with her owne goodwill hir fyrmely tyde" (10–12). The hind, however, is not just an erotic object, for she is "the gentle deare" "so goodly wonne" (7, 14), a form of economic reward. In poetic terms, meanwhile, the sonnet reclaims Petrarchan legacy and glory, both Italian and native. Besides, given the dense biblical echoes of sonnet LXVII, Spenser's hind simultaneously embodies a promise of divine meed.[110] What he is about to enjoy amalgamates eroticism, economy, sacrality, and textual production.

Fittingly, this meed is aligned with gift rather than "toile." The events of the sonnet transpire after "weary chace" in which the lover sees "the game from him escapt away" (1–2). Like Wyatt's, his work of hunting is "long pursuit and vaine assay" (5), so when the hind submits herself to his will, he cannot conceal his astonishment: "Strange thing me seemd to see a beast so wyld, / so goodly wonne with her owne will beguyld" (13–14). Indeed, all action would appear to be the hind's, yet her will, John King argues, "accords with the right operation of that human faculty in accordance with divine grace."[111] In the Easter sonnet that immediately follows (LXVIII), the love the speaker and his mistress share is figured as a metaphor of the absolute gift of divine self-sacrifice. Christ made "triumph ouer death and sin" (2) and "diddest dye" for humanity (6); the poet and his lady are "with thy deare blood clene washt from sin" (7), and their love becomes "the lesson which the Lord vs taught" (14). This implies, Anne Lake Prescott writes, that "grace and love are unearned...coming to us *despite* our lack of deserving."[112] Reflecting back on the self-surrendering hind of LXVII, this offers another reminder that the origin of the poet's meed (be it the lady's body, wealth, or poetic achievement) is the measureless divine gift.

Unlike Wyatt's sonnet, however, where an encounter with the divine threatens the existence of both the subject and his poem, in Spenser the sacred is realized in the secular domain of human existence, and the gifts of love, salvation, and economic recompense unfold in writing. If Wyatt's sonnet dreams of disintegrating into an immaterial "wynde," Spenser's lover holds in his hands a "hynd" whose description echoes that of the book of the *Amoretti* itself from the opening sonnet. There, he envisioned his "trembling" "leaues" and "lines" as bound by the lady's "lilly hands"; here, in a gender chiasmus, her "trembling" body is bound by his hand ("I in hand her yet halfe trembling tooke, /

with her own good will hir fyrmely tyde" [LXVII.11–12]). His meed is not only his bride, or her dowry, or salvation, but also the elusive text on which he has been at work since the beginning of the sequence. Yet it comes as a gift rather than an earned reward (this becomes particularly palpable if we recall the multiple intertextual debts Spenser incurs in writing this sonnet, not to mention the unpayable debt of language itself); it does not pay the poet for work but instead offers a material, temporal space in which divine inspiration can be revealed.

Postbetrothal sonnets develop the idea of the lover's meed as a multifaceted object of complex economic, sexual, poetic, and sacral desire. In LXXIV, Spenser famously thanks three Elizabeths—his mother, his queen, and his beloved—for the "guifts of body, fortune and of mind" (4), linking all three women "that three such graces did vnto me giue" (14) with different aspects of meed. At first sight, the forms of meed represented by the three women appear to be in conflict. The queen (Elizabeth Tudor) is associated primarily with pecuniary reward and poetic fame ("my soueriegne Queene most kind, / that honour and large richesse to me lent" [7–8]). By contrast, the gift of his beloved and soon-to-be-wife (Elizabeth Boyle), "by whom [his] spirit out of dust was raysed: / to speake her prayse and glory excellent" (10–11), suggests grace that overcomes the allure of the flesh ("dust") and thus opposes the transient wealth promised by the queen, although the images of elevation may also imply penile tumescence, that is, erotic meed. At the same time, by crediting his mother with his "body" (4) and "being" (5) and thus life, the poet opposes her to the queen, who is incessantly associated with violence and death throughout the *Amoretti*.[113] When his mother's gift of "body" is revealed as "dust," however, it finds a contrast in his beloved's gift leading his spirit "out of dust" to God. Conflicts proliferate, and the sonnet appears to pit queen against mistress, mother against queen, and mistress against mother. However, its principal movement is that of resolution, for it seeks to erase these conflicts through the text of the poem itself: the identity of the three women's names (all three are called Elizabeth) superimposes the varieties of meed associated with each upon the others. Sexual pleasure becomes one with economic reward, life is equated with death, and the heavenly merges with the worldly. Crucially, this meed emerges through "most happy letters fram'd by skilfull trade" (1): the poet's "trade"—writing—facilitates exchange ("trade") between diverse flows of desire and becomes the terrain where this polymorphic meed can be formulated and enjoyed.

In blazonic sonnets LXXVI, LXXVII, and LXXXI, Spenser likewise anticipates a form of meed that blurs the lines between economic, erotic, and spiritual satisfaction. In LXXVII, the lady's breasts appear as "twoo golden apples of vnualewd price" that lie in "a siluer dish" on "that table...so richly spredd" (6, 5, 13). In LXXXI, returning to the mercantile rhetoric of sonnet XV, Spenser compares the beloved's breast to a ship loaded with expensive goods (an economic object): "Fayre when her brest lyke a rich laden barke, / with pretious merchandize she forth doth lay" (5–6), and her mouth becomes "the gate with pearles and rubyes richly dight" (10). But at this point in the sequence, the Spenserian lover's meed clearly exceeds "mede mesurelees," for the lady's body, in addition to being a source of sexual and economic pleasures, is also "the sacred harbour of that heuenly spright" (LXXVI.4). As William Kennedy writes, in these blazons "what begins as a visual tour of the beloved's body, a debased Petrarchan blazon, releases the speaker's sacral imagination."[114] The poems simultaneously deploy several frameworks of desire (sexuality, economy, religion), constantly shifting perspective in order to unleash the multiple energies of meed.

But when it would appear that the project of the *Amoretti* is complete and the lady's love, together with an agglomeration of other forms of reward, is secured and manifested through the poetic text, the reader is presented with one of the most enigmatic elements of Spenser's sequence— the carefully choreographed final separation of the lovers (sonnets LXXXVII–LXXXIX). English sonnet sequences in general, Carol Neely suggests, are characterized by open-endedness.[115] The case of the *Amoretti* is different, however, because its narrative of courtship and betrothal demands closure. Yet having gone from Petrarchan desolation to an assurance of conjugal bliss, Spenser suddenly (and inexplicably) thrusts his speaker back to ground zero of courtly writing—a lover pining hopelessly for his unattainable beloved. This enigmatic move clearly violates the textual logic of the collection and has invited a number of interpretive solutions—technical, numerological, psychological, and biographical.[116]

But does the loss of possession also metapoetically signify the impossibility of attaining non-Langlandian meed? To a degree, it is possible to answer this question in the affirmative if we connect the Spenserian lover's erotic frustration to the precarious vision of meed shattered by conflicting desires. For even as the postbetrothal sonnets celebrate the harmonious multiplicity of meed, they carry fissures within it. In the late blazons, to take the most obvious example, Spenser's "sensual fantasy threatens to warp the poet's view of the lady in favor of fleshly rather than spiritual qualities."[117] Sonnet LXXVI betrays the speaker's anxiety about his ability to control his sexual appetite: "How was I rauisht with your louely sight, / and my frayle thoughts too rashly led astray"; "Sweet thoughts I enuy your so happy rest, / which oft I wisht, yet never was so blest" (5–6, 13–14). Likewise, sonnet LXXXIV, addressing the lover's "pure affections" and "modest thoughts breathd from wel tempred sprites" (5, 6), reasserts his lady's status as an allegory of divine gift: "Onely behold her rare perfection, / and blesse your fortunes fayre election" (13–14). Yet the lover's desires are far from virtuous. Addressing himself, he insists that "not one sparke of filthy lustfull fyre / breake out, that may her sacred peace molest," and "ne one light glance of sensuall desyre: / Attempt to work her gentle mindes unrest" (1–4).[118]

In this reading, the lover's loneliness in the final poems of the *Amoretti* becomes, to use Christopher Warley's perceptive phrase, "an extension of the contradictions present throughout the sequence."[119] That is, Spenser's sequence would appear to admit defeat in its attempts to construct a textual space in which meed would overcome the shattering influence of Langlandian parsing and present a workable unity of reciprocity and gift, sexual and religious desires, work and grace. Suggestively, instead of being united with his beloved and enjoying the "meede" of "endlesse honor," in sonnet LXXXVI—which immediately precedes the three separation sonnets—Spenser blames a "venemous toung" whose "poysoned words and spitefull speeches" "in my true loue did stirr vp coles of yre" and demands that "shame be thy meed" (1, 4, 8, 13). It is utterly plausible that Spenser curses an unknown slanderer whose lies caused a temporary separation of the lovers.[120] However, the closest imaginative parallel to this shaming of the tongue is Spenser's own image of the poet Malfont undergoing a degrading punishment in book 5 of *The Faerie Queene* (his "tongue was for his trespasse vyle / Nayled to the post, adiudged so by law").[121] The tongue that was supposed to earn the author of the *Amoretti* the "meede" of "endlesse honor" here embodies the despair of poetic nonfulfillment. Undoing the work of semantic recuperation, sonnet LXXXVI restores to "meed" its Langlandian connotations of depravity and vice.

But it is also possible to read the final sonnets of isolation less as symptoms of the Spenserian subject's failure to attain meed and more as products of a dialectic of measure and *un*measure inscribed within the notion of meed itself. In Langlandian usage, meed is an excessive symbolic unit whose radically "mesurelees" linguistic economy is predicated upon a superabundance of meaning. In contrast to the medieval poet's attempts to circumscribe its sprawling significatory potential, Spenser embraces the semantic chaos of meed, charging it with erotic, economic, salvific, and poetic value. But if the *Amoretti* derives its inspiration from an impulse to pursue multiple forms of meed at once, the calculated measures of Spenser's poetry ("leaues, lines, and rymes")—a product of the restricted economy of limited resources—are bound to come into conflict with the unruly excesses of meed. The measure of the *Amoretti* is undermined—or, to use a surprisingly apposite term from the thought of Maurice Blanchot, "unworked"—by the intractable *un*measure of meed.¹²² These sonnets of separation, then, indicate the poet's reluctance to terminate the process of textual dilation, and the indeterminacy of the *Amoretti*'s conclusion speaks not of Spenser's bankruptcy in his ambition to attain non-Langlandian meed but, rather, of the endless potentiality of writing about it. Confronted with meed, instead of abandoning his text (like Wyatt), or completely de-aestheticizing it as a wasteful verbal effort (like Langland), Spenser makes the measureless nature of meed and the ensuing impossibility of an ending part of his aesthetic project. *Un*measure becomes a central element of his measured work. This constitutes one more step in the process (begun in the opening sonnet) of imagining his poetic text as belonging simultaneously to the general economy of unrestricted giving and the limited economy of scarcity. Meed being a synonym of excess, the work of meed—the work of love, of writing, of faith—is endless.

To embody meed, the *Amoretti* needs to be measureless because the gifts of language, of poetry, of grace belong to the order of excess and will never be exhausted by a single Petrarchan sequence. It must become a book that, according to Blanchot, "collects an extreme capacity for rupture, a limitless anxiety, one that the book cannot contain.... Such a book, always in movement, always on the verge of scattering, will also always be gathered in all directions, through dispersion itself and according to the division essential to it, which makes it not disappear but appear, maintaining this dispersion so the book can accomplish itself."[123] By insisting upon the elusiveness of poetic closure, the *Amoretti* asserts the limitless promise of poetry as the poet's true meed.

Pursuing Meed in *Emaricdulfe* and *Parthenophil and Parthenophe*

Emaricdulfe (1595), written by "E. C.," about whom nothing is known, is just another write-by-numbers Elizabethan sonnet sequence.[124] Yet its concerns are similar to those of the *Amoretti*, which allows us to set Spenser's poetic agenda against another sonnet sequence preoccupied with poetic labor and poetic meed. Similar to the *Amoretti*, E. C.'s beloved in *Emaricdulfe* is represented as an embodiment of divine grace:

> Al those that write of heauen and heauenly ioyes,
> Describe the way with narrow crooked bendings,
> Beset with griefe, paine, horror and annoyes,
> That till all end haue neuer perfect endings.
> The heauen wherein my thoughts are resident,
> The paradice wherein my heart is sainted,
> Through street-like straight hie-waies I did attempt,
> Nor with rough care nor rigorous crosse attainted.
> I must confesse faith was the only meane,
> For that wich some for want thereof did misse,

Only thereby at length I did obtaine,
And by that faith am now instal'd in blisse:
There sleepe my thoughts, my heart there set thy rest,
Both heart & thoughts thinke that her heauen is best. (XXI)

Although part of a Petrarchan sequence, the sonnet hardly registers erotic desire at all. With the exception of a punning reference to "her heauen" in the last line, the poet is preoccupied exclusively with the spiritual. Boasting to the reader of his "blisse," E. C. claims that his faith made sure that he could find a direct pathway toward a "paradice wherein my heart is sainted." If there is ambiguity about what the lover's object of desire is, it is rather feeble: his love is first and foremost a divine experience. Unlike Spenser, whose meed functions as an assemblage of erotic, economic, salvific, and poetic aspirations, E. C. seems happy to purify as much as possible his vision of Emaricdulfe—in his sonnets, she is portrayed as a heavenly mistress whose reciprocity offers a direct and unequivocal sign of grace.

In this regard, it is interesting to compare E. C.'s translation of Desportes's *Diane* I.XXXII—"What meane our Merchants so with eger minds / To plough the seas to finde rich iuels forth?"—with Spenser's version. Similar to *Amoretti*'s XV, E. C.'s version (uncannily placed at number XV in *Emaricdulfe* as well) adds to the concluding couplet a sentiment absent in Desportes—"Her other parts (proud *Cupids* countermate) / Exceed the world for worth, the heauens for state." But E. C.'s sonnet is less flexible than Spenser's translation in equating the beloved with the sacred. By insisting that the lady's "other parts," which we are likely to identify as her genitalia, are "*Cupids* countermate" (i.e., rival, antagonist), E. C. in fact seeks to divorce the poem from any suggestion of eroticism. Where Spenser builds his sonnet XV up toward a synthetic polyvalence of the beloved's attractions, the author of *Emaricdulfe* sanitizes the Petrarchan image of his lady and concludes his version of the poem with an affirmation of her divine powers (she exceeds "heauens for state").

The sacralization of the lady has an important corollary for the status of writing in E. C.'s sequence. In the *Amoretti*, I have argued, writing operates at once as a means and a product of the divine. In *Emaricdulfe*, meanwhile, the work of writing and the experience of the sacred are rigorously dissociated. In sonnet XXI quoted above, E. C.'s faith-inspired direct route to "heauen and heauenly ioyes" is contrasted with the crooked paths of other lovers: while he relies solely on faith ("faith was the only meane"), others have to turn to the long and painful process of (poetic) labor without guaranteed results ("Beset with griefe, paine, horror / That till all end haue neuer perfect endings"). In subsequent sonnets, E. C. proceeds to disparage his own verse as "rough-hewed lines, these ragged words / That neuer stil'd from the Castalian spring…Nor neuer learn'd with pleasant tune to sing" (XXII) and to distance himself from "moderne Laureats of this later age, / That liue the worlds admirement for your writ, / And seeme infused with a diuine rage," hoping instead to "to cote…/ Her graces with my learnings scarsitie" (XXIII).

Earlier in the sequence, he expressed hope that his pen and muse "Shall now learne skill my Ladies fame to raise…/ And honour her with more immortall praise" (sonnet IV), and in the penultimate poem he is adamant that "with immortall flowres of poesie" he will "deck my inuention for thy dignitie: / With heauenly hymnes thy more then heauenly parts / Ile deifie, thy name commands such dutie" (sonnet XXXIX). But the last sonnet in the sequence shatters this ambition. There he expects other poets like Daniel and Spenser to immortalize his beloved; what he reserves for himself is idle contemplation:

> *Delias* sweete Prophet shall the praises singe
> Of bewties worth exemplified in thee,
> And thy names honour in his sweete tunes ring:

Thy vertues *Collin* shall immortalize,
Collin chast vertues organ sweetst esteem'd,
When for *Elizas* name he did comprise
Such matter as inuentions wonder seem'd.
Thy vertues hee, thy bewties shall the other
Christen a new, whiles I sit by and wonder.   (XL)

While Spenser promises his beloved, "my verse your vertues rare shall eternize" (LXXV.11), E. C.'s sequence contrasts writing and virtue. In the prefatory epistle, E. C. describes *Emaricdulfe* as "an idle worke I had begun, at the command and seruice of a faire Dame...so sweete a Saint"; and he expresses hope that his friends will "excuse my vnlearned writing, in regard you may be assured I am no scholler, as dooth appeare by this my worthles verse." By the last poem this attitude comes full circle. Although, like Spenser's Elizabeth, his beloved may be sanctified, his relationship with his mistress is located outside the process of poetic labor, his verse completely disconnected from the work of salvation. His bliss is obtained through faith, and his verse neither contributes toward achieving the goal nor offers proof of such attainment. In contrast to Spenser, who constantly tries to discern new possibilities for involving his verse in multiple experiences, E. C. is happy to achieve spiritual bliss through the work of faith, leaving poetry to others. In fact, writing is something he is compelled to perform by duty: "Both heart, and pen, and muse shall thinke it dutie, / With sigheswolne words to blaze her heaue[n]ly beutie," he declares early in the sequence (sonnet IV). Remarkably, in *Emaricdulfe* "meede" is a form of service that the poet renders to the lady: "Then for thy wisedomes well deseruing meede, / In loues pure dutie thou shalt ay command mee" [sonnet XVIII]). She is the one who obtains meed from the lover in the form of his forced textual labor infinitely disengaged from divine aspirations. If for Langland the "mesurelees" wasting of words may offer a negative analogy to the "mede mesurelees" of divine grace, for E. C. there is no common measure whatsoever between his sacred desires and his "rough-hewed lines" and "ragged words."

A radically different form of meed is developed by Barnabe Barnes in *Parthenophil and Parthenophe* (1593).[125] Notwithstanding a few clichéd references to the beloved's divine nature in the early sonnets—her "sainctlike bewtie" (sonnet XLIV.5) and her angelic speech ("euery word she speakes [is] an Angels grace" [sonnet XXVI.12])—Barnes's lover explicitly denies her any link with the sacred. By accusing her of cruelty, he claims that although her actions "make thee saint-like," her "hard hart makes all these graces weedes" (sonnet XXVIII.13–14). The meed he seeks is purely worldly. Moreover, from the start his desire is coded in economic and sexual terms: "How great a wast, of mynde and bodies weale / Now meltes my soule!" (sonnet X.12–13). Loving Parthenophe is a form of economic loss incurred by his unsatisfied desire:

> These eyes thy bewties tenants, pay due teares
> For ocupation of myne hart thy free hold:
> In tenour of loues seruice (if thou behold)
> With what exaction it is helde through feares,
> And yet thy rentes extorted, dayly beares,
> Thou would not thus consume my quiets gold.
> And yet tho couetous thou be, to make
> Thy bewtie rich, with renting me so roughlie
> And at such sommes, thou neuer thought doest take,
> But still consumes me, then thou doest misguide all:
> Spending in sport for which I wrought so toughlie.
> When I had felt all torture and had tryed all,
> And spent my stocke through streane of thine extortion
> Oh that I had but good hopes for my portion.   (sonnet XX)

The purpose of this extended legal metaphor is to highlight the nature of Parthenophil's experience of love as constant and unrelenting depletion of his "stock." If being in love with Parthenophe is akin to holding a tenancy, the terms of this arrangement are extortionist. The rents the lady's "couetous" beauty demands from the lover threaten to consume the latter in an ever-insatiable "streane" of exorbitant "sommes" of devotion "exacted" from him. Against a mistress who seeks to enrich her virgin self, Parthenophil is left bare and helpless, despite having "felt all torture and had tryed all." In this asymmetrical relationship, his desire becomes a form of useless expenditure, a process of wasting resources without any recompense from the lady.

The lover's interminable despair—after all, the beloved's name Parthenophe (from the Greek παρθένο, virgin) precludes any possibility of reciprocity—is reminiscent of Wyatt's sonnets. There is, however, an important difference in the ways Wyatt and Barnes develop precarious subjectivity faced with the measurelessness of erotic experience. If the Henrician poet seeks to withdraw (abeit unsuccessfully) from what he sees as an irrecoverable waste of his libidinous energy or, in "Who so list to hounte," to replace it with the equally formidable divine gift of death, the Elizabethan sonneteer is more concerned with recovering his losses. Having yielded his heart to Parthenophe, he expects her to reciprocate the gesture: "Oh make exchange, surrender thine for myne," he demands rudely (sonnet XV.7). His tone becomes more insistent as the sequence progresses: in sonnet 73, reminding the mistress that she has endless resources in her possession ("Why did rich nature graces graunt to thee, / Since thou art such a niggard of thy grace"?), he craves his portion of the riches: "Graunt me some grace, for thou with grace art wealthie / And kindely mayst afforde some gratious thing" (1–2, 9–10). Instead of the "thankelesse meede" of serving her (sonnet XXV.12), he desires a rich meed of sexual pleasure.

Barnes's version of Desportes's erotico-economic blazon is illuminating precisely because it foregoes all the gestures toward the beloved's celestial status made by Spenser and E. C., restoring to the English poem the French original's preoccupation with material wealth and sexual desire and simultaneously reinforcing its Langlandian overtones:

> I wish no rich-refinde Arabian gold,
> Nor Orient Indian pearle rare natures wonder,
> No Diamondes th'Aegiptian surges vnder,
> No Rubyes of America deare sold,
> Nor Saphyres which rich Affricke sandes enfold,
> Treasures far distant, from this Isle a sunder,
> Barbarian Iuories in contempt I hold:
> But onely this, this onely Venus graunt
> That I my sweet Parthenophe may get:
> Her heires no grace of golden wyers want,
> Pure pearles with perfect Rubines are in set,
> True Dyamondes in eyes, Saphires in vaynes,
> Nor can I that soft Iuory skinne forget:
> England in one small subiect such containes. (sonnet XLVIII)

The sonnet features a curious mirror structure, where the first half of the poem is at once negated and affirmed by the remainder of the text. The opening seven lines set up expectations that the speaker is about to renounce the allure of material possessions. But when his true desires are revealed, the poem goes on to incorporate all the previously repudiated economic riches into the map of her sexual body. The poem folds in on itself, interlacing eroticism with economism as the lover's only meed. As the sonnet is driven forward by a single line of argument, so is the lover consumed by a single desire to possess Parthenophe. In this, it comes closest to Will's reaction to the spectacle of Mede in Langland's erotico-economic blazon. Fittingly, at the end of the sequence, Parthenophil concludes a sonnet on the seven deadly sins by describing himself as "couetous [for] I neuer meane can keepe" (sonnet XCVII.12). Barnes willingly and knowingly succumbs to "coveitise of mede." Parthenophil's desire for meed—his obsession with reciprocal economic and sexual gestures—determines the status of writing in Barnes's sequence. In Langland, Wyatt, and E. C. poetry is posited—albeit by different routes—as a form of wastefulness; in Spenser, when he imagines his poetry as a pathway toward salvific experience, a means to an end, this pathway's success is contingent upon its nature as a manifestation of divine grace. For Parthenophil, however, writing becomes an investment that is bound to yield a return:

> Write write, helpe helpe, sweet muse and neuer cease
> In endlesse labours pennes and papers tyer
> Vntill I purchase my long-wish't desier:
> Braynes with my reason neuer rest in peace,
> Wast breathlesse wordes, and breathfull sighes increase,
> Till of my woes remorsefull you espye her,
> Till she with me, be burnt in equall fier.
> I neuer will from labour wittes release
> My sences neuer shall in quiet rest
> Till thou be pitifull, and loue alike. (sonnet XVIII.1–10)

Despite addressing an unresponsive, pitiless mistress who threatens to render writing a hopeless, profitless, wasteful activity, Parthenophil expects this scriptive labor to purchase him the sexual graces of his beloved. In this world of limited resources, writing is instrumentalized and turned into an element of reciprocity.

Parthenophil's desire for a meed of erotic and economic riches culminates in the final poem of his collection, a triple sestina in which he fantasizes using black magic in order to rape Parthenophe and thus finally get what he believes he deserves (sestine 5). In sonnet CV, the last in the collection and placed immediately before the pornographic sestina, Parthenophil elaborates the transition: having found Parthenophe "ruthlesse, and vnkinde," he decides to change "the tenour of my louely dittie: / By whose enchaunting sawes, and magicke spell / Thine hard indurate hart, I must compell" (9, 12–14). "Changing the tenour of [his] louely dittie," of course, is a shift in the genre from sonnet to sestina. But for Barnes it is accompanied by a change in the role of poetry within the economy of desire. He begins the sestina in the hope that his verse will finally become the ultimate tool of sexual gratification; in fact, he rejects poetry and instead utters "enchaunting sawes, and magicke spell," which should make his words effective and gainful. With earlier sonnets of unrequited yearning apparently rejected as a "wast" of "breathlesse wordes" and "increase" of "breathfull sighes" (sonnet XVIII.5), the final poem of the sequence is designed to bring Parthenophil the desired return on his verbal investment. In addition to serving as an instrument of obtaining reward, the sestina also reiterates Parthenophil's denial of sacrality as a form of meed. The rites he performs for Hecate—"This wine aboute this aulter, to the furies / I sprinkle... About this alter, and rich incense kindled / This lace and *Veruine* to loues bitter furies / I binde" (sestine 5.14–15, 32–34)—clearly suggest "inverted Christian ritual."[126] In turn, the ritual makes the poem "the only logical conclusion of that state of mind that gives preeminence to the physical fulfillment of desire"[127]—at the expense of all other forms of meed.

In the end, however, Parthenophil's dream of sexually enjoying Parthenophe as part of the restricted economy of exchange is undone by the discursive forces of meed. The concluding envoy, "Tis now acquitted: cease your former teares, / For as she once with rage my bodie kindled, / So in hers am I buried this night" (sestine 5.109–11), reveals more than Parthenophil would wish to disclose. Invoking the legalistic rhetoric of earlier sonnets, he insists that the lady's debt has been paid ("acquitted"); whatever obligations toward him she may have incurred in the long process of his wooing and writing have been wiped off in the act of sexual consummation. As the last line signals, however, the stakes in this relationship with meed are too enormous to be contained within the circle of limited exchange. The enjoyment of erotic meed leaves the lover dead and his text "exhausted"—"rhythmically flabby, rhetorically limp."[128] For Bataille, transgressive sexuality, especially that which takes an orgiastic, sacrilegious form, defies the idea of efficacy and belongs instead to the general economy of useless consumption and loss.[129] But we know as much from Langland: the opening blazon articulates a link between "coveitise of Mede" and death; and we can sense a similar threat of annihilation when Parthenophil's fantasy of rape draws to a close. Reaching out to touch the "mede mesurelees" of erotic excess, Barnes's Petrarchan lover discovers the lethal danger of obtaining meed.

Parthenophil's vulnerability once again reminds us that the Langlandian legacies continue to haunt the writing of meed even after 200 years. This chapter has by no means presented an exhaustive history of the word "meed" in premodern English poetry, but what it has demonstrated is that the energies that pulsate within the early modern Petrarchan visions of meed bear an unmistakable medieval imprint. The tensions between the economies of work and of the gift, the incommensurability between the human and the divine giving and taking, the impossibility of determining whether poetry belongs to the world of measured scarcity or to the world of measureless excess—all the contradictions that the Mede episode of *Piers Plowman* brings to the fore and makes a matter of poetic analysis are still embedded in the memory of English poetic discourse in the late Tudor period. When Renaissance poets like Wyatt, Spenser, or Barnes make their Petrarchan lovers come face to face with a desire for meed, their imaginative constructions incorporate vestiges of the

Langlandian symbolic economies. Across two centuries of poetic history, their Petrarchan voices echo the concerns articulated by the medieval poem. The specific modulations these voices take differ from one another. Wyatt shuns the meed of inordinate sexual and economic desires only to find his selfhood imperiled by a close proximity to the meed of God's grace, whereas Spenser in the *Amoretti* attempts to break the barriers between measureless and measured meed, between sexuality and God, between the work and the gift. In comparison to Spenser, both E. C.'s and Barnes's sonnets engage in a simplification of meed as both sequences purge Langland's concept of its contradictions, shrinking its expanse to religious salvation and sexual gratification, respectively. But in all these scenarios of desiring subjectivity, the language of self-articulation evinces a striking degree of interlacement between the Renaissance codes of Petrarchism and the medieval codes of meed, so that the Langlandian poetic imagination emerges as constitutive of early modern English Petrarchan identities.

Two

Chaucerian Melancholy in Renaissance England

Surrey's "Songes and Sonettes"
and Sidney's "Astrophil and Stella"

In a frequently invoked passage from *An Apologie for Poetrie* (c. 1580), Sir Philip Sidney reflects upon the lamentable state of contemporaneous English poetry, contrasting it unfavorably with the splendor of the days gone by. He wonders why "England (the Mother of excellent mindes) should bee growne so hard a stcp-mothcr to Poets, who certainly in wit ought to passe all other." Sidney finds it especially depressing because "heertofore Poets haue in England also flourished... And now that an ouer-faint quietnes should seem to strew the house for Poets, they are almost in as good reputation as the *Mountibancks* at *Venice*."[1] In light of these remarks, the choice of poets that Sidney allows into his exemplary vernacular canon becomes particularly intriguing. According to Sidney, "*Chaucer*, vndoubtedly, did excellently in hys *Troylus* and *Cresseid*; of whom, truly, I know not whether to meruaile more, either that he in that mistie time could see so clearely, or that wee in this cleare age walke so stumblingly after him....I account the *Mirrour of Magistrates* meetely furnished of beautiful parts; and in the Earle of Surries *Liricks* many things tasting of a noble birth, and worthy of a noble minde. The *Sheapheards Kalendar* hath much Poetrie in his Eglogues: indeede worthy the reading, if I be not deceiued."²

By mentioning two relatively recent texts (*The Mirror for Magistrates* and Spenser's *Sheapheardes Calender*) and two poets of the past (Geoffrey Chaucer and Henry Howard, Earl of Surrey), Sidney opens up a curious diachronic perspective on English poetry. Given the rhetoric of motherhood and originary loss that Sidney previously employs to describe the barren poetic landscape around him, such reverence toward the dead Chaucer (leaving Surrey aside for the moment) hardly comes as a surprise. As Thomas A. Prendergast demonstrates, the institutionalization of Chaucer as the father of English poetry in the fifteenth and sixteenth centuries was inextricably linked with "an aesthetics of melancholia" — the process of mourning Chaucer's death and supplying, as it were, the body of his works in lieu of his dead body.³ But what precisely does Sidney the poet invest in this melancholic bridging of past and present that we find in Sidney the critic? Is this allusion to Chaucer's authority by an Elizabethan poet merely a rhetorical ploy attempted by a vernacular desperately in need of a legitimatizing pedigree, one that ultimately attests to the incommensurability between Chaucer's medieval poetics and early modern literary strategies?⁴ Does the shift in writerly and readerly attitudes to Chaucer that occurs by the end of the fifteenth century — a historicizing distancing of the Chaucerian canon as a past recoverable through restorative humanist explication but no longer open to direct imitation, one that entails "the gradual closing down of the Chaucerian text and the increasing difficulty of 'writing'

Chaucer...directly and unabashedly"[5] — prevent early modern poets from engaging with Chaucerian poetics the way Thomas Hoccleve and John Lydgate did? Or does the vernacular genealogy Sidney imagines to run from Chaucer through Surrey endorse a definable relevance that the Chaucerian text possessed for Sidney himself? After all, as Richard Firth Green observes, in terms of courtly aesthetics the line between Chaucer and Sidney is "unbroken."[6]

The argument of this chapter, in a nutshell, is that Sidney's remarks about the dead Chaucer and Surrey illuminate some aspects of his own Petrarchan practice. In *Astrophil and Stella*, I suggest, Sidney deploys a subtly Chaucerian form of writing: constructing his poetic subject through a series of slippages of identity (including a simultaneous assertion and disavowal of Petrarchism), Sidney reactivates the mode of discourse that Chaucer crafts in *The Book of the Duchess* — a mode, I argue, intrinsically linked to the operations of melancholy. At the same time, this chapter maintains that Sidney's access to Chaucerian subjectivity is mediated by the Petrarchan and anti-Petrarchan poetry of Surrey ("the Earle of Surries *Liricks*"), which was available to Sidney and other sixteenth century readers in Richard Tottel's miscellany *Songes and Sonettes written by the right honorable Lorde Henry Haward late Earle of Surrey, and other* (1557).[7]

Sidney's potential engagement with Tottel's collection has never been taken seriously, even though a copy of it likely was in the Sidney household library.[8] Mid-twentieth-century studies were outright dismissive of Tottel's *Miscellany* (and thus of Surrey) as a dead end of an earlier poetic tradition rather than a harbinger of the Elizabethan age.[9] Two decades later Anne Ferry still argued that Sidney's "own verse...shows no sign of direct imitation of Surrey, or Wyatt."[10] More recently, William Kennedy claimed that Sidney's estimate of Surrey is the product of class consciousness that has no bearing on his poetic practice: "The terms in which he canonizes Surrey as one of the nation's premier poets along with Chaucer and Spenser reflect his aristocratic perspective.... In *Astrophil and Stella*, however,...[he] echoes the energy and dynamism of Wyatt's lyrics at the expense of Surrey's polish."[11]

Yet as Andrew Hadfield states, "In many ways Surrey was the obvious choice for Sidney to use as a model for the lyric," including the Henrician poet's being "keen to experiment with numerous forms of versification" and his self-conscious nationalism as a poet.[12] Developing these remarks, I argue in this chapter that it is not just a noble birth that Sidney and Surrey share but a poetic mind as well — a literary self that derives its lineage from Chaucer's courtly melancholy, with its ambivalent attitudes to courtly identity and poetic language. In making this argument, I also expand Wendy Wall's reevaluation of Tottel's collection as a source of productive poetic strategies for later sixteenth century writers, as "*the* handbook for Elizabethan poets."[13] My contention is that Chaucer's medieval poetics of subjectivity explored in *The Book of the Duchess* provides a vernacular template for the Petrarchan voice found in Surrey's section of *Songes and Sonettes*. Tottel's *Miscellany* solidifies the Chaucerian positionality of a melancholy speaker for English poetry and passes it on to Sidney, whose *Astrophil and Stella*—itself of a collection of songs and sonnets[14]—ties together the Chaucerian and the Petrarchan threads of the English vernacular discourse. Accordingly, the chapter opens with an analysis of melancholy selfhood in *The Book of the Duchess*, an interpretation that I then interrupt for an overview of melancholy theory from Aristotle to Kristeva in order to situate the Chaucerian subject within its discursive and imaginative context. The subsequent sections analyze the vestigial presence of Chaucerian melancholy in *Songes and Sonettes* and *Astrophil and Stella*, which in both collections manifests itself through the instability of poetic selfhood and the perennially unfinished work of anti-Petrarchan subversion.

This chapter thus concerns itself with several discursive continuities—those between medieval courtly poetry and its Renaissance counterpart; between the first and the second generations of English Petrarchists; and between the premodern and the postmodern ideas of what constitutes the melancholy self. If the previous chapter looked at how the discursive memories of Langlandian meed affect the relationship between subjectivity and economic desire in several early modern Petrarchan projects (Wyatt, Spenser, Barnes, E. C.), this chapter turns to the medieval—Chaucerian—substrate that striates the constructions of melancholy selfhood in two central Elizabethan Petrarchan sequences, Surrey's *Songes and Sonettes* and Sidney's *Astrophil and Stella*. My goal is not merely to assert the centrality of the figure of melancholy to the scenarios of subjectivity in Chaucer, Surrey, and Sidney. Rather, by gleaning evidence from both medical and literary texts, I intend to show that the poetics of melancholy presupposes a distinct form of subjectivity, one ravaged by instability and expressing itself in a frantic proliferation of new identities; and that in English Renaissance Petrarchism the melancholy subject takes a markedly Chaucerian shape. What follows thus elaborates the central thesis of this book regarding the pervasive presence of medieval forms of poetic imagination in English Petrarchan texts of the early modern period.

Locating the Chaucerian Subject

The *Book of the Duchess*—the first of Chaucer's major poems (c. 1369–72)—is written in the first person. Ardis Butterfield has called it "the first narrative poem in English to start with 'I'";[15] and Renaissance readers knew it as the

Dreame of Chaucer in William Thynne's 1532 edition and *The dreame of Chaucer, called the Dutchesse* in Thomas Speght's edition of 1598.[16] However, its complex, multilayered narratorial organization denies any open-and-shut determinacy as to the poem's subject position. It opens with a complaint of the narrator, a man who for the past eight years has been afflicted with a mysterious malady.[17] To while away the night, he asks for a book of "romaunce" to be brought to him, in which he reads the Ovidian story of Ceyx and Alcyone. Upon finishing the tale, he finally goes into uneasy slumber accompanied by a most peculiar dream. In his dream, he finds himself, on a bright May morning, in a room in which windows and walls are decorated with scenes from courtly literature from the story of Troy to the *Romance of the Rose*. Hearing a hunting horn, the dreamer rides out and witnesses a hunt for the "hert" in progress. The "hert" steals away from all the hunters, however, and the dreamer wanders into a forest, where he encounters a knight dressed in black—a young nobleman stricken with grief and complaining to himself about the loss of his beloved.[18] The rest of the poem consists of a series of verbal exchanges between the dreamer and the man in black: the former inquires about the causes for the latter's distress and attempts to offer consolation, but repeatedly fails to comprehend the elaborate allegories of desire and death that the man in black offers as an explanation. It takes the dreamer some time to grasp the reason of the other's sorrow, but after the final moment of recognition, the two men part, and the dreamer awakens and decides "to put this sweven [i.e., dream] in ryme" (1332).

Although the first-person pronoun is appropriated by a number of personages, the primary contenders for the status of poetic subject in the *Book of the Duchess* are the dreamer and the man in black, with the apparent centrality of the lovelorn knight countered by the metanarrative powers of the otherwise vacuous dreamer. With this rupture in the poetic self being so easily identifiable, it might be tempting to discuss the dreamer and the man in black in diacritical terms, as nonlover/lover, reader/poet, gentleman/aristocrat, original/conventional, English/French. If the man in black is consumed by love and grief, and if his preferred means of communication is the refined language of French courtly poetry, the dreamer, in contrast to Chaucer's French sources, appears to lack any kind of amorous or literary experience and to comprehend only colloquial English.[19] Likewise, any historicist reading of the poem is bound to acknowledge the social gulf separating the narrator and his patron, John of Gaunt.[20] Finally, the *Book of the Duchess* can be imagined as Chaucer's ironic critique of the French norms of love and of literary courtliness. By misunderstanding (or pretending to misunderstand) the man in black, the dreamer exposes the unoriginality and impotence of the nobleman's poetic language.[21] What better way is there to comment on courtly poetry than to pull lover and writer apart and equip the latter with a mind capable of incisive critique of the former's discourse?

However, the structure of the poetic "I" in the *Book of the Duchess* eschews such rigidly assigned roles. The narrator-turned-dreamer already suggests a destabilized identity rather than a coherent antithesis to the man in black, but there are additional puzzling analogies between the dreamer and the man in black that involve the two in what Louise O. Fradenburg describes as relations of "replication" and "reproduction."[22] Both are masculine subjects, and yet each is feminized in some way.[23] The narrator identifies with Alcyone, the female character of the "romaunce" he reads, and imitates her sorrow and her actions (95–100, 231–69), whereas the man in black is so engrossed in his grief that he identifies with his deceased lady White, up to a point where he passes out in an attempt to re-create her death and therefore bodily form ("Hys sorwful hert gan faster faynte / And his spirites wexen dede; / The blood was fled for pure drede" [488–90]). His excessive mourning bordering on self-destruction also echoes that of Alcyone, who, having discovered that her husband is dead, dies from sorrow (213–14).

Both men display signs of what appears to be a form of melancholy. The poem's opening meticulously catalogs the narrator's many symptoms—lack of sleep ("for day ne nyght / I may not slepe wel nygh noght" [2–3]), loss of interest in life ("I take no kep / Of nothing" [6–7]), phantasmatic workings of downcast imagination ("For sorwful ymagynacioun / Ys alway hooly in my mynde" [14–15]). These are easily identifiable markers of melancholy, so the ruthless self-diagnosis he offers—"and thus melancolye / And drede I have for to dye" (23–24)—is largely redundant. But the man in black is beset by a similar affliction caused by the loss of his beloved wife, White, a traumatic event that places him past all cure: "Ne hele me may phisicien, / Noght Ypocras, ne Galyen" can help (571–72). Like the dreamer, the man in black suffers from insomnia ("my slep [ys] wakynge" [611]), apathy ("My lyf, my lustes, be me loothe" [581]), and an acute death wish ("That me ys wo that I was born!" [566]).[24] Whether the dreamer and his interlocutor suffer from the same species of melancholy is contestable. Chaucer's primary source, Jean Froissart's *Le paradis d'Amour* (1361–62), is narrated by a sleepless and sick lover, which has led some critics to identify the narrator's sickness in Chaucer's poem as love melancholy as well.[25] Others refuse to apply automatically the mechanics of the French text to the *Book of the Duchess*, suggesting that the narrator in fact is a clinical case of head melancholy or *melancholia canina*.[26] I shall return to the question of diagnostics in the next section; what I want to stress here is the noticeable similarities between the symptoms displayed by the narrator and the man in black as further evidence of a transcendence of difference between the two.

Further, both the dreamer and the man in black are implicated in experiences of textuality, so that reading and writing become intricate techniques of constructing their respective identities. The narrator emerges out of an act of reading: explicitly, when he reads the Ovidian romance; and implicitly, in the sense that the opening lines of the *Book of the Duchess* create an effect of unmistakable *déjà lu*—something both the poet and his readers will have come across in numerous *dits amoureux*.[27] Soon, however, the Ovidian story is retold for the reader by the narrator (who does not rely on an off-chance that his audience will be familiar with the *Ovide moralisé*), whereas the tradition of *dits amoureux* takes a physical shape in the figure of the man in black. Likewise, the man in black, as we learn from his piteous narrative, began his career as a reader through the process of courtly education ("I was able to have lerned tho, / And to have kend as wel or better, / Paraunter, other art or letre" [786–88]), but by the time of his meeting with the dreamer he is already a producer, not merely a consumer, of courtly poetry. He is introduced to the reader when he is about to perform "a lay, a maner song" (471), and he recites the first poem he wrote for his beloved (1175–80). Moreover, the identity of the one character arises in the process of textualizing the self of the other: the dreamer consolidates his selfhood by incorporating the man in black into his text, whereas the man in black articulates his identity through the French tradition of courtly poetry, which of course constitutes the narrator's primary source for his dream vision.[28] With his white face and black garments, the knight is a written page. In a self-exposing gesture, he compares himself to a "whit wal or a table" (780) waiting to be written to come into existence, and the dreamer describes him as "tretable" (533), as though in reference to one of the courtly scenes that adorn the walls of the room where the dreamer awakens into his dream.[29]

Finally, these slippages in the order of subjectivity also manifest themselves in the poem's ambivalent engagement with the discourse of French courtliness. The *Book of the Duchess* is strangely Francophobic and Francophilic at once. In traditional accounts, Chaucer moves "toward a realism that suggests comic disenchantment," looking "for the real expression of passion in the courtly prison from which [he] had not yet escaped"; as a result, we witness "the maturing of a poet, his emancipation from a clichéd genre that had long lost its vitality."[30] But if Chaucer, as many critics insist, broadcasts the inadequacy of French courtly language throughout the poem, why does his alienation from the vocabulary and grammar of *dits amoureux* not lead him to rejecting them altogether? Indeed, in the *Book of the Duchess* images, characters, rhetorical figures, and other conventions of French tradition are exposed as hollow, aimless, even unintelligible, and yet they continue to provide Chaucer with the only system of poetic signification, whatever its limitations.[31] As Deanne Williams astutely remarks, "the *Book of the Duchess* records a nostalgia for this previous unity [of French culture] even as it enacts its breakdown."[32]

What we discover in the *Book of the Duchess*, then, is not a binary opposition between a common, loveless, ironic, original English poet and an aristocratic, conventional, Francophile lover struggling with each other for dominance over the text of the poem. Rather, Chaucer's poem undertakes a radical obfuscation of the limits of individual subjectivity (narrator becomes Alcyone who becomes the dreamer who becomes the man in black who becomes his dead beloved, etc.). Each self in the *Book of the Duchess* is in constant dialogue with a constellation of other subjectivities; it is always "the object that invades and disrupts the other's subjectivity."[33]

As a result, distinction between self and other becomes largely untenable. Any self in the text is irrevocably ruptured: the "I" of the poem is simultaneously waking and dreaming, desiring and writing, aristocratic and middle class, masculine and feminine, English and French.

This poetic configuration is closely associated with the discourse of melancholy. As I have already pointed out, this malady afflicts the two masculine subjects at the heart of the poem. Yet melancholy operates on a much broader scope in the *Book of the Duchess:* the workings of melancholy not only serve up the dream vision's subject matter, they underpin the destabilized Chaucerian subject and help account for the poet's uneasy relationship with the tradition of French courtly poetry. In the next section, I locate the perennially elusive Chaucerian subjectivity in the context of various theoretical writings of melancholy, both pre-modern and modern. What I attempt to demonstrate is that melancholy represents a powerful cultural mechanism that orchestrates the dynamic of splintered selfhood in Chaucer's poem, but also that it extends, both temporally and discursively, into other text and contexts, including Renaissance Petrarchism and modern psychoanalysis, highlighting the enduring fascination of our culture with the potentialities of the melancholic psyche.

Toward a Poetics of Melancholy

The first question to ask is, what melancholy? As we have seen, there is no critical consensus about the nature of the maladies that trouble the narrator and the man in black. Against the critics who seek to contrast them as suffering from two different types of melancholy (or even from two different afflictions altogether), one could argue that although in antiquity melancholy per se and lovesickness (also known as *amor hereos*) formed two different constellations of medical thought, over the course of the medieval and early modern periods the two had come to occupy differently inflected positions within the same class of disorders. In fact, as Donald Beecher and Massimo Ciavolella note, already in antiquity there is "little doubt about the general association of the diseases raised by black bile [i.e., of melancholic nature] with the perturbations caused by inordinate passion."[34] Pseudo-Aristotle's *Problems* (between the third century BC and sixth century AD) opens its discussion of the melancholic temperament with a famous question that connects melancholy and creativity: "Why is it that all men who have become outstanding in philosophy, statesmanship, poetry or the arts are melancholic, and some to an such extent that they are affected by the diseases arising from the black bile?"[35] What Pseudo-Aristotle is describing here is genial melancholy, a corporeal predisposition toward nobility of the mind. In the next passage, however, he ties creative melancholy to erotic desire: "wine makes men inclined to love, and Dionysus and Aphrodite are rightly associated with each other; and the melancholics are usually lustful."[36] Still, it was not until the arrival in the medieval West of the Arabic medical writings by al-Rāsi (Rhazes), 'Ali ibn al-'Abbās (Haly Abbas), and 'Abdullāh Ali Sinā (Avicenna), largely based on Aristotle and Galen, that a link between melancholy and lovesickness was formalized. The text that revolutionized European thinking about the two afflictions was Constantine of Africa's *Viaticum* (c. 1065), a translation of Ibn al-Jazzār's *Zād al-musāfir* with inclusions from other Arabic sources. This book, as well as the commentaries it solicited among Europe's educated elites (by Gerard of Berry, Giles of Santarem, and Peter of Spain), fused erotic longing and melancholic symptomatology into one disorder.[37] Little changed for the Renaissance mind. As Marion A. Wells notes, "by the time we reach the early modern period, the connection between lovesickness and melancholy becomes inescapable."[38]

The logic behind this alignment can be found in the Galenic theory of the humors. This subject has received plenty of critical attention, especially in the last two decades, so a few remarks will suffice.[39] Galenic medicine operated on the assumption that the health of a human body depended on a fine balance of the four principal humors: blood, phlegm, choler, and black bile. The main cause of melancholy was an excessive presence in the organism of black bile (*melaina chole*), a cold, dry, and sluggish substance. As Thomas Walkington in *The optick glasse of humors* (1631) writes, "Of al the 4 this humor is the most vnfortunate and greatest enemy to life, because his qualities being cold and drie do most of all disagree from the liuely qualities, heate and moisture."[40] Black bile was a natural element in the body, and bodies where it was predominant were diagnosed as having a melancholic complexion (or disposition). But an excess of black bile could be produced unnaturally, by burning any of the four humors, which produced unnatural melancholy, or melancholy adust. "Melancoly or blacke choler is deuyded in to two kyndes," says Sir Thomas Elyot in *The Castel of Helthe* (1541). "Naturall, whyche is the dregges of pure bloud, and is knowen by the blacknes... and is verily colde and drye. Unnaturalle, whyche procedeth of the adustion of choleric mixture, and is hotter and lighter, hauying in it violence to kyll, with a daungerous disposition." The latter occurs "in foure kyndes, eyther it is of naturall melancoly aduste, or of the more pure parte of the bloudde aduste, or of choler adust, or of salt fleume [i.e. phlegm] adust."[41] As Timothie Bright notes in his *Treatise of Melancholie* (1586), "besides the complexion inclining to such temper, this matter [black bile] is increased by perturbation of mind, by temper of aire, and kind of habitation, and that humour which otherwise would yeeld a nutritiue iuyce...by this occasion is turned into these dregges of melancholie."[42]

Through unnatural melancholy, lovesickness came to be categorized as one of the subspecies of melancholy per se because the heat of inordinate passion contributed to an increased production of the melancholy humor in a lover's body. In the words of Jacques Ferrand from *Erotomania* (1610), through violent perturbations in the lover's mind, "the bloud becomes adust, earthy, and Melancholy, as in all other violent passions, except joy, according to *Galen*, by which meanes diverse have fallen into strange and desperate diseases; growing Melancholy, Foolish, Mad, Cynicall, Wolvish."[43] Although in its early stages love is not a melancholic disease, prolonged unrequited desire produces results identical to other forms of atrabilious disturbance.[44] Not surprisingly, Andreas Laurentius in his *Discourse...of Melancholike Diseases* (1599) prescribes the same course of dietary treatment to all melancholics, including lovers: "then must wee handle these amorous persons in such maner, and after the same order which I haue appoynted for the melancholike..., and almost with the very same remedies."[45] In other words, to distinguish, terminologically and etiologically, between different kinds of melancholy is somewhat to go against the tenets of pre-modern medicine.[46] The latter approaches erotic passion, political acumen, creativity, and atrabilious sadness as a cluster of related medical, social, and cultural issues. As Drew Daniel suggests, in a useful corrective to the tendency to compartmentalize early modern melancholy, the very essence of melancholy is instability and multiplicity, which "disorganizes the concept but also paradoxically introduces a secondary kind of consistent incoherence, or generative indeterminacy, into the expression of melancholy itself."[47]

The point where this inconsistent consistency of melancholy comes to the fore is the question of ruptured subjectivity. Gerard of Berry describes lovesickness, arising "because the entire attention and thought, aided by desire, is fixed on the beauty of some form or figure," as an imbalance among the estimative, imaginative, and concupiscible faculties of the mind "misled by sensed intentions into apprehending non-sensed accidents."[48] Such a disturbance privileges an object and disrupts "the mutually dependent processes of imagination and estimation," which in turn "draws attention to the fundamental ontological instability of the subject."[49] Several centuries later Laurentius also finds the debilitating effects of melancholy in the patient's obsession with an object: "Melancholie therefore is a dotage, not coupled with an ague, but with feare and sadnes. We call that dotage, when some one of the principall faculties of the minde, as imagination or reason is corrupted." A lover, Laurentius continues, "doteth continually vpon this object, runneth after his shadow, and is neuer at rest. There are now some certaine yeares past, since I saw a gentleman ouertaken with this kinde of melancholie, he talked being alone vnto his shadow, he called it, welcomed it, kissed it, ranne after it euery day."[50] Ficino imagines the work of desire as an invasion of the self by an object of love: "after I have lost myself [in love], if I recover myself through you, I have myself through you; if I have myself through you, I have you before and more than I have myself, and I am closer to you than myself, since I approach myself in no other way than through you as an intermediary."[51]

Ruptured selfhood is also a site of rapprochement between the pre-modern discourse of melancholy and the modern discourse of psychoanalysis. Within the discourse of melancholy, there is a certain genealogical continuity at work that allows diverse iterations of melancholy and the questions they grapple with to preserve their analytical core within different cultural contexts and systems of knowledge.⁵² In many instances, psychoanalysis not so much offers an explanatory mechanism that radically departs from pre-modern theory as it crystallizes the insights of pre-modern writers. That is, pre-modern and postmodern approaches to melancholy constitute parts of a single textual history; both Galenic humoralism and Freudian psychoanalysis are textual fictions that may have lost much of their clinical validity but remain powerful cultural codes that facilitate an understanding of other fictions, such as Chaucer's *Book of the Duchess*, Surrey's *Songes and Sonettes*, and Sidney's *Astrophil and Stella*. Accordingly, I consider the psychoanalytic writings by Freud and Kristeva on melancholy not as theoretical postulates but as imaginative constructions that are manifestations of the same compelling discursive tradition. As Franco Berardi notes, "Freudian and Lacanian theories, as any other mythology of the soul, need to be taken for what they are: creations of self-imaginations, projects of exploration in the unconscious which create their own territory while narrating it."⁵³ In place of contrasting historicism and psychoanalysis, I propose a triangulation of melancholy discourse that reads Freud, pre-modern poetry, and early medical writers as involved, in equal shares, in the production of discursive figurations of melancholy.

Freud's description of the mechanism of melancholy connects it with the loss of an external object and the consequences this loss has for the ego:

> The free libido [resulting from the loss] was not displaced onto another object; it was withdrawn into the ego. There, however, it was not employed in any unspecified way, but served to establish an *identification* of the ego with the abandoned object. Thus the shadow of the object fell upon the ego, and the latter could henceforth be judged by a special agency, as though it were an object, the forsaken object. In this way an

object-loss was transformed into an ego-loss and the conflict between the ego and the loved person into a cleavage between the critical activity of the ego and the ego as altered by identification.[54]

The tension between the subject and the (lost) object is introjected into the subject; in turn, this results in the splitting of the ego into two agencies that perform the roles of censorious subject and object under scrutiny within the limits of the same "I." In this, Freud argues, "one part of the ego sets itself over against the other, judges it critically, and, as it were, takes it as its object."[55] The melancholic self is thus essentially split between subject and object within itself. Central to Freud's vision of melancholy, however, is the idea that the initial introjection of the object into the ego results in the ego's transformation through the process of identification. In his later work, *The Ego and the Id*, Freud not only posits the melancholic split within the self between the subject and the internalized object as central to the production of the ego through object-identification ("the transformation of an erotic object-choice into an alteration of the ego"), but goes as far as speculating that this identification, rather than a singular occurrence, is a continuous process that renders the self fundamentally unstable: "If [object identifications] obtain the upper hand and become too numerous, unduly powerful and incompatible with one another, a pathological outcome will not be far off. It may come to a disruption of the ego in consequence of the different identifications.... Even when things do not go so far as this, there remains the question of conflicts between the various identifications into which the ego comes apart, conflicts which cannot after all be described as entirely pathological."[56] Every self is intrinsically melancholic, and every self is a constant process of identification. The melancholic subject is thus "nowhere properly itself, given that it never avoids yielding to an identification and always confuses itself in some way with another (an alter ego—but one that is neither other nor self)."[57]

Early modern theorists of melancholy had discovered this long before Freud, however. A stock remark among them is that melancholic persons are haunted by fantasies of identification. According to Levinus Lemnius's *Touchstone of Complexion* (1576), "the Mela[n]cholike iuyce...disquieteth the mynde, wyth sundry straung apparitions, and phantasticall imaginations."[58] The word "imaginations," however, operates as the early modern equivalent of Freudian "identifications." As Laurentius captures this mechanism of melancholic mimesis, "this disquieting and distracting of themselues, ariseth out of the diuersitie of matters which they propound and set before themselues, for receiuing all manner of formes." Melancholics imagine themselves to be someone or something else, for any impression in a melancholic, he continues, "suffereth not it selue easily to be blotted out...if they happen to commonly to looke vpon some pitcher or glasse (which are things very vsuall and common) they will iudge themselues to be pitchers or glasses."[59] Walkington in *The optick glasse* describes melancholic minds as "imagining that they see and feele such things, as no man els can either perceiue or touch."[60] Not only see and feel, but they identify with such things, we might add, for Walkington goes on to relate a series of anecdotes about melancholic imaginations: one, he writes, "tooke a strong conceit, that he was changed into an earthen vessell, who earnestly intreated his friends in any case not to come neare him, lest...he might be shakt or crusht to peeces"; whereas another "did affirme, his whole body was made of butter, wherefore hee neuer durst come neere any fire, least the heate should haue melted him."[61] Burton, echoing his numerous predecessors, also stresses a propensity among melancholics to imagine themselues a wild array of things and persons. Melancholics, he muses, "conceave so many phantasticall visions, apparitions to themselves, and have such absurd apparitions, as that they are Kings, Lords, Cocks, Beares, Apes, Owls; that they are heavy, light, transparent, great, and little, senselesse and dead," which "can bee imputed to naught else, but to a corrupt, false, and violent Imagination."[62]

If we turn to the *Book of the Duchess*, we see how the poem's protean subject embodies the logic of melancholy. The severance of the narrator's psyche into dreamer and man in black encapsulates the initial ego-splitting, particularly if we focus on the metapoetic problematic in their relationship. The critical agency becomes detached from that segment of the dreamer's ego that identifies with an object (in this case, French courtly culture), and the outcome of this bisection is a psychic dialogue between two aspects of his self, with the dreamer placing the man in black in an object position of critique. After the initial rift in the poetic "I," however, each sliver of the ego in turn becomes further divided. The dreamer takes on new identities while the man in black, too, empties his self and displaces it with the feminine ego of his deceased wife, White. Denigrating the existent self, the Chaucerian subject pluralizes his identity across a range of forms, each of those substitute identities undergoing further splintering, which produces the overall effect of a kaleidoscope of identifications.

The mechanism of melancholy also sheds light on the relationship of unfinished detachment that Chaucer's poem maintains with the discourse of French courtliness. Melancholy engenders a type of writing that not only imagines a dissolution of selfhood but disavows its own discursive history even as it remains inextricably bound to it. According to the logic of melancholy, a rejected identification is never discarded completely; its residue remains part of the self. Freud describes a melancholic ego as "a precipitate of abandoned object-cathexes...[that] contains the history of those object choices."[63] Julia Kristeva applies this to verbal and artistic practice: "depressed persons do not forget how to use signs. They keep them, but the signs seem absurd, delayed, ready to be extinguished."[64] Melancholic writing, in other words, never unfolds through total displacement. What appears discarded becomes disavowed history that returns and continues to determine the new discursive and subjective formations erected out of the debris of melancholic devastation. In the face of an impending complete erasure of the self, a melancholic poet, seeking to continue as a writing subject, creates an utterance out of the ruins of language, integrating, in subversively unexpected ways, the failed, inadequate signs into this poetic performance. This poetry of melancholy always includes its own irretrievable history, its own dispersal between the past and the present.

Faced with signs that are no longer bound by the naturalizing powers of the system of writing, with poetic vocabulary and grammar that, upon being translated from French into English, have departed from their enunciatory context, the Chaucerian subject nonetheless discovers that preserving this inadequate system of signs offers the only path to sustaining any kind of legible poetic identity. The French sources cannot be superseded by an unadulterated English utterance. Rather, exposed as failed by the melancholy subject, they are reintegrated into a new language of English courtliness and thus constitute a (disowned) part of its history. Melancholic discourse at once moves forward and looks back, just as the man in black at the end of Chaucer's poem, presumably consoled and cured by a conversation with the dreamer, returns to his castle; and the narrator (together with the reader) is catapulted back to the beginning. Although the melancholic Chaucerian subject appears to reject French courtly subjectivity in the *Book of the Duchess*, he reappropriates it for a new performance of the self. This new poetic "I" constructed out of dysfunctional language still contains traces of the old selfhood, however, resulting in a form of writing that simultaneously reiterates and subverts its own discursive past. This form of identity is what Chaucer bequeaths to Tudor Petrarchans.

Petrarchan Melancholy in Surrey's *Songes and Sonettes*

If indeed Sidney in his *Apologie* expresses his admiration for the Surrey of Richard Tottel's 1557 *Songes and Sonettes*, the poetic voice that the collection presents deserves closer attention. While earlier studies conceptualized the Tottel volume as a comparatively random sampling of Henrician and Marian verse,[65] the recent work by Paul Marquis has alerted readers to the early modern editor's obsessive attention to the minute details of his textual arrangements.[66] Tottel's collection reorders Surrey's disparate songs and sonnets into a coherent narrative of loss and desire with a unique poetic voice, an important precursor to Elizabethan sonnet sequences. The upshot of this reorientation is a new image of Surrey's poetic self: rather than a conventional, if urbane and adroit, Petrarchan versifier that Surrey still occasionally appears to be to the critics,[67] in Tottel's *Miscellany* he is a daring, original poet who constructs a knotty, disturbed subjectivity, at once Petrarchan and anti-Petrarchan—a subjectivity unstable in a Chaucerian way.

Chaucer is a persistent presence in Surrey's verse. As William Sessions suggests, Surrey's poetry develops out of an admixture of continental (both classical and early modern) and native (predominantly Chaucerian) legacies.[68] Also, Surrey's canon contains repeated references to Trojan history and thus inevitably to Chaucer's *Troilus and Criseyde*.[69] This Chaucerian presence materializes particularly acutely in Tottel's *Miscellany*. The two opening poems in *Songes and Sonettes* ("The sunne hath twise brought furth his tender grene" [1] and "The soote season, that bud and blome forth brings" [2]), while voicing Petrarchan sentiments, allude explicitly to trademark Chaucerian beginnings, and at the close of the section, in his epitaph on Thomas Wyatt "W. resteth here" (35), Surrey again invokes Chaucer as the exemplary—dead—English poet. In a recent essay, Amanda Holton argues that these Chaucerian allusions in the collection are superficial and that "some of the most important aspects of Chaucer's work are strongly resisted in the *Miscellany*, either ignored, dismissed or challenged," in particular the medieval poet's "interest in variety of voice, his sympathetic engagement with women...and his interest in female speech."[70] Tottel's collection on the whole is more misogynistic than Chaucer's oeuvre, but I cannot agree with Holton about the absence of variety of voice in Surrey's *Songes and Sonettes*, including gender instability. As I argue, the Surrey section in the collection is profoundly Chaucerian in that it is underwritten by a vernacular melancholy; this melancholy governs the construction of Surrey's poetic subjectivity and determines his relationship with Petrarchism. One of the first English Petrarchans, Surrey is simultaneously one of the first English anti-Petrarchans, but also one of the preeminent Tudor Chaucerians, inasmuch as his anti-Petrarchan discourse reactivates a subject position previously stamped on the vernacular by Chaucer's poetics of melancholy.

The term "anti-Petrarchism" requires a brief commentary. Admittedly, its analytical value is limited because resistance to Petrarch's formal and ideological strategies and deautomatization of Petrarchan writing emerge alongside the normative Petrarchan model. Petrarch himself engages in a self-reflexive critique of his erotic and textual desires, creating possibilities for later poets to reconfigure the received model; and in a sense all poetry after Petrarch revises, reinterprets, and reshapes its source.⁷¹ "If Petrarchism itself questions the conventions it establishes," remarks Barbara Estrin, it is not surprising that subsequent poets "inherit the unease at its core."⁷² As Christopher Warley brilliantly shows, the very opposition of "conventional Petrarchism" and "original anti-Petrarchism" is a product of nineteenth century social, national, and cultural sensibilities, an analytical apparatus largely alien to Renaissance poetry itself.⁷³ Consequently, it is all but impossible to distinguish between deferential Petrarchan imitation and anti-Petrarchan rejection. This is reflected in the recent vocabulary for dealing with the ambiguities of Petrarchan writing, most notably Heather Dubrow's "counterdiscourses of Petrarchism," a phrase designed to suggest a complex variety of ways in which English poetry criticizes, resists, and rewrites Petrarchism.⁷⁴ Still, limitations of the term "anti-Petrarchism" notwithstanding, I retain it in this chapter to designate sustained attempts to dismantle the normative patterns of Petrarchan writing, attempts that not only involve a rigorous self-critique of the Petrarchan subject but threaten to sabotage the very foundations of identity charged with performing it.

Surrey's *Songes and Sonettes* opens with the monologue of a melancholic subject:

> The sunne hath twise brought furth his tender grene,
> Twise clad the earth in lively lustinesse:
> Ones have the windes the trees despoiled clene,
> And ones again begins their cruelnesse,
> Since I have hid under my brest the harm
> That never shall recover healthfulnesse.   (1.1–6)

The text identifies the speaker as a bearer of a secret wound of melancholy long hidden under his breast. This wound, ancient and yet forever fresh, is what determines the subject, making him—like Chaucer's narrator and the man in black—a case history, a narrative to be recounted. The title supplied by Tottel urges us to read the text as a love poem ("Descripcion of the restlesse state of a louer, with sute to his ladie, to rue on his diyng hart"), which would suggest that the lover's trauma was caused by unrequited love. Yet for the speaker himself, what engenders his melancholy is not so much the loss of the object of desire as the loss of his ego: "And in my minde I measure pace by pace, / To seke the place where I my self had lost" (1.34–35). His wound is then the glaring absence of selfhood—absence that, uncannily, functions as the foundation of his identity articulated through attempts to rediscover the lost self (for example, in acts of remembrance) or to configure its substitute out of the remnants of irretrievable subjectivity.[75] His is a wound at once unavailable and present ("Lo, if I seke, how I do find my sore: / And if I flee, I cary with me still / The venomd shaft" [1.46–48]).

Shortly before the poem ends, however, the speaker is revealed to be a love poet ("I may plaine my fill / Unto my self unlesse this carefull song / Print in your hart some parcell of my tene" [1.49–51]), so the self he claims to have lost can be identified as Petrarchan. This sets up the ensuing narrative of *Songes and Sonettes* as an account of its poetic subject's paradoxical existence between Petrarchism and its abandonment, as a record of a Petrarchan poet who is alienated from his Petrarchan genealogy. It is only appropriate that the wound of lost selfhood is inextricably tied with the speaker's poetic speech being impeded by melancholy: "For I, alas, in silence all to long, / Of mine old hurt yet fele the wound but grene" (1.52–53). The trauma of lovesickness has swallowed the lover's ability to speak the language of Petrarchism, paralyzing his utterance into silence. Moreover, this melancholic inarticulacy spills into the form of the poem itself: what lovesickness does to the speaker, Surrey does to his own text.

Amid the clichéd Petrarchan figures of fire and ice ("What warmth (alas) may serve for to disarm / The frosen hart, that mine in flame hath made" [1.9–10]), the poet subverts the operation of this key Petrarchan trope: "Strange kindes of death, in life that I do trie: / At hand to melt, farre of in flame to burn" (1.17–18). At hand to melt? Not freeze? Replacing the traditional Petrarchan "cryopyric"[76] antithesis that contrasts burning and freezing with an asymmetrical opposition of melting and burning—one barely sustainable in terms of difference—Surrey effectively undermines the rhetorical foundations of Petrarchism with its carefully balanced poetics of oxymoron.[77] Surrey is capable of employing the same antithesis in an orthodox manner (e.g., "In standing nere my fire, I know how that I freze: / Far of I burn" [4.41–42]), which makes this deviation all the more significant.

Two points invite commentary here. First, instead of abandoning the rhetorical figure altogether, Surrey's sabotages it by retaining it in his discourse yet depleting it of poetic efficacy. Surrey's use of the trope, to adopt Paul de Man's formulation, "simultaneously asserts and denies the authority of its own rhetorical mode."[78] He turns the dysfunctional oxymoron into a blind spot over which a reader trained in Petrarchan diction will inevitably stumble, at once recognizing it and appreciating its deformity. This makes the poem an embodied example of the "strange kinde of death, in life" that Surrey (with Tottel's help) scripts for the lover-poet whose lost Petrarchan identity can only be recovered through acts of maimed Petrarchan writing. In this "strange kinde of death, in life," he simultaneously is and is not a Petrarchan poet. The very first text in what is widely recognized as an essentially Petrarchan collection openly disfigures Petrarchism. Second, this stripping of poetic language of meaning is linked to the speaker's death ("Strange kindes of death, in life that I do trie"). Fixation on the self as lost object brings with it a taste of termination, and the horizon of expectations thus created by the first poem not only places its subject in the territory of melancholy, with its unfixedness of the self and linguistic incapacitation, but also introduces the death of the subject as one of the themes. The rhetorical self-injury Surrey inflicts in the quoted lines thus forms part of a larger scenario of melancholic devaluation of the self: "the dead language [that melancholics] speak," Kristeva writes, ". . . foreshadows their suicide."[79] Rather than an aberration or a scribal error, this subversion of Petrarchan rhetoric becomes a symptom of Surrey's poetics of melancholy, anticipating his eventual disintegration of Petrarchan identity.

The narrative of Surrey's *Songes and Sonettes* indeed oscillates between denial and acceptance of Petrarchism as the language of self-articulation. In "When somer toke in hand" (5), a poem that Tottel aptly entitles "Complaint of a lover that defied love, and was by love after the more tormented," the lover attempts to adopt a non-Petrarchan identity by rebelling against Cupid, although his effort proves futile. Instead of regaining health and psychic stability, his self is further lacerated by Cupid: "That I, me thought, was made as whole as any man alive, / But here I may perceive mine errour all and some, / For that I thought that so it was: yet was it still undone" (5.38–40). Echoing the speaker's failure to extricate himself from Petrarchism, Surrey's section continues with a cluster of immaculate Italianate sonnets (6–14), including such faithful renderings of Petrarch as "Love, that liveth, and raigneth in my thought" (6), "Set me whereas the Sunne doth parche the grene" (12), and "I never saw my Ladie laye apart" (13), which at the formal level contrast vividly with the poulter's measures and iambic tetrameters of the first five poems.

Placed among these texts is "When Windsor walles susteyned my wearied arme" (11), in which the speaker recalls standing on the edge of the castle wall and contemplating suicide: "My vapord eyes suche drery teares distill, / The tender spring which quicken where they fall, / And I half-bent to throw me down withall" (11.12–14). Though Tottel makes an attempt to posit this sonnet as an amorous piece, the title "How eche thing save the lover in spring reviveth to pleasure" sits uneasily with this poem that juxtaposes images of the spring ("The blossomd bowes with lusty Ver yspred, / The flowred meades, the wedded birdes so late / Mine eyes discover" [11.4–6]) with an acute, self-destructive grief for a lost companion, most likely the poet's childhood friend Henry Fitzroy the Duke of Richmond, an illegitimate son of Henry VIII.[80] Surrey's sentiment soon becomes even more apparent in the pastoral elegy "So cruell prison how could betide, alas" (15), written, presumably, while Surrey was imprisoned in Windsor for a quarrel with another courtier. This text also mourns Richmond's death and wistfully looks back on the past days of joy when "I in lust and joy, / With a kinges sonne, my childishe yeres did passe, / In greater feastes than Priams sonnes of Troy" (15.2–4). Reiterating the melancholic tenor of the collection (i.e., nostalgic longing for the originary plenitude of the past: "O place of blisse, renuer of my woes" [15.45]), the poem also recasts this problematic in an explicitly literary mold, signaling *The Knight's Tale* and the *Aeneid* as key subtexts of the poem and imagining the lost object in terms of Chaucerian poetry.[81]

With the two Windsor poems, Surrey's *Songes and Sonettes* also opens up a field of experimentation with the gender politics of Petrarchan love. The texts commemorating Richmond's death delineate what Stephen Guy-Bray calls a "homoerotic space" — an exegetical locale where the long-standing tradition of classical elegy, Chaucerian vernacular chivalry, and the poet's own intimate friendship with Richmond all stipulate a palpable degree of same-sex desire.[82] By mourning the death of a childhood friend, Surrey takes on the role of a grieving suitor and displays "the melancholia of unrequited love."[83] Preserving, in other words, the structure of Petrarchan desire, the poet eliminates the gender difference between subject and object, which delivers a blow to the conceptual foundations of Petrarchism. Moreover, immediately following Surrey's erotically charged elegies for Richmond are two texts that also critique the Petrarchan gender matrix, "O happy dames, that may embrace" (17) and "Good Ladies: ye that have your pleasures in exile" (19). In both of these, "the female voice is ventriloquised through a Petrarchan diction conventionally attributed to the male lover."[84] "O happy dames" is especially interesting in this regard as it represents a female response to, or rewriting of, Petrarch's sonnet 189 "Passa la nave mia colma d'oblio," famously translated by Thomas Wyatt as "My galley charged with forgetfulnesse" (and printed in *Songes and Sonettes*).[85] Of course, there is the ready biographical explanation that the poems were written by Surrey for his wife in order to give voice to the pain of separation during his military service in France.[86] But read alongside the homoerotic Windsor poems, the female-voiced texts become poetically—that is, within or against Petrarchism—charged shifts. Feminizing the monolithic model that affords little textual power to the feminine voice,[87] Surrey presents Petrarchan genders as dialectically interrelated positions that grant the speaker an escape from the rigidity of binarism, exploring "possibilities of identification across genders facilitated by desires that are not limited by heterosexual choice."[88] What takes place in this section of *Songes and Sonettes* is thus a "queering" of Petrarchism: Surrey's mode of writing in these poems explores gender incoherence "poetically produced through the subject's difference from itself and thus through the unfixing of some of the subject/object poles of sexual difference in the Petrarchan lyric tradition."[89] These poems celebrate the uncertainty of the language of Petrarchan love and explore liminal spaces between the gender poles. But within the narrative of Surrey's anti-Petrarchan experimentation, the subject's self-queering constitutes another aspect of the revisionary work that the melancholic poet-lover dissatisfied with the Petrarchan self available to him directs at his subjectivity.

This process culminates in the ultimate rejection of the Petrarchan "I," a destruction of the subject that Surrey performs spectacularly in what I take to be the central text of Tottel's *Miscellany*, "In winters just returne" (18). There the reader finds himself inside a Chaucerian script, one in which a shepherd, the speaker in the text, on a cold winter morning, hears a cry that he unmistakably identifies as belonging to a lover: "And as it is a thing, that lovers have by fittes, / Under a palme I heard one cry, as he had lost his wittes. / Whose voyce did ring so shrill, in uttering of his plaint" (18.5–7). The shepherd rushes toward the sufferer to offer consolation ("With teares, for his redresse, I rashly to him ran" [18.27]). In return, this "dying lover refused upon his ladies unjust mistaking of his writing," as Tottel characterizes him in the title, recounts his story of amorous delight turned to pain:

> Who joyed then, but I? who had this worldes bliss?
> Who might compare a life to mine, that never thought on this?
> But dwelling in this truth, amid my greatest joy,
> Is me befallen a greater losse, than Priam had of Troy.
> She is reversed clene, and beareth me in hand,
> That my deserts have geven her cause to breke this faithful band.
> And for my just excuse availeth no defence,
> Now knowest thou all.   (18.49–56)

Having solicited the shepherd's promise to vouch for his truthfulness, the hapless lover dies: "Thus, in his wofull state, he yelded up his ghost" (18.65). The melancholy of unrequited love finally claims its victim, and the speaker has nothing left to do but bury the dead lover "Where Creseids love, king Priams sonne, the worthy Troilus lay" (18.78), joining together Chaucer and Petrarch in a bizarre act of poetic grief.

The structure of the poetic "I" in Surrey's text closely replicates the one found in the *Book of the Duchess*, in which an aristocratic lover-poet becomes the object of observation and critique for a socially and culturally inferior non-lover and nonpoet. Surrey's shepherd dully acknowledges his low status: "I am (quod I) but poore, and simple in degree: / A shepardes charge I have in hand, unworthy though I be" (18.35–36). However, the most startling element of the poem is that the subject who dies appears to be the same aristocratic Petrarchan lover whose role Surrey has heretofore performed in *Songes and Sonettes*. The Petrarchan poetic self that Surrey has questioned, undermined, and "queered" in a number of texts, in "In winters just returne" is undone altogether.

Writhing in pain, the lover blames his demise on the machines of courtly discourse:

> Thou cursed pen (sayd he) wo worth the bird thee bare,
> The man, the knife, and all that made thee, wo be to their share.
> Wo worth the time, and place, where I so could endite.
> And wo be it yet once againe, the pen that so can write.
> Unhappy hand, it had ben happy time for me,
> If, when to write thou learned first, unjoynted hadst thou be.
> (18.15–20)

The motif first introduced in the opening text of Tottel's *Miscellany*—that a deconstruction of love poetry foreshadows the death of the lover—is finally realized 18 poems later. Here the Petrarchan self becomes the victim of the very mechanism of poetry that engenders it. In blaming the writing tools and their material histories—the "cursed pen," "the bird," the "man" and "knife and all that made thee"—Surrey unleashes the energies of violence and death that were inherent in the technologies of inscription in early modern culture.[90] His death is at the same time poetic: literalizing the Petrarchan metaphor of a dying lover, the text takes the rhetorical resources of Petrarchism to the limit. Watching his own poetic subjectivity break down, Surrey fulfills the oath of absolute loyalty he earlier swore to the lord of love: "Yet from my lorde shall not my foote remove. / Swete is his death, that takes his end by love" (6.13–14). It is also crucial that this self-undoing of Petrarchan subjectivity is realized through a recourse to Chaucerian imaginative resources. In rewriting the Petrarchan lover and the censorious poet as the man in black and the dreamer from the *Book of the Duchess*, Surrey makes his anti-Petrarchan modality an element of the national poetic tradition and explicitly connects Petrarchism to an English vernacular past.

But melancholic writing loses in order to perpetuate: an abandoned self or discourse is kept present in memory so that it can continue to underpin new articulations of subjectivity. Melancholy, shattering the structures of Petrarchan discourse and imploding the poetic self, still preserves them, often in distorted forms, in utterances that follow. Surrey's Petrarchan self-annihilation is no exception: although the poet-lover is dead, his identity lingers on, and the self of the humble shepherd, the new "I" that the poem apparently offers as a solution to the Petrarchan crisis, is transformed into a semblance of exactly what it was recruited to replace. Recounting the impact of the lover's death on him, the shepherd suddenly rewrites himself as a Petrarchan swain:

> For pitye though my heart did blede, to se so piteous sight,
> My blood from heat to colde oft changed wonders sore:
> A thousand troubles there I found I never knew before.
> Twene drede and dolour, so my sprites were brought in feare,
> That long it was ere I could call to minde, what I did there.
> (18.68–72)

Kneeling over the dead body of the Petrarchan poet, the shepherd finds himself engulfed in erotic melancholy. He perceives this as a new subjectivity (what he "never knew before"), but the reader notices that it has in fact been transferred from the dead lover. If Surrey's poetic suicide aimed to undermine Petrarchism, the new—non-Petrarchan—identity the shepherd is supposed to embody calls this act of anti-Petrarchan defiance into question, for this new self is still written in the language of Petrarchism. What emerges at the end of the poem is a hybrid self in which the Petrarchan lover acts like a parasite clinging to the host identity of the shepherd. Just as the tomb erected for the dead lover ("By him I made his tomb, in token he was true" [18.79]) becomes an indelible monument to Petrarchism, Surrey's poem preserves Petrarchan selfhood by recording its destruction.

Indeed, no melancholic farewell is ever final, and as subsequent poems demonstrate, the subject's love wound never quite goes away. Having followed his Petrarchan subject to his death, Surrey finds himself resuscitating the rhetorical figures and images that the sequence has previously associated with Petrarchan love:

> As oft as I behold and see
> The soveraigne beauty that me bound:
> The nyer my comfort is to me,
> Alas the fresher is my wound.
> As flame doth quench by rage of fire,
> And runnyng stremes consume by raine:
> So doth the sight, that I desire,
> Appease my grief and deadly payne.   (24.1–8)

The excerpt is interesting because here Surrey again, at the moment of invoking his speaker's melancholy wound, undertakes a deconstruction of the Petrarchan diction, producing an effect similar to what he achieves in the opening poem of the collection. He translates the lines from Petrarch's *Canzoniere* 48.1–2 "Se mai foco per foco non si spense / né fiume fu giamai secco per pioggia" ("If fire was never put out by fire, nor river ever made dry by rain"} as "As flame doth quench by rage of fire, / And runnyng stremes consume by raine." While in Petrarch's original fire and rain are kept in a balance within themselves, in Surrey's version flame eliminates fire and water is consumed by rain. Formally clinging to the rhetoric of the *Canzoniere*, Surrey subverts the Petrarchan trope and deprives it of its signifying capacity. An act of melancholic writing, this dissonant poem both engages and rejects Petrarchism; it is neither purely Petrarchan nor anti-Petrarchan as it flickers on both sides of the discourse.

Surrey's melancholy obsession with poetic death continues in a series of four poems on the death of Sir Thomas Wyatt (33–36). Surrey envisions Wyatt as the new archetypal English poet who "reft Chaucer the glory of his wit" (35.14), a paragon of manliness, honor, and nobility pinned against the deplorable and corrupt courtly environment.[91] Tellingly, though, this (homoerotic) invocation of a *dead* poet is accompanied by yet another reshaping of Surrey's own poetic selfhood: lamenting Wyatt's untimely death and elevating him as the new object of imitation, Surrey, as though oblivious of his own self, assumes Wyatt's identity, especially in "W. resteth here, that quick could never rest" (35). Dropping all singular first-person pronouns, departing from his own polished style, and adopting Wyatt's rough meter and diction, Surrey professes an uncanny fidelity to Wyatt's spirit, which "reveals itself more subtly through Surrey's pervasive implication that Wyatt himself is the creator of the poem."[92] Through imitating Wyatt's subjectivity, Surrey uses the apparatus of melancholy identification in order to further dismantle his poetic self.

These later poems restate a certain inescapability of the subject from internal division brought about by lovesickness; pointing to a resolution, they contain caveats that belie the promise of recuperated selfhood. Presented with a self-image, the poet sees the same melancholy wound that has determined the elusive shape of his subjectivity since the opening lines of *Songes and Sonettes:* "That nought I finde displeasaunt in my sight: / But when my glasse presented unto me / The curelesse wound that bledeth day and night" (39.11–13). Even if the wound should heal, the scars will remain, as Surrey himself affirms, openly quoting Wyatt: "Yet Salomon said, the wronged shall recure: / But Wiat said true, the skarre doth aye endure" (40.5–6). Such is the fate of all who are lovesick. In the words of Laurentius, "being taken away [from their love object], the diseased partie will finde himselfe marueilously relieued, though notwithstanding there may remaine behinde some certaine prints and skarres in the bodie."[93]

The concluding text of Surrey's *Songes and Sonettes* encapsulates this poetics of melancholy, with its unresolved conflict within the self and a form of writing torn between remembering and forgetting:

> The fansy, which that I have served long,
> That hath alway bene enmy to myne ease,
> Semed of late to rue upon my wrong,
> And bad me flye the cause of my misease.
> And I forthwith dyd prease out of the throng,
> That thought by flight my painfull hart to please
> Som other way: tyll I saw faith more strong:
> And to my self I said: alas, those daies
> In vayn were spent, to runne the race so long.
> And with that thought, I met my guyde, that playn
> Out of the way wherin I wandred wrong,
> Brought me amiddes the hilles, in base Bullayn:
> Where I am now, as restlesse to remayn,
> Against my will, full pleased with my payn.   (41)

Bidding farewell to an illusion (erotic? political? poetic?) that has long tormented him, the speaker only finds himself trapped in Boulogne, where he is "restlesse to remayn /

Against [his] will." Liberation turns out to be another form of imprisonment, physical and textual. By labeling the poem "The fansie of a weried lover," Tottel also redirects the reader's attention back to Surrey's uneasy dialogue with Petrarchism. If this last poem finalizes the poet's departure from the Petrarchan fantasy, the choice of the sonnet form—curiously, one that could be said to conform to neither the Italian nor the English pattern—is at the very least puzzling. Also, apparently having dealt away with Petrarchan diction and put it behind him, Surrey's "weried lover" concludes with a Petrarchan figure par excellence, "full pleased with my payn." The poem's anti-Petrarchan ethos negates its Petrarchan form, but the discourse of Petrarchism continues to dictate the terms in which the poet's rejection of his Petrarchan identity is written. This ambivalence, however, is deeply entrenched in the poetics of melancholy. In melancholy, "identification becomes a magical, a psychic form of preserving the object...[and] the lost object continues to haunt and inhabit the ego as one of its constitutive identifications."[94] The lost, or rejected, Petrarchan self in Surrey's poetry is never expunged from discourse but only fantasized as abandoned. It is always present in the background, as memory, offering a point of reference against which anti-Petrarchan identifications can ever take place. Encased in the tomb Surrey's Petrarchan protagonist shares with Chaucer's most famous lover, moreover, it proclaims its vernacular genealogy, signaling a tight interlacement between Petrarchan suffering and Chaucerian melancholy in early modern English culture.

The Subject of Melancholy in *Astrophil and Stella*

Astrophil is a melancholic and he knows it. Boasting enviable medical knowledge, he turns sonnet 23 into an exercise in self-diagnosis:

118 Renaissance Texts, Medieval Subjectivities

> The curious wits, seeing dull pensivenesse
> Bewray it selfe in my long setled eyes,
> Whence those same fumes of melancholy rise,
> With idle paines, and missing ayme, do guesse.
> Some that know how my spring I did addresse,
> Deeme that my Muse some fruit of knowledge plies:
> Others, because the Prince my service tries,
> Thinke that I thinke state errours to redresse.
> But harder Judges judge ambition's rage,
> Scourge of it selfe, still climbing slipprie place,
> Holds my young braine captiv'd in golden cage.
> O fooles, or over-wise, alas the race
> Of all my thoughts hath neither stop nor start,
> But only *Stella's* eyes and *Stella's* heart.[95]

The speaker makes no mystery of the humoral causes of his affliction, blaming it on the atrabilious vapors ("those same fumes of melancholy") that make him sad and pensive. He admits, however, that his symptoms can have different etiological explanations, confirming my earlier remarks about the elusiveness of boundaries between various kinds of melancholy, both natural and unnatural. It is possible, he playfully suggests, that his melancholy is of a scholarly nature, the product of plying "the fruit of knowledge," just as it is possible that his condition could be linked to his political career and attempts "state errours to redresse." Lemnius, invoking the classical Aristotelian formula, notes that those subject to melancholy most often include "those that be Magistrates and Officers in the Commonwealth, or Studentes which at vnseasonable times sit at their Bookes & Studies. For through ouermuch agitatio[n] of ye mynd, natural heat is extinguished, & ye Spyrits aswell Animall as Vitall, attenuated and vanish away: whereby it co[m]meth to passe, that after their vitall iuyce is exhausted, they fall into a Colde & Drye constitution."[96] Or perhaps Astrophil's melancholy stems from "myssing and beyng disappointed of some great desyre and expectation, which they hoped & had, of some thing to come to passe"[97]—from what Sidney calls thwarted "ambition's rage...still climbing slipprie place." After all, elsewhere in the sequence Astrophil confesses the sin of "*Ambition*" (27.11) and admits that "to my birth I owe / Nobler desires, least else that friendly foe, / Great expectation, weare a traine of shame" (21.6–8).[98]

In the end Astrophil brushes these explanations aside, positing his unrequited love for Stella—erotic melancholy—as the mechanism that orchestrates the dynamic of his selfhood. By his own account, he has been injured by Cupid's blow ("Not at first sight, nor with a dribbed shot / Love gave the wound, which while I breathe will bleed" [2.1–2]) and now bears an incurable wound that threatens his own life and the existence of those around him ("Flie, fly, my friends, I have my death wound; fly" [20.1]). He is so morbidly fixated on the object of his desire, Stella, that minute details of her appearance, demeanor, and speech become his raison d'être, betraying a mighty disturbance in the estimative faculty of his brain: "I would know whether she did sit or walke, / How cloth'd, how waited on, sighd she or smilde, / Whereof, with whom, how often did she talke" (92.9–11). This results in a nexus of symptoms that reinforce the mimetic verisimilitude of the diagnosis. Astrophil is sleepless (32, 39, 40, 99), most likely due to the "blacke and darke fumes of melancholie, rising vp to the braine, whereof the fatansie forgeth obiectes, and disturbeth the sleep of melancholy persons."[99] He sighs and cries abundantly (61, 67, 95, 104, Song 8) and prefers solitude and silence to company ("Because I oft in darke abstracted guise / Seeme most alone in greatest companie, / With dearth of words, or answers quite awrie" [27.1–3]). All of these are textbook qualities of a melancholic, since one "shall finde [him] weeping, sobbing, sighing, and redoubling his sighes, and in continuall restlesnes, auoyding co[m]pany, louing solitarines, the better to feed & follow his foolish imaginations."[100] The principal color of Astrophil's world is black (the words "black" and "darke" occur 38 times in the sequence). Like other melancholics, he has "in [his] braine a continuall night"; in his inner world, "a darknes & cloudes of melancholie vapours...obscure the clearenes."[101]

Perhaps it is because these manifestations of lovesickness are so salient and self-evident that critics have all but ignored the subject of melancholy in *Astrophil and Stella*.[102] After all, if all Petrarchan lovers are melancholic, why would a thematic explication of Astrophil through this lens be a fruitful scholarly enterprise? However, melancholy not merely supplies a subject matter for Sidney's cycle but also determines its textual logic, namely, a fragmentation of the "I" and its dissolution into a series of quasi-theatrical performances of identity. In this sense, the melancholy that saturates Sidney's *Astrophil and Stella* is of a Chaucerian brand. Admittedly, the claim of Sidney's fractured subjectivity is old news. In the words of Gary Waller, in *Astrophil and Stella* we find ourselves "in the presence of a continually decentered self that searches for fixity through the endless dissemination of language."[103] What I seek to demonstrate in the following pages, however, is that in Sidney's *Astrophil and Stella* it is melancholy that prevents the subject from sustaining a coherent, stable identity. Additionally, melancholy elucidates the speaker's uneasy relationship with the tradition of Petrarchan writing. The ambivalent position *Astrophil and Stella* assumes vis-à-vis Petrarchism arises out of a writing premised on simultaneous disavowal and preservation of a literary discourse—a poetics of melancholy.

From the start, Sidney's sequence harbors a melancholic rupture of identity, of an ego turning on itself. The name of the cycle's protagonist, Astro/Phil, is one of the crucial sites that embody the logic of melancholic object-introjection and identification outlined above. The speaker identifies with

Stella, which is reflected in the Greek version of her name (Astra) being incorporated into that of the desiring speaker, while at the same time the compound Astro/Phil couples Philip (Sidney) and his textual creation, Astrophil. In the past 50 years critics have spilled a great deal of ink trying to untangle the intricacies of the relationship between Sidney and Astrophil. The imperfect alignment of the two was first formulated as a theoretical problem by Theodor Spencer in 1945; he identified the poetic interplay between Sidney and Astrophil as the central concern of the sequence of *Astrophil and Stella*.[104] In S. K. Heninger Jr.'s later formulation, "the poet, Sidney, can watch the lover, Astrophel, in the act of loving and can make observations and insinuate inferences about his success. By the same token, Sidney can also comment upon Astrophel's practice as a poet."[105] For the most part, this split between Sidney's and Astrophil's voices has been read in terms of ethical criticism, with Astrophil taken as a negative example of passion that Sidney himself does not condone. Critics have pointed out such ideological frameworks as Christian intolerance of sin, Renaissance courtier ethics, and Protestant attitudes to married love and adultery.[106] Although the grounds on which Sidney and Astrophil can be contrasted may vary from study to study, the idea of *Astrophil and Stella* as an examination by the poet of his textual projection holds a particular attraction to the Sidney readers.

This model also aligns with the self-critique that characterizes melancholic subjectivity, when (to recall Freud again) "one part of the ego sets itself over against the other, judges it critically, and, as it were, takes it as its object" ("Mourning and Melancholia," 247). One of the most striking instances of Sidney's ego-cleavage is sonnet 34, where the two agencies engage in a polemic about the values of courtly love and amorous poetry:

Come, let me write, "And to what end?" To ease
A burthned hart. "How can words ease, which are
The glasses of thy dayly vexing care?"
Oft cruel fights well pictured forth do please.
"Art not asham'd to publish thy disease?"
Nay, that may breed my fame, it is so rare:
"But will not wise men thinke thy words fond ware?"
Then be they close, and so none shall displease.
"What idler thing, then speake and not be hard?"
What harder thing then smart, and not to speake?
Peace, foolish wit, with wit my wit is mard.
Thus write I while I doubt to write, and wreake
My harmes on Ink's poore losse, perhaps some find
Stella's great powrs, that so confuse my mind.

This schism in textual identity closely follows the pattern of melancholic splitting: incorporating the loved object (Stella) into the speaker's ego results in the emergence of two forces within the self, one loving and the other censoring the love. There are echoes here of the dreamer's conversation with the man in black from the *Book of the Duchess* as well as of Surrey's shepherd witnessing the agonies of a Petrarchan poet. However, similar to what we have seen in Chaucer and Surrey, the distinction between the two aspects of the "I" is rendered deliberately suspect. Behind the ostensibly dialogic organization of the sonnet, it is easy to overlook the fact that such differentiation is rather problematic. For readers of the early modern editions of Sidney, the poem would have appeared even more disturbing since the absence of quotation marks made the distinction of the two voices all but impossible. But even today this internal conversation betrays a massive instability that accompanies every use of "I" in the sequence: Sidney/Astrophil are both forced to fall back on the same pronoun in order to express their subjectivity. "Thus write I while I doubt to write," Sidney (or Astrophil?) exclaims, and the substitutability of the signifier besets both projects, of writing and of poetic reflection.

To use Edward Berry's succinct wording, in *Astrophil and Stella*, "Sidney creates a poetic form in which both the speaker and authorial voice are radically ambiguous."[107] Though occasional slippages from the first to the third person pronoun ("Therewithall away she went, / Leaving *him* so passion rent, / ... That therewith *my* song is broken" [Song 8, 101–02, 104; emphasis added]), suggest that autoreflexive work undeniably takes place within the poetic subject, Sidney's "attempts to distinguish himself from the speaker are at best limited."[108] In Chaucerian terms, Astrophil is not just the man in black under the microscope of Sidney the dreamer. One "I" is always difficult to differentiate from another ("I am not I, pitie the tale of me" [45.14]); every self is and is not the same at once. When the speaker cries, "I might, unhappie word, ô me, I might, / And then would not, or could not see my blisse" (33.1–2), we presume that he refers to the subtleties of early modern modality, but the same reading—and the same tag of "unhappie word"—can be applied to the first-person pronoun. Because of "*Stella's* great powrs, that so confuse [his] mind" (34.14), Astrophil's ego defies coherence and becomes a series of misrecognitions, what Sidney himself calls "those civill warres" in him (39.7).

As in Chaucer's poem, however, the dispersal of subjectivity in *Astrophil and Stella* is not confined to a poet/lover split. The mechanism of melancholia, both pre-modern and modern, involves an endless process of identification within the limits of the same self, not so much erasure of the original self but a continuous rewriting of the ego through a series of assumed identities. All these identifications are driven by the subject's desire to fulfill his wish—in Sidney's case, to obtain Stella. But it appears, Borch-Jacobsen remarks, "as if wish fulfillment did not so much consist in *having* the object as in *being* the one who possesses it: a slight difference, an initially imperceptible nuance that liberates the fabulous space of fantasy in which a world of heroes is already stirring."[109] *Astrophil and Stella* is indeed a "world of heroes"—it is built around a continuous splintering of the ego into multiple sub-subject positions, producing a self "always in the process of *being* fashioned" and resulting in "the poems' ever-changing rhetorical texture, which records the transformation of a poetic Proteus."[110]

The first sonnet in *Astrophil and Stella* is perhaps the most famous statement of such relentless dispersal of identity:

> Loving in truth, and faine in verse my love to show,
> That the deare She might take some pleasure of my paine:
> Pleasure might cause her reade, reading might make her know,
> Knowledge might pitie winne, and pitie grace obtaine,
> I sought fit words to paint the blackest face of woe,
> Studying inventions fine, her wits to entertaine:
> Oft turning others' leaves, to see if thence would flow
> Some fresh and fruitfull showers upon my sun-burn'd braine.
> But words came halting forth, wanting Invention's stay,
> Invention, Nature's child, fled step-dame Studie's blowes,
> And others' feete still seem'd but strangers in my way.
> Thus great with child to speake, and helplesse in my throwes,
> Biting my trewand pen, beating my selfe for spite,
> "Foole," said my Muse to me, "looke in thy heart and write."

The opening lines explore a conflict between true loving, authenticity, inwardness, poetic originality, and anti-Petrarchism on the one hand ("'Fool,' said my Muse to me, 'looke in thy heart, and write'"), and writing, falsity, exteriority, and stock Petrarchan poetics ("Oft turning others' leaves, to see if thence would flow / Some fresh and fruitfull showers upon my sun-burn'd brain. / But words came halting forth, wanting Invention's stay") on the other. But as the sonnet progresses, the initial rupture is pushed aside by an avalanche of what an early modern medical text would call the protagonist's "phantasticall imaginations." The speaker slips from a lover to a writer, then from an assiduous reader of poetry to a truant schoolboy, before becoming a birthing woman, self-loathing, anxious, and in pain, and turning back into a writer.

The sequence as a whole enlarges this melancholic dynamic by staging a histrionic proliferation of new forms of subjectivity. If in the opening sonnet Sidney's melancholic subject (like Surrey before him) depreciates his gender, in the next poem his national identity and social position are undone: "Now even that footstep of lost libertie / Is gone, and now like slave-borne *Muscovite*, / I call it praise to suffer Tyrannie" (2.9–11), a desperate cry of belittled selfhood also repeated in 47: "What, have I thus betrayed my libertie? /...or am I born a slave, / Whose necke becomes such yoke of tyranny?" (1, 3–4; cf. 29.14, 86.9). The speaker further identifies with proverbial heroes of classical mythology such as Narcissus, Paris, and Hercules (82); and from an educated and sophisticated courtier becomes an immature schoolboy (1, 3, 46, 56, 73, 79).[111] As a diligent Neoplatonic lover, he identifies with Stella herself (36, 87, 90, 94, 107).[112] If in the opening sonnet Astrophil is with child, in 37.2 his thoughts go into labor and by 50.10–11 he has been delivered of stillborn babies.

Even Astrophil's humanity is placed under erasure. In his *Apologie* Sidney confesses that Pugliano, his riding master in Vienna, with his praises of horsemanship made him wish to be a horse, "if I had not beene a pecce of a Logician before I came to him, I think he would haue perswaded mee to haue wished my selfe a horse."[113] In *Astrophil and Stella*, however, he *is* a horse:

> I on my horse, and *Love* on me doth trie
> Our horsemanships, while by strange worke I prove
> A horsman to my horse, a horse to *Love*;
> And now man's wrongs in me, poor beast, descrie.
> ....
>   and while I spurre
> My horse, he spurres with sharpe desire my hart:

He sits me fast, however I do sturre:
And now hath made me to his hand so right,
That in the Manage myselfe take delight. (49.1-4,10-14)

The speaker here not only imagines himself an animal but also delights in his beastly condition. It is, however, not so difficult for Sidney to be a horse since his Greek name Philippos ("horse-lover") already incorporates an equine identity; as a readily available alter ego and half-namesake for the poet, Astrophil is always already a horse.[114] Elsewhere in the sequence, Astrophil, realizing that his human body can ill assist him in his desire to possess Stella, dreams of dehumanizing self-transformations into a double of Stella's puppy (59) and a lascivious parrot ironically named Philip (87; cf. 108.6-8), for they both have free physical access to Stella. A number of pre-modern medical tracts name among manifestations of melancholy oblivion of the human self and appropriation of an animal identity instead. "Some thinke," Burton writes, "they are beasts, wolves, hogges and cry like dogges, foxes, bray like asses, and low like kine."[115] Burton's words echo Ficino's observation that in the madness of love "a man is brought down below the species of man and in some degree is changed from a man into a beast."[116] Indeed, he who loves Stella "all selfnesse he forbeares" (61.7).

It then becomes possible to characterize Astrophil's melancholic self, or any melancholic self, as "essentially theatrical."[117] Untrammeled by a stable discourse or subject position, such a melancholic ego, Kristeva writes, "asserts itself on the field of artifice: there is a place for the "I" only in play, in theater, behind the masks of possible identities."[118] But the psychoanalytic notion of melancholy as a thespian merry-go-round of identifications merely revives the pre-modern understanding. Like drunkards, Lemnius writes, melancholics "are ledde with many affections and phansies, gybing and gesturing as though they were Stage Players."[119]

To see a melancholic, Burton agrees, is to "see a man turne himselfe into all shapes like a Camelion, or as *Proteus, Omnia transformans sese in miracula rerum*, to act twenty parts and persons at once, for his advantage, to temporize and vary like *Mercury* the Planet, good with good, bad with bad; having a several face, garb, & character for every one he meets; of all religions, humours, inclinations."[120] This aptly describes Astrophil, who takes on the roles of first a tragic (46) and then a comic (51) character; and the choice of genres here is not accidental. Bright compares the progress of melancholy with "the comedy turned into tragedy, pleasantnes into fury, & in the end, mirth into mourning" while in unnatural melancholy, caused by the burning of blood through internal heat, "euery serious thing for a time, is turned into a iest, & tragedies into comedies, and lamentation into gigges and daunces."[121] Burton, in lieu of his introduction to the matter of love melancholy, announces, "I am resolved...boldly to shew my selfe in this common Stage, and in this Tragecomedy of Love, to Act severall parts, some Satyrically, some Comically, some in a mixt Tone, as the subject I have in hand gives occasion, and present Sceane shall require or offer it selfe."[122] Early readers did in fact characterize *Astrophil and Stella* as tragicomedy. Thomas Nashe, in his preface to the 1591 edition describes it as a "Theatre of pleasure, for here you shal find a paper stage streud with pearle, an artificial heau'n to ouershadow the faire frame, & christal wals to encounter your curious eyes, whiles the tragiccommody of loue is performed by starlight.... The argument cruell chastitie, the Prologue hope, the Epilogue dispaire."[123]

This melancholic performance of the self also accounts for *Astrophil and Stella*'s discontinuous form torn between lyric and narrative.[124] The insufficiency of the self manifested in the opening sonnet of the sequence makes a search for alternative identities the driving force behind the development of the plot. While individual poems deconstruct Astrophil's lyric subjectivity (class, nationality, gender, humanity), the overarching narrative, if intermittent, is that of apparently chaotic gliding from one identity to another. Each individual subject-position that Sidney constructs in *Astrophil and Stella* comes under erasure and is temporarily replaced with another, which generates an effect of narrative development. Despite a strong diegetic plot with a beginning, climax, and conclusion, however, teleological character development in *Astrophil and Stella* is an illusion: instead of solidifying the self through narrative linearity, Astrophil is engaged in an endless kaleidoscopic performance of shattered—and therefore lyric—subjectivity that fails to coagulate into a fixed "I." As Marion Campbell formulates it, "No consistent psychological or narrative structure can be identified in *Astrophil and Stella* because the poem...dramatizes the process of creating a self and of narrating that self's history without those processes ever crystallizing into the product of a self created or a story told."[125] Rejecting the linearity of narrative and thus the stability of a subject-position in the symbolic order, Sidney in *Astrophil and Stella* instead opts for an unfinished—melancholic—form of lyric subjectivity that defies closure and prevents the narrative from reaching a final resolution.

The closest Astrophil comes to stabilizing his identity is when Stella agrees, conditionally, to share his love ("For *Stella* hath with words where faith doth shine, / Of her high heart giv'n me the monarchie" [69.9–10]), dispersing the gloom of melancholy. Crying in ecstasy, "I, I, ô I may say, that she is mine" (69.11), Astrophil, through the frenzied repetition of the signifier (in various forms "I," "me" or "my" occurs 15 times in the sonnet), appears to organize multiple subject-positions into one coherent self. His bliss, however, is short lived. After sonnet 86, which registers "[a] change of lookes" in Stella (86.1), Astrophil's previous symptoms come back with a vengeance. He is again smothered with sighs ("Only true sighs, you do not go away" [95.12]) while "the blacke horrors of the silent night, / Paint woe's blacke face so lively to [his] sight" (98.9–10). He again embraces self-loathing ("let mine owne conscience be / A still felt plague, to selfe condemning me: / Let wo gripe on my heart, shame loade mine eye" [86.2–4]) and guilt: "I have (live I and know this) harmed thee, / Tho worlds quite me, shall I myself forgive?" (93.10–11). In the last sonnet, Astrophil is as far as ever from a stable identity. His body and soul are unceremoniously snatched by sorrow and despair:

> When sorrow (using mine owne fier's might)
> Melts downe his lead into my boyling brest,
> Through that darke fornace to my hart opprest,
> There shines a joy from thee my only light;
> But soone as thought of thee breeds my delight,
> And my yong soule flutters to thee his nest,
> Most rude despaire my daily unbidden guest,
> Clips streight my wings, streight wraps me in his night,
> And makes me then bow downe my head.   (108.1–9)

Disjointed, physically and emotionally manipulated, self-mutilating (sorrow uses his "owne fier's might"), emasculated by an act of symbolic castration ("Most rude despaire.../ Clips streight my wings"), possibly subhuman, wrapped into the darkness of the night, Astrophil remains engulfed in the realm of melancholy that subverts identitarian stabilization. As elsewhere in the sequence, Astrophil's self here is a site where various identifications continue to vie with one another.

The final sonnet is doubly significant because it also epitomizes Sidney's uneasy relationship with Petrarchism and anti-Petrarchism. There, looking in his heart, Astrophil discovers "the conventional image of the Petrarchan lover, caught in an endless cycle of joy and despair."[126] This may come as a surprise because among identities that *Astrophil and Stella* subverts perhaps none is more crucial than that of a Petrarchan poet. In sonnet 15, the speaker contrasts his method with that of countless Petrarchan "apes": "You that do Dictionarie's methode bring / Into your rimes, running in rattling rowes: / You that poore *Petrarch's* long deceased woes" (5–7). The poet envisions Petrarchism as a system of signs, lifeless and largely meaningless, that anyone can discover in a "Dictionarie" of amorous poetry, such as Tottel's *Miscellany* or Thomas Watson's Ἑκατομπαθία—Elizabethan handbooks for love writing at which, as William Kennedy suggests, Sidney levels his attack in these lines.[127] When later Sidney assures Stella that he lacks poetic ambition ("thinke not that I by verse seeke fame, /...I wish not there should be / Graved in mine Epitaph a Poet's name" [90.1, 7–8]), he again emphasizes what form of poetic subjectivity he strives to avoid: he does not want to frame his poetic nest "in Lawrell tree" (90.6)—that is, to follow Petrarch. It would appear, in other words, that Sidney's speaker, like Surrey before him, vigorously refuses identification with Petrarch.

That is not what Sidney's first readers thought, of course. Among numerous fictional titles Sidney received soon after his death (as though in compensation for an almost lifetime of waiting for a real one) was that of "our English *Petrarke*." It was reportedly coined by Sir Walter Raleigh and repeated in 1591 by Sir John Harington in his translation of *Orlando furioso*.[128] Soon after that Burton recruited Sidney's lovesickness to illustrate the connection between melancholy and artistic inspiration, placing Sidney right next to Petrarch. Speaking about "all the other Symptoms of Lovers," Burton claims that they invariably "turne to their ability, Rimers, Ballet-makers, and Poets...as Nevisanus the Lawyer holds, *there never was any excellent Poet, that invented good fables, or made laudable verses, which was not in love himselfe...Petrarchs Laura* made him so famous, *Astrophels Stella*."[129]

So is Sidney a Petrarchan or an anti-Petrarchan?[130] One answer to this central crux of the Sidney scholarship—the ambivalence of *Astrophil and Stella* toward Petrarchism—is the poetics of melancholy. While Astrophil's claims of Petrarchan self-denial seem to contrast vividly with the very idea of creating an exquisite Petrarchan sequence, both are tightly interlocking elements in a system of melancholic writing that Sidney redeploys in *Astrophil and Stella*. It is the insufficiency of Petrarchan subjectivity that orchestrates the thematic and formal intricacies of the sequence: looking for a new poetic identity, the speaker deconstructs the amorous ego offered to him by the discourse of Petrarchism. But, as we have already seen in Chaucer and Surrey, the poet ends up reiterating the same Petrarchan subjectivity that he sought to avoid in the first place. The lost, or rejected, Petrarchan self Astrophil presumably leaves behind is never discarded completely—rather, this residual identification remains part of the self's archeological sedimentation. As Judith Butler reformulates the Freudian insight, in melancholy "there is no loss and, indeed, no negation. Melancholia refuses to acknowledge loss, and in this sense 'preserves' its lost object as psychic effects."[131] That is why Sidney's phantasmatic melancholic wound—like Surrey's wound that reappears at the end of Tottle's volume—never heals. Simultaneously abandoned and retained, the rejected Petrarchan identity continues to exercise its influence over the subject's writing.

As Maria Prendergast observes, Sidney's reluctance to assume the authority of originality "discloses Astrophil's underlying concern that, by identifying himself with a radical poetics of originality, he may drift progressively into a solipsistic space which ultimately alienates him from any coherent, unified conception of self."[132] The poetics of melancholy obviates this dilemma. *Astrophil and Stella* exposes the limitations of Petrarchan discourse, yet the very sustainability of its subject-position depends on the preservation of this rejected language embedded, if in a disguised, surreptitious form, within the poetic utterance. Consequently, the failed system of poetic signification is not rejected altogether but incorporated instead in a poetic sequence that, in a characteristically melancholic manner, makes it impossible to distinguish between Petrarchism and anti-Petrarchism. Sidney's Petrarchan sequence is melancholic in the sense that its fragmentation, dispersal, and instability form the necessary conditions for its functioning as a viable if struggling discourse, which makes it hostile to and yet ultimately dependent upon its own discursive history.

Immediately after Sir Philip Sidney's tragic death in 1586 near Zutphen in the Netherlands from an all too literal (and yet erotically charged) musket wound in the left thigh, the process of creating the Sidney legend began.[133] That the 1591 publication of *Astrophil and Stella* inaugurated a fashion for Petrarchan sonnet sequences is beyond doubt, and thus the proud title of England's Petrarch is Sidney's by right.[134] What is less obvious, however, is that the invention of self-reflexive Petrarchism in English, one that critiques the language of love poetry, can be exclusively assigned to Sidney.[135] As I have attempted to demonstrate here, the shattered subjectivity Sidney espouses in *Astrophil and Stella,* one torn between loving and writing and constantly in pursuit of a chronically elusive stability, is also inscribed in the English vernacular by Chaucer and Surrey—poets with whom Sidney (if his own testimony carries any weight) felt a special bond.

Taken on its own, Sidney's sonnet sequence is a daring project of an early modern poet who, by his own praxis of anti-Petrarchan writing, opens new ways for articulating the self and thus looks into the future. If, however, instead of disinheriting Sidney in poetic terms (and thus reenacting some of the most unpleasant instances of his biography) we replace autonomy with lineage and open *Astrophil and Stella* to a dialogue with earlier texts, the role that the Chaucerian poetics of melancholy plays in its discursive configuration becomes more pronounced. It is this poetics that determines that no matter how much Sidney's sequence may insist upon its independence from Petrarchism, it cannot operate outside of the territory regulated by Petrarchan discourse without running the risk of total dissolution in anti-Petrarchan asymbolia. By the same token, *Astrophil and Stella* vigorously resists its Chaucerian history and yet adopts the same pattern of poetic subjectivity that Chaucer shapes in the *Book of the Duchess* and Tottel's Surrey redeploys in his *Songes and Sonettes*. The Sidneian "I" does not simply transpose the Petrarchan self into English but rather, projecting it onto vernacular discourse, joins a process of symbolic accretion that adds a historical, even nostalgic, dimension to its articulations of subjectivity. Sidney's Petrarchan melancholy, in other words, is articulated in Chaucerian terms. Simultaneously forgetting and remembering Chaucer, *Astrophil and Stella*, in its frenzied but ultimately doomed quest for poetic originality, displays the key principle of the poetics of melancholy and thus reaffirms the relevance of the medieval imagination to the project of early modern English Petrarchism.

THREE

Sovereign Love, Medieval and Early Modern

The Arts of Marriage in the Casket Sonnets and "The Kingis Quair"

Having considered the workings of medieval substrate in some of the canonical examples of English Renaissance Petrarchism (Wyatt, Surrey, Sidney, Spenser), in this chapter I turn to a relatively obscure Petrarchan text that only recently began to attract scholarly attention — the casket sonnets. The casket sonnets are a short sequence of 12 French poems (11 sonnets and an envoy) attributed to Mary Stuart, Queen of Scots, which were first published in London in 1571 amid the political crisis over Mary's presence in England following her deposition and flight from Scotland. The sonnets, both the French originals and the accompanying crude (and not always accurate) Anglo-Scots translations, appeared in a political pamphlet called *Ane Detectioun of the duinges of Marie Quene of Scottes*.[1] The book claimed that the poems had been written by Mary and presented them as evidence of the transgressions she had allegedly committed while on the Scottish throne, with a view both to justify Mary's removal from power and to advance the argument against her as Elizabeth's successor to the crown of England.

It is easy to see why the casket sonnets might represent something of an anomaly that resists absorption into the paradigm of early modern English literary culture. The uncertainty of their authorship; their implication in the charged political affairs of early modern England and Scotland that inevitably redirects attention from the poems to their context; the French language of their originals and, worse still, the glaring imperfections of the Anglo-Scots versions; the poet's gender and, as a consequence, a reversal of the traditional Petrarchan scenario of desire—all these factors appear to jeopardize the casket sonnets' standing in the history of early modern English Petrarchism. But at the same time, while the casket sonnets were not the first sonnet sequence in English published under a woman's name (that honor goes to Anne Locke's 1560 *Meditation of a Penitent Sinner*, a lengthy paraphrase in sonnet form of Psalm 51), they were the first sequence of *love* sonnets ever to appear in Elizabethan England. Moreover, for several decades following their publication, they remained "one of the most widely circulated examples of poetry under a feminine signature in the period."[2] Despite their dubious authorship, national hybridity (as Cathy Shrank writes, they display "a pseudo-Scottish voice, easily comprehensible to an English reader, but marked with selected Scottishisms"[3]), or aesthetic shortcomings, the casket sonnets represent an important chapter in the history of early modern poetry.

What sets the casket sonnets apart from other Elizabethan sonnet sequences is, in fact, not their foreign provenance or their inversion of the conventional Petrarchan gender roles. Rather, it is the language of matrimony in which the female lover chooses to articulate her subjectivity as well as the royal status of the speaker that put the casket sonnets in a position of hostility to mainstream Petrarchism. Much of the drama of the sequence emerges out of the speaker's acrimonious rivalry with her beloved's wife, with five out of twelve poems directly addressing this conflict. Given that the Petrarchan tradition is indispensible for understanding their poetic subject, especially if we accept that Mary was indeed the author of the poems,[4] in their fantasies of matrimonial alliance and consummation of marriage, the casket sonnets enact a palpable contrast with the suppression of fleshly pleasure in orthodox Petrarchism. Although Edmund Spenser's *Amoretti* (1595) is often credited with overhauling the Petrarchan language of unrequited desire in order to express the Protestant idea of marital bliss, in Elizabethan England the casket sonnets were the first to explore the possibility of articulating matrimonial desires through the conventional resources of Petrarchan poetry.

However, in the casket sonnets the deployment of Petrarchism to speak of marital love is further complicated by the fact that their lover also presents herself as a sovereign queen entrusted with the care of her kingdom. In other words, in Mary's poetry the violation of Petrarchism by an intrusion of matrimonial sexuality correlates with a form of politicization of the Petrarchan tradition. The appropriation of Petrarchan eroticism as an allegory of political submission to the female monarch was one of the defining features of the lyric tradition of Elizabeth's reign. Philip Sidney, Edmund Spenser, Samuel Daniel, Henry Constable, and other Elizabethan sonneteers frequently resorted to the Petrarchan rhetoric of disempowerment and adoration to formulate their positions as subjects of the queen.[5] But Mary's casket sonnets enact a reconfiguration of this form of discourse. Expressions of monarchical selfhood, the casket sonnets use the Petrarchan language of submission and domination to probe from a sovereign's perspective questions of princely power and its relationship to the subjects, of passion and rule, and of the limits of political and sexual authority, all considered in the sequence through the prism of matrimony.

This conjunction of sexuality and politics, of matrimony and monarchy in the casket sonnets, constitutes my object of interest in this chapter. Mary's articulation of her unique royal subjectivity in the casket sonnets is achieved mainly through a radical disruption of sovereign marital bonds, for the lover of Mary's sonnets is portrayed as a woman willing to sacrifice marital alliance for the sake of unregulated passion, even though this leads to an abnegation of her claims to monarchical power. As I argue in this chapter, this scenario of subjectivity needs to be elucidated through the prism of the pre-modern Anglo-Scots tradition of allegorical sovereign marriage; and my aim here is to suggest that the ideologeme of matrimony survives in the language of sovereign eros from the fifteenth century literary and cultural imagination into the Elizabethan period. I begin this chapter with an analysis of matrimonial desires in Mary's Petrarchan poems, which I then contrast with the English politics of the 1560s and 1570s, notably Elizabeth's matrimonial maneuverings and the English queen's deployment of Petrarchism as a tool of self-articulation vis-à-vis marriage. As elsewhere in the book, however, I seek to transcend the interpretive frame of early modern culture and politics by suggesting a medieval genealogy for the articulation of Mary Stuart's royal subjectivity in the language of Petrarchism. I read the treatment of royal marriage in the sonnets as an antithesis to the valorization of chaste sovereign love in a late medieval poem, *The Kingis Quair*, traditionally attributed to James I Stewart (1394–1437). Royal poetry (to adopt Peter Herman's useful term) is not an exclusively early modern phenomenon;[6] and as I show below, the casket sonnets reactivate in a Petrarchan framework the concerns about sexuality, law, and sovereignty voiced by the medieval poem, recalling a long-standing discursive tradition that underwrites articulations of monarchical erotic and political desires from the early fifteenth to the late sixteenth century.

The Poetics of Sovereign Marriage in the Casket Sonnets

In order to elucidate the poetic and ideological implications of the erotic energies saturating the casket sonnets, it is useful first to consider the circumstances of their publication and reception. Although the title page of the book in which they appeared bore neither place nor date of printing, and the author's name was masked behind the initials "G. B.," it is doubtful that the politics behind *Ane Detectioun of the duinges of Marie Quene of Scottes* or the names of those who had had a hand in bringing it out in print were much of a mystery to early modern English readers. The "G. B." of the title page stood for George Buchanan (1506–82), a Scots Protestant humanist scholar and writer (and at one point a poet at the court of Mary);[7] and *Ane Detectioun* was a stylized Anglo-Scots translation (in all probability by Thomas Wilson) of Buchanan's Latin *Detectio* written around 1568 to justify the Scottish lords' rebellion against the queen and her subsequent deposition by accusing her of numerous "duinges"—sexual intemperance, adultery, and conspiracy to commit murder.

Both the *Detectio* and *Ane Detectioun* recounted and interpreted the events that had taken place in Scotland in the winter and spring of 1567.[8] Born in 1542, Mary Stuart was the daughter of and heir to James V of Scotland. Married to the French Dauphin François, she spent her early years at the royal court in France, embracing the language and culture of the Catholic realm. After the dauphin's sudden death, in 1561 she returned as Catholic queen to Scotland, a country that had establish Protestantism as its official religion the previous year. There, notwithstanding a strong opposition from both the Scottish nobility and the English government, in 1565 she married Henry Stewart, Lord Darnley, the son of the Earl of Lennox. As a result of this union, the future James VI/I was born in 1566. The marriage soon collapsed, however. Darnley, who had been growing estranged from Mary and increasingly unhappy with the degree of royal power she was willing to grant him, allowed himself to be involved in a plot against the pregnant Mary. Although he soon changed sides and betrayed his co-conspirators, it did not save him: he was assassinated in 1567.

During this prolonged period of crisis, Mary—probably even before she was a widow—had grown attracted to James Hepburn, Earl of Bothwell, who was rumored to have played a more than episodic role in Darnley's death. Desiring to place the queen further under his control, Bothwell abducted Mary and brought her to Dunbar Castle, where he allegedly raped her. She married him shortly after, which spelled the beginning of her end as Scots monarch. A union with her husband's suspected murderer rendered Mary just as guilty in the eyes of many, first of all her political enemies, who did not fail to capitalize on this opportunity. After a broad coalition against Mary and Bothwell was formed, Bothwell fled the country and Mary was imprisoned in the island fortress of Loch Leven and shortly afterwards forced to abdicate in favor of James. She escaped to England, where she was promptly imprisoned and remained in captivity until her execution in 1587.

Although *Ane Detectioun* dealt with the Scots affairs, for all intents and purposes it was an English text, printed and distributed in England with the backing of William Cecil's government and evidently aimed at an English audience. If Buchanan's *Detectio*, a catalog of Mary's alleged crimes such as her adulterous affair with Bothwell and her role in Darnley's death, sought to justify the deposition, the English pamphlet had an additional goal of neutralizing Mary's threat to the English interests, namely, to preempt her claim to the English throne (Mary's grandmother was a sister of Henry VIII married to James IV of Scotland).[9] James E. Phillips claims that *Ane Detectioun* was "completely a product, in its published form, of English activities to discredit Mary without violating Elizabeth's official attitude of benevolent neutrality toward her reluctant guest," and John D. Staines describes the pamphlet as "the most significant tool of Cecil's policy of covertly destroying Mary's reputation."[10]

Wilson's translation of Buchanan's *Detectio* was the centerpiece of Cecil's smear artillery, but the English *Detectioun* also incorporated a lengthy defense of their actions on behalf of the Scottish lords (so-called *Actio*) and the "casket letters"—a body of several letters and poems, presumably in Mary's own hand, discovered in a silver casket, which subsequently gave the poems their current moniker.[11] These sonnets had first surfaced during the 1568 York commission, whose mandate was to explore the charges of adultery and murder against Mary brought forward by the Scots, although the English were only allowed to view the papers unofficially *in camera*.[12] Yet the English presumably made copies of the letters and poems, and by 1571 Cecil had decided to release them to a wider audience. The poems were advertised as authentic writings of the deposed queen: "Certaine French Sonnettes writtin by the quene of Scottes to Bothwell befoir hir Mariage with him, and (as it is sayd) quile hir husband lyuit, But certainly befoir his diuorce from hys wife as the wordes tham selues shew, befoir quhom she here preferreth her selfe in deseruing to be beloued of Bothwell"

(Qiiij^r). *Ane Detectioun* thus invited the audience to read the sequence—in which the female speaker confesses her desire for her male beloved and dwells on her rivalry with his wife—as incriminating evidence of Mary's adulterous love affair with Bothwell (who at the time of the events was still married to one Jean Gordon), positing love and marriage as the key terms through which any interpretation of the sonnets must proceed.

Some historians are skeptical toward the sonnets' authenticity. John Guy spends a good deal of his recent biography of Mary trying to discredit them as forgeries, though other scholars are more open to the possibility that they are genuine writings of the Scots queen.[13] The voice of a monarch, however, is never entirely his or her own; rather, it is a product of negotiation between representational and interpretive forces. As Helen Hackett writes, images of monarchy are found between "their deliberate construction and promotion by central governmental authority, and their creation by a public projecting their own desires and anxieties."[14] This is particularly true in the case of Mary Stuart, whose troubled reign and fall quickly became a matter of contentious polemic that was played out in the textual sphere in the form of pamphlets, histories, and poems produced and consumed on both sides of the conflict.[15] Even if the letters and sonnets were forgeries (and both Scottish and English politicians had sufficient motive to fabricate them), or if they were altered in a major way to suit the political needs of those who wished to discredit Mary, the casket sonnets actively participated in the construction of Mary's subjectivity for the early modern English imagination.

In these circumstances, expressions of desire in the casket sonnets assume a distinctly political significance, and the vicissitudes of Petrarchan language—the volatile oppositions of spirit and body, of truth and appearance, of suffering and pleasure, of power and submission—become constitutive elements of Mary's self-representation as a queen. Already in the first sonnet, the energies of passion are recognized as a pernicious force that threatens to disrupt the fabric of social relations that determine her status in the world:

> O Goddis haue of me compassioun,
> And schew quhat certaine profe
> I may geif, which shall nat seem to him vaine,
> Of my loue and feruent affectioun.
> Helas, is he nat alredy in possessioun
> Of my bodie, of hart, that refusis no payne,
> Nor dishonour in the life vncertaine,
> Offence of frendes, nor worse afflictioun,
> For him I esteme al my frends les then nathing,
> And I will haue gude hope of my enemeis.
> I haue put in hasard for him both fame & conscience,
> I will for his sake renounce ye world,
> I will die to set him forwart.
> Quhat remayneth to gief proofe of my constancie? (Rij^v–Riij^r)

The poem is preoccupied with finding ways to offer proof of the lover's "constancie"—a Petrarchan legacy of nonvariability and devotion to the beloved sometimes viewed as the casket sonnets' key influence on women's sonnet writing in Renaissance England.[16] But in the course of the poem, constancy undergoes a semantic transformation, from a kind of virtue that consolidates the lover's subjectivity (as she says in the second sonnet, "I haif na vther desire, / But to make him perceiue my faythfulnes" [Riij^r]) into a pathological flaw that eventually becomes a source of "dishonour" and "offence" for the speaker. The sonnet opens with an invocation to the gods ("O Goddis haue of me compassioun, / And schew quhat certaine profe / I may geif.../ Of my loue and feruent affectioun") and, shortly before the end, includes a promise to "renounce ye world" for the sake of her love, so it could be argued that Mary imagines passion as a transcendent experience. This stance, however, is contrasted with the explicit admission that her relationship with the lover is rooted in physicality: "Helas, is he nat alredy in possessioun / Of my bodie, of hart, that refusis no payne." (Like other Petrarchan lovers, Mary finds a masochistic pleasure in her sufferings as both her body and her heart willingly accept the physical and emotional pain.) And once introduced, the motif of profane pleasure swells until it monopolizes the sonnet's field of signification. By the end of the poem, Mary is prepared to lose the goodwill of her supporters for the sake of her love, which as a consequence would encourage the actions of her political enemies, and to renounce her reputation ("fame") and her self-identification ("conscience") in favor of desire. The unwavering passion Mary feels for her beloved becomes a dangerous attachment whose menace lies precisely in its constancy.

What becomes clear as the sequence progresses, however, is that Mary defines this constant "loue and feruent affectioun" against the institution of marriage. In the second sonnet, the speaker mentions her rival for the affections of their beloved as someone whose passion is neither constant nor authentic, "That he sall know my constancie without fiction, / Not by my weeping, or faynit obedience, / As other haue done: but by vther experience" (Riij^r). But it is the following poem that announces marriage as the ultimate dividing line between the two women:

> Sche for hyr honour oweth you obedience:
> I in obaying you may receiue dishonour,
> Nat being (to my displesure) your wife as she.
> And yit in this poynt she shall haue na preheminence.
> Sche useth constancy for hyr awin profite:
> For it is na litle honour to be maistres of your goodes,
> And I for luifing of you may receiue blame,

> And will nat be overcumme by hyr in loyall obseruaunce.
> Sche has no apprehension of your euyll,
> I feare so all appearing euill that I can haue na reste:
> Sche had your acqueintance by consent of hyr freindes,
> I against al thair will haue borne you affection.
> And nat the lesse (my hart) you doubt of my constance,
> And of hir faithfulnes you haif firme assurance. (Riij^{r-v})

As the opening verses suggest, the lover is dismayed by the discrepancy between her rival's and her own marital positions. Her antagonist enjoys the honor of a legitimate marriage while the speaker laments her compromised, even dishonorable position as lover. At the same time ("And yit"), the speaker seeks to elevate her own affectivity as a valid counterpoint to the institution of wedlock; and the next sonnet opens with a charge of frigidity and impassivity leveled at the beloved's wife:

> Quhen you lovit hyr she usit coldnesse,
> Gif you suffrith for hir luif passioun,
> That commith of to greit affectioun of luif,
> Hyr sadnes schew the tristesse of hyr hart,
> Taking na pleasure of your vehement burning. (Riij^v)

Despite his "greit affectioun of luif" and "vchcmcnt burning," the wife remained cold and melancholy during intercourse, unable to match his sexual appetite. When the speaker claims that the rival is therefore not "worthy of sic husband and Lord" and that she "hath neuer weyit nor estemit / One so greit hap" (Riij^v), these remarks imply that, rather than the wife who fails to recognize the good fortune of her husband's sexual prowess ("one so greit hap"), it is the speaker who can fully emulate his desire with her own "loue and feruent affectioun" and ever increasing "burning" (Riiij^r). The speaker's only desire, as she spells it out in the tenth sonnet, is to "serue and loue you truely, / And to esteme all wan hap lesse then nathyng, / And to follow your wyll wyth myn" (Riiii^v). (This last line possibly contains a bawdy proto-Shakespearean pun on "wyll" and "myne" as the male and female sexual organs, reinforcing the speaker's desire to prioritize sexual passion over social codes of propriety.) Constant references to the speaker's willingness to "esteem all [her] frends les then nathing," to "put in hasard for him both fame and conscience," and to "receive blame" for loving him (Riij^r) suggest that, for her, passionate intimacy with the object of desire holds a more powerful appeal than the bonds of family and society.

At the same time, as the ninth sonnet indicates, the speaker never quite foregoes the allure of marriage, even though her version of it is founded upon erotic violence and an inverted temporality of conjugal union:

> For him also I powered out many tearis,
> First quhen he made himselfe possessor of thys body.
> Of the quilk then he had nat the hart.
> Efter he did geue me one vther hard charge,
> Quhen he bled of his blude great quantitie,
> Through the great sorrow of the quilk came to me that dolour,
> That almost caryit away my life, and the feire
> To lefe the onely strength that armit me.
> For him since I haif despisit honour,
> The thing onely that bringeth felicitie.
> For him I haif hasardit greitnes and conscience,
> For him I haif forsaken all kin and frendes,
> And set aside all vther respectes,
> Schortly, I seke the aliance of you onely.   (Riiij^v)

The sonnet splits into two unequal parts corresponding roughly to the octave and sestet division of the French text. The octave contains references to two violent acts, one directed at the speaker and the other at her beloved, both of which can be read as allusions to the particulars of Mary and Bothwell's dangerous liaison. The opening three lines seem to imply a forced sexual act, apparently rape, that the beloved commits against the speaker ("he made himselfe possessor of thys body / Of the quilk then he had nat the hart"), although the past tense somewhat alleviates the traumatic import of this revelation (he did not have her heart then, but he presumably has it now). These lines have been traditionally interpreted as a cryptic mention of Mary's abduction and rape by Bothwell in May 1567, although there were rumors that she was complicit in the affair.[17]

But what follows this muted admission of sexual violence perpetrated against the speaker is a picture of her beloved bleeding in "great quantitie." Again, a biographical reading is possible: Bothwell was indeed wounded in border skirmishes at Liddisdaill on October 1566, and Mary was widely reported to fear publicly for his life.[18] However, the complex and indeed abstruse imagery of the sonnet resists such unequivocal exegesis. For the two acts of violence are, to an extent, bound together by the fourth line, "Efter he did geue me one vther hard charge," which seems to correlate not only with the emotional distress the beloved's wound may have caused her but with his attack on Mary as well. Although separated from the allusion to rape by a syntactic and visual break, the fourth line also suggests that the beloved assaulted the speaker in a frictionlike manner, which throws the process of reading back to the opening image of her violated body. Yet bizarrely, what follows is an image of the beloved—not the speaker—bleeding profusely, and insofar as this "one vther hard charge" is already implicated in the opening act of erotic violence against Mary, his own injuries become a consequence of the rape. In other words, the sonnet appears to invert the conventional logic of rape, implying that the rapist is likewise hurt in the process. Mary's tears for herself mingle with her tears for Bothwell even as their broken bodies emerge out of the octave as intertwined in their violent act of passion. Symptomatically, Buchanan's account in *Ane Detectioun* also envisions the first sexual encounter between Mary and Bothwell as an aggressive exchange of erotic blows: on the first occasion, Bothwell "forced hir against hir will," but the next night it was the queen's turn to "reaquite force with force and to rauish hym agayne" (Bij^{r-v}). Aptly, the lines that follow this mirror image of rape—one in which it is the attacker who bleeds while the victim fears and sheds tears for her assailant's life—again explicitly articulate an immoral, asocial passion that threatens to disrupt all kinds of bonds as status, family, and society are sacrificed for the sake of desire.

However, in the last line of the sonnet the speaker states that she is in search of an "aliance" with her beloved, the word she has previously deployed (in the fourth sonnet) to describe her rival's marriage to their shared object of desire. The speaker's relationship with him thus also forms a kind of wedlock, a suspicion reinforced by a reference to "consent" in the following poem ("in the subiectioun / Of quhome I will without any fictioun, / Live and die, and this I consent" [Riiij^{v}]).[19] In fact, of the three elements of a legitimate early modern English marriage (consent, exchange of gifts, and consummation), the casket sonnets enact two, moving dangerously close to becoming a record of an actual marriage. But in this marriage consummation is not only committed through rape but in fact precedes the verbal act echoing marital vows. The casket sonnets, even as they retain the rhetoric of marriage, imagine it as an instance of violent sexuality that wounds the bodies and erodes the social identities of those who engage in it. Sarah Dunnigan argues that the casket sonnets break away from the Petrarchan tradition by forging "a new language of the desecrated female body which enters into dialogue with the other implicit neo-Platonic desires of the sequence."[20] I would stress, however, that the act of

Sovereign Love 149

desecration of Mary's body is closely associated with the marital dynamic in the sequence. Sexual violence is inscribed in the casket sonnet as an antithesis to normative marital sexuality and as a form of consummation of marriage, placing the codes of unrequited love under double pressure. Adapting the figures of pain and pleasure to the perspective of a woman physically violated by her object of desire but also celebrating the act of violence as part of a deviant marriage ceremony, the casket sonnets implode the foundations of Petrarchism.

The text of *Ane Detectioun* made sure the marital scenario of the casket sonnets resonated with the narrative of Mary's marriage to Bothwell, running a political commentary on the events and, implicitly, on the poems. Buchanan and Wilson treated Mary's third marriage as the key motive of her actions. She murdered her husband Darnley, *Ane Detectioun* claims, so "that the saim filthy mariage with Bothwell might be accomplished" (Miij^v), a marriage also described as "vnmatrimoniall matrimonie" (Fiij^v) and "maist wickit weddyng" (Giij^r). In fact, their hasty union is presented as an act even more heinous than the adultery that preceded it: according to *Ane Detectioun*, for Bothwell "to become a husband [was] to hir greater schame than he was befoir an adulterer" (Fj^v). In contrast to this abominable marriage between the lecherous queen and her lover, the union between Mary and Darnley is described by Buchanan as a "kinde society of mariage" (Biij^r) which Mary destroyed when she murdered her husband: "a sister hath butcherly slaughterit hyr brother, a wief her husband, a Quene her King" (Niiij^v). Admittedly such rhetoric blatantly twisted the facts of Mary and Darnley's family life and misrepresented the widespread attitudes to the marriage in Scotland (and England).[21] But in its impulse to proclaim "the sanctity of marriage,"[22] *Ane Detectioun* required an ideal form of royal matrimony against which Mary's subversive sexuality—including the desires voiced in the casket sonnets—could be measured and condemned.

One might argue that for Buchanan and Cecil to reveal Mary's failings as a wife was part of a more complex attack that involved portraying her as a woman who "cannot control her passions and therefore cannot fulfill the demands of a *rex stoicus*, a king who governs with strict moral rectitude, without regard to his passions."[23] The writers of *Ane Detectioun* describe Mary as "a woman burning in hatrid of hir husband, and in loue of ane adulter, and in baith these diseasis of corrupt affactionis unbridelit" (Hiij^r). As a point of departure, they take an equation of erotic self-control and political power, where the virtue of private governance over the ruler's passions is reflected in the public governance of his subjects and kingdom. As Michel Foucault writes, "this virtue that functions as an example and a sign of superiority does not owe its political value simply to the fact that it is an honourable behavior in everyone's eyes. In reality, as far as the subjects are concerned, it reveals the form of relationship that the prince maintains with himself. This is an important political point because it is this relationship with the self that modulates and regulates the use the prince makes of the power he exercises over others."[24] Failure to govern oneself translates into inability and unworthiness to govern others. As Sir John Fortescue noted in *A learned commendation of the politique lawes of Englande*, "For who can be more myghty or more free then he that is hable to conquere and subdue not onely others but also himselfe? Whiche thinge a kynge whose gouernaunce is politike can doo and euer doth."[25] Not surprising, for the authors of *Ane Detectioun* the dangers of unregulated emotion also become a threat to Mary's identity as a sovereign: "In all her wordes and doyinges," the pamphlet exclaims, "sche neuer kept any regard, I will nat say of Quenelike maiestie, but nat of matronlike modestie"; and she spent her days "in unprincely licentiousnesse" (Bi^{r-v}). That in Mary's case combining sovereignty and vehement libidinous emotions ends in a catastrophe does not mean that such a unity is not achievable in theory, nor can it be argued that early modern culture universally endorsed the inhibition of emotion and promoted the neo-Stoic ideal.[26] But the ethical agenda of *Ane Detectioun* explicitly espouses a standard of emotional restraint that clashes violently with Mary's alleged behavior.

What is also not to be missed is that in early modern political theory the anxiety over a woman ruler's inability to control her passions and retain power is often channeled through the language of marriage. John Knox's attack on female rule in *The First Blast of the Trumpet* (1558) was directed, *inter alia*, at women who "have burned with such inordinat lust, that for the quenching of the same,they have betrayed to strangiers their countrie and citie;...and some have killed with crueltie their owne husbandes and children."[27] His words proved prophetic a decade later, when the situation the authors of *Ane Detectioun* had on their hands replicated Knox's scenario to the letter: Mary not only "burned with such inordinat lust" that she sacrificed her royal duty and office for Bothwell, but she was claimed "to have killed with crueltie" her husband, Darnley, for the sake of quenching her desire. John Ponet, another Marian exile, relates in his *Shorte Treatise of Politike Power* (1556) the story of Romilda, the wife of the duke of Lombard, who falls in love with king Cacanus after the latter kills her husband in battle and besieges the city. Against "all honestie and womanly shamefastenesse, she woeth him [Cacanus] to be her husbande: and hauing no regarde of the loue that eueri honest creature ought to beare to his countrey, she promiseth to geue him citie, countrey, iewelles, goodes, and what so euer she could polle of her subiectes, and make for him, so that he wolde marie her."[28] In both instances, it is the perversion of marital bonds on the part of a woman monarch that carries the biggest threat to the political fate of the realm; and echoes of such stories of women who killed their husbands and betrayed their kingdoms for the sake of sexual desire resound throughout the text of *Ane Detectioun*.

The casket sonnets offer their own proof of the incompatibility of Mary's sexual behavior with the idea of royal self-regulation. In the second sonnet, the lover openly sacrifices the attributes of royal power for the sake of desire:

> Into his handis and in his full power,
> I put my sonne, my honour, and my lyif,
> My contry, my subiects, my soule al subdewit
> To him, and has none vther will
> For my scope, quhilk without deceit,
> I will folow in spite of all enuie
> That may ensue: for I haif na vther desire,
> But to make him perceiue my faythfulnes,
> For storme or fayre wedder that may come,
> Neuer will it chainge dwelling, or place.
> Schortly I sall geif of my trueth sic profe,
> That he sall know my constancie without fiction,
> Not by my weping, or faynit obedience,
> As other haue done: but by vther experience. (Riij^r)

Another token of the lover's "constancie," this sonnet is an expansion of the Petrarchan figure of disempowerment and submission to the beloved. Her only desire, she claims in sonnet 10, is "to serue and loue [him] truely," so he "shall knaw wyth obedience, / Not forgetting the knawlege of my leal deuty, / The quhilke I shall study to the fine that I may euer please you" (Riiij^v). These and other instances of self-abasement betray Mary's readiness to relinquish her own will and be governed by her object of desire.[29] Yet the royal status of the speaker (made abundantly clear by the reference to her "contry" and "subiects") complicates the Petrarchan scenario of subjection. Petrarch is happy to accept subjection to Laura, whom he envisions as the "enthroned monarch in [his] heart" ("chi nel mio cor siede monarcha").[30] The lover in Mary's sonnets, by contrast, realizes that her office ("deuty") requires submission from others, but she chooses to invert the roles presupposed by the traditional scenario of sovereign-subject relationship, embracing instead unconditional service as her attribute. Critics are unanimous in their interpretation of what this inversion entails. For Herman, "Mary uses her position as monarch to undermine her position as monarch...to articulate her personal subjectivity while destroying her political subjectivity"; for Dunnigan, the poems serve as "an erotic assertion, or rather negation, of political desires"; and for Staines, they "detail Mary's perverse subjection of herself, and her nation, to her passion for a man."[31] Instead of being checked by her royal status, Mary is shown to be willing to forfeit her political power in order to satisfy her erotic impulses.

Importantly, however, the submission to desire that leads to a disintegration of Mary's royal identity in the second sonnet is again linked with the institution of marriage. By putting into the hands of her beloved her son, honor, life, country, subjects, and soul, the speaker not only shows disregard for her reputation (and possibly flirts with eternal damnation), but in abandoning her son and heir for the sake of her beloved, she puts at risk the future of her dynasty. If one of the purposes of sovereign marriage is the continuation of a bloodline in order to secure the stability of the realm, Mary's erotic desires clearly deny any value to the notion of a legitimate marital alliance. When in the penultimate poem she addresses her beloved as "my hart, my bloud, my soule, my care" (Sj^r), she merely repeats the sentiment expressed throughout the sequence: for Mary, her passion has displaced her obligations to her subjects, her religion, her family, and her kingdom. It is her beloved who becomes the sole focus of Mary's political duty ("care"), and as she submits herself to him entirely, the conventional considerations of royal marriage are banished from the text of the casket sonnets, giving way to a fantasy of illicit sexual pleasure.

Royal Marriage in Elizabethan England: Politics, Poetry, Allegory

If *Ane Detectioun*'s negative commentary on Mary's involvement in Darnley's murder and her alliance with Bothwell provided a local perspective on the problematic of royal marriage in the casket sonnets, there was also a wider political and cultural context for the poems printed under Mary's name. In the England of 1571, the images of a queen seeking an adulteration of marriage through a risky "aliance" with her ravisher not only pointed toward the recent events north of the border, they also spoke to the domestic English politics of the 1560s and early 1570s, specifically what had become "the central political issue of the decade"—Elizabeth's own marriage and succession to the throne of England.[32] Dunnigan argues that Mary's amatory desires in the casket sonnets should be read against "Elizabeth's carefully managed eroticisation."[33] But the language of sovereign marriage in Mary's poems also alludes to the dense fabric of conjugal rhetoric that had surrounded the English queen from the moment of her coronation. As we know in retrospect, Elizabeth remained single, adopting the role of the virgin queen, but such an outcome did not appear inevitable in the 1560s. She was widely expected and exhorted to marry. In his 1558 letter to Elizabeth, Archbishop Matthew Parker urged the young queen to marry: "Marriage we all wish to see your godly affection inclined to, whereby your noble blood might be continued to reign over us to our great joy and comfort, whereby the great fears of ruin of this your ancient empire might be prevented, and destruction of your natural-born subjects avoided... all your natural subjects in general most effectuously do crave at your hand to see you entered into the blessed state of wedlock."[34] On several occasions (1559, 1563, 1566, and 1576) Parliament petitioned her to take a husband and thus settle the succession question.[35] Although in her answer to the 1559 petition Elizabeth claimed that "in the end, this shall be for me sufficient: that a marble stone shall declare that a queen, having reigned such a time, lived and died a virgin," in 1563 she did an about-face and promised the Commons, "if I can bend my liking to your need I will not resist such a mind." Likewise, she is remembered to have promised the Parliament in 1566, "I say again, I will marry as soon as I can conveniently, if God take not away him with whom I mind to marry, or myself."[36]

The decade preceding the publication of the casket sonnets in *Ane Detectioun* had seen several courtships of Elizabeth by foreign princes. In addition to Philip II of Spain (Mary Tudor's widower) and James Hamilton, Earl of Arran and Duke of Châtelherault, who both flirted with the idea of marrying Elizabeth soon after her ascension, Elizabeth in this period was the object of earnest suits by Eric XIV of Sweden (1559–62); the Archduke Charles (1563–67); Henry, Duke of Anjou (1570–71); and Francis, Duke of Alençon (1572–1578, 1582).[37] We cannot know whether Elizabeth never had any intention to marry or simply failed to find a candidate she considered suitable, but her meticulously choreographed matrimonial projects guaranteed that the public discourse surrounding the queen in the 1560s and 1570s was imbued with talk of her impending marriage.

The issues of Elizabeth's marriage and succession elicited a rich body of literature that, with varying degrees of subtlety, argued for and against matrimony, in favor of a foreign or an English, a Catholic or a Protestant husband for Elizabeth, or simply handpicked a preferred candidate.[38] It is hard to tell whether by releasing the casket sonnets and highlighting their problematic of marriage through textual glosses the masterminds of *Ane Detectioun* were deliberately referring to Elizabeth's marital maneuverings, let alone commenting on a particular matrimonial project. Nevertheless, it is useful to remember that Cecil played a vital part in the publication of the casket sonnets and was closely involved in the government's attempts to settle the questions of Elizabeth's marriage and succession as well.[39] What is safe to assume is that the casket sonnets were deployed to present the readers with a distinct scenario of royal matrimony—a scenario risky, disturbing, and dangerous both to a (hypothetical) female monarch and her kingdom, a scenario involving unbridled sexual passion, adultery, and legally questionable marriage. In order to marry her lover, the speaker of the casket sonnets abandoned her royal identity, her power, and the future of her dynasty, her son; for him she rejected honor and familial ties. Moreover, as readers were bound to know, Mary's criminal union with Bothwell had indeed left the country torn by civil strife and the future of the kingdom in doubt. By contrast, though Elizabeth still lacked an heir, her future marriage—provided she avoided the pitfalls of Mary's infatuation—was expected to secure succession. The casket sonnets provided Elizabeth with a kind of mirror for magistrates that showed her the dangers associated with an ill-suited royal marriage. It is hard not to speculate that after Mary's "aliance" with her lover was made public through the printing of the casket sonnets, marriage became an issue much more rife with risk and uncertainty for Elizabeth as well.

The contrast between the two queens can be further illustrated by looking at how Elizabeth I drew on the language of

Sovereign Love 157

Petrarchism in the context of sovereign marriage. Rosalind Smith suggests that the impact of Mary's sonnets on English poetry was "to problematize women's participation in the sonnet sequence as a genre."[40] Yet the circulation in the public sphere of Mary's poetry, with its visions of violent sexuality and its disdain for the institution of marriage, had more local ramifications that affected the uses of Petrarchan poetics in expressions of sovereign eros. A poem attributed to Elizabeth demonstrates a form of royal selfhood markedly (and perhaps consciously) different from the one articulated in the casket sonnets:

> I grieve and dare not show my discontent;
> I love, and yet am forced to seem to hate;
> I do, yet dare not say I ever meant;
> I seem stark mute, but inwardly do prate.
>   I am, and not; I freeze and yet am burned,
>   Since from myself another self I turned.
> My care is like my shadow in the sun—
> Follows me flying, flies when I pursue it,
> Stands, and lies by me, doth what I have done;
> His too familiar care doth make me rue it.
>   No means I find to rid him from my breast,
>   Till by the end of things it be suppressed.
> Some gentler passion slide into my mind,
> For I am soft, and made of melting snow;
> Or be more cruel, Love, and so be kind.
> Let me or float or sink, be high or low;
>   Or let me live with some more sweet content,
>   Or die, and so forget what love e'er meant.[41]

The poem is entitled "Elizabeth: On Monsieur's Departure" in one of its seventeenth century manuscripts, and it has been widely accepted in critical discourse that the poem, written in the early 1580s, marks the end of the marriage negotiations between Elizabeth and her last suitor, Duke of

Alençon, the "Monsieur" whose "departure" the speaker of the poem laments, although there is also a possible Essex connection as well.[42] It is possible that the poem may have been composed in the wake of an elaborately contrived engagement ceremony, in the course of which Elizabeth exchanged vows and rings with the Duke of Alençon, only to retract her promise to marry him the following day.[43]

On the surface of things, the poem is nothing but a collection of Petrarchan commonplaces: with the speaker at once burning and freezing, loving and hating, mute and eloquent, floating and sinking, the text exemplifies the Petrarchan mode.[44] But the probable context and date of its composition—a poem by a desiring queen written in the unhappy aftermath of a failed courtship—make it an intriguing parallel to the politics and poetics of royal marriage in the casket sonnets. In Mary's poems as they appear in *Ane Detectioun*, the Petrarchan framework collapses against the surge of erotic desire. The quest for spiritual fulfillment turns into an experience of acute bodily pleasure, eroticism becomes a form of cruelty, the balance of submission and empowerment is undone by a crisis of royal identity, and the virtue of constancy is rewritten as a pathway to dishonor and self-destruction. Moreover, the counterpoint to the isolation of Petrarchan desire she finds in a fantasy of marriage is similarly flawed, for Mary's marital union with her beloved is enacted through the violence and ignominy of rape. The speaker's self thus finds itself perpetually dislocated: as she is clinging to the constancy of erotic passion, her identities as Petrarchan lover, as wife, and as sovereign all break down, leaving her in a position of erotic, poetic, and political vulnerability and helplessness.

In contrast, the poem ascribed to Elizabeth strives to contain its currents of energy within the formal and imaginative structures of Petrarchism. The queen's fervent erotic desire is unmistakable ("I love...I freeze and yet am burned...No means I find to rid him from my breast")—in fact, Elizabeth's love is no less constant or ardent than Mary's, for she openly admits that her desire can only terminate with her death ("by the end of things it be suppressed") and even indulges in sexual innuendo (her love "stands, and lies by [her]"). Besides, "the allusion to the marriage vow"[45] in the third line ("I do") and the reference in line 6 to another self ("Since from myself another self I turned"), which in early modern England was occasionally used to denote a spouse,[46] both suggest that this desire has a conjugal dimension. However, the passion that takes a violent form in the casket sonnets in Elizabeth's poem is channeled into a balanced (if precariously wired) rhetorical performance. By neither disavowing nor parading her desire (she is "forced to seem to hate"), the English queen creates a textual space where passion and restraint vie with each other but neither gains the upper hand, maintaining an uneasy equilibrium of contrarieties.

The last stanza outlines a choice between a "gentler passion" that would result in "some more sweet content" for the lover, and the devastating force of violent desire that could potentially "sink" the lover, forcing her to "die, and so forget what love e'er meant" (possibly with bawdy connotations of "die" as orgasm). The latter is the same eroticism that destroys the lover of the casket sonnets, but while Elizabeth's poem acknowledges love's unlimited power over the speaker, her text institutes a series of defenses that preserve her identity. Where the exiled Scots queen rejoices in the shattering pain of erotic experience, her English cousin does everything in her power to minimize the intensity of sexual violence. Through a careful coordination of antithesis and parallel, Elizabeth constructs a rhetorical armature that, despite its potential fragility, carries the lover through largely unimpaired. Ending on an open note of indecision, this is a poem of intense ambiguity that prevents any major disruption to the lover's identity. The temporal organization of her love is equally enigmatic: the marital vow "I do" presupposes a future to her love, but the past verbal forms scattered across the poem ("I ever meant... I turned...I have done") indicate that this passion is something to be forgotten. Mixing futurity and pastness, fervor and restraint, Elizabeth orchestrates a kind of rhetorical split that ensures that her subjectivity, albeit tested by the passion, is not destroyed. Although for some critics this is a sign of the speaker's weakness as a sovereign, when read against the casket sonnets, "On Monsieur's Departure" comes across as a text that, even as it acknowledges multiple pressures building around the speaker, preserves her royal subjectivity.[47] At once a revelation of conjugal desire, a commitment to maintain her identity despite the vicissitudes of passion, and an effective Petrarchan performance, Elizabeth's poem retraces the dangerous path of the casket sonnets yet clearly avoids their main missteps. Elizabeth and Mary, both courtly poets, demonstrate two diametrically opposed approaches to inscribing marital passion in the language of Petrarchism. Undoubtedly, Mary's audacious revision of the Petrarchan model is historically and poetically significant; her sexualization and conjugalization of unrequited love opened new ways for thinking and writing about Petrarchan love in English, especially for women poets. But it is also clear that in the context of Elizabethan politics and society, Mary's poetics of royal divestment, which associated her "with disorder and danger,"[48] was unsustainable as a form of monarchical writing.

There is another important aspect to the contrast between Mary and Elizabeth. Beyond considerations of actual affection, marriage, and progeny, in pre-modern England sovereign marriage also operated as an imaginative construction that joined the ruler and his or her kingdom by way of allegorical marital alliance, or "sovereign love"—a symbolic affective bond between monarch and subjects that guarantees perpetuation of their joint political project.[49] The origins of this rhetorical strategy in Judeo-Christian culture can be found in the Song of Songs. A sensuous erotic poem tracing the flows of desire between two speakers soon to be joined in marriage (traditionally identified as Solomon and a Shulamite), this biblical text was interpreted as an allegory of the union between Israel and God and, in the Christian West, following Origen, as a figurative expression of Christ's marriage to the church or to the individual Christian soul.[50] This interpretive tradition, despite Protestantism's skeptical attitude to allegory, retained its vitality and validity in post-Reformation England as well.[51]

On the secular plain, the biblical imagery of erotic bonding between two lovers on the cusp of a conjugal alliance was also appropriated in the pre-modern period to represent a monarch's relationship to the realm.[52] In the English context, an illuminating theoretical example of such thinking is found in Tigurinus Chelidonius's *Most Excellent Hystorie of the Institution and Firste Beginning of Christian Princes*, a political treatise published in English the same year as *Ane Detectioun* (1571).[53] It included a chapter in which the author castigated incontinence in princes and commended "the dignitie and excellencie of marriage, which is the very remedie that God hath ordained against this vice" (182). Chelidonius exhorted princes to marry "as well as for continuance of their race, as also for the comforte of the imperfection of mannes nature" (183), and also admonished them against adultery, calling on princes to "vnderstande how excellent and precious a thing marriage is, which beeing polluted and violated is pourged by the effusion of mans bloud, and authorised therevnto by Justice" (189). Even more directly, the English version, addressed to "the moste highe and most excellent Princess, Elizabeth," exhorted the young queen to avoid

"that abominable and filthie sinne of incontinencie" through "that holy and honourable state of matrimonie" (Aiij^v).
Yet the main lesson for the early modern ideology of royal marriage of Chelidonius's book is found in the allegorical significance it assigns to marriage: "what is more agreable to Nature than mariage?" he asks. We shall discover, he continues, in "all workes of Nature a certayne printe, Image, and purtraite of marriage...by the ayde, solace, comfort and fauor of this matrimoniall societie, all thinges are maintained, conserued, and continued" (189–90). Marriage here is posited as the privileged form of analogy that, to quote Foucault again, "can extend, for a single given point, to an endless number of relationships.... Through it, all the figures of the whole universe can be drawn together."[54] Similarly, in Chelidonius's view, the marital analogy molds the relationship between distinct elements of the universe, such as heaven and earth, but also, given the political nature and intended audience of the treatise dedicated to Elizabeth, between ruler and his subjects.[55] The language of Chelidonius's *Hystorie* is echoed in *Ane Detectioun*, which bemoans Mary's "violating of matrimonie" because marriage not only "doth truely conteine a great misterie" but "compriseth within it all inferior kindes of duties, sa being broken it ouerthroweth thaim all." Whosoever "nat anely violateth, but also despiseth [marriage], he doth nat ouerthrow all the foundations of humayne fellowschip, but as mickle as in him lyeth, dissolueth and confoundeth all order of nature" (Niiij^r). Like Chelidonius, the authors of *Ane Detectioun* imagine marriage as the key figure underlying all relations, the dissolution of which threatens the very foundations of natural and political order.

Tudor rulers adopted the allegorical language of sovereign marriage as a vibrant rhetorical tool, despite Kantorowicz's offhand remark that prior to James VI, "the marriage metaphor seems to have been all but non-existent."[56] Although critics have—understandably, in the context of the queen's gender—focused on Elizabeth's uses of the conjugal metaphor,[57] English political discourse relied on the marriage trope in order to articulate the relationship of sovereign and nation throughout the sixteenth century. The very foundation of the Tudor rule took place through matrimony because Henry VII's most legitimate claim to the throne was through his marriage to Elizabeth of York. Dedicating his *Union of the Two Noble and Illustre Famelies* (1548) to Edward VI, Edward Hall posits "the vnion of the noble houses of Lancaster and Yorke, conioyned together by the godly mariage of your moste noble grandfather, and your verteous grandmother" as the originary point of the Tudor dynasty: "as kyng henry the fourthe was the beginning and rote of the great discord and deuision; so was the godly matrimony, the final ende of all discencions, titles, and debates."[58]

Although the matrimony in question is a historical event, its significance clearly exceeds the local boundaries of human bodies, even royal, and touches upon the future fate of the nation. During Henry VIII's reign, Richard Morrison in 1539 wrote of "that louely bonde, which god hath ordeyned and sette in nature, to holde together, to preserue and mayntene a thynge in this worlde for mans welth and safetie most needfull, ciuyle ordinaunce, obeysaunce of the members to the hed, of the subiectes to theyr souerayne."[59] Henry's daughter Mary Tudor was quoted as saying, during Thomas Wyatt the Younger's 1554 rebellion against her proposed marriage to Philip of Spain, that this "seconde mariage shoulde greatly aduance this realme (wherevnto she was firste maried) to much honour, quiet, and gaine. For (quod her grace) I am alreadie maried to this common weale, and ye faythful membres of the same, the spousall rynge whereof I haue on my fynger, which neuer hitherto was nor shal hereafter be leaft of."[60] Elizabeth herself in 1559 famously answered, in similar terms, the Common's petition that she marry: "'I am already bound onto a husband, which is the kingdom of England, and that may suffice you.'" After that, she is said to have showed them "the ring with which she was given in marriage and inaugurated to her kingdom in express and solemn terms."[61] Although this report is possibly spurious,[62] it nonetheless underlines the significance of the figure of sovereign marriage for the Tudor political imagination. A poem printed the same year speaks in Elizabeth's voice:

> Here is my hand,
> my dere lover Englande
> I am thine both with mind and hart
> For ever to endure,
> Thou maiest be sure
> Untill death us two depart.[63]

Notwithstanding the instability of gendered and familial roles in these formulations, the figure of a passionate bond between subjects and monarchs is pervasive. At once contrary to and synonymous with the sovereign's literal marriage, the allegorical union legitimizes the rule of the Tudors.

If this rich rhetorical and imaginative environment is brought to bear upon the casket sonnets, their private conjugal desires will engage all the complexities associated with sovereign marriage in Tudor England. The casket sonnets, let us recall, portray Mary as a ruler willing to disrupt matrimonial bonds and replace them with an adulterous "aliance" predicated on sexual aggression and resulting in dissolution of all social, familial, and political connections. Read allegorically, however, Mary's union with her lover exposes the kingdom that she embodies to violation, rape, and dishonor. Of course, the injuries to her lover's body, which he synecdochally sustained in an act of sexual activity with her, may simultaneously allegorize Mary's unfortunate subjects and her kingdom, suffering because of their queen's profanation of the bonds of sovereign love. In either reading, Mary's desires are detrimental to the political fate of her realm and people, for they pervert the affective link between the sovereign and her kingdom. This creates a sharp contrast to Elizabeth's ruminations, in "On Monsieur's Departure," on the choice between the erotic desire for her fleshly lover (her "care") and the other form of passion ("Some gentler passion slide into my mind, / For I am soft ... let me live with some more sweet content"). This other attachment, while still libidinous, forms an opposition to the Petrarchan longing and can be read as the queen's bond with her kingdom. If Mary makes her beloved her sole "care" ("my hart, my bloud, my soule, my care" [Sj^r]), Elizabeth, "constrained by the responsibilities and cares of monarchy,"[64] chooses the "care" of her subjects and kingdom over the experience of physically painful (burning and freezing) union with her Petrarchan lover. Abandoning the project of marriage with the Monsieur, she opts for the conjugal alliance with her subjects.

In fact, allegorical sovereign marriage becomes the criterion for contrast between Mary and Elizabeth in a pamphlet against the 1569 Revolt of the Northern Earls, which sought to replace Elizabeth with Mary Stuart on the English throne. The rebellion itself was involved with questions of matrimony since it was closely linked to, if not provoked by, the plans to marry the exiled Scots queen to the Earl of Northumberland.[65] The allegorical form of sovereign marriage offers the author of the pamphlet, Thomas Norton, yet another tool of contrast between Elizabeth and Mary. Claiming that Elizabeth is "by al right the soueraigne Ladie and Maistresse of us al, and of you too," Norton notes, "Her highnesse is the Husband [sic] of the common weale, maried to this realme, and the same by ceremonie of ring as solemnely signified as any common mariage is...Shall they seuer the knot of loue and agreement betwene her and them, and yeld their bodies to a notorious adulter, and yet saye they breake no bonde of this sacred wedlocke?"[66] What Norton accused Mary of in 1569 became even more evident in 1571, when the casket sonnets presented their speaker, identifiable as Mary, as bent on dissolving the conjugal ties with the realm and replacing them with a depraved "aliance" built on lust, violence, and scandal.

The Art of Love in *The Kingis Quair*

Thus far, this chapter has been delineating the early modern contextual space in which the problematic of sovereign marriage in the casket sonnets takes place. As I have argued, the poems printed under Mary Stuart's name in *Ane Detectioun* present a radical scenario of Petrarchism in which libidinous impulses are indulged to a point where they overrun the speaker's identity as sovereign. Driven by passion, the lover of the casket sonnets destroys her royal selfhood and constructs an imaginative space of perverse marital love embodied in erotic violence and characterized by a disdain for traditional considerations of marriage. This form of selfhood unfolds in a striking contrast with the images of Queen Elizabeth's marriage, both as a dynastic alliance and an allegorical union with the realm. However, it is not only the gleanings from the early modern period that illuminate how far the casket sonnets stray from the idealized model of sovereign marriage. Poetic history offers an equally illuminating counterpoint to Mary's articulation of passionate subjectivity. An expression of royal eros, Mary's Petrarchan poems have a medieval antecedent in Anglo-Scots literature—*The Kingis Quair* (the king's book), a Chaucerian prison poem written sometime in the 1420s or 1430s and usually attributed to James I Stewart.[67] It is a relatively short (1,379 lines) courtly dream vision in rhyme royal, aptly characterized by A. C. Spearing as an "erotic pseudo-biography"—incidentally, a label that usefully lends itself to the casket sonnets as well.[68] Written as a recollection of the speaker's past misfortunes, the first-person poem opens with the speaker reading the *Consolation of Philosophy* and deciding to write down his own history in a book. He recounts a passage over turbulent sea, capture and imprisonment, then recalls seeing, through his cell window, a beautiful lady in the garden and falling in love with her. The speaker then falls asleep and in his dream appears before two goddesses, Venus and Minerva, who promise him earthly happiness if he agrees to abide by the laws of moral love. He then, still in his dream, encounters Fortuna, who lifts him high upon her wheel, but the speaker is abruptly awakened to reality as his dream vision ends. As the goddesses promised, the lover soon finds bliss with the lady from the garden and is granted release from captivity. A formulaic envoy sends the book into the world and recommends it to his poetic precursors, Chaucer and John Gower.

Although scholars debate the authorship of the text, the Selden manuscript (preserving the unique copy of the poem) paratextually assigns it to James I: it contains a colophon that reads, "Explicit etc. etc. Quod Iacobus primus scotorum rex Illustrissimus," a claim reiterated by a sixteenth century rubric in the manuscript, "heirefter followis the quair Maid be King Iames of Scotland the first callit the Kingis Quair and Maid quen his Ma*iestie* wes in Ingland."[69] Annals of Scots history contain references to James I as poet-king: Walter Bower in his *Scotichronicon* (1440–47) describes the king as "another Orpheus" and claims that "he applied himself with eagerness sometimes to the art of literary composition and writing," whereas John Mair's 1521 *History of Greater Britain as well England as Scotland* mentions James's "ingenious little book about the Queen [written] while he was yet in captivity and before his marriage."[70] Of course the historical and philological value of these attributions is dubious, yet their potential to guide interpretive choices must not be overlooked. According to Olga Fradenburg, "whether or not [James] wrote the *Quair*—or any other poem, for that matter—some important fifteenth-century writers and readers wished to believe that he did; and that wish is itself of historical significance."[71] Equally important, the fictional adventures that befall the protagonist of the poem—the speaker's youth, his sea voyage away from his native land abruptly interrupted by his enemies, his imprisonment and then liberation—echo emphatically the events of James's own life. As heir to the unstable Scottish throne, in 1406 young James was secretly dispatched to France, but he was captured by pirates en route and handed over to the English, whose prisoner the Scottish prince (but de facto Scottish king following the death of his father, Robert III) remained until his release in 1424.[72] As Joanna Martin notes, "it is evident that its author intended the reader to recognize the prince's trials in the events described."[73] In any case, recent criticism of *The Kingis Quair* has primarily considered the poem in light of pre-modern Anglo-Scotts kingship.[74]

Despite obvious differences in form, genre, and historical provenance, *The Kingis Quair* and the casket sonnets display intriguing connections, such as hybrid national identity[75] and their presumed authors' carceral experience.[76] What interests me here is that both works investigate the significance of sovereign marriage to their projects of erotic and political subjectivity, contributing their voices to the complex process of constructing kingship in the pre-modern Anglo-Scots political imagination. As a prison poem, *The Kingis Quair* pays particular attention to the nuances and connotations of different forms of incarceration, and the poem's diegetic progress is from captivity to freedom. The speaker recalls being put "in strayte ward and in strong prisoun" (169), and he describes himself as "a sely [i.e., pitiable] prisoner" who is "within thir cald[e] wallis thus ilokin" (306, 478). Likewise, he portrays falling in love with the lady in the garden as captivity: "sudaynly my hert became hir thrall / For euer, of free wyll" (285–86). At the end of the poem, however, the parallelism of the lover's actual imprisonment and courtly captivity is disrupted: the protagonist obtains physical liberty, "Eke quho may in this lyfe haue more plesance / Than cum to largesse from thraldom and peyne?" (1275–76), yet this liberation is inextricably tied with another form of submission: "In lufis [i.e. love's] yok that esy is and sure, / In guerdoun of all my lufis space [i.e., as reward for the extent of all my love], / Sche hath me tak, hir humble creature" (1346–48).

While this image may appear incongruous with the poem's resolution, the reader's potential anxiety is alleviated if we assume the poem "to have had a public purpose in marking [James's] marriage to the English princess Joan Beaufort, cousin of Henry VI, which was a crucial factor in the political negotiations leading to James's release from captivity."[77] James's continued erotic submission encodes the promise of a conjugal union. However, this "lufis yoke" of marriage fulfills a very specific function in the emotional universe of *The Kingis Quair*. It harnesses the erotic energy of the lover's initial response to the lady (as the prolonged blazon [316–36] suggests) into a royal identity that balances passion and restraint. The speaker explicitly links his earlier misadventures with a lack of self-rule that characterizes his youth:

> Thou [sely] youth, of nature indegest,
> Vnrypit fruyte with windis variable
> . . . .
> Thus stant thy confort in vnsekernesse,
> And wantis it that suld thee reule and gye.   (92–93, 99–100)

As a young man, he lacked reason to govern himself:

I mene this by myself, as in partye.
Though nature gave me suffisance in youth,
The rypenesse of resoun lak[it] I
To gouerne with my will.   (106–09)

Love for the lady in the garden, though initially conceived in erotic terms, offers him a chance to correct his ways and to procure instruments of self-rule. When he appears before Venus and asks for a remedy against his unrequited love and political setbacks, she advises him to be patient and restrained: "therfore humily / Abyde and serue and lat Gude Hope the gye" (739–40). James receives further instruction from Minerva, the goddess of Reason, who agrees to give him her "lore and disciplyne" (896):

As, gif thy lufe be sett all-uterly
Of nyce lust, thy trauail is in veyne.
And so the end sall turne of thye folye

To payne and repentance—lo, wate thou quhy?
Gif thee ne list on lufe thy vertew set,
Vertu sal be the cause of thy forfet.

Tak him [i.e., God] before in all thy gouernance,
That in his hand the stere has of you all,
And pray vnto his hye purueyance
Thy lufe to gye.   (898–907)

Passion has to be modified by reason and Christian ethics; such is Minerva's counsel to James. By abiding by the laws of virtuous love and by practicing rigorous emotional self-discipline, James will attain political and moral liberty. He is released "by the mene [i.e., means] of Luffis ordinance" (1277), which "shows an authority limited by laws rather than ruling by willfulness."[78] When he accepts the restraints of the law, James's earlier sensuous desires become, to use Fradenburg's useful formulation, a form of "legalized passion."[79] In this respect, *The Kingis Quair* offers a stark contrast to the pathways of sovereign love pursued by the casket sonnets. Rather than attempt to balance desire and restraint, Mary makes pleasure the kingpin of her subjectivity. Where James seeks to unite reason and passion and thus advocates love as an "enriching quality for public office,"[80] Mary rejects reason for the sake of unbridled desire, ignoring the threat it poses to her royal power.

Yet the key difference between James and Mary is their respective visions of sovereign marriage. Crucially, within the space and time of the poem, James's marriage is never consummated. The text concludes with a promise of conjugality, yet the speaker's erotic desire—much like in Elizabeth's "On Monsieur's Departure"—remains unfulfilled. By contrast, the speaker of the casket sonnets rejects reasoned passion and the legality of marriage for the sake of her desire and celebrates a union consummated through rape, for which she forfeits her claim to the crown. Both royal speakers yearn for a marriage, but while James's "lufis yok" places the erotic union with his beloved in an uncertain future temporality, thus insisting on chastity, Mary's "aliance" with Bothwell functions as an afterthought to an adulterous and violent sexual relationship in which both lovers are disfigured by passion.

The difference is not accidental. One of the main precepts of royal self-articulation in the language of married love is that conjugal sovereign desire must remain inaccessible. In her reading of the Song of Songs Julia Kristeva writes, "Supreme authority, be it royal or divine, can be loved as flesh while remaining essentially inaccessible; the intensity of love comes precisely from that combination of received jouissance and taboo, from a basic separation that nevertheless unites...at no point is sexual intercourse carried out."[81] Indeed, for all the titillating eroticism of the Song of

Songs—the lovers' explicit corporeal fantasies and intense physical longing—the mis-en-scène of the biblical text is that of "sexual arousal at the not quite immediate prospect of fulfillment."[82] That both *The Kingis Quair* and "On Monsieur's Departure" uphold this taboo on consummation only highlights its violation in the casket sonnets. Significantly, the last two of the casket poems can be seen as an attempt to return the speaker's desire to an unrequited state of anticipation: "All the night quhair I lye and languishe here, / My hart being ouerset wyth extreme feare / Seing absent the butte of my desire," Mary exclaims in the penultimate poem, and the following envoy opens, "Not seing you as you had promisit / I put my hand to the paper to write" (Si^r). These complaints may echo some verses from the Song of Songs that express a similar sentiment: "In my bed by night I soght him that my soule loued: I soght him, but founde him not" (3.1); "I opened to my welbeloued: but my welbeloued was gone, & past: my heart was gone when he did speake: I soght him, but I coulde not finde him: I called him, but he answered me not" (5.6). But while these sonnets make an effort to reinstate sovereign love as a passionate but unconsummated bond between the speaker and her beloved, the damage inflicted by prior revelations of rape and adultery cannot be undone. If anything, the speaker's insistence on separation in the last sonnets may be construed as a form of allegorical lament over her loss of political power and her kingdom.

The same contrast plays out in the allegorical dimension of the poems. *The Kingis Quair*'s anticipation of a sovereign marriage simultaneously signifies Scotland's impending union with James after his release and return to the royal throne in Edinburgh. As a reward for erotic and moral self-government, James obtains freedom and his object of desire while at the same time, through allegorical marriage, he reclaims his kingdom. C. S. Lewis's summary of the poem's significance—that in *The Kingis Quair* "the poetry of marriage at last emerges from the traditional poetry of adultery; and the literal narrative of a contemporary wooing emerges from romance and allegory"—thus tells only half the story.[83] Even as the historical singularity of James's passion defictionalizes the conventional figures of amatory discourse, it allegorizes the royal marriage as a sublime articulation of the structures of monarchical rule.

Out of this anticipated marriage, James emerges as a future king of Scotland. From this perspective, the "lufis yok" of *The Kingis Quair* perhaps should be read not allegorically but figuratively, to adopt Eric Auerbach's terminology, as one of the two events linked together by a relationship of anticipation and fulfillment. As Auerbach writes, in a figurative relationship between events, "the first signifies the second, the second fulfills the first. Both remain historical events; yet both, looked at in this way, have something provisional and incomplete about them; they point to one another and both point to something in the future, something still to come."[84] Key in Auerbach's view is the emphasis on incompletion, on a time yet to come. Between marriage and enthronement, James's poem speaks of a future, and a similar kind of future is promised by "I do" in Elizabeth's poem. By contrast, in the casket sonnets any possibility of a future is foreclosed when the allegorical bonds tying Mary to her subjects are dissolved through uninhibited *aphrodisia*, which leaves the kingdom in a state of ravishment by sovereign desire. Mary's version of sovereign love is completed in the act of consummation. As a result, not only bodies, both figurative and real, are maimed but Scotland also slips from the sovereign's grasp as her royal identity crumbles.

Still, the presence in both *The Kingis Quair* and Mary's casket sonnets of a crucial connection between royal sexuality and royal power—envisioned in terms of literal and allegorical conjugal union—indicates the importance of sovereign love to the pre-modern Anglo-Scots poetic and political imagination. The points of reference between the medieval and the early modern texts suggest the existence of a recognizable and reinscribable form of textual subjectivity that operates in the English vernacular and dictates its terms to those who write sovereign desire. Granted, within this discursive tradition the casket sonnets form a distinct antithesis to James's poem (as well as to Elizabeth's post-courtship lyric). But by tapping the imaginative resources of this tradition, the early modern poems weave together fragments of Petrarchan discourse and medieval courtly poetry, producing a hybrid form of royal selfhood. When the casket sonnets, in their quest for a conjugal union, however execrable and disgraceful, overturn the Petrarchan poetics of unrequited desire, they reactivate the discursive potential of the medieval fantasies of sovereign marriage, such as *The Kingis Quair*. The poetic subject of the casket sonnets, in other words, carries within it elements of both Petrarchism and the medieval poetic imagination, merging the two strands of discourse together in a performance of selfhood simultaneously unique and deeply imbricated in the traditions of pre-modern Anglo-Scots poetry.

FOUR

Petrarchan Afterlives of Erotic Legality

Love and Law in Lydgate, Daniel, and Drayton

After looking at the vernacular memories haunting the languages of economy, melancholy, and sovereign marriage in Elizabethan Petrarchism, this chapter will turn to the representations of legal selfhood in Samuel Daniel's *Delia* (1592–1623) and Michael Drayton's *Idea* (1594–1619). I will read them as palimpsests preserving traces of legal subjectivities articulated in a number of medieval English poetic texts. In the past decades, there has been a steady scholarly interest in the relationships between early modern literature and the law, and the presence of legal figures in English love poetry has received its share of critical attention. For the most part, however, scholars have approached the uses of legal figuration in English sonnet sequences as fully determined by the historical law of the period—as a reflection of various Elizabethan concerns with the legal status of property, treason, royal prerogative, or land holding.[1] There are compelling reasons to go down that critical path. For one, Petrarch's *Canzoniere* rarely exploits the potentialities of legal figuration. The notable exception is poem 360 ("Quel antiquo mio dolce empio signore"),[2] an allegorical commentary on theorizing desire in legal terms. This poem was translated into English by Thomas Wyatt as "Myne olde dere enmy" in the 1530s, and at the end of the century by I. C. as "Loues Accusation at the Iudgement-seate of Reason."[3] Beyond that, there are only scattered references to Laura's unkindness as transgression that the lover nonetheless pardons, albeit not as readily as her other offenses ("et perdono / più lieve ogni altra offesa" [37.89–90]); to the stealing of his heart in the process of loving ("furando 'l cor" [135.25]; "mio cor dolce rapina" [167.5]); and at one point to Laura's coldness as the prolonged murder of the lover ("mille volte il dì m'ancida" [172.12]). There is, however, nothing that would approach the comprehensive investment in legal diction that characterizes a great many Elizabethan sonnet sequences, such as *Delia*, *Idea*, or *Zepheria* (1594). From this angle, the pervasive appearance of legal language in early modern Petrarchan discourse is an idiosyncratic development in Elizabethan poetry, a situation that invites and indeed encourages contextualizing the sonnets in the minute particulars of Elizabethan legal culture.

Without questioning the validity of that approach, this chapter seeks to suggest a parallel method of reading the figures of law in Elizabethan sonnets. What follows takes as its broad interest the history of legal figuration in pre-modern English love poetry, and its specific focus, as elsewhere in the book, is on the dynamic of continuity and change within the English poetic imagination from the late medieval to the Petrarchan age. I read the legal figures deployed in the sonnets of Daniel and Drayton through the prism of diachronic history as belated and often distorted but still recognizable permutations of the medieval tradition of the poetic laws of love. The latter form of discourse configures a universe in which passion falls within the purview of the law and can be posited as a legal matter. It is manifested in English poetry in a number of texts, but in this chapter I consider some of its most representative examples—John Lydgate's *Temple of Glas* and *Complaynte of a Louers Lyfe* as well as the anonymous *Assembly of Ladies*. Medieval juridico-erotic poetry leaves an imprint on English vernacular discourse in the shape of a distinct form of legal subjectivity—subjectivity bound to an erotic jurisdiction where desire is at once the object and the limit of the law.

Through reading *Delia* and *Idea* alongside these medieval English texts I seek to elucidate not only the native genealogy of the legal figures in the sonnets but also the crucial transformations that take place in English juridico-erotic poetry in the course of the fifteenth and sixteenth centuries. My central claim in this chapter is that the transition from medieval to Petrarchan is characterized by a palpable shrinking of the jurisdictional space of effectively independent erotic legality under pressure from positive (mainly common) law. This change affects the imaginative patterning of juridico-erotic poetic discourse, but it also triggers a form of discursive resistance to this colonization. I further argue that in some instances the trends in legal figuration that became dominant in the late sixteenth century were already at work in medieval English poetry. Oscillating between early modern (Daniel, Drayton) and medieval (Lydgate, *The Assembly of Ladies*) poetic texts, this chapter continues to build imaginative connections between English Petrarchism and its vernacular antecedents. As a result, the medieval discursive substrate once again emerges as indispensible not only to the understanding of individual poetic texts but also for grasping the broader currents of literary history.

Legal Nostalgia in Samuel Daniel's *Delia*

When Thomas Newman brought out the first pirated edition of Sir Philip Sidney's *Astrophil and Stella* in 1591, he included, in addition to an incomplete version of Sidney's sequence, a handful of poems by other writers, including Samuel Daniel, Fulke Greville, and Thomas Campion.[4] Among them was a curious sonnet that has since been attributed to Daniel:

> Way but the cause, and giue me leaue to plaine me,
> For all my hurt, that my harts Queene hath wrought it,
> Shee whom I loue so deare, the more to paine me,
> Withholds my right, where I haue dearely bought it.
> Dearly I bought that was so highly rated,
> Euen with the price of bloud and bodies wasting,
> Shee would not yeeld that ought might be abated,
> For all shee saw my Loue was pure and lasting,
> And yet now scornes performance of the passion,
> And with her presence Iustice ouerruleth,
> Shee tels me flat her beauty beares no action,
> And so my plea and proces she excludeth:
> What wrong shee doth, the world may well perceiue it,
> To accept of faith at first, and then to leaue it.[5]

The sonnet's central conceit exploits the idea of law as a libidinous attachment, where a legal right can be construed as a form of jouissance and where passion and legality are posited as structural and imaginative equivalents.[6] It represents unrequited love as an occasion for taking action against the lady, with the hope that the lover's grievance can be redressed in a court of law. The speaker opens the proceedings by asking his audience to consider the matter at hand ("Way but the cause, and giue me leaue to plaine me"), then follows with a list of his injuries: the lady, he argues, "withholds [his] right" to what he bought "dearly," even "with the price of bloud and bodies wasting"; and she "would not yeeld that ought might be abated," despite the speaker's "pure and lasting" love.

The argument is studiously prepared and well delivered, but when the sonnet reaches its tentative *volta* at the end of the second quatrain, together with the lover we become painfully aware that the law's promise of remedy is hollow. The lover's meticulously assembled legal suit flounders because the lady not only "scornes" this legal "performance of the passion," but her sheer "presence" "Iustice ouer ruleth," justice being the main object of the law. As Thomas Wilson puts it, "when men desire the law, for triall of a matter, they meane nothing els but to haue Iustice."[7] Her beauty, the lover discovers, "beares no action" and "[his] plea and proces she excludeth." The lady overrides the law, and a legal suit cannot be brought in this matter. The poem thus configures a gendered contrast between the lover and his mistress. The former displays a remarkable faith in the institution of the law and its power to adjudicate matters of love; the Petrarchan lady, on the other side, explicitly positions their erotic relationship outside the law as she highlights the inapplicability of legal categories to intimacy. To use the sonnet's own language, she maintains the nonactionability of love. As is elegantly demonstrated by the form of the sonnet, in which the masculine vigor of legal diction is artfully undermined by the exclusively feminine rhymes, the lady's beauty, the lover's desire, her rejection, his suffering, all the delights and vulnerabilities of erotic passion form an antithesis to the idea of law.[8]

But the legal crisis in Daniel's sonnet simultaneously encodes a poetic crisis. The poem's legal language is shot through with overtones of the technical vocabulary of classical rhetoric, such as *causa* (a subject of litigation, a case before the court, a formal accusation, but also a hypothetical rhetorical exercise) and *actio* (performance or delivery of a speech).[9] The sonnet, in other words, is an instrument of pleading. But by implicating the "performance" of the lover's passion in the failure of his "cause," Daniel diagnoses the poem's own rhetorical insecurities. That the sonnet "beares no action" can be construed in two senses: it may signify the impossibility of launching a suit against the lady (legal crisis) and at the same time speak to the deficiency of the lover's rhetorical means and his inability to deliver his argument in verse (poetic crisis). The collapse of the lover's suit simultaneously registers a degree of dissonance between Daniel's legal argument and the poem's textual devices. From this perspective, the sonnet's opening invitation to "way...the cause," from an appeal to a legally minded audience to evaluate the juridical merits of the lover's case, turns into a challenge to the reader to consider the potential sustainability of the poem's central conceit—a metaphor of love as litigation. The subject of the sonnet, then, is juridico-erotic poetry itself, so unpacking the poem's legal frictions will go some way to suggest an outline of the pre-modern history of English love poetry invested in the idea of the law.

How can one read the nonactionability of love in Daniel's sonnet? What is certain is that there does not appear to be anything wrong with the lover's legal case. Daniel's technical language is precise and correct and his argumentation corresponds to the practices of the English law. What the lady has committed against the lover is presented as some kind of civil "wrong," so that the lover, in the words of an early modern legal dictionary, "hath cause, or may bring an action for some dutie due to him, as an action of debt upon an obligation,...trespasse of goods taken away, beating, or such like, for whose recovery he is driven to his action."[10] Indeed, the early modern English action of debt would be the most plausible reading of the lover's "cause." Claiming that the lady "withholds [his] right" to what he has "dearly bought," Daniel's lover invokes the formulaic common-law writ of debt ordering the defendant "to render or yield up a sum of money, or a quantity of fungibles, which he owed to and unjustly withheld from the plaintiff" ("Praecipe A. quod juste et sine dilatione reddat B. centum solidos quos ei debet et injuste detinet ut dicit").[11] In early modern English law, a sale gone bad (the lover twice stresses that he "dearly bought" what he demands from the mistress) most commonly generated an action of debt.[12] The same action was also available in cases of interpersonal violence ("beating, or such like"), which Daniel may imply when claiming that the lady has "hurt" him up to the point of his "bloud and bodies wasting." It is worth mentioning that the writ of debt could also be used to bring action for beach of a promise to marry,[13] so its appearance in a sonnet describing erotic rejection is not surprising.

Such massive investment in the law renders its collapse (starting with the third quatrain) all the more spectacular. But if the lover is failed not by an incompetent judge or erroneous writ, this legal and poetic crisis must arise out of deeper uncertainties about the boundaries of authority between law and love. The most obvious answer is to assume that the nonactionability of love in the poem is a sign of impending modernity. The present age is quick to believe that the irrational, nongovernable, private sphere of love is incompatible with, and not containable by, the discipline and dispassion of the public law; intimacy always goes beyond any attempt to codify it in a rigid institutional language. We moderns tend to imagine love as "the very negation of the ideas of law and legality," where "love is all that law cannot and may not be."[14] Petrarch himself at one point in the *Canzoniere* shares this sentiment when he exclaims incredulously, "Who can put a rein on lovers or give them laws?" ("Chi pon freno a li amanti o dà lor legge?") (222.9). Yet Daniel's sonnet is fascinating precisely because it displays none of this antagonistic love-as-the-other-of-law mentality: on the contrary, for all the lover's skepticism, even despair, we are struck by his undiminished faith in the power of the law to redress erotic grievance. So tightly are the discourses of law and of love entwined that for the speaker erotic subjectivity becomes inseparable from legal subjectivity; in the couplet, he continues to speak legal language even though the law has failed to provide remedy.

What the lover discovers, then, is the limit not of law, or a law, but of the law that he seeks redress from in this particular instance—namely, the common law. It is not that there is no legal action, process, or pleading possible in the domain of passion in principle; on the contrary, the speaker's faith in the power of law to arbitrate matters of erotic intimacy is evident everywhere in the sonnet. Rather, Daniel's legal desires are thwarted by a jurisdictional miscalculation, by recourse to a law whose repertoire of available remedies is unable to accommodate an erotic grievance. It is a characteristic of the English common law that the number of procedures available to one who has been wronged is severely limited, and one's legal rights are often contingent on the existence of remedies.[15] Crafting an impeccably competent writ of debt, the speaker attempts to back it up with the facts of his love being "pure and lasting," which results in his suit being dismissed due to a jurisdictional mismatch. In this light, it is hardly surprising that the lover's amorous "hurt" is not recognizable in the eyes of this form of law. Perfectly intelligible to those conversant in the language of love poetry, this cause is deprived of meaning once it is expressed in the categories of the common law.

Daniel's sonnet, in other words, hesitates on a threshold of two legal modalities. In one, love constitutes a proper matter for the law; in the other, love is subjected to the operations of the institutionalized positive law. However, the former jurisdiction remains an unfulfilled legal fantasy for the lover (he desires but does not access its resources), whereas the latter, despite its ostensible juridical feasibility, effectively denies the lover his amorous right. Put otherwise, the sonnet's confusion stems from its being suspended between two different forms of legal subjectivity, for the lover at once imagines himself as a subject of the common law and a subject of erotic law. Although the latter appears to fall within the jurisdiction of the common law, it ultimately proves incompatible with it. I propose that we read the layering of juridical attitudes in the sonnet—its longing for an erotic legality, its unfruitful turn to the common law, perhaps even its brooding apprehension of a divergence of love from law—temporally, as a "field of force in which the dynamics of sign systems of several distinct modes of production can be registered and apprehended."[16] What I suggest is that the sonnet articulates as its central contradiction the conflict between historically distinct models of eroticism's relationship with the law. The lover's dream of a law that governs passion then becomes a form of legal nostalgia, contrasted with the law's inescapable present that denies love a position within the juridical order.

Such a vision of legal temporality is presented even more explicitly in sonnet 26 from *Delia* proper (1594):

> Whilst by her eyes pursu'd, my poore hart flew it,
> Into the sacred bosome of my deerest:
> She there in that sweete sanctuarie flew it,
> Where it presum'd his safetie to be neerest.
>   My priuiledge of faith could not protect it,
> That was with blood and three yeres witnes signed:
> In all which time she neuer could suspect it,
> For well she sawe my loue, and how I pined.
>   And yet no comfort would her brow reueale me.

No lightning looke, which falling hopes erecteth:
What bootes to lawes of succour to appeale mee?
Ladies and Tyrants, neuer lawes respecteth.
  Then there I dye, where hop'd I to have liuen;
  And by that hand, which better might haue giuen.

The sonnet's ostensive goal is to affirm the contrariety of love and law. Daniel compares his heart to a sparrow that flies into Delia's "sacred bosome," hoping to find safety there. But, against the law of sanctuary, the mistress slays his heart, which leads the lover to a despondent conclusion, "What bootes to lawes of succour to appeale mee? / Ladies and Tyrants, neuer lawes respecteth." This would suggest that cases involving erotic desire, reciprocity, and rejection defy legal authority; they belong to a sphere where positive laws do not obtain. This would be a surface reading, however, for as in "Way but the cause," this sonnet's legal organization is somewhat more complicated than a simple dichotomy of love and law. The poem is constructed on an underlying premise that love does fall within the purview of the law. The lover's heart presumes its "safetie" in the sanctuary of the beloved's breast, which he posits as a legal right, a "priuiledge of faith" certified by his "blood and three yeeres witness." The shock of the sonnet comes the moment the lover's realizes that his lady will not recognize this right and, more generally, the laws of love, shattering the inviolability of the asylum.

But crucially for my argument, the lover's undoing comes as a result of a historical fallacy. The law that he presumes will guarantee his legal right to intimacy is modeled on the law of sanctuary—an ancient legal practice that permitted a person to take refuge in a church (Delia's "sacred bosome") or some other designated place of asylum. The Middle Ages, deriving their legal ideas about sanctuary from multiple sources (canon law, Roman law, common law), balanced temporal and ecclesiastical jurisprudence to articulate a workable if conflicted attitude to sanctuary. Sanctuary was commonly sought by a person who committed a crime, although often what Daniel calls the "lawes of succour" were invoked by those pursued by their enemies.[17] In Elizabethan England, however, the law of sanctuary was if not exactly an anachronism then at least a fading legal reality. The attack on the ecclesiastical privilege of sanctuary had begun under Henry VII and continued under his son Henry VIII, who radically narrowed the scope of the sanctuary privilege. He increased the number of exceptions to the law (the categories of subjects who could not seek asylum and the kinds of crime that, if committed, forfeited one's right to asylum); delegitimized many of the sanctuaries; and put a limit on how many fugitives each legal place of sanctuary could hold.[18] Although the law of sanctuary was not formally abolished until 1623, at the time of Daniel's *Delia* ecclesiastical asylum in England had been stripped of much of the authority it had enjoyed in the medieval period.[19]

As a consequence, by figuring the juridical space in which love has a legal standing through the language of ecclesiastical law of sanctuary, Daniel engages in a form of legal medievalism. The poet nostalgically presents erotic legality as a withering tradition that yields under the pressure of impeding modernity. The latter entails a decay of the laws of love and a rise of erotic lawlessness, which Daniel associates with femininity and tyrannical rule. We have witnessed a similar move in "Way but the cause," where the lover laments the "hurt, that [his] harts Queene hath wrought" him, opening a possibility for the failure of the law to be read as a consequence of the lady's absolutist ambition. Elsewhere in *Delia* he protests that his "aspyring will, / Was not to dispossesse her of her right: / Her soueraignty should haue remained still" (31.9–11).

In an influential reading of Elizabethan love poetry in the context of the Inns of Court, Andrew Zurcher links such instances of the rhetoric of sovereignty in other Elizabethan sequences prior to Shakespeare to the "legal-constitutional issues" of Elizabeth's reign, specifically, questions about the limits of prerogative power.[20] That argument is attractive, although Zurcher may overstate his case regarding the pervasive influence of absolutist ideology on the sonnets of Sidney, Daniel, and others and their attendant lack of interest in the common law.[21] As we have seen with Daniel, even in an early sonnet he is quite capable of articulating his legal subjectivity in the language of the common law, and as I shall demonstrate, late medieval poetry also displays systematic borrowings from the same pool of imaginative resources, including land law and tort.

Moreover, while Daniel's sonnet may indeed imply that royal prerogative has something to do with erotic intimacy being denied legal standing, the poem is just as concerned with legal history—namely with the vanishing of love from the jurisdictional grid. Seized by a historical longing, Daniel's lover inscribes an idealized vision of erotic legality as a thing of the past, as a fragment of a recognizable but no longer attainable configuration of legal forces. He stages the dissolution of the sacred space of sanctuary and its reclassification as part of a different order of law; in legal terms, the move bemoans the loss of jurisdictional independence on the part of desire and its incorporation in the juridical order of the common law. In this sense, one cannot fault Daniel's poetic strategies for being inappropriate: the historical elimination of sanctuary in England was in part due to the struggle for jurisdictional authority between the church and the king, between the canon law and the common law, even though, as recent revisionist studies have suggested, the victory the common law of the royal courts enjoyed in this process had much to do with the sympathetic attitudes of those on the side of the canon law.[22] In Daniel's nostalgic vision, in other words, the present is radically different than the past: erotic law as an independent legal domain is associated with the Middle Ages; by contrast, early modernity seeks to absorb matters of erotic intimacy under the rubric of positive law.

This view of jurisdictional evolution is paradigmatic of broader historical processes occurring in pre-modern English love poetry invested in the idea of the law. As we move from the medieval to the Elizabethan period, we witness an incremental displacement of an effectively separate erotic jurisdiction into other jurisdictions, predominantly the common law, until we reach the ultimate divergence of eroticism and legality synonymous with modernity. Accordingly, if we wish to grasp the juridical desires of Elizabethan sonneteers in their historical and poetic specificity, the medieval tradition of the laws of love offers vital insights into the shifting mechanisms of inscribing selfhood at an intersection of desire and law in pre-modern English poetry.

Desire, Judgment, and Jurisdiction in the Courts of Love

While the laws of love to which Daniel's lover implicitly appeals may strike one as a metaphorical construction, such laws are in fact an episode of legal history. As some records indicate, in twelfth century France, at the court of the Countess of Champagne and then at the court of Queen Eleanor, there existed the so-called *cours amoreuses*—assemblies composed of ladies who reviewed and adjudicated cases involving the relationships of love between the sexes, such as what punishment should be meted out to a courtly lover for failure to reciprocate, how to arbitrate a breech of erotic trust, how to remedy a misplaced affection, or which lover will be the right choice for a given lady. Their principal archaeologist and champion Peter Goodrich characterizes these courts as a "minor jurisdiction," a semiautonomous system of legal thought in which the rights and wrongs of desire are debated and arbitrated on their own terms: here, passion can be judicially regulated, desire can achieve justice, and erotic transgression is punishable by erotic law. In this jurisdiction, love has its own legal identity distinct from other positive law; it is a law "neither of the established monarchical state nor of the church but of a feminine public sphere and concerned exclusively with disputes relating to the art of love and relationships between lovers."[23]

In addition to being a legal phenomenon, however, the courts of love belong to literary history. Over the course of the Middle Ages, they generated a body of courtly literature dedicated to amorous jurisprudence. Perhaps the most famous example of a literary text setting out to record the proceedings of the courts of love is Andreas Capellanus's *De amore* (1176), which incorporates reports on a number of representative cases tried before the erotic tribunals and the legal precepts ("the rules of love") that determined the judgments.[24] *De amore*, however, is not the only such text in medieval literature. References to erotic jurisprudence appear in the Occitan *Cort d'amor* (c. 1200), Guillaume de Machaut's *Remède de fortune* (c. 1340) and *Le jugement du roy de Behainge* (c. 1345), Christine de Pisan's *Le livre de trois jugements* (c. 1400), and Martial d'Auvergne's *Les arrêts d'amour* (c. 1460).[25] Petrarch's canzone "Quel antiquo mio dolce empio signore" belongs to the same tradition, so C. S. Lewis is justified in his characterization: as he writes of the Italian canzone and Wyatt's translation, "if the original had been lost and Wyatt were not known to be the author, no one would dream of classifying the poem as anything but medieval."[26] In fact, much of what we know about the laws of love is derived from literary sources, beginning with Capellanus. This explains the somewhat skeptical appraisals of these juridical assemblies' claims to historical validity. Howard Bloch, for example, shrugs this whole tradition off as "a tedious no-man's land between pseudo-document and literary text."[27] Similarly, Richard F. Green dismisses the aristocratic courts of love as "pure allegory," arguing that "around an original kernel of truth was built up a complex fiction which should be treated with a good deal of circumspection."[28]

Yet to insist on the fictional status of the laws of love is not the same as to deny their legal and cultural significance. They represent, Goodrich writes, "an attempt to think through the most pervasive, the most political and the most immediate problems of social intercourse and institutional life, namely the relationship between the sexes conceived neither as a war of the sexes nor as a play of power and possession but rather as a question of reciprocal recognition and mutual right."[29] The judgments of love explore the very possibility of thinking about passion in juridical terms, probing the limitations and potentialities of the law. They "expose," to adopt Bruce Holsinger's formulation of the relationship between law and literature, "logical or cognitive gaps unacknowledged or undertheorized within official legal culture and exploit them through the alternative medium of literary language."[30] The poetic courts of love imagine a form of law that compensates for the structural impossibilities of the positive law (its inflexibility of procedure or blindness to such matters as emotion) and at the same time presents a vision of love as a governable force whose at times devastating effects can be offset by a system of legal norms and regulations. It is, in fact, erotic legality's opposition to other forms of law that primarily accounts for its close relationships with literature and art. Jean Baudrillard's remark that "the sphere of play is always the aesthetic sublimation of labour's constraints" is apposite here.[31] According to Goodrich, literature "suggests other possibilities for law, other means of expression of law and more profoundly conceptions of value and of justice that draw upon a wider variety of experiences of gender, sexuality, ethnicity and lifestyle than are currently available within the closed vision of an embattled legal profession and its mythology of a juristic science."[32] That is, rather than simply recycle historical legal practice, the laws of love posit poetry and rhetoric as privileged sites of the legal imagination. Even as they gesture toward historical institutions, agents, and norms, they fantasize a dissident vision of perfect law, a social collective desire for a certain form of legality.[33] The laws of love delineate their own jurisdiction on the margins of institutionalized law as an artifice, as a poetic endeavor that facilitates a critique of both juridical and poetic discourses.

For Goodrich, the literary courts of love represent a site of resistance to the ideological and formal rigidity of positive law. Reclaiming them for legal history means rewriting the history of law "in the terms of the traditions and texts—the emotions, the lives—that have been suppressed and excluded from doctrine and its representations of institutional history."[34] I see, however, erotic legality as a useful category of literary history, one that illuminates some of the changes and continuities in English poetry from the late medieval to the Elizabethan period. There appear to be no historical records of such courts of love in medieval England.[35] Yet, one cannot ignore a distinct strain in late medieval English poetry that places desire under the sign of the law, such as Geoffrey Chaucer's *Parliament of Fowls* (1370s–1380s), Sir John Clanvowe's *The Book of Cupid, God of Love* (also known as *The Cuckoo and the Nightingale*) (1386–91), Thomas Hoccleve's *Epistle to Cupid* (1402), John Lydgate's *Temple of Glas* and *Complaynte of a Louers Lyfe* (both c. 1400–20), the anonymous *Assembly of Ladies* (1450–85), and the slightly later William Neville's *The Castell of Pleasure* (printed 1518) and the comic *Court of Love* (c. 1530s). By either pondering the nature of Cupid's laws (Clanvowe, Hoccleve) or staging elaborate legal sessions in which the lovers are judged on the merits of their passions (Lydgate, *Assembly*, *The Court of Love*), these texts explicitly theorize love's status in the legal domain.

Lydgate's *Temple of Glas* (c. 1400–1420s) offers perhaps the most sustained exploration of erotic legality.[36] In this dream vision, the narrator, in his sleep, is "rauysshid in spirit in [a] temple of glas" (16) dedicated to Venus, where he finds a myriad of lovers pleading with the goddess. The dreamer's attention is drawn to a young lady who kneels before the deity:

> And al hir wil, to Venus þe goddes,
> Whan þat hir list hir harmes to redresse.
> For, as me þou3t, sumwhat bi hir chere,
> Forto compleyne she hade gret desire:
> For in hir hond she held a litel bil,
> Forto declare þe somme of al hir wil,
> And to þe goddes hir quarel forto shewe. (313–19)

Lydgate clearly places the act of supplication within a legal paradigm; and the lady, when she voices her complaint, insists on its status as a technology of law, asking the goddess, "So þat my bil 3our grace may atteyne, / Redresse to finde of þat I me compleyne" (333–34). The heading *Supplicatio mulieris amantis* found in some manuscripts of Lydgate's poem only intensifies the character of her "bil" as a formal legal complaint.[37] The lady protests being bound against her will to someone she does not love ("For I am bounde to þing þat I nold; / Freli to chese þere lak I liberte" [335–36]) and dreams of discovering a space in which she and her lover could enjoy their mutual passion:

> For he þat haþ myn hert[e] feiþfulli,
> And hole my luf in al honesti,
> With-oute chaunge, al be it secreli,
> I haue no space wiþ him forto be.
> O ladi Venus, consider nov & se
> Vnto þe effecte and compleint of my bil,
> Siþ life and deþ I put al in þi wil. (363–69)

Remarkably, however, this space of intimacy is presented as orchestrated by law. That she lacks her object of desire is conceived of in terms of legal possession ("What I desire, þat mai I not possede; / For þat I nold, is redi aye to me, / And þat I loue, forto swe I drede" [350–52]); and this injustice, the lady claims, is "Again al ri3t, boþe of god and kynd" (343). When Venus promises to remedy her grievance, the resolution also takes the form of a legal judgment ("And so, my dou3ter, after 3our grevauns / I 3ov bihote 3e shul haue ful plesaunce" [417–18]). Venus asserts that the happiness of the lovers is, in fact, a legal right: "Ye most of ri3t haue consolacioun" (425). The goddess then proceeds to give assurance to the lady: "3e shal haue ful poss[ess]ion / Of him þat 3e cherissh nov so wel, / In honest maner, wiþ-oute offencioun" (427–29).

At this point, the poem's focus shifts toward the lady's lover, who suddenly finds himself assaulted by what he fears is unrequited desire for her. Being in love immediately translates into being incorporated into the order of erotic law as he is "cau3t vnder subieccioun / Forto bicome a verre homagere / To god o[f] loue" (570–72). "Hanging in balaunce betwix hope & drede, / Withoute comfort, remedie or rede" (641–42), he is forced to adopt a legal subjectivity and "deuyse / His pitous quarel" in which he asks Venus for "redresse of [his] sorow" (698–99, 701). After he pleads "þis case" and "mater" (722, 827), the goddess likewise grants him "ful redresse of all þat 3e nov fele" (865). She directs him to disclose his desire to the lady, who, following Venus's advice, accepts the lover. In the process, the reader is again reminded that for Lydgate erotic intimacy forms a category of law. "Witnes on Venus, þat knoweþ myn entent," the lady exclaims, "Fulli to obei hir dome and Iugement, / So as hir lust disposen and ordeyne" (1078–80), and Venus warns her that to betray her suitor would constitute a "wrong" (1131).

Lydgate's *Temple of Glas* thus imagines love as something that can be remedied, altered, and directed by a law. But crucially, it posits erotic legality as largely lying outside the jurisdiction of traditional courts and laws. While Lydgate's language is an accurate reflection of English legal discourse ("redresse," "bil," "quarel," "possession," "offencioun," "wrong," "iugement"), it lacks specificity that would tie it to an institution or a form of litigation. Some commentators have taken the lady to be trapped in an unhappy marriage and seeking adulterous love outside of it (or even her husband's death).[38] If true, that would further confirm that Venus's law is untouched by historical law, and that the laws of love constitute a polemical alternative to the ecclesiastical legal discourse on matrimony. In that case, Lydgate's position is close to that of Capellanus, who writes that "if the parties concerned marry, love is violently put to flight," in addition to formulating the first rule of love as "Marriage is no real excuse for not loving."[39] The laws regulating marriage (and thus property rights) and the laws of love belong to different legal orders.

Lydgate's insistence that Venus's court operates via a "bil" (317, 333, 368) or "quarel" (319, 699) also repays closer attention. "A written statement of a case; a pleading by the plaintiff" (*OED* n., 3.4a), in medieval and early modern English law a bill was a mechanism to initiate legal proceedings directly in a royal court, bypassing the formulaic presentment by writ. At common law, in order to commence action, the plaintiff had to make a complaint in the Court of Chancery, which issued a suitable writ and sent it to the appropriate court. Playing on the tensions between the courts of King's Bench and Chancery, bills offered litigants more flexible (and often less expensive) legal options for accessing the structures of justice. Similar to bills were *querelae*—informal complaints (often in French) submitted to one of the king's central courts in cases where there was no common-law writ of trespass available.[40] While not directly oppositional to the common law, suits by bills and *querelae* carried with them overtones of resistance to the central system of litigation.

Lydgate, in other words, mines the resources of juridical culture in order to give the proceedings at the court of Venus an unmistakably legal form, yet the cases considered by this erotic law are a far cry from the matters dealt with by the courts of Lancastrian England. What is at stake in Venus's judgments does not concern land titles, chattels, illegitimacy, trespass, or constitution, the traditional areas of the common and canon law. Instead, they apply themselves to the rights and wrongs of passion, probing whether this or that form of love is just in the eyes of Venus. Maintaining a degree of legal realism that ensures recognition of the poem's narrative as a juridical affair, *The Temple of Glas* highlights its departure from positive law. Judgments of love here function as a parallel system of law, identifiable as a form of legal practice but one claiming a degree of jurisdictional autonomy from other courts. It is significant that in *The Temple of Glas* the laws of Venus are administered in a clearly marked juridical and physical space of the glass temple, which is "circulere / In compaswise, Round bentaile wrouȝt" (36–37). To witness the administration of this law, the dreamer has to cross several symbolic boundaries: to fall into a "sodein dedeli slepe" (14), to be transported in his oneiric state to "this grisly, dredful place" (23), and finally to enter the temple itself ("I fond a wiket, and entrid in as fast / Into þe temple" [39–40]).

As Bradin Cormack points out, "jurisdiction amounts to the delimitation of a sphere—spatial (state, city, or manor; domestic, maritime, or foreign), temporal (proximate or immemorial past; regular or market days), or generic (matters spiritual or matters temporal; promise or debt)—that is the precondition for the juridical as such, for the very capacity of the law to come into effect."[41] Lydgate's poem fully explores this notion of jurisdiction as a category of demarcation, for love here claims a legal autonomy by initiating an ontological, spatial, and therefore legal severance from the agglomeration of other jurisdictions.

Additionally, this erotic law asserts independence through the category of gender. In Thomas Hoccleve's *Epistle to Cupid* (1402), a translation of Christine de Pisan's *L'epistre au dieu d'amours*, the women incensed by the treacherous behavior of men remind them that the laws of Cupid are a feminine prerogative: "clerkis," they claim, "folk excyten by hir wikked sawes, / For to rebelled ageyn *vs* and *our* lawes."[42] *The Temple of Glas* advances a similar argument. As several critics have shown, exploring femininity is one of Lydgate's central considerations in *The Temple of Glas*.[43] What has not received much attention, however, is that the operation of law in the poem is contingent on the exclusion of the masculine. Although the dreamer observes two heterosexual lovers voice their complaints, the focus is clearly on the lady and her legal bond with Venus. In fact, the young man's suit is a consequence of Venus's legal decisions; he is incorporated into the order of this law almost against his will. Although Cupid is mentioned several times, there is a sense that he represents the dark aspects of the law of love associated with pain and suffering and merely works as an instrument of enforcing Venus's judgment. Having assured the lady that her suit will be granted, the goddess adds, "I mene of Cupide, þat shal him so distres / Vnto yo*ur* hond, wiþ þe arow of gold, / That he ne shal escapen þou3 he would" (444–46). The tableaus in the temple of glass that the dreamer describes at the beginning of the poem (55–142) also tend to focus on female characters that have cause for grievance against their lovers (Dido, Medea, Penelope, Alceste, Griselda).

The gendered nature of erotic law suggested in *The Temple of Glas* is expanded in another medieval poem, the anonymous *Assembly of Ladies*.[44] An account of its female narrator's dream, the poem records her journey to Plesaunt Regarde, a place she, along with her companions, is invited to visit in order to submit her complaint to Lady Loiaulte. This lady is vested with the authority to rectify amorous wrongs: "Ther is no grief nor no maner offence / Wherin ye fele your hert is displeased / But with hir help right sone ye shul bien eased," the narrator is promised (124–26). As we learn from the bills read to Loiaulte by her secretary (this court, like Lydgate's court of Venus, operates through "billis"), the grievances considered may include "promesse made with feithful hert and wil / And so broken ayenst al maner skille / Without desert" (585–87); recompense in situations when a lady "had bien gwerdoned for hir service, / Yit nothyng, as she takith it, pleyne" (591–92); remedy against a lover's lack of "stabilnesse" (606); or satisfaction of a desire for "goode comfort [a lady's] sorow to appese / That she myght live more at hertis ease" (671–72). Having witnessed the hearing of such bills, the narrator submits her own complaint and is assured of a remedy, "And in al this wherein ye fynde yow greved / There shal ye fynde an open remedy, / In suche wise as ye shul be releved" (722–24), even though the final redress is delayed until some future time.

There is no consensus among the critics about the nature and status of law in *The Assembly of Ladies*. Wendy Matlock, downplaying the amorous aspects of the petitioners' complaints, pursues a historicist reading of the poem; she argues that the proceedings at the court of Loiaulte mimic the major flaws of the Lancastrian legal system, such as procrastination of the court officials, interminably delayed suits, and the courts' frequent reluctance to render a final decision.[45] Julia Boffey, by contrast, while acknowledging that the women's petitions are not always related to erotic relationships and do not unequivocally represent "women's particular grievances against men," suggests that *The Assembly of Ladies*, like *The Temple of Glas*, explores the connection between law and love. As she writes, these texts offer "idealizing fantasies of social assimilation or integration, where courts are models of well-ordered and concord-dispensing harmony."[46]

For me, the court of Lady Loiaulte functions as a separate jurisdiction of love that acknowledges the existence of other structures of legality but insists on its own independent ontology. Like Lydgate's *Temple of Glas*, the anonymous poem unfolds in a dream location; and in this dream-world, Loiaulte's "court" (198, 720) is a "dayes journey" away (214), while the edifice itself is "rounde about was closid with a wal" (230). (The English word "court" is derived from the Latin *cohors*, which signifies "enclosure.") Like other legal architecture, including the glass temple, Loiaulte's court "advertizes itself as a select and exclusive space in which a monopoly over the administration of justice according to rational precepts is supposed to reign."[47] Everyone who is admitted to the castle is distinguished chromatically from those who do not belong to this legal system: "al youre felawes and ye must com in blewe" (116). The castle, like the temple of glass, is an example of what Michel Foucault calls "heterotopias"— places "which are something like counter-sites, a kind of effectively enacted utopia in which the real sites, all the other real sites that can be found within the culture, are simultaneously represented, contested, and inverted. Places of this kind are outside of all places, even though it may be possible to indicate their location in reality."[48] Similar to heterotopias, the sites of erotic law in *The Temple of Glas* and *The Assembly of Ladies* represent the reality of medieval legal culture, yet they also enact a utopian challenge to the structures of positive law. Accessible to select lovers and thus real, at the same time the sites of Lady Loiaulte's castle and Venus's temple embody society's dream of a counterlaw that treats the relationship between the sexes without directly involving the positive legal categories of ownership or trespass.

Mainly, however, the legal independence of the jurisdiction of love in *The Assembly of Ladies* is achieved through the process of gender proscription.[49] It is an all-female court from which men are excluded categorically. Upon invitation to attend a legal session, the narrator inquires whether she and her friends should ask their male companions to come with them. "Nat one," Perseveraunce sternly objects, "may come among yow alle" (147). Plesaunt Regarde's personnel consist entirely of feminine personifications—Perseveraunce (messenger), Diligence (guide), Contenaunce (gatekeeper), Discrecioun (chief purveyor), Aqueyntaunce (lodgings officer), Largesse (steward), Bealchiere (marshal of the hall), Remembraunce (chamberlain), and Avisenesse (court secretary). By the same token, the scenes on the walls of the castle depict female characters only (456–69). Although it has been argued that the gendered space in *The Assembly of Ladies* is in fact an oppressive locale that marginalizes women and perpetuates masculine authority,[50] I would propose that spatial and sexual restrictions in this medieval poem contribute to the production of jurisdictional autonomy. Within the carefully delineated feminine spaces of the glass temple and Plesaunt Regarde, love becomes a legal matter in its own right. Imitating some of the historical conditions of the fifteenth century English legal system, *The Temple of Glas* and *The Assembly of Ladies* aspire to a jurisdictional independence as they imagine a form of legality capable of regulating desire and correcting the wrongs in the sphere of intimate relationship, which they envision as bearing distinctive marks of territorial and sexual difference from institutionalized law. It is a legal domain that has its own laws that focus on a complex of actions and relations (desire, loyalty, truthfulness, courtesy) that largely escape the attention of other forms of legality (unless they directly impinge on their administration of justice, such as perjury affecting criminal procedure), its own distinct transgressions (breach of trust, lack of constancy, nonreciprocity), and a separate form of judgments.

Against this background Daniel's legal nostalgia for a medieval past assumes a more concrete shape. Daniel's sonnets, such as "Way but the cause" and "Whilst by her eyes pursu'd," are engaged in negotiating a viable imaginative space for love as a proper juridical matter. The amorous wrongs suffered by the lover call for legal action, and the laws of love similar to those articulated in *The Temple of Glas* and *The Assembly of Ladies* might provide a forum where his erotic "cause" could be considered as a matter for the law. Daniel's sonnets are clearly aware of this legal possibility since their desiring subjects yearn for a form of the law that could accommodate their failure to achieve reciprocity. Both lovers, in other words, imply the existence of the rules and courts of love where passion not only posits legal questions but also receives legal answers. Yet this appeal to the laws of love is accompanied by an admission of their anachronistic irrelevance. Erotic legality is discredited as juridical antiquarianism, for in the legal present erotic law is denied viability and its autonomous jurisdiction is displaced into the domain of the common law. Suspended between the two legal systems, Daniel's sonnets harbor the dreams of the laws of love as an independent domain even as these laws are repressed and erased by a surge of legal modernity.

Murder and Passion in Drayton's *Idea*

If Daniel's *Delia* associates the vision of erotic law as a separate jurisdiction with a medieval legal past, coveted but unreachable, Michael Drayton's *Idea* (1599–1619) represents a different type of investment of the poetry of erotic desire in the language of the law. What we witness in Drayton's sequence is a further dismantling of the very idea of love as a proper subject for jurisprudence, evident from the persistent displacement of amorous legal matters into the jurisdiction of positive, primarily criminal, law. Consider, for example, sonnet 2:

> My heart was slaine, and none but you and I:
> Who should I thinke the Murther should commit?
> Since, but your selfe, there was no Creature by,
> But onely I, guiltlesse of murth'ring it.
> It slew it selfe; the Verdict on the view
> Doe quit the dead, and me not accessarie:
> Well, well, I feare it will be prov'd by you,
> Th'evidence so great a proofe doth carrie.
> But O, see, see, we need inquire no further,
> Upon your Lips the scarlet drops are found,
> And in your Eye, the Boy that did the Murther,
> Your Cheekes yet pale, since first he gave the Wound.
>   By this I see, how-ever things be past,
>   Yet Heav'n will still have Murther out at last.[51]

The lady's disdain for the lover figured as murder is a topos of love poetry, including Petrarch's *Canzoniere* (Laura "mille volte il dì m'ancida," Petrarch complains [172.12]), and Drayton is not alone among Elizabethan sonneteers to turn to this metaphor. Sir Philip Sidney's *Astrophil and Stella* (published in 1591) addresses the cruel Stella as "Deare Killer" and accuses her of being a "murdering Tyran." In Henry Constable's *Diana* (1592), the treachery of the lover's eyes corrupted by beauty leaves his heart exposed to fire, and his eyes are tried for murder in the court of Reason: "*Loue*, sith by fire murdred my hart was found, / Adiudged them in teares for to be drownd." William Smith in his sequence *Chloris* (1596) admonishes his mistress, "Then all too late my death thou will repent, / When murthers guilt thy conscience will torment"; and Bartholomew Griffin in his *Fidessa* (1596) similarly complains that his lady murders him but "feareth not foule murthers guilt." By the same token, the lover of Robert Toft's *Laura* (1597) moans, "murtherer th'art of this poor life of mine."[52] Taking as a starting point the Ovidian notion that sexual desire can potentially destroy its subject, these poets reframe the pervasive erotic violence of Petrarchism as a legal problem.

But Drayton's sonnet goes further than any of these examples in exploring the technologies of legal figuration. Murder here is not an accidental occurrence of a clichéd trope but a central metaphor that organizes the totality of the sonnet's imaginative expanse. Besides, Drayton breathes new life into the trope by attaching a remarkable degree of mimeticism to his language. The poem replicates one of the two methods of initiating a criminal prosecution available in the early modern period, the appeal of felony brought forward by an individual appellant (the other form was trial by indictment put forward by the crown, although the two were not mutually exclusive).[53] The appeal represents a formal charge against the lady and her accomplice, Cupid, and is followed by an inquest, which includes drawing a list of witnesses and suspects and weighing the evidence, culminating in the discovery of the signs of the lady's culpability, the "scarlet drops" of blood on her lips. While not identified as such, the intended audience of the sonnet would appear to be a panel of the jurors who are asked to consider the facts of the case. The sonnet had clearly digested the growing emphasis on the jury's role in the discovery and evaluation of evidence that had come to characterize the criminal trial in Elizabethan England. If medieval juries were self-informing entities that relied on their knowledge of the case and the defendant, by the end of the sixteenth century, "while in theory juries might still take into account what they already knew, in practice they in most cases simply weighed the evidence presented at trial."[54] Even the foundations of the sonnet's poetic language—the imaginative transformation of the pain of amatory rejection into a figure of homicide—finds a parallel in early modern legal thought. The late sixteenth century was characterized by attempts to attach premeditated malice, the principal condition of murder, to intentional criminal acts that did not have murder as their object but still resulted in death.[55] In objective terms, the lady's dismissal of her lover cannot be characterized as a felony, yet for the Elizabethan legal mind, the intention behind the rejection could be reconceived as a form of transgression (most likely against the laws of love) and ultimately reinterpreted as homicidal.

In one sense, Drayton's sonnet is similar to *The Temple of Glas* and *The Assembly of Ladies* in that it derives the meaning of intersubjective relationships from the lexicon of the law. Human actions and emotions—the lady's rejection and the lover's sorrow—are figured as a felony and the subsequent process of accusation, investigation, and trial. The elusive matter of erotic intimacy is materialized as a matter of criminal procedure. But at the same time, Drayton's sonnet marks a departure from the world of the fifteenth century poems. Although the language of law continues to determine the network of social bonds between the lovers, the source of its signification is dramatically shifted. Where in the medieval texts passion forms a proper matter for the law, and the laws of love are administered in a clearly marked juridical and physical sphere, in the Elizabethan poem love lacks a distinct legal identity. The imagery of criminal procedure spreads from the core figure of rejection as murder and asserts jurisdiction over the domain of passion. The idea of a law that can respond to desire remains intact, but the transgressions are defined according to a different system of legal imagination. The very substance of what constitutes a proper matter for erotic law has undergone a subtle but undeniable change. In Drayton's Petrarchan sonnet, love is legible at law only insofar as it is a felony and a process of prosecution; it cannot constitute itself in the order of the law as passion but has to engage in mimicry of other forms of legality in order to be recognized as a legal matter. The rhetorical authority of erotic law has been restructured and reoriented toward positive law.

For comparison, when in the *Temple of Glas* the young man, feeling the painful force of desire, claims that "Thus am I murdrid & slain at þe lest" (634), the phrase is not submitted as part of his legal suit to Venus. Similarly, in Capellanus's *De amore*, the question of murder by rejection comes up in a conversation between a lady and her suitor. He threatens her: "If, then, you send me away and without the hope of your love, you will drive me to an early death, after which none of your remedies will do any good, so you may be called a homicide"; and she responds, "I have no desire to be called a homicide."[56] Here murder is a literal crime detached from the world of erotic legality. The lady's terse change of tone suggests a shift from the register of courtly love (and courtly law) to the discourse of criminal law. For Drayton's lover, on the contrary, such jurisdictional maneuver is a foreclosed option because from the outset the jurisdiction of love is absorbed into the domain of positive law.

Drayton's insistence on using contemporary criminal law as a source of his legal imagery yields even more striking results in sonnet 46:

> Plaine-path'd Experience, th'unlearneds guide,
> Her simple Followers evidently shewes
> Sometimes what Schoole-men scarcely can decide,
> Nor yet wise Reason absolutely knowes:
> In making tryall of a Murther wrought,
> If the vile actors of the heynous deed
> Neere the dead Body happily be brought,
> Oft't'ath been prov'd, the breathlesse Coarse will bleed.
> She comming neere, that my poore Heart hath slaine,
> Long since departed (to the World no more)
> Th'ancient Wounds no longer can containe,
> But fall to bleeding, as they did before:
>   But what of this? Should she to death be led,
>   It furthers Justice, but helpes not the dead.

Similar to sonnet 2, this poem seeks justice in love by relying on the resources of the English criminal law. Its central conceit is based on the practice of cruentation (also known as the ordeal of the bier)—the touching of the corpse by a suspected murderer, where the bleeding of the corpse was believed to point out the culprit. A form of divine intervention, cruentation manifested the "indignation" of the corpse at the sight of its killer, with the victim's blood "crying out" against the murderer, even though its primary juridical purpose must have been to deter potential perpetrators from committing their crimes rather than to identify actual murderers. The faith in the power of cruentation to advance the cause of justice was based on the analogical belief in the powers of sympathy and antipathy, although in some instances the explanations for the bleeding were based on science rather than providence.[57] Although the superstition had been known in antiquity (it is mentioned in Pseudo-Aristotle's

Problems), it became a judicial procedure in early medieval times and remained part of English criminal investigation well into the seventeenth and occasionally eighteenth century.[58] Such historical figures as Francis Bacon and James VI/I were prepared to believe in the validity of cruentation. Even though, as Malcolm Gaskill writes, such "magical methods of discovery were legally unreliable and offensive to Protestant orthodoxy, in practice they were frequently tolerated, especially if the authorities had little else to go on in the way of solid evidence."[59]

By using the image of cruentation, Drayton once again turns to contemporary legal practice as a source of figuration. As in sonnet 2, criminal law becomes the primary discourse through which the Petrarchan subject conceptualizes his relationship with the mistress. Although the sonnet is suffused with erotic undertones (an intercourse encoded in the lady's proximity to his heart's body, the ejaculatory dream of blood gushing out of his wounds), the desire for intimacy and sexual release is represented according to the logic of criminal procedure. He hopes, in other words, that the historical positive law of felony will meditate on the circumstances of his erotic relationship with the lady and will settle the matter by assigning culpability and compensation. The sonnet's rhetorical brilliance, however, does not save the lover from failure in this undertaking. As we have seen in Daniel's "Way but the cause," historical positive law—the English common law—falls short of providing the lover with workable instruments to attain redress for erotic grievance, and Drayton's Petrarchan poems are no different in this regard.

Sonnet 2, if read as an address to the jury, already plants seeds of uncertainty about the common law's reach into the domain of passion and desire. One consequence of the changing role of the juries (from providing local knowledge about the crime to assessing the evidence presented by the prosecution) was the growing independence and activism of the jury panels, who increasingly chose to reject the evidence and refused to indict if they were not persuaded by the crown's attorneys.[60] There is, in other words, a distinct historical possibility that the audience of the jurors in sonnet 2 might reject the lover's appeal of felony due to insufficient or inconclusive evidence presented by him. By sonnet 46, however, no ambiguity remains. Common law may, Drayton exclaims, pronounce justice rendered in the sphere of criminal jurisdiction, but it obviously and glaringly lacks the capacity to answer the lover's demand of erotic redress: it "furthers justice, but helpes not the dead." Where Daniel finds consolation in legal nostalgia by imagining a past when matters of love were successfully decided at law, Drayton is reduced to venting his frustration at the present times' legal ineffectiveness in addressing erotic wrongs, even as he continues to invest in the imaginative structures of the common law in his attempts to bring the lady to justice.

Such adherence to the language of the common law is an indicator of the position Drayton's sequence occupies in the history of juridico-erotic poetry. His sonnets bespeak a tight interlacement of the language of the common law and the discourse of desire—or, in historical terms, a displacement of erotic legality as a separate jurisdiction into the domain of the common law. "If love has its own laws," Goodrich writes, "then it makes little rhetorical sense to subject love to a law, to rules, to rights and obligations that are identical in form to the public norms that govern mercantile [and, one might add, criminal] relations."[61] Indeed, in subjecting erotic intimacy to the full hold of criminal procedure, Drayton's "murder" sonnets register the disappearance of love's own laws and the rise of positive law as the key imaginary mechanism of regulating relationships between the sexes. The laws governing passion are held in abeyance by the laws of felony.

The claim that the sixteenth century witnessed a gradual displacement of the poetic laws of love into the domain of the common law is congruent with legal history. The key aspect of English legal culture in the period was the rise of the common law to a position of doctrinal, procedural, and jurisdictional hegemony. James Simpson describes English literature's transition from the medieval to the early modern in jurisdictional terms. According to Simpson, "the sixteenth century witnessed a contraction and simplification of a much more complex 'medieval' jurisdictional field"; sixteenth century love lyrics, for him, are "symptomatic of the single power in whose sway those poems are held."[62] Simpson writes of Wyatt and Surrey, but his argument can be extended to later Elizabethan poets like Daniel and Drayton as well, especially if we unpack the main trajectory of the jurisdictional attrition that characterizes the sixteenth century. As Cormack notes in his study of early modern literature in conjunction with jurisdictional history, "while at the beginning of the Tudor period it was possible to imagine English law substantially in terms of interrelated spheres of juridical activity, by the mid-seventeenth century the common law of the central royal courts was fully present to the culture as the dominant source of juridical norms."[63] In other words, it is the rise to supremacy of the common law, primarily at the expense of the ecclesiastical jurisdiction, that determines the direction of legal history in Tudor England. Simpson's argument is of course a simplification, for in Elizabethan England the common law continued to share the juridical space with at least a dozen noncommon law jurisdictions (ecclesiastical courts, courts of equity, admiralty, manorial courts, etc.), each with its different trial methods and legal standards.[64] Still, as the century progressed, the juridical and jurisprudential capacities of the civil and the canon law were significantly diminished.[65] What the common law tried to achieve was not to eradicate other legal traditions but rather to gain control over them. Operating largely through the writs of prohibition, the central common-law courts (King's Bench and Common Pleas) kept other courts within their jurisdictional orbit.[66]

Attendant upon this process of assimilation of erotic legality into the order of the common law is the conspicuous reversal in Daniel's and Drayton's sonnets of the gender-exclusionary model that characterized the medieval poems. In Lydgate's *Temple of Glas* and especially in *The Assembly of Ladies*, the amorous jurisdiction derives its legitimacy and authority, in addition to spatial delimitations, from its exclusively feminine contingent of lawgivers, lawyers, and litigants. Men are all but excluded from the proceedings; when they do take part in the erotic tribunals, as the young lady's lover does in Lydgate's *Temple of Glas*, their role is to acquiesce to the force of feminine erotic law. In both Daniel and Drayton, in contrast, the law clearly is a masculine prerogative. Women here are ostracized by the law; figured as perpetrators, they are transformed into signs of legal discourse through a judicial process initiated and carried out by masculine victims, plaintiffs, appellants, jurors, and officers of the court.

The difference is not accidental, for the common law chose to institute itself as a "prose that was if not always resistant to the images of femininity, was nonetheless unremittingly hostile to the 'other sex.'"[67] This is not to suggest that under common law women were excluded from the legal process; on the contrary, there was a significant female participation in litigation in Elizabethan England across a variety of jurisdictions, including common-law courts. However, as historical data suggest, female litigants to a significant degree preferred courts of equity over common-law courts because the latter imposed palpable limitations on female legal agency and in many instances were keen on suppressing and silencing women waging law altogether.[68] The early modern subject of the common law was markedly masculine, and the official discourse of the common law operated based on a male standard, an attitude that was particularly pervasive in the sphere of criminal prosecution, including homicide.[69] In this light, the imposition of common-law criminal jurisprudence on the courts of love can be read as an important chapter in the long history of denial, repression, and erasure of an alternative (feminine) jurisdiction by the force of mainstream (masculine) legal tradition in England.

It is important, however, not to lose sight of the more than faint vestiges of medieval poetry still discernable in this triumph of legal modernity in Drayton's sonnets. The desire to posit love as a legal matter, despite Drayton's fascination with contemporary practices of criminal law, is in its essence a medieval phenomenon, if a markedly belated one in Elizabethan England. Despite the discontinuity of the imaginative technologies (laws of love versus criminal law), there is a categorical continuity to the idea that legal construction of desire is a valid jurisprudential principle. Subha Mukherji remarks that by the seventeenth century the amorous jurisdiction becomes "an anachronism" in English literature.[70] But such sweeping dismissal of erotic legality, such insistence on the vanishing without a trace of the laws of love from the late Elizabethan poetic landscape ignores instances of translation, displacement, and conversion of erotic laws from a separate domain into other jurisdictional territories and modalities. Drayton's relations with his mistress, in the aftermath of her slaying his heart and then being detected through the trial of the bier (among other means), are in some deep underlying sense a residual species of the laws of love, however distorted and unrecognizable. Notwithstanding the assimilation of the laws of love under the increasingly aggressive common law, inasmuch as there is hoping for erotic legality traceable in early modern discourse, the jurisdiction of love continues to exist within the discursive structures of positive law. No matter how marginalized and suppressed, medieval legal energies continue to flow through Renaissance poetry, reaffirming the legitimacy of the Middle Ages for the early modern period.

Love, Poetry, and the Limits of Common Law

As I have suggested, the proliferation of common-law imagery in Elizabethan sonnets can be associated with the changes to the jurisdictional palette of early modern England. Drayton's homicidal sonnets in particular indicate the dwindling authority of the laws of love. It is important to note, however, that the reconfiguration of juridico-erotic discourse I have been sketching in these pages is not a radical innovation of the Elizabethan age but, at least to a degree, an extension of medieval poetic practices. For already in Lydgate's *Complaynte of a Louers Lyfe* (also known as *The Complaint of the Black Knight* and written at about the same time as *The Temple of Glas*), the laws of love yield some of their jurisdictional status to the common law.[71] By articulating unrequited desire in the language of the common law, in some important respects the *Complaynte* anticipates many of the discursive strategies adopted by Elizabethan Petrarchans almost two centuries later.

The structure of Lydgate's poem closely imitates Chaucer's *Book of the Duchess*: the narrator, wandering through the forest, overhears the sorrowful complaint of unrequited love ("the colde of ynwarde high dysdeyn" [239]) uttered by a nobleman. The anguished lover is recorded as pleading for a redress of his grievance (the lady's nonreciprocity), but his suit is constructed in very different categories from *The*

Temple of Glas. As the knight relates, Daunger and Dispite have conspired with Envye and Enemyte "ayens al ryght and lawe, / Of her malis, that Trouthe shal be slawe" (250–52, 257–59). Murder indeed features prominently in the episode as the sorrowful lover repeatedly alludes to his own unlawful killing: "O Lorde of Trouthe! to The I calle and clepe: / How may Thou se thus in Thy presence, / With-out[e] mercy mordred Innocence?" (285–87); "And thus I am for my trouthe, alas! / Mordred and slayn with wordis sharp and kene, / Gilt[e]les, God wote, of al trespas" (512–14). Murder is just one of the crimes perpetrated against the desiring knight, however. Mal-Bouche slanders him ("And Male-bouche gan first the tale telle, / To sclaundre Trouthe of Indignacion [260–61]), as a result of which False displaces Trouthe and assumes possession of his property: "And Falsnes now his place occupieth, / And entred ys in-to Trouthes londe, / And hath therof the ful possessyoun" (266–68).

It is not easy to untangle the jurisdictional architectonic of the episode. That the speaker is a lover would suggest that he addresses the god of love, Cupid; indeed, at some point he exclaims, "O God of Love! vnto the I crie, / And to thy blende double deyte / Of this grete wrong I compleyn[e] me" (453–55). After all, all the injustices that he suffers are merely multiple facets of his lady's disdain, and "Venus and the god Cupide" are blamed for his misfortunes (436). But he repeatedly redirects his suit to the "Lorde of Trouthe" (285), the "ryghtful God...that art of Trouthe souereyn" (269, 288); and it is not clear whether the god of love and the god of truth are the same, for the former offers assistance to falsehood rather than truth, "Of God of Love, that fals hem so assure, / And trew, alas! dovn of the whele be falle" (304–05). It would appear that the lover puts himself into a double legal bind, positing himself as a subject of divine and erotic law at the same time. But even more intriguing is the fact that the lover's grievances consist almost entirely of a series of causes actionable under the common law: slander, murder, and disseisin (displacement of the rightful owner of land, wrongful dispossession).[72] In fact, Lydgate's language is so specific that some scholars have identified the litigant knight as Henry Bolingbroke, exiled and deprived of his lands by Richard II.[73]

The lover's legal case, in other words, is inscribed at an intersection of several jurisdictions, with Cupid's law and the common law placed at the heart of the juridical knot. He explicitly asks how it is possible that "Falshed shuld haue iurysdixioun / In Trouthes ryght, to sle him gilt[e]les?" (271–72). This traversal of jurisdictional domains, I would argue, simultaneously bespeaks a synthesis and a conflict. For on the one hand, the multiplicity of legal attachments in the poem invokes the early medieval idea of different kinds of human law being but a reflection of the overarching framework of divine law, which involves all forms of legality in an analogical relation of resonance with one another.[74] Prior to the dissolution of bonds between positive human law and divine law in the postmedieval period, the law of love, just like criminal law, forms part of an integrated whole.[75] As such, even though the Lydgatean lover's appeal of murder unfolds within the domain of Cupid's law, in the final instance both operate as analogues of divine justice delivered under the auspices of the "Lorde of Trouthe." But at the same time, the uncertainty that obtains in the Lydgatean lover's positioning vis-à-vis various systems of law reflects the process of jurisdictional disintegration and attrition, as a result of which the sphere of erotic legality is gradually placed under erasure by the growing territorial ambitions of the positive (common) law. Richard Green traces the impact on literary texts of the transition from local to central law, from reliance on communal oral traditions of truth-seeking to the centralization of the legal process by the royal courts' bureaucratic machine in the late fourteenth and early fifteenth centuries.[76] Green does not consider Lydgate's poem, but the lover's "trouthe" seems to be a casualty of similar historical processes. His "trouthe" being assaulted by common-law crimes and trespasses thus becomes an allegory of literary history in which the separate jurisdiction of erotic legality is being infiltrated by the common law and disappears from the imaginary map of juridical potentialities.

However, at the same time as it anticipates the common law's claims to jurisdictional primacy as well as its masculinist domination (there are no apparent female personifications in the text), Lydgate's *Complaynte of a Louers Lyfe* formulates a strategy of rhetorical insubordination that opens up pathways to resisting this process of suppression of erotic legality. That the central trope of the passage is the metaphor of murder by disdain is clear, but the figurative status of this murder is more problematic. The episode follows the interactions of several personifications of abstract qualities (Daunger, Dispite, Envye, Enemyte, Male-bouche, Mys-beleve, Falsnes, Cruelte, Disdeyn, etc.); the lover himself, as the poem progresses, is translated into a personification of Trouthe. What murder denotes in this context is a form of juridical relationship between these personifications (i.e., Daunger and Dispite conspire with Envye and Enemyte in order to commit the murder of Trouthe), similar to other forms of legal actions in the episode (dispossession of lands, slander, etc.). Consequently, as a predicate to personified characters, murder acquires a degree of realness that renders the figure almost literal. But although it appears that the metaphor of murder all but escapes figuration, its literalization still takes place within a world populated by personifications—tropes configured through a nonarbitrary relationship between signifier and signified. Personification characters are contiguous with the words from which they derive (Daunger/danger), and this creates a refractory effect of *mise en abyme* that throws into relief the possible defiguralization of murder.

As James Paxson writes, personification is a "figure always telling something about figuration itself."[77] By setting the homicidal metaphor among personifications, Lydgate's poem foregrounds an ontological distinction between different levels of textual figuration, testing the significatory mechanisms of various rhetorical agglomerations. As a result, *Complaynte of a Louers Lyfe* not only places the figurative language of murder under scrutiny and opens juridico-erotic discourse up to a critique, but it opposes the movement of colonization and suppression of the domain of erotic legality by positive law (murder and trespass). Faced with the prospect of marginalization and eventual erasure of the laws of love, the text of Lydgate's poem mobilizes rhetorical self-reflexivity as a deterrent to the advancement of the common law.

Medieval poetry passes this form of discursive resistance on to Elizabethan Petrarchans, for the murder sonnets from Drayton's *Idea* belong to the same type of self-reflexive writing as Lydgate's *Complaynte of a Louers Lyfe*. In particular, sonnet 2, for all its legal mimeticism, estranges the symbiosis of *ars juridica* and *ars poetica*. From the point of view of juridical discourse, it can be read as articulating a murder charge against the lady in a legal setting, at an inquest in front of a magistrate. However, that the victim of this homicide is the speaker's own heart lends a slightly macabre (and simultaneously comic) tone to the proceedings. Read literally—and given Drayton's attention of realistic detail in the sonnet, his "maniacal exactitude of language," to use Roland Barthes's phrase for such mimetically verisimilar descriptions,[78] reading the sonnet literally cannot be dismissed as a viable interpretive option—it makes the poems a rhetorical impossibility, for the voice of the poem is the voice of the same lover whose heart has been slain and for whom he now demands justice.

The speaker assumes the role of a forensic orator and deploys prosopopeia, a figure that (among other things) "raiseth againe as it were the dead to life, and bringeth them forth complaining or witnessing what they knew."[79] He gives voice to the victim, except that he is the victim himself (as the poem seems to imply in the strangely unsettling line "the Verdict on the view / Doe quit the dead"). One, it is reasonable to assume, cannot be a murder victim and make an appeal of the crime at the same time, although, as Gaskill demonstrates, such seemingly supernatural evidence would be in line with the beliefs and practices of English justice in the late sixteenth and early seventeenth centuries. As he writes, in the absence of forensic science, "in early modern England, the dead had to speak for themselves," so English culture had developed various technologies of postmortem communication that "enabled victims to testify against a murderer post mortem...the victim was effectively brought back from the dead in order to act as the plaintiff."[80] These included cries of murder, in which the victims of homicide, speaking *in extremis*, used the last dying moments of their lives to identify their killers, and ghosts returning from the grave and denouncing their murderers, a popular device of cheap print literature.[81] But what is an aberration at law is the essence of poetry. While a poem spoken by a corpse, Diana Fuss writes, apparently "denotes an extravagant rhetorical conceit, an impossible literary utterance," it in fact represents "a general attribute of all lyric poems, verse suspended between the animated voice of the speaker and the frozen form of the poem that preserves it."[82] While the elision of the subject of enunciation and the subject of the enounced might bring the operation of criminal law abruptly to a halt, in Drayton's sonnet it creates an opportunity for poetic discourse to investigate its own process of signification and thus assert its authority over the discursive field.

This of course is based on a willful misreading of Drayton's text, one that literalizes the legal figures in the sonnet and makes the heart's homicide a criminal matter. But in the opposite scenario, one in which figuration is sustained, law fares not much better, for in that case legal discourse is unmasked as thoroughly dependent on poetic diction: it is only insofar as the murder of the heart is marked as a trope, as a rhetorical connivance, that the law can function properly through the forensic prosopopoeia that draws a distinction between the orator and the victim and allows the former to conjure up the victim and speak for the dead. And in the reverse scenario, as I have suggested, if the figural reality of the sonnet asserts itself as total reality and literary discourse is bypassed en route to legal literalism, the death of the heart spells the death of the speaker so that the whole legal coordination of present and absent voices (lawyer and victim) becomes an utter impossibility. Like Lydgate, Drayton, by experimenting with prosopopoeia, shows us "how rhetorically complex the literary representation of self and voice is, because that representation is seen to operates within a network of rhetorical agendas."[83] Whether the speaking "I" is to be construed as alive or deceased, the sonnet is an aesthetic provocation to the law because it reveals the latter's dependence on poetic figuration to make its case of murder.

Drayton further exposes the rhetorical limits of the law and the liberating potential of poetry in sonnet 50:

> As in some Countries, farre remote from hence,
> The wretched Creature, destined to die,
> Having the Judgement due to his Offence,
> By Surgeons beg'd, their Art on him to trie,
> Which on the Living worke without remorse,
> First make incision on each mast'ring Veine,

> Then stanch the bleeding, then trans-pierce the Coarse,
> And with the Balmes recure the Wounds againe;
> Then Poyson, and with Physike him restore:
> Not that they feare the hope-lesse Man to kill,
> But their Experience to increase the more:
> Ev'n so my Mistres workes upon my Ill;
> 	By curing me, and killing me each How'r,
> 	Onely to shew her Beauties Sov'raigne Pow'r.

Returning to the gruesome forensic imagery of the earlier poems, the sonnet continues Drayton's interest in imagining a legal space for the relationship of intimacy; and as in the other sonnets, the site of killing is presented as the territory where sexuality can enter the order of the law. But while the poem's originary figure is the same metaphor of murder by disdain, here Drayton undertakes a series of rhetorical transformations that further expose the processes of figuration and question the authority of the law. The gender and legal roles in the sonnet are reversed: the lover becomes the condemned criminal ("Creature destined to die, / Having the Judgement due to his Offence") while the lady is associated with the order of the law. The lover's murder itself is revisited as a legal act, whereas the law that demands the execution is no longer the masculinized common law of England. Instead, the sonnet's simile takes the lover to a heterotopia of "some Countries, farre remote from hence," another jurisdiction where the law that governs love unfolds in a feminine sphere. Where Daniel's nostalgia is primarily temporal, Drayton's longing for erotic legality takes a geographical shape.

In other words, while the sonnet's legal language gestures back to the more conventional uses of the murder metaphor in *Idea* (sonnets 2 and 46), in this case Drayton turns the figure inside out: murder becomes lawful execution, the common law is displaced by an alternative form of legality associated with femininity, and the execution pointedly avoids death as his wounds are "recure[d]" and poison introduced into his body is countered by an antidote. The poem erects several lines of resistance against the imaginative and rhetorical advancement of the common law. Although the jurisdiction of love is no longer available to the lover, he still manages to frustrate the encroachment of the common law by transferring his legal relationship with the lady into an alternative domain distinct from both the English criminal law and the medieval laws of love. Crucially, however, this transfer is linked to the art of poetry: this alternative legal universe is built through an "Art" that makes an "incision" on the lover's body, imitating an act of writing. As the law writes on the subject's body, Drayton's subject rewrites this law on the body of the poem, questioning the authority of its figures in the process.

In concluding this chapter, I would like to reiterate the central argument of this book: that in our considerations of early modern Petrarchan poetry, medieval poetics offers an invaluable analytical tool, and the subject of erotic law offers a particularly compelling illustration of this claim. "To enter into relations with the law," Derrida writes, "is to act as if it had no history or at any rate as if it no longer depended on its historical presentation. At the same time, it is to let oneself be enticed, provoked, and hailed by the history of this non-history. It is to let oneself be tempted by the impossible: a theory of the origin of law, and therefore of its non-origin."[84] Indeed, although the subjects of erotic law in Daniel's and Drayton's sonnets may appear to have no history beyond the synchronic context of the Inns of Court and common-law rituals of Elizabethan England, there is a distinct diachronic aspect to these performances of legal selfhood. The language in which these Petrarchan subjects write themselves is derived from the medieval laws of love, however altered and recoded this language may be. Daniel's and Drayton's early modern lovers remain medieval subjects of erotic law. When it comes to interpreting legal figures in Elizabethan Petrarchism, a focus on poetic history—on literary tradition, on discursive memory, on textual genealogy, on rhetorical continuity—in addition to legal history repays the effort. By taking account of fragments of the poetic past that animate the articulations of desire in the language of the law in the sonnets, we can elucidate some of the complexities of the evolutionary processes that characterize English love poetry from the medieval to the early modern, arriving at a more accurate picture of the poetry of the past.

FIVE

Medieval Pathologies of Affect

Reading Hoccleve and Henryson
in Shakespeare's "Sonnets"

If traces of medieval poetics of subjectivity can be discovered in a host of English Petrarchan sonnets sequences, from Philip Sidney's *Astrophil and Stella* and Edmund Spenser's *Amoretti* to Samuel Daniel's *Delia* and Michael Drayton's *Idea*, could this argument be extended to a poetic text that seems to epitomize the Renaissance break from the medieval past—*Shake-speares Sonnets* (1609)? The question itself is fraught with risk. Shakespeare is nothing if not modern in his sonnets, and thus to entertain the idea that medieval poetics may be relevant to his sequence would be, on the surface of things, counterintuitive. It is true, of course, that Joel Fineman's *Shakespeare's Perjured Eye*—including its central thesis that in the sonnets Shakespeare develops, out of the tired tradition of poetic praise, a "new poetics and, along with this, a new first-person poetic posture"[1]—has not aged well and no longer holds the same sway as it did in the 1980s and early 1990s. A host of subsequent critics have highlighted the important links between poetic traditions of the Renaissance, in particular Petrarchism, and Shakespeare's sonnets.[2] The argument of Shakespeare's modernity in general has come under serious scrutiny in recent years, with a series of critical projects tracing how the English medieval past—subject matter, formal devices, religious, political, and philosophical ideas—affected Shakespeare's work and was in turn affected by him.[3] But despite this exciting proliferation of "medieval Shakespeares," the conviction of Shakespeare's inextricable modernity largely remains "institutionally embedded."[4] This is particularly true for Shakespeare's nondramatic poetry and even more so for the sonnets as their notable absence from the recent critical discussions of Shakespeare's imaginative rendezvous with the Middle Ages continues to speak to our investment in the idea of the sequence's inviolate modernity.[5] The post-Finemanean slogans of the 1990s—that in the sonnets Shakespeare "created an /I/ markedly different from anything before him"[6] and "discovered a newly complex system of expression, unprecedented in the Renaissance lyric"[7]—are no longer formally endorsed, but it would appear that their underlying tenets continue to inform tacitly our responses to Shakespeare's sequence.

Meanwhile, the sonnets themselves are rather conscious of their historical responsibility:

> When in the Chronicle of wasted time,
> I see discriptions of the fairest wights,
> And beautie making beautifull old rime,
> In praise of Ladies dead, and louely Knights,
> Then in the blazon of sweet beauties best,
> Of hand, of foote, of lip, of eye, of brow,
> I see their antique Pen would haue exprest,
> Euen such a beauty as you maister now.
> So all their praises are but prophesies

> Of this our time, all you prefiguring,
> And for they look'd but with deuining eyes,
> They had not still enough your worth to sing:
> For we which now behold these present dayes,
> Haue eyes to wonder, but lack toungs to praise.[8] (106)

This is a "backward-looking sonnet,"[9] in the sense that it seeks to define Shakespeare's own place vis-à-vis preceding literary history. The poem's principal imaginative fulcrum is the conflict between the poetic practice of the past ("Chronicle of wasted time" written in an "antique Pen") and the writing of "these present dayes"—that is, Shakespeare's own sonnet(s). The sonnet thus "meditates upon poetry of the past" and "relates the present to the Middle Ages."[10] A great deal of critical energy has been spent trying to determine the text or texts that Shakespeare may have had in mind while writing it. The lines in question have been read as references to "medieval annals and romance," "old chivalric literature," "old minnesingers and trouvères,"[11] and Chaucer, as well as records of the poet's desire to distance himself from Spenser's *The Faerie Queene* and from the English Petrarchan tradition in general.[12] But such identifications, while immensely useful, are either hostile toward Shakespeare's vernacular past or rather reductive in their specificity. The language of the sonnet, meanwhile, is pointedly abstract; it is inviting rather than foreclosing, suggestive rather than restrictive. It does not name names; all it does is acknowledge the existence of a poetic precedent with which the early modern discourse has somehow to come to terms.

There are, moreover, certain dangers in acts of periodization. According to one of Frederic Jameson's postulates of modernity,

> The foregrounding of continuities, the insistent and unwavering focus on the seamless passage from past to present, slowly turns into a consciousness of a radical break; while at the

same time the enforced attention to a break gradually turns the latter into a period in its own right.... The more we seek to persuade ourselves of the fidelity of our own projects and values with respect to the past, the more obsessively do we find ourselves exploring the latter and its projects and values, which slowly begin to form into a kind of totality and to dissociate themselves from our own present as the living moment in the continuum.[13]

In other words, for Jameson the very act of periodization institutes a rupture between modernity and its past, petrifying the latter into a closed-off totality that, whatever our insistence on its relevance to our current situation, remains divorced from the living present. Shakespeare's sonnet, however, departs from the fatalistic rigidity of Jameson's claim. The speaker imagines his "blazon of sweet beauties best, / Of hand, of foote, of lip, of eye, of brow," a genre that gestures unequivocally toward Renaissance Petrarchism,[14] as though underwritten by descriptions of "Ladies dead, and louely Knights" derived from the "Chronicle of wasted time." These past "discriptions" are "prophesies" of Shakespeare's texts, "prefiguring" the parameters of early modern poetry. The sonnet argues that the poetry of "these present dayes" is in fact sustained by past articulations of passion written with an "antique Pen." For while we moderns may enjoy a far superior subject matter ("your worth"), we still "lack toungs to praise," the latter the prerogative of the ancients. It is not that we cannot write poems because we are "tongueless," as Vendler argues;[15] it is, rather, that we cannot write poems in "toungs" and "rime[s]" other than those borrowed from "wasted time." Even Fineman has to admit that although in this sonnet "the young man, by convention, necessarily gets the better of it...a kind of odd and self-conscious literary retrospection" attaches itself to the poem.[16] Or, as I have been suggesting in this book all along, articulations of desire in

Renaissance Petrarchism still bear traces of medieval forms of discourse. While the subject matter may have changed, the poetic "toungs" remain heirs to vernacular literary traditions. The poet casts himself "as a pillager of the past, as a browser through old manuscripts who puts dusty clichés to fresh uses,"[17] but the focus on the "fresh uses" may obfuscate the ineluctability of the "dusty clichés" that continue to provide the poet with a vehicle for expressing his desire. If Jameson's despair grows out of our failure to retain the past as part of our living present, Shakespeare's own unmistakable pessimism, on the contrary, stems from insufficient modernity—the writer's inability to extricate his discourse completely from the remnants of a past poetic tradition.

In this final chapter, I investigate some of the medieval "toungs" at work in Shakespeare's sonnets—points where Shakespeare's "novel subject," as Fineman reluctantly admits, "carries with it the memory of that which it displaces."[18] My focus is Shakespeare's articulation of his desiring subject in the language of disease, and as I argue here, in Shakespeare's sonnets the uses of this Petrarchan trope—love as a sickness that delights the lover, as Petrarch says ("il mal che me diletta et non me dole")[19]—preserve memories of two distinct imaginative frameworks developed in medieval English poetry. One of these entails a figurative alignment of bodily infirmity, erotic desire, and pecuniary lack present in some of Shakespeare's young man sonnets. As I suggest, it contains discursive vestiges of English medieval begging poetry exemplified most powerfully by "La male regle" by Thomas Hoccleve (c. 1368–1426). The other medieval scenario of subjectivity that I analyze in this chapter appears in the dark lady sonnets in the form of the speaker's pathological desire for a diseased female body that threatens to pollute the speaker. In this case, Shakespeare reactivates the aesthetic of disgust so vividly articulated in *The Testament of Cresseid* by

Robert Henryson (c. 1425–1506), where the speaking subject is also drawn toward a pathological, "foul," feminine object of desire. While I do not necessarily argue for either author's inclusion in the catalog of Shakespeare's imaginary library,[20] both fifteenth-century poems contributed to the production of vernacular poetic resources—the "toungs" that enabled articulations of sick amorous subjectivity in Shakespeare's sonnets.

The double valence of the sonnets' medieval engagements is reflected in the structure of this chapter. It begins with a reading of how the Petrarchan trope of erotic sickness in Shakespeare's verse reactivates the technologies of poetic selfhood characteristic of medieval begging poetry, then follows it with a discussion of how the same figure of the disease of love in the dark lady sonnets carries out its vernacular dialogue with Henryson's poem. The chapter thus adopts the traditional division of Shakespeare's sequence into the young man (1–126) and the dark lady (127–54) sonnets that has been in place since Edmond Malone's 1780 edition of the collection.[21] The division has been the subject of some incisive critiques in recent decades, but in the context of this book it represents a useful analytical move.[22] Valerie Traub writes that "despite some gender ambiguity in modes of linguistic address, male and female *bodies* are cathected quite differently in these poems."[23] Traub is concerned with gender identity, but I appropriate her formulation to describe the presence of the two separate medieval strains within the imaginative fabric of Shakespeare's sonnet sequence. Yet despite the differences between the two forms of the sonnets' historical engagement, they both further develop the central argument of this book that in early modern England the Petrarchan language of subjectivity is adulterated by vernacular memories of discourse. A radically modern text, Shakespeare's sonnets extract their identity from multiple discursive traditions, and as this chapter demonstrates, medieval English poetry is one of them.

Medieval Begging in the Young Man Sonnets

The imagery of disease and decay is pervasive in the first 126 sonnets, where Shakespeare repeatedly identifies with the position of impairment. The speaker is represented as ravaged by some kind of physical, moral, or legal defect, and he endows the beloved with a potential to rehabilitate his imperfections:

> O for my sake doe you wish [with?] fortune chide,
> The guiltie goddesse of my harmfull deeds,
> That did not better for my life prouide,
> Then publick meanes which publick manners breeds.
> Thence comes it that my name receiues a brand,
> And almost thence my nature is subdu'd
> To what it workes in, like the Dyers hand,
> Pitty me then, and wish I were renu'de,
> Whilst like a willing pacient I will drinke,
> Potions of Eysell gainst my strong infection,
> No bitternesse that I will bitter thinke,
> Nor double pennance, to correct correction.
> Pittie me then deare friend, and I assure yee,
> Euen that your pittie is enough to cure mee. (111)

The dynamic of this poem unfolds from the speaker's self-presentation in the language of deficiency toward a promise of remedial action contingent upon the beloved's reciprocation. The first two quatrains implicate the lover in the shame of wrongdoing, through references to "harmfull deeds" and the "brand" his name receives. Despite his attempts to deflect guilt onto Fortune ("the guiltie goddesse of my harmfull deeds"), the subject is forced to acknowledge that his public persona is tarnished in ethical and legal terms. The third quatrain, however, makes an abrupt shift to medical vocabulary, portraying the speaker as "a willing pacient" drinking "potions of Eysell gainst [his] strong infection," hoping to cure his disease. The internalization of guilt is crystalized in the image of "the Dyers hand" working its way under the skin; and this transfer of defect inwards, inside the lover's body ("in-fection"), also invites the reader to revisit the "harmfull deeds" of the first quatrain and possibly rethink it as an aspect of physical suffering as well. If the last line of the third quatrain returns the reader to moral and legal terminology ("Nor double pennance, to correct correction"), the couplet reasserts the sonnet's reliance on the language of medicine as a source of its signification.

Such legal and medical self-abasement unfolds against the possibility of rehabilitation through the young man's love. The Shakespearean lover hopes to be restored—as well as morally corrected—by his friend's reciprocity, which is imagined as a process of healing in the last two lines. As a result of this juxtaposition, the lover and the young man come to occupy the two poles on an axis of bodily infirmity: in sharp contrast to the speaker plagued by moral and physical disease, the beloved is represented as a source of purity and health. Granted, the subject's movement toward identification with the object is the key intersubjective strategy of love poetry. As Fineman writes, "identification of praising subject with praised object is a staple in the repertoire of praise," where the subject's "identity or unity...is already prefigured for him in the compact wholeness of the beloved."[24] In the tradition of epideictic poetry, Shakespeare's lover finds a counterpoint of ideality in the form of his friend who offers a glimpse of "a masculine noble imaginary."[25] What *is* striking about Shakespeare's sonnet is its insistence that this traditional mechanism of identification be conceptualized in medical terms, as a movement from affliction to health.

Sonnet 37 complicates this opposition of the sick lover and his fair friend. This poem introduces an additional dimension to this framework of subjectivity and imagines the speaker, in contrast to the young man, not only as physically imperfect but as financially lacking as well:

> As a decrepit father takes delight,
> To see his actiue childe do deeds of youth,
> So I, made lame by Fortunes dearest spight
> Take all my comfort of thy worth and truth.
> For whether beauty, birth, or wealth, or wit,
> Or any of these all, or all, or more
> Intitled in their [thy?] parts, do crowned sit,
> I make my loue ingrafted to this store:
> So then I am not lame, poore, nor dispis'd,
> Whilst that this shadow doth such substance giue,
> That I in thy abundance am suffic'd,
> And by a part of all thy glory liue:
> Looke what is best, that best I wish in thee,
> This wish I haue, then ten times happy me.

The core work the poem performs is the production of medical and economic difference between the lover and his beloved, combined with the articulation of the former's desire for this difference to be elided. The lover whose voice we hear is not explicitly presented as sick, but he is clearly disabled and corporeally frail, whether by age ("decrepit"), accident ("made lame by Fortunes dearest spight"), or simply the power of desire, like Petrarch, whose encounter with Laura's beauty leaves him lame or limping, "che zoppo n'esco" (214.24). At the same time, the fact that the speaker at some point in the sonnet has a fantasy of no longer being "poore" points toward economic deprivation. His object of desire, in contrast, is in possession of "worth and truth /...beauty, birth, or wealth, or wit /...or more / Intitled in [his] parts." Shakespeare portrays his friend as the ideal site of economic and bodily plenitude, sharply opposed to the lover who is consumed not only by erotic desire but by financial instability and physical sufferings as well. An act of love between the two, therefore, will give the speaker access to the material and cultural riches and thus restore him to physical and financial health and social acceptability: "I make my loue ingrafted to this store / So then I am not lame, poore, nor dispis'd." When he is "suffic'd" in the young man's "abundance," his corporeal lack and pecuniary insufficiency are rehabilitated.

Sonnet 37 does not strike one as overly Petrarchan, and yet an interlocking of erotic desire with pecuniary longing and debilitating disease can be traced back to Petrarch's poetry. *Canzoniere* 328 presents a vision of unrequited love figured simultaneously as disease and poverty, when Laura's death leaves the Italian poet sick and economically wrecked:

> Qual à già i nervi e i polsi e i pensier egri
> cui domestica febbre assalir deve,
> tal mi sentia, non sappiend' io che leve
> venisse 'l fin de' miei ben non integri.
> Li occhi belli, or in Ciel chiari et felici
> del lume onde salute et vita piove,
> lasciando i miei qui miseri et mendici. (lines 4–10)

[As one about to be assailed by tertian fever already feels his muscles, pulse, and thoughts weaken, so I felt, although I did not know how swift the end of my imperfect wealth would come. Her beautiful eyes, now in heaven bright and happy in the light that rains salvation and life, leaving my eyes here wretched and poor.]

There are, however, some important differences between Petrarch's use of the image of erotic, economic, and medical deprivation and its function in Shakespeare's sonnet 37. Obviously, while the former directs its plaint at a conventional heterosexual beloved, Shakespeare's homoerotic poem shifts the gender of its addressee, expressing passion for a young man. But more crucially, if the Italian sonnet is firmly rooted in the tradition of courtly love, Shakespeare's young man sonnets are involved in the homosocial culture of patronage and as such articulate a hierarchical relationship between patron and client in an attempt to solicit favor.[26] As Arthur Marotti usefully notes, "Shakespeare presented himself in these poems as the insecure petitioner who seeks the continuing favor of a patron in order to enjoy social (and probably financial) rewards."[27] Many of the sonnets are thus in "quest for the reciprocities of love within the conditions of social inequality that are intrinsic to relations of service": uttered by a speaker wallowing in his abject state, they are expectations of what looks suspiciously like monetary reward from a social superior.[28] In Shakespeare's sonnets, then, desire becomes an object of textual commodification, although Heather Dubrow is correct to warn us against reducing Elizabethan Petrarchism wholesale to a mere trope of economic or political interests: Marroti's influential argument notwithstanding, love *is* love.[29]

As a result, in his "sick and poor" sonnets Shakespeare adapts what is in essence a courtly, Petrarchan trope—an alignment of desire, disease, and pecuniary appetite—to a specific social and economic situation. As economic historians might argue, this eroticized voicing of financial and sexual deprivation in Shakespeare's verse constitutes an example of "a whole literature of economic complaint," a new product of the sixteenth century and the printing press.[30] But this interpretation would ignore the poetic forces at work in poems such as Shakespeare's sonnet 37. For English literary history contains an earlier instantiation of this form of poetic subjectivity—medieval petitionary, or begging poetry. There, the poet makes a claim, though often camouflaged, on his royal or aristocratic addressee to recompense him for his poetic, bureaucratic, or personal service.[31] What makes this type of writing particularly apposite to my discussion of Shakespeare's sonnets is that, as Antony Hasler points out, one of the key verbal resources for such poetic self-articulation is the rhetorical interlacement of desire, poverty, and disease. In a skeletal form, these medieval speakers represent themselves as poor and in pain while constructing their patrons as embodiments of health and financial plenitude. In this subtype of begging poetry, Hasler writes, the poet speaks "under the sacrificial sign of an explicit recognition and internalization of deficiency, the mimesis of a willed embrace of frailty and defect" so that "the flawed subject is moved into a position of imaginary stability and coherence through encounters with a patronal surrogate."[32] These sickly court beggars write in the hope that identification with the wholeness of their patrons will restore them to financial and bodily health.

Late fourteenth and fifteenth century English poetry offers several examples of petitionary texts that ingeniously interweave the discourses of courtly love, disease, and money. "The Complaint of Chaucer to His Purse" by Geoffrey Chaucer (ca. 1399) wittily figures the purse as a courtly lady:

> To yow, my purse, and to noon other wight
> Complayne I, for ye be my lady dere.
> I am so sory, now that ye been lyght;
> For certes but yf ye make me hevy chere,
> Me were as leef be layd upon my bere;
> For which unto your mercy thus I crye,
> Beth hevy ageyn, or elles mot I dye.[33]

In all probability aimed at King Richard, Chaucer's poem is a plea for money, yet the speaker's financial insecurity is figured as a form of courtly disease. What he seeks is a remedy against this financial sickness in the form of a purse filled with money ("Beth hevy ageyn, or elles mot I dye"), which—given the courtly disposition of the poem—will also provide an ad hoc sexual orifice and alleviate his libidinous urges.

John Lydgate's "Letter to Gloucester" (ca. 1433) similarly personifies the poet's empty purse as a mortally sick patient:

> Riht myhty prynce, and it be your wille,
> Condescende leiser for to take,
> To seen the content of this litil bille,
> Which whan I wrot, myn hand I felte quake.
> Tokne of mornyng, weryd clothys blake
> Cause my purs was fal in gret rerage,
> Lynyng outward, his guttys wer outshake:
> Oonly for lak of plate and of coignage.[34]

The speaker presumes to address his powerful patron ("myhty prynce") because he has succumbed to a malady of an empty purse. Here poverty and disease again form an imaginative symbiosis, representing the poet as afflicted with a rhetorically ambivalent distress of ill health and lack of money. And although the poem appears to concern itself exclusively with money, like in Chaucer there are subtle erotic undertones in the image of the poet's "purs."[35] The patron, by contrast, is associated with a restorative potential of health and finances: "But ye, my Lord, may al our soor recure, / With a receyt of plate and of coignage" (lines 39–40).

But perhaps the most fascinating instance of this form of discourse is Thomas Hoccleve's "La male regle" (c. 1400–10).[36] This poem is a written petition addressed to Thomas Neville, Lord Fournivall, the historical treasurer of the exchequer, in which Hoccleve cites his financial troubles and requests payment of the annuity due to him. The text originates in the historical circumstances in which Hoccleve and other clerks in the Office of the Privy Seal found themselves when Henry IV's government had suspended payments of annuities for 1404–05.[37] As such, it is presented to its audience "as a token of a writer's esteem which a noble patron should reciprocate by the gift of money."[38] If the money so desired by Hoccleve should ever be disbursed, it will be paid as a direct result of his poetic text. As the speaker bluntly states,

> Lo, lat my lord the Fourneval, I preye,
> My noble lord þat now tresoreer,
> From thyn hynesse haue a tokne or tweye
> To paie me þat due is for this yeer,
> Of my yearly x li. in th'eschequeer. (417–21)

However, this direct appeal to Fournivall does not occur until line 417 of this 448-line poem. Instead, much of the text imitates the discourse of a sick man addressing Lord Health and supplicating the latter to restore the speaker to well-being:

> O precious tresor inconparable!
> O ground and roote of prosperitee!
> O excellent richesse commendable
> Abouen all þat in eerthe be!
> Who may susteene thyn aduersitee?
> What wight may him auante of worldly welthe,
> But if he fully stande in grace of thee,
> Eerthely god, piler of lyf, thow helthe?
>
> Whil thy power and excellent vigour,
> As was plesant vnto thy worthynesse,
> Regned in me, and was my gouernour,
> Than was I wel, tho [then] felte I no duresse.
> Tho farsid [filled] was I with hertes gladnesse.
> And now my body empty is, and bare
> Of ioie and ful of seekly heuynesse,
> Al poore of ese and ryche of euel fare. (1–16)

Hoccleve's poem oscillates between economic and medical discourses, producing a text in which "the literal sickness of body and metaphorical sickness of purse are intricately interwoven from beginning to end."[39] Health here becomes an economic category ("precious tresor," "prosperitee," "richesse," and "welthe"), whereas money — or the absence thereof — is conceptualized through the lens of corporeal frailty or wholeness, as sickness or health (his economic body is "bare / Of ioie" and "ful of seekly heuynesse," "poore of ese and ryche of euel fare"). His sufferings, as the poet elegantly phrases it later in the text, are caused by the "force of the penylees maladie" (130), a "seeknesse," he adds, "as wel of purs as body" (337–38).

But even as Hoccleve's subjectivity emerges out of an alignment of bodily sickness and monetary hardship, "La male regle" also repeats "the familiar rhetorical outlines of courtly love poetry, the abject posture of the lover-poet before the beloved, replaced by the professional poet and his patron."[40] As the imaginary site of bodily and financial restoration, Lord Health becomes the object of desire for the speaker, who often draws on the courtly vocabulary of erotic passion. By declaring early in the text, "Thy loue is lyf" (19), the speaker assumes the role of an unrequited lover who has been separated from his beloved ("what thow art now wel remembre I can" [27]). The final appeal to the allegorical god of health is particularly illuminating:

> My body and purs been at ones seeke,
> And for hem bothe, I, to thyn hy noblesse,
> As humblely as þat I kan, byseeke,
> With herte vnfeyned, reewe on our distresse.
> Pitee haue of myn harmful heuynesse.
> Releeue the repentant in disese.
> Despende on me a drop of thy largesse.
> Right in this wyse if it thee lyke and plese. (409–16)

In these lines, not only is the addressee expected to act as a courtly lady (to "reewe" on the speaker's "distresse" and "pitee" his "harmful heuynesse") but also, by placing the speaker in the position of a supplicant lover, the stanza rewrites his bodily ailment as a malady of love, where the grace and mercy of his Lord Health ("Now kythe on me thy mercy and thy grace" [406]) is the only thing that can "releeue...disese," that is, cure him. A begging clerk turns into a courtly lover afflicted with an erotic malady that simultaneously disguises and proclaims his appetite for money.

The trajectory of figuration adopted by the medieval poets—from actual poverty and sickness toward the language of desire—is an inversion of the rhetorical mechanisms of Shakespeare's begging sonnets, where disease and penury are first and foremost tropes of unrequited desire. That is, if the medieval begging poems originate in the poets' dire situations (real or feigned) and assume a courtly stance as a persuasive rhetorical device, early modern sonnets, regardless of the economic or social ambitions lurking behind the codes of Petrarchan writing, are inescapably grounded in the language of love, which they channel through the language of economic and medical woes. This may partly explain the radical shift in tone from the witty performances of comically abject medieval poets to the macabre agonies of Shakespearean Petrarchism: if you really need the money, you might as well be witty and entertaining.[41] Still, despite the reversed trajectories of tropology, these poetic efforts result in analogous structures of textual identity. At some point, it becomes difficult to distinguish between the verbal self created by Shakespeare's sick and destitute Petrarchan lover and identities imagined by the poor and afflicted civil servants toiling away at the Ricardian and Lancastrian courts. Whatever the unique social, historical, and poetic circumstances of Chaucer, Hoccleve, and Lydgate on the one hand, and of Shakespeare on the other, the language of their pathological self-examinations displays a remarkable degree of transperiodic commonality.

What this reading suggests, in other words, is that the poetics of selfhood formulated by English medieval begging poetry constitutes part of a discursive continuum to which Shakespeare's version of Petrarchism also belongs. In the young man sonnets, Shakespeare reappropriates the technologies of Petrarchan desire to conceptualize the speaker's relationship with his patron as a fantasy of a sick and impoverished lover's identification with his beloved, who is imagined as an epitome of economic splendor and corporeal well-being. But by opening the language of Petrarchan love to the economic considerations of the late Elizabethan culture of patronage, in the act of writing the poet simultaneously provokes into action medieval energies that saturate the poetic discourse at his disposal. The vernacular medieval poetics of corporeal infirmity and pecuniary deprivation latch themselves onto the Petrarchan figures of debilitating and depleting desire, delivering a hybrid form of subjectivity in which the Renaissance language of selfhood bears distinct traces of medieval begging. That is, Shakespeare's Petrarchan subjectivity preserves the structural core of an earlier vernacular model of poetic identity. As a result, the sonnets of sickness and poverty from the young man group find themselves in a position of historical dislocation: at once a product of Elizabethan rhetorical and political culture, the high-water mark of the Renaissance in England, and a version of medieval begging poetry, they disrupt the boundaries of traditional periodization and thrust English Petrarchism into a dialogue with its vernacular past.

The Shakespearean Subject, Medieval and Modern

The argument that in the young man sonnets Shakespeare's Petrarchan subjectivity retraces the contours of the textual identities constructed by medieval beggars invites further questioning of Shakespeare's modernity and, in broader terms, of the modernity of English Petrarchan subjectivity in general. What exactly makes the Shakespearean subject modern? And what makes the Hoccleavan and Lydgatean form of selfhood medieval? Fineman predicates what he calls "the invention of poetic subjectivity" in Shakespeare's sonnets upon the speaker's rejection of the object and his discovery of "the resonant hollowness of a fractured verbal self" in the differential domain of language.[42] This claim is an expansion of a pivotal (if agonizingly brief) essay by John Freccero, who argues that the innovation of Petrarchism consists of a reification of the linguistic sign and erosion of referentiality; this occasions the subject's separation from the object of desire by impenetrable confines of nonreferential linguistic solipsism.[43] "It is not at all clear," Gordon Braden comments on this point, "that what Petrarch worships in worshiping [Laura] is not the activity of his own creative imagination."[44] In Petrarchism, language and poetry intrude between the subject and the object of desire, replacing the latter with words and locking the former in a refractory hall of textual production. The verbal text, instead of mediating a relationship with the object of desire, becomes the sole "ground for the constitution of the self."[45] By contrast, medieval culture is more concerned with a transcendence of language for the sake of the object, and medieval selfhood emerges out of an encounter with an extraneous entity that engenders the self as a response to its demands—"the dialectic between an inward subjectivity and an external world" which, Lee Patterson writes, "provides the fundamental economy of the medieval idea of selfhood."[46] Where Dante's Beatrice gestures beyond the textual fabric of *La vita nuova* toward divine grace, Petrarch's Laura is nothing but an effect of verbal signification within the poet's idolatrously opaque text.

If we apply this theoretical opposition to the contrast between Shakespeare's begging poems and the earlier iterations of this form of textual subjectivity, however, the results are inconsistent. When we consider how the language of disease and restoration is implicated in the mapping out of subject-object relationships both in Shakespeare's sonnets and the medieval texts, it becomes almost impossible to pit the medieval against the early modern. Nancy Selleck articulates a brilliant challenge to Fineman's argument of solipsistic subjectivity in the sonnets. Shakespeare's Petrarchan poems, Selleck writes, are characterized by "their insistence on the self's dependence on its engagement with a *subjective* other, an other who cannot be controlled or stabilized—in short, an other who cannot be subsumed by the self...[their insistence] on continually reembracing the other rather than on turning inward."⁴⁷ She does not label this quality of Shakespearean selfhood as essentially medieval, yet the poet's begging sonnets, by bringing into focus the relationship between the needy subject and the plentiful object, display something of an anachronistic historicity. Medieval begging texts, with their dreams of medical, economic, and erotic reciprocity, presuppose the existence of two poles: the sickness- and poverty-ridden body of the poet, produced by deprivation; and the antithesis it finds in the splendor and perfection of the addressee, be it patron, physician, lover, or some combination of the three. The same can be said about sonnet 37, which is clearly produced by a desire—a desire whose structure remains medieval in its nature—for a beautiful, wholesome, and affluent beloved who will restore the frail and destitute lover to health and prosperity.

Yet even when Shakespeare is at his most medieval, as he is in sonnet 37, there are clear signs of encroaching modernity that disturbs the dialogic relationship of selfhood. For despite the lover's belief in his patron's recuperative powers, the restoration fantasized in the sonnet is illusory. The young man's perfection contains many qualities (health, prosperity, status, sexual gratification), but these qualities are the product of (the poet's) writing (they are "Intitled in their parts" [37.7]). Moreover, reciprocity between the two—"I make my loue engrafted to this store" (8)—similarly unfolds in writing as the pun on γράφειν *(graphein)* (Greek for writing) indicates.

As Christopher Warley suggests, the client-patron relationship "only exists ideally, in the speaker's lyric."[48] Both the patron's abundance and the process of restoration are, then, an effect of the poet's skillful handling of discourse. Thus if the object of desire is but an imitation of the idea of plenitude ("Whilst that this shadow doth such substance giue, / That I in thy abundance am suffic'd"), the act of healing also becomes a simulacrum.[49]

Moreover, suspicion that the object of the speaker's passion may be as flawed as the speaker himself occurs in other sonnets as well. In sonnet 33, the beloved is compared to the sun that can contaminate those around him, presumably including the speaker: "Suns of the world may staine, when heauens sun staineth" (14). Sonnet 34 likewise represents the beloved as the source of pollution, possibly venereal disease: "Why didst thou promise such a beautious day, / ...To let bace cloudes ore-take me in my way, / Hiding thy brau'ry in their rotten smoke" (1, 3–4).[50] Of course, in these examples as elsewhere in the young man sonnets, Shakespeare "is being suggestive, not conclusive," and we thus cannot "dismiss the beloved as irredeemably cankered."[51] Still, these images do imply the possibility of the beloved's status as a malicious pathogen that threatens the speaker's health.

In addition, the speaker often uses similar metaphors to describe himself and the young man, especially when dealing with physical or ethical corruption. In sonnet 12, thinking of the young man's inevitable death, the speaker invokes "lofty trees...barren of leaues" (5). Yet, in sonnet 73, the speaker's self-portrait rehearses the same image: "That time of yeeare thou maist in me behold, / When yellow leaues, or none, or few doe hange / Vpon those boughes" (1–3). Similarly, the lover's decaying body is likened to a crumbling building in sonnet 146: "Why so large cost hauing so short a lease, / Dost thou vpon thy fading mansion spend?" (5–6). But earlier, in sonnet 95, the same trope is applied to the male beloved: "Oh what a mansion haue those vices got, / Which for their habitation chose out thee, / Where beauties vaile doth couer euery blot" (9–11). Both the speaker and his perfect friend conceal "blots" and carry "infection" (36.3, 95.11, 67.1, 111.10). These verbal echoes between the speaker's representations of himself and his beloved create a subtle network of associations that subvert the original difference between the lover and his patron, enclosing the two in a Petrarchan web of linguistic mirroring. The distinction between self and other is irreparably compromised, producing a subjectivity that articulates itself by relying on its internal verbal resources rather than on the presence of an other. Through this fascination with the subject's narcissistic discourse, modernity reasserts itself in Shakespeare's sonnets.

The dual temporal dynamic of subject-object interaction that operates in Shakespeare's sonnets, namely, their simultaneous adherence to the medieval model of recuperative transcendence and to the Petrarchan short-circuit of language that folds back on the subject, is exemplified by sonnet 118:

> Like as to make our appetites more keene
> With eager compounds we our pallat vrge,
> As to preuent our malladies vnseene,
> We sicken to shun sicknesse when we purge.
> Euen so being full of your nere cloying sweetnesse,
> To bitter sawces did I frame my feeding;
> And sicke of wel-fare found a kind of meetnesse,
> To be diseas'd ere that there was true needing.
> Thus pollicie in loue t'anticipate
> The ills that were, not grew to faults assured,
> And brought to medicine a healthfull state
> Which rancke of goodnesse would by ill be cured.
> But thence I learne and find the lesson true,
> Drugs poyson him: that so fell sicke of you.

The sonnet's big question concerns the beloved's ambivalent relationship with health and sickness. The young man's original characteristic is "sweetnesse" (and arguably health), but as the poem progresses the lover realizes that it is his object of desire that makes him sick, describing himself in the end as one "that so fell sicke of you." From a locus of perfection to a locus of sickness, the beloved undertakes a kind of semantic somersault. It is also worth noting, however, that the beloved's initial sweetness is "nere cloying," where "nere" could mean both "ne'er" (never) and "near," marking the object of desire as a possible source of the speaker's disease earlier than the last line. The speaker's error was to believe that his passion for the beloved was a form of wholesomeness, but the text of the poem proves the supposition to have been false.[52] The treatment he received was aimed at a healthy body, whereas he, by way of his desire-as-sickness, was sick all along. The beloved then appears to be a source of sickness, not health. And yet, provided the original medical logic of the sonnet is sound (i.e., you can "sicken to shun sicknesse" and your illness can "by ill be cured"), the beloved simultaneously holds the power to cure the sick lover.

Out of these semantic instabilities, the object of desire in sonnet 118 emerges as a kind of *pharmakon*: cure that kills, poison that restores health.[53] The result is a poem of dual allegiance: at one level, it upholds the medieval scenario of patronal therapy, positing the young man as the source of restoration and health. But at the same time, a counter current of Petrarchan energy destroys the illusion of plenitude promised by the object of desire. When both lover and patron assume attributes of lack, distinctions between subject and object fade, and the sonnet enacts negative identification, obviating the possibility of the begging lover's transition from deficiency to wholeness. At once a medieval begging poem and a statement of Petrarchan self-referentiality, sonnet 118 traverses the pre-modern literary landscape, resisting confinement in either literary period.

However, the same indeterminacy of historical attribution obtains if we take a closer look at Hoccleve's "La male regle." There one finds inchoate yet tangible forms of the linguistic and poetic order that we habitually associate with Petrarchism. Although the poem ostensibly enacts a stark contrast between the needy and sick poet and his exemplary patron, in some respects the possibility of identificatory recuperation is subverted in Hoccleve's text in ways that anticipate Shakespeare's Petrarchan solipsism. Hoccleve's "penylees maladie" is a consequence of what he insistently calls his "misreule" (290), failure to regulate his body and its appetites. His physical sufferings stem from eating and drinking at London taverns, which has brought him to this pitiful state and made him a "mirour...of riot and excesse" (330). His visits to taverns and lewd houses, in turn, lead to an empty purse, and by way of a circular logic this lack of funds prevents any improvement in his health: "By coyn, I gete may swich medecyne / As may myn hurtes all, þat me greeue, / Exyle cleene, and voide me of pyne" (446–48). This further exacerbates his sickness, but it is the same sickness "as wel of purs as body" that "hath refreyned / [Him] fro tauerne and othir wantonnesse" (338–39)—that is, his disease of an empty purse has in a sense safeguarded him from temptations. As Robert Meyer-Lee notes, for the speaker of "La male regle" money is "both the vehicle and cure of his 'misreule.'"[54] But that implication makes the speaker's somatic and financial disease a form of moral health, so that restoration of his financial well-being will likely lead to further excess and, in turn, disease. Lord Health becomes a menacing figure promising the petitioner not (or not only) wholeness but further suffering and deprivation.

Furthermore, the homoerotic relationship between the poet and Lord Health is complicated by the intrusion of Sickness, a female personification. Sickness is called a "fo" to both speaker and his lord (22, 52), yet her relationship with Lord Health is less straightforward. When the speaker exclaims, "If þat thy fauour twynne from a wight, / Smal is his ese and greet is his greuance" (17–18), he indicates that his affliction is a gift from Health rather than Sickness. But if disease is controlled by Lord Health as much as corporeal well-being is, it makes Sickness at once an antithesis and a semantic extension of Health. Like Shakespeare's *pharmakon,* then, Hoccleve's addressee and object of desire is at once salubrious and harmful, remedy and poison. Tellingly, the rhetoric of the speaker's relationship with Health and with Sickness defies a clear-cut opposition. In the same way that the poet metaphorizes Health as wealth, he describes his relationship with Sickness through a monetary trope: "Seeknesse, y meene... / Habundantly þat paieth me my wage" (118–19). Besides, if Sickness, who is linguistically and conceptually imbricated in Health, is also a prosopopeic projection of Hoccleve's own disease, we can question the very status of Lord Health as an object extraneous to the speaker's subjectivity rather than an effect of the latter's plaintive discourse. In other words, instead of providing the beggar poet with a stable point of imaginary plenitude, "La male regle" engages him in an endless semantic play of *différance* that anticipates the auricular echo chambers of Petrarchism. Hoccleve's relationship with his patron takes on a provisional Renaissance quality, plunging the subject of "La male regle" into a proto-Shakespearean nightmare of an unfulfilled promise of restorative identification.

What emerges out of such a medievalizing reading of Shakespeare's sonnets is the impossibility of compartmentalizing poetic history in the strictly ordered strata of the past and the modern. Shakespeare's invention of poetic subjectivity turns out to be a recollection of an earlier form of poetic identity, whereas Hoccleve's medieval self-articulation proves strikingly modern in some respects. The medieval beggars and the Shakespearean subject belong to the same discursive tradition that, entwining the figures of disease, erotic longing, and economic favor, produces a subjectivity ravaged by different kinds of desire, a subjectivity citable and adaptable in different contexts. The remarkable thing about this tradition is that within its boundaries it is extremely difficult to organize individual texts in a temporal or structural progression. It is not only that Shakespeare recites a largely medieval script of identity while Chaucer, Lydgate and Hoccleve anticipate certain aspects of Petrarchan and post-Petrarchan subjectivity; the complexity and intricacy of the subject's relationship with the object of plenitude do not necessarily increase as we move from the medieval to the Petrarchan poems. Instead of presenting a linear history of subjectivity, the nominally earlier and later poems scatter themselves across the temporal axis, encouraging an exchange of imaginative resources among diverse poetic voices.

The Aesthetics of Disgust in the Dark Lady Sonnets

In contrast to the young man's dubious position between sickness and health, the dark mistress plays a clearly defined role in Shakespeare's sonnets. In the second sub-sequence, the object of love herself and the passion she arouses in the lover become the primary instances of sickness, the originary points of the speaker's erotic affliction. But the dark lady's involvement in the lover's disease is twofold. First, she acts as an exogenous pathogen that infects the speaker in an act of erotic intimacy, and second, the sonnets pathologize the speaker's erotic attachment to the lady by presenting this desire as a form of deviant, perverse attraction, with the sick nature of this eroticism itself becoming a form of disease.

Sonnet 141 explores the relationships between these two figurations of disease:

> In faith I doe not loue thee with mine eyes,
> For they in thee a thousand errors note,
> But 'tis my heart that loues what they dispise,
> Who in dispight of view is pleasd to dote.
> Nor are mine eares with thy toungs tune delighted,
> Nor tender feeling to base touches prone,
> Nor taste, nor smell, desire to be inuited
> To any sensuall feast with thee alone:
> But my fiue wits, nor my fiue sences can
> Diswade one foolish heart from seruing thee,
> Who leaues vnswai'd the likenesse of a man,
> Thy proud hearts slaue and vassall wretch to be:
>> Onely my plague thus farre I count my gaine,
>> That she that makes me sinne, awards me paine.

The poem's explicitly medical vocabulary is concentrated in the couplet, where the lover claims that what his desire for the lady has bought him is nothing but "plague" and "paine," and the origin of this affliction in sensual "sinne" makes the speaker's sufferings symptoms of an erotic disease he has contracted from the lady. This is not an isolated occurrence, for in another dark lady sonnet, the disease of love is also portrayed as a result of malicious intersubjective transference: in sonnet 137, under the influence of love, the speaker's "heart and eyes.../...to this false plague are...now transferred" (13–14). Branded as the source of the lover's infection, the dark lady assumes her position in the sequence as a dangerous agent of pollution and contamination.

The rhetoric of contagion has a long history in Western theories of love. Ficino in his *Commentary on Plato's Symposium* (1484) refers to love as "amatory infection," not dissimilar from "itch, mange, leprosy, pneumonia, consumption, dysentery, pink-eye, and the plague."[55] Closer to home, a shepherd in Barnabe Googe's *Eclogues* (1563) rails against love which "all infects the blood about / and boils in every part," whereas Barnabe Barnes in *Parthenophil and Parthenophe* (1593) refers to his mistress's "womanlike contagion" as source of his erotic sickness.[56] It is, however, useful to remember that figures of infectious venereal disease took on a more specific medical meaning in early modern England, a country ravaged by an epidemic of syphilis.[57] Shakespeare's interest in this disease is well documented.[58] To take the most famous example, sonnet 154 pictures a well in which a Nymph dips Cupid's "heart inflaming brand" (2). The well has since become "a bath, and healthfull remedy, / For men diseasd" (11–12), but the curative effect of this bath has failed to restore the speaker to health: "I my Mistrisse thrall, / Came there for cure and this by that I proue, / Loues fire heates the water, water cooles not loue," he laments (12–14). As several commentators have observed, this describes one of the commonest methods of treating syphilis in the period—the use of sweating baths.[59] In fact, the "plague" the speaker claims to have contracted from his mistress in sonnet 141 was one of the early modern ways to designate the French disease.[60] Shakespeare's accusations that his mistress has infected him with erotic malady are also attuned to the gender politics of early modern syphilis. As Kevin Siena demonstrates, early modern venercology "showed an overwhelming tendency to present women as causal agents, to discuss contagion almost solely in terms of male victims, and to present images of women as deceptive and dangerous, female biology as pathological and dirty."[61] Just as in early modern medical discourse the culpability in heterosexual contagion was routinely assigned to the female partner, Shakespeare's mistress is portrayed as the infectious source of the lover's "plague" and "paine."[62]

Of course, fascinating as these historical parallels between Shakespeare's sonnets and early modern syphilography are, they merely redeploy the familiar tropes of love poetry. The point I would like to stress is that the images of erotic infection in sonnet 141, syphilis or otherwise, form part of a more radical and ingenious rhetorical configuration of disease. The reference to contagion in the couplet ("Onely my plague thus farre I count my gaine, / That she that makes me sinne, awards me paine") comes on the heels of, and in this sense offers a commentary on, a detailed catalog of the beloved's "errors." Thus, by casting in medical language the revolt of the "fiue sences" that the lady triggers in the speaker, Shakespeare turns his lover's attraction toward a repulsive object of desire into a pathology. Meticulously striking out one sense after another as a source of enjoyment, the poet removes conventional pleasure from the sonnet, emphasizing instead the lover's revulsion at his mistress. The original disgust of the eyes is lent to the other members of the sensorium, none of which "desire to be inuited / To any sensuall feast" with the mistress. The lady's appearance, voice, taste, smell, and skin all reject the idea of beauty and erotic appeal.[63] But while the lover may "dispise" her repulsive features, "dispight" all his loathing, the dark lady nonetheless succeeds in exciting his desire (his heart "in dispight of view, is pleasd to dote"). Although the visual, auricular, tactile, gustatory, and olfactory impressions nauseate the lover, his heart cannot overcome its passion for this ugly object. Quite the contrary, the lady's "errors" become the lover's eros.

This opens for the subject the possibility of a counterpleasure—a form of enjoyment characterized, as Karmen MacKendrick writes in her study of unorthodox forms of jouissance, by the "disruptive refusal of the usual meanings of pleasure (stimulation leading to gratification)" and the "tendency to displace by intensification."[64] Such counterpleasures deviate from the culturally prescribed trajectories of development and latch themselves onto atypical and unsuitable objects. Indeed, what the Shakespearean lover pursues is a form of counterpleasure in which beauty is displaced by ugliness and desirability is corrupted by disgust. And as the medical references in the couplet remind us, such attraction toward a repulsive object also constitutes a form of perverse, pathological affect—a form of disease. He is sick not only because she has infected him with "plague" (or syphilis, if we want to insist on the historicist reading), but also because his love is a sick counterpleasure: he desires what cannot be desired under the auspices of reason—an unattractive body that "leaues vnswai'd the likenesse of a man."

In sonnet 150, the poet makes this emotional oxymoron of repugnance and attraction the central object of poetic rumination:

> Oh from what powre hast thou this powrefull might,
> VVith insufficiency my heart to sway,
> To make me giue the lie to my true sight,
> And swere that brightnesse doth not grace the day?
> Whence hast thou this becomming of things il,
> That in the very refuse of thy deeds,
> There is such strength and warrantise of skill,
> That in my minde thy worst all best exceeds?
> Who taught thee how to make me loue thee more,
> The more I heare and see iust cause of hate,
> Oh though I loue what others doe abhor,
> VVith others thou shouldst not abhor my state.
> If thy vnworthinesse raisd loue in me,
> More worthy I to be belou'd of thee.

Structured as a series of unanswered questions, the poem records the speaker's frenzied musings on the sick nature of his desire, where disgust and irresistible attraction are mingled. How is it possible, he wonders, to love someone so odious? Where does her power ("this powrefull might") to move his heart to passion despite her imperfections ("VVith insufficiency my heart to sway") come from? These are not idle questions, for they concern the very nature of love in the dark lady sonnets. The speaker desires a woman totally devoid of any attractive qualities; on the contrary, her repulsive—possibly diseased—features ("things il") and moral failings should repel. For him, however, even "the very refuse of [her] deeds," including the phrase's potential medical overtones,[65] serves as an aphrodisiac. The lover's sick passion for an object of disgust becomes a disturbing technique of subjectivity.

That the Shakespearean lover desires "what others doe abhor" speaks to the paradoxical ability of disgust (and of related emotions such as abhorrence and abomination) to combine aversion and attraction.[66] Modern theorists have variously referred to this fascinating quality of disgust as "a certain macabre allure...an eroticism of disgust," "a vortex of summons and repulsion," "the allure of the disgusting," and "the ambivalence of attraction and repulsion."[67] But already in Shakespearean England, Benedict Robinson suggests, disgust operated as "at once desire's opposite and a form of desire."[68] Delving into this paradox of disgust as counterpleasure, Shakespeare articulates a precarious form of subjectivity that teases the limits of normalcy and stability. Traces of medical language in the sonnet ("becomming of things il...refuse of thy deeds") again remind us that we are dealing with a pathology of affect: loving "what others doe abhor" is a perverse, queer form of eroticism that can only be conceived of as a disease. The common presumption, Carolyn Korsmeyer argues, is that "there is no enjoyment that a sane person would take in the irredeemably disgusting."[69] Hence we see the concluding self-pathologizing gesture draw a parallel between the dark lady's possibly sick and definitely sickening body and the lover's own disease: "VVith others thou shouldst not abhor my state." The love between the speaker and the mistress becomes a mechanism of inscribing sameness (abhorrence) among two equally disgusting bodies. The lover's disease stems from the lady's power to infect him with the "plague" of desire, but his perverse desire for a repulsive mistress plunges him deeper into the abyss of sickness.[70]

This pathological process, however, is tightly entangled with the lover's verbal activity. Consider sonnet 147:

> My loue is as a feauer longing still,
> For that which longer nurseth the disease,
> Feeding on that which doth preserue the ill,
> Th'vncertaine sicklie appetite to please:
> My reason the Phisition to my loue,
> Angry that his prescriptions are not kept
> Hath left me, and I desperate now approoue,
> Desire is death, which Phisick did except.
> Past cure I am, now Reason is past care,
> And frantick madde with euer-more vnrest,
> My thoughts and my discourse as mad mens are,
> At randon from the truth vainely exprest.
>   For I haue sworne thee faire, and thought thee bright,
>   Who art as black as hell, as darke as night.

Booth squeamishly describes the sonnet as a "gross expansion" on the tradition in which "love or the beloved is likened to a disease."[71] Indeed, much of the sonnet records the lover's unpalatably pathological state. The ambiguous syntax of the opening quatrain shifts the attributes of sensuous insatiability and its devouring effects back and forth, from the subject to the disease and then back to the subject, with his love fever longing for what causes and fuels the disease ("longing still / For that which longer nurseth the disease"), and the disease in turn nourishing itself on the subject who "doth preserue the ill." The subject is complicit in his own malady: by consuming the disease, he offers his own body to be eaten by it, whatever the precise historical diagnosis may be.[72] But the couplet ("For I haue sworne thee faire, and thought thee bright, / Who art as black as hell, as darke as night") interrupts the lover's self-pathologizing monologue, introducing the object of desire ("thee") into the history of illness. In this instant, both the lover's bodily sufferings ("feauer") and his madness ("frantick madde with euer-more vnrest, / My thoughts and my discourse as mad mens are") are touted as initiated by the mistress; she is charged with engendering the speaker's moribund condition. The sonnet again reminds us that the pleasure the speaker takes in his mistress's abhorrent body ("black as hell, as darke as night") is a form of disease.

But in addition to suggesting that the cause of the lover's malady lies in the act of suspending abjection, the couplet also explores the role language plays in a situation where enjoying an abhorrent object becomes a source of pleasure. Niklas Luhmann describes the historical process by which idealization, a code of love in which passion finds its justification in the supreme qualities of the beloved (e.g., medieval courtly love or Petrarchism), is replaced by another, paradoxical, regime of passion where the beloved's beauty or virtue no longer plays a key role in the arousal of desire but, rather, the power of the lover's imagination creates an erotic attitude toward an object otherwise considered unattractive.[73] Similarly, in Shakespeare's sonnets, by creating a verbal tapestry that belies the dark lady's ugliness—such as in sonnet 147's final couplet—the lover overcomes his abhorrence.[74] Fineman reads this verbal gesture of accentuating the difference between reality (what *is*) and text (what *is thought and sworn*) as Shakespeare's formulation of a new poetics of linguistic and sexual difference, a "novel desire *of* language" itself.[75] But his argument ignores the pathological aspect of the desire the poem articulates. The lover succumbs to a debilitating disease of love as a result of his paradoxical linguistic activity. Although the third quatrain also suggests that linguistic corruption may be a consequence or a symptom of the disease, the logical operator "for" in the couplet cancels this possibility, positing nonveridical discourse as the origins of the lover's affliction, his "feauer" produced by the work of poetic language. While for Cynthia Marshall "the poem is ultimately less concerned with physical, moral, or emotional effects of the 'disease' than with its debilitating effects on 'discourse,'"[76] I would suggest, conversely, that sonnet 147 is preoccupied with the debilitating effects that language and discourse may have on the lover's health. It is not that his language is corrupted because of the lover's fever; rather, he is sick with fever because language—an instrument of the imagination that makes overcoming disgust possible—has corrupted him. Other poems in the sequence articulate a similar argument. In sonnet 150 the dark lady's disturbing power to compel the lover to lust after her abhorrent body is also posited as an aesthetic ruse, as "such strength and warrantise of skill." And in sonnet 137, because the lover "put[s] fair truth vpon so foule a face," "to this false plague are [his eyes] now transferred" (12, 14). Poetry, in other words, is complicit in this pathology of affect.

But if the lover's pathological desire for the dark lady requires language in order to emerge, so is the birth of language contingent upon the presence of a sick and sickening female body around which poetic discourse can be constructed. If there were no dark lady—no disgusting object, no source of plague, no nauseating infection emanating from her body—there would be no need for poctry. Put otherwise, Shakespeare's poetics reveals itself to be ultimately dependent on the dark lady's "foule" ugliness. As Naomi Baker shows, in early modern English literature, the poetics of revolting eroticism is closely linked with a celebration of masculine creativity. Articulating male desire for an unattractive female body becomes a way to explore the potentialities of artistic representation: "The representation of (female) physical ugliness is thus crucial to the construction of (male) art and the male artist, a prerequisite for the display of his redemptive creativity."[77] We witness a similar dynamic at work in Shakespeare's sonnet sequence. What sets Shakespeare apart from his contemporaries in this regard, however, is his insistence on encoding his artistic prowess in a language of disease. This disease of love is made possible through verbal manipulation ("fairing the foule with Arts faulse borrow'd face" [127.6]), but for this poetry to take place at all, the poet requires the revulsion of his beloved's physical and moral ugliness, which continues to persist in his discourse as the originary locus of poetic desire. The complex imagery of sickness associated with the dark lady remains a constant mental object against and "dispight" which his subjectivity unfolds. The very possibility of poetry in Shakespeare's sonnets is predicated on pathology.

Shakespearean Pathologies *avant la Lettre:* Henryson's *Testament of Cresseid*

It is tempting to read the poetics of disgust in Shakespeare's sequence as a prefiguration of modern aesthetics, akin to Fineman's "novel desire *of* language." It is, however, not without precedent in English poetry, and to support my argument I would like to turn to Robert Henryson's *Testament of Cresseid* (c. 1494)—or *The Testament of Creseyde,* as it was known to early modern English readers.[78] At just 616 lines, *The Testament* is a remarkable poem. Henryson undertakes a continuation of Chaucer's *Troilus and Criseyde* (c. 1381–86) but ends up writing an original proto-Renaissance postscript to the Trojan legend.[79] But from the more narrow perspective that constitutes my concern in these pages, he codifies for the English vernacular imagination a poetics of disease in which the sick—and sickening—feminine body functions as an object of desire for the masculine subject and as a reluctantly acknowledged source of poetic inspiration.

Henryson's poem picks up where Chaucer left off.[80] The narrator, having finished reading *Troilus and Criseyde*, opens up another book that traces Creseyde's destiny after her separation from Troylus. Abandoned by Diomede, she becomes a prostitute in the Greek camp, denounced by everyone but her father. In her exasperation, she blames Venus and Cupid for her misfortunes and immediately after that falls into a trance and has a dream vision. In it, the seven planetary gods, incensed at what they perceive as Creseyde's ingratitude, condemn her to leprosy. Upon awakening, Creseyde in horror discovers her physical ugliness caused by the disease. She moves into a leper house, where by accident she is spotted by Troylus riding past, although the two do not recognize each other. When his identity is revealed to her, stricken with guilt and remorse, she composes her own testament and dies. Upon hearing the news of her death, Troylus erects a tomb for her and engraves an epitaph on its walls. Henryson concludes his poem by warning other women to mark Creseyde's actions and her fate.

The central imaginative movement of the poem is Creseyde's transformation from a paragon of beauty to a repulsive mass of leprous flesh and the ensuing surge in the intensity of disgust. The initial change deals with moral revolt, although the distinction between physical and moral ugliness is uncertain in medieval texts as the former frequently functions as a trope of the latter.[81] When Crescyde becomes a prostitute in the Greek camp, "fayre Creseyde / the floure and a per se / Of Troy and Grece," Henryson exclaims, is forced "to chaunge in fylthe al [her] femynite / And be with fleshly luste so maculate" (78–81). Once the ideal of a courtly lady, Creseyde is now a whore among the Greeks, "takyng [her] foule plesaunce" (83). As she herself says, by all her former lovers she is "excluded / as abiecte odyous" (133). Soon these moral "fylthe" and "foule plesaunce" turn into physical ugliness as the gods engage in their retributive justice. Cynthia's punishment of leprosy is particularly devastating:

> Thy christal eyen menged with blode I make
> Thy voice so clere vnplesaunt heer and hace
> Thy lusty lere [i.e., complexion] ouerspred with spottes blake
> And lumpes hawe [i.e., lead-coloured] appering in thy face
> Where thou comest eche man shal flye the place
> Thus shalte the go beggyng fro house to hous
> With cuppe and clapper lyke a lazarous. (337–43)

The stanza, through graphically disturbing images of gradual corporeal deterioration, imagines the transformation of a female body from health and beauty to sickness and decay. By the time Creseyde awakes from her dream, she is disfigured beyond recognition: her skin is marred by "spottes blake," her eyes are filled with discharge mixed with blood, and hideous "lumpes" have formed on her face. She also loses her voice, which completes this picture of physical decomposition.

This description of Creseyde holds well alongside the actual images of medieval leprosy. Susan Zimmerman paints the following picture of a medieval leper: "nerve–numbed or wasted limbs, suppurating lesions, and a contorted or mangled face, with thickened lips and swollen eyebrows...a distinctive, fetid breath (caused by multiple secondary infections); and...a hoarse, unnatural voice (attributable to damaged nerves in the larynx and vocal cords)."[82] Such parallels with the text of *The Testament* demonstrate, as a number of scholars have pointed out, Henryson's knowledge of the symptomatology of the disease.[83] Incidentally, early modern readers of Henryson's poem may have interpreted Creseyde's disease differently. In the sixteenth century, with the relative decrease of leprosy and advent of syphilis, the omnivorous French disease incorporated many of the medical and cultural connotations of its medieval counterpart. As Sander L.

Gilman writes, while by the late sixteenth century leprosy had "all but vanished" in western Europe, "its iconography remained as part of the popular storehouse of images of disease and pollution and was immediately attached to the new disease of syphilis."[84] And while attempts to argue that Henryson infects his heroine with syphilis have been received skeptically (syphilis had not reached Scotland until 1497, at least several years after the assumed date of *The Testament*),[85] earlier literary and medical texts did contribute to mapping out the imaginative and discursive repertoire of the new French disease.

Yet Henryson's description of Creseyde's revoltingly diseased body is not a medical document but a literary event. Essentially, it is an anticourtly statement, a counterblazon. *The Testament*, a continuation of Chaucer's romance, openly acknowledges its origins in the tradition of courtly love. So when Henryson's text reduces Creseyde, the exemplary medieval courtly lady, to a compendium of signs of bodily corruption, the aim is not only to shock the reader with gruesome details or dazzling clinical knowledge but to disturb the discourse of erotic ideality through an insistence that revolt and attraction can be joined in the same form of subjectivity. As a modern critic puts it, leprosy is "the quintessence of disgusting disease";[86] and Henryson's own text links Creseyde's sickness and revulsion. As Cynthia summarizes the gods' sentence, Creseyde is "In al her lyfe with payne to be opprest / And tourment sore / with sikenesse incurable / And to al louers be abomynable" (306–08). But while Creseyde's loathsome, hideous, foul body would appear completely detached from the discourse of erotic attraction, Henryson's counterblazon, through a direct reference to the discourse of courtly love, explores the operations of desire within the structures of disgust. In this, Henryson's *Testament* anticipates the pairing of attraction and revulsion in Shakespeare's Petrarchan sonnets.

The Testament traces the flows of a pathological desire intertwined with disgust by focusing on the attachments that the two principal male characters—Troylus and the narrator—form with Creseyde. The case for Troylus's sick desire for Creseyde is in some ways the more obvious one, given that Henryson's poem is a postscript to their love affair. In one of the most influential readings of the relationship between Creseyde and her former lover, Felicity Riddy uses Julia Kristeva's theory of abjection to argue that Troylus's subjectivity is delineated through the exclusion of Creseyde. To recapitulate briefly, for Kristeva the abject is a form of the disgusting (refuse, putrefaction, and death), which she associates with the maternal body. In order for the boundaries of subjectivity to be consolidated, the abject is expelled from the body as the nonself, the Other: "The abject is not an ob-ject facing me, which I name or imagine...what is *abject*, on the contrary, the jettisoned object, is radically excluded and draws me toward the place where meaning collapses...refuse and corpses *show me* what I permanently thrust aside in order to live."[87] In other words, the subject is formed through expunging the abject, but the identity achieved this way is brittle and can easily be shattered, for abjection always continues to threaten to disturb the order of subjectivity. Although "ejected beyond the scope of the possible, the tolerable, the thinkable," the abject nonetheless lurks there—"beseeches, worries, and fascinates desire....[Abjection] disturbs identity....Excrement and its equivalents (decay, infection, disease, corpse, etc.) stand for the danger to identity that comes from without: the ego threatened by the non-ego, society threatened by the outside, life by death."[88]

To return to the poem, according to Felicity Riddy's interpretation, Creseyde's leprous body is abject, and the text, by repeatedly expunging her (to her father's home then to the leper house then to the grave), enacts a "struggle to constitute a stable masculine identity," in which Creseyde is "cast out [for the sake of] making masculinity.... She has to have been exiled, repudiated, and stricken with disease so that Troilus can lay claim to the 'humanitie' which she attributes to him."[89] Although this reading is attractive, it ignores the emotional bond between Troylus and Creseyde that is never fully dissolved and, one could argue, in fact reestablished in Henryson's poem. The most powerful expression of this erotic connection comes at the moment of their chance meeting, when Troylus, looking at the abominable shape in front of him, for some inexplicable reason thinks of Creseyde and the desire for her that once possessed him:

> Yet than her loke into his mynde he brought
> The swete vysage / and amorous blenkyng
> Of fayre Creseyde / somtyme his owne derlyng.   (502–04)

As Henryson explains, the image of an object can be stamped upon one's imagination ("The ydol of a thyng in case may be / So depe depe enprynted in the fatansy" [507–08]); Troylus's memory brings back to his mind the original image of Creseyde as a "swete" and "amorous" object of passion. But this act of memorial reconstruction destabilizes the taxonomy of ugliness and beauty in the lover's mind: it "deludeth the wyttes outwardly / And so appereth in forme and lyke estate / With in the mynde / as it was figurate," Henryson writes (509–11). The effect of Troylus's act of recollection is that Creseyde's image becomes a trope ("in the mynde...figurate"), a sign of what it is not. Her ugliness now signifies her lost beauty, so her "swete visage / and amorous blenkyng" become legible through her leprous flesh, the "byles blake" (339) that "ouerspred in her visage" (395). Through the work of memory, eroticism is inscribed right at the center of disgust. It is also worth noting that what Troylus feels for Creseyde is called "affectioun" (as other lepers exclaim after she receives the money, "yon lorde hath more affectioun / howe euer it be / vnto yon lazarous / Than to vs al" [530–32]).

The word may appear innocuous enough, but four stanzas later Creseyde herself uses it to condemn her own ruinous sexual desires: "My mynde on flesshly foule affectioun / Was enclyned to lustes lecherous" (558–59).

What the encounter between Troylus and Creseyde offers the readers, in other words, is a sketch of proto-Shakespearean paradoxical desire in which the lover's imagination overcomes the improbability of passion at the sight of ugliness. Looking at the abominable leper in front of him and remembering Creseyde, Troylus finds his body in a fit of erotic sensation:

> A sparke of loue than tyl his hert couth spring
> And kyndeled his body in a fyre
> With hote feuer / in swette / and trymblyng
> Him toke / whyle he was redy to expire
> To beare his shylde his brest begon to tyre
> Within a whyle he chaunged many a hewe
> And neuertheles nat one another knewe. (512–18)

Here Henryson more or less admits that Troylus desires Creseyde, although it is impossible to determine whether the onrush of passionate desire he feels is limited to the mental image and is not tainted by the repulsive attraction of the decomposing flesh in front of him. In any case, the encounter between Troylus and leprous Creseyde is charged with affective intensity. The two former lovers do not recognize each other, but the reader cannot fail to recognize in this scene Troylus as the prototypical subject of erotic desire.

As in Shakespeare's sonnets, however, the interaction between a desiring subject and a disgusting object is carried out in terms of pathology. Riddy is adamant that in Henryson's poem leprosy is "troped as a judgment on Cresseid, and not a contagion...isolated, [she] should infect herself."[90] But the actual text of Henryson's poem points in the opposite direction, for in the process of his encounter with Creseyde,

Troylus's desire takes a form of disease as his allegedly unassailable body falls prey to sickness. He finds himself "in a fyre," he suffers from "hote feuer" and "trymblyng," he sweats, loses stamina, changes "many a hewe," and is "redy to expire." Riddy sees this as a sign of his body being "youthful, sexual, and male."[91] However, to me this seems to be a misreading of the passage. Not only is Henryson's language pointedly medical here; his vocabulary is sinister. What is being described in these lines is a debilitating, destructive disease that puts Troylus's body at risk. Troylus's vision of his own fate in Chaucer's romance—"I woot that whan ye next upon me se, / So lost have I myn hele and ek myn hewe" (5.1402–03)—is realized at the end of Henryson's poem, when we watch his encounter with Creseyde translate into an experience of sickness.

What is the nature of Troylus's disease? On the one hand, it is possible to read his disease as a consequence of pathological intersubjectivity that links the two bodies through contagion.[92] *The Testament* puts Troylus and Creseyde in close contact that suspends disgust, which might suggest that Creseyde's disgusting body operates as the polluting source of Troylus's disease. But on the other hand, as Shakespeare's dark lady sonnets remind us, the disease may be not only metonymic (a result of contagion) but metaphoric as well: it is a figurative response to a "sparke of loue" kindled by the presence of a disgustingly septic body, and as such it bespeaks the pathological character of this kind of eroticism. The passion that seizes Troylus at the sight of the leprous Creseyde cannot be characterized in terms other than perversion and sickness. Of course, Shakespeare's sonnets, in making the same aberrant sexual appetite for a revolting female body a matter of poetic reflection, in terms of complexity and poetic daring are removed quite significantly from Henryson's poem. The latter merely adumbrates the tentative contours of subjectivity haunted by pathological affect in the English poetic imagination. Nonetheless, in articulating his questions about the disease of love in the sonnets, Shakespeare reveals his dependence on this poetics of disgust in the production of which Henryson's text is directly involved, with the Renaissance poet's reflection on abject desire predicated upon its prefiguration in vernacular literary discourse.

The proto-Shakespearean scenario of pathological eroticism that marks the desiring subject's attraction to an object of disgust as sickness is also explored in *The Testament* through the narrator's relationship with his heroine. It is easy to miss, behind both the linguistic pyrotechnics of Henryson's description of Creseyde and the Chaucerian legacy that urges us to focus on her relationship with Troylus, that the poem's first-person speaker also forges a libidinal bond with Creseyde's abominable body. The narrator, Catherine Cox suggests, "seems at once to desire and to detest her....He rejects the body of the feminine, yet desires it; he resents his own dependency, and punishes the feminine because his desire cannot be satisfied without her."[93] His desire for Creseyde may be tenuous and elusive, but it represents one of the key poetic strategies in Henryson's text.

By assuming the role identical to that of Chaucer's narrator in *Troilus and Criseyde*, the speaker already identifies with the latter's imperfectly concealed passion for Creseyde. Speaking of Chaucer's romance, Henryson's narrator writes,

> Of his distresse me nedeth nat reherse
> For worthy Chaucer in that same boke
> In goodly termes / and in ioly verse
> Compyled hath his cares who wyl loke.   (57–60)

But whose "distresse" and "cares" does he have in mind, those of Troylus or of Chaucer? Both readings are grammatically possible; if we accept the latter, *Troilus and Criseyde* becomes a record of Chaucer's unrequited love for his heroine.[94] Given that Henryson's narrator clearly wants us to see a continuity between himself and Chaucer, the earlier poet's libidinous impulses are transferred onto him. In fact, much of what Henryson's narrator does seems to be driven by mimetic desire.[95] For instance, his final words in the poem, "Sithe she is deed / I speke of her no more" (616), echo Troylus's only direct speech in the poem ("I can no more / She was vntrewe / and wo is me therefore," he utters upon hearing of her demise [601–02]), which also indicates that the narrator is harboring dreams of replacing the Trojan knight as Creseyde's designated lover.

Even more tellingly, just like Troylus does when faced with a mass of decomposing flesh that once was his beloved, the narrator, in his lament on the severity of Creseyde's punishment, resorts to the power of memory and chooses to recall the lost splendor of her courtly desirability:

> O crewel Saturne / frowarde and angry
> Harde is thy dome / and to malycious
> Of faire Creseyde / why haste thou no mercy
> Whiche was so swete / gentyl / and amorous
> Withdrawe thy sentence and be gracious
> As the were neuer / so sheweth through thy dede
> A wrekeful sentence gyuen on Creseyde.   (323–29)

Despite Creseyde's impeding transformation into an ugly body of leprous flesh, in his references to her the narrator continues to cling to the rhetoric of beauty, recalling Creseyde's qualities as a courtly lady ("swete," "gentyl," and "amorous"). This passage also draws attention to the role of poetry in the paradox of erotic disgust. Fineman, in connection with Shakespeare's desire for the dark lady, calls such nostalgia for absent beauty the "regretting difference from that which it presents, provoking a desire for that which, as representation, it necessarily absents."[96] A similar dynamic is at work in Henryson's text, where courtly language continues to harbor erotic desire in the empty textual spaces between the images of corruption and decay. Her ruined appearance is inscribed through "spottes blake" (339) and "byles blake" (395), the color of ink in which the poet is writing, but the unfilled white areas of the page are still governed by memories of courtly love. While Creseyde's body is a source of abomination and revulsion, poetry has the power to overcome disgust; it is "literature," Kristeva observes, that facilitates a "sublimation of abjection."[97] By placing the language of courtly attraction alongside the disgusting images of leprosy, Henryson's poem implies the existence of a link between the odious, sick feminine body and the birth of poetic discourse.

But as with Troylus, the cathexis between the narrator and the leprous Creseyde is marked by pathology. From the start, the speaker articulates himself through the categories of disease and health. Once a servant of Venus ("loues queen / To whom somtyme I hyght obedience" [22–23]), he hoped that his "faded herte of loue she wolde make grene," but he cannot pray to the goddess "for great colde" and is forced to hide in his chamber, abandoning all hope of resuscitating his former passion. He admits that in "a man of age" like himself, "though loue be hote," "it kyndleth not so soone as in youthheed," and his "corage [is] duf and deed" despite his recourse to "phisyke [medicine]" (22–35). The speaker, oscillating between the figurative and the literal dimensions of heat and cold, is recognizable as a sick subject of desire. In Henryson's version, it is not love that causes the lover's sickness but, rather, the speaker's inability to desire that becomes the malady of love and requires a cure. Yet, in spite of such a rearrangement of the classical trope, the subject of the poem is still produced at an intersection of disease and passion.

As a result, the opening of *The Testament* constructs "a disabled body that is in need of restoration or cure,"[98] to which the revolting figure of the diseased Creseyde provides a parallel image. Granted, the narrator's erotic malady is removed from both Troylus's sickness (which can be read as directly caused by Creseyde's pathogenic proximity), and the Shakespearean subject's disease of love (which is explicitly identified as a form of erotic infection spread by his contagious mistress). In *The Testament* the speaker's malady is not leprosy, nor does he contract it from Creseyde. Yet, strangely, the two characters share a number of symptoms. Saturn condemns Creseyde to melancholy and poverty:

> I chaunge thy myrthe in to melancoly
> Whiche is the mother of al pensyuenesse
> Thy moyster and thy hete / in to colde and dry
> ....
> To great disease / thy pompe and thy richesse
> Into mortal nede and great penurie
> Thou suffre shalte / and as a beggar dye.   (316–18, 320–22)

These marks of Creseyde's impending illness, however, replicate the signs of the narrator's abject condition at the beginning of the poem. Although he sets his narrative in the spring (the middle of Lent), he is shivering from the cold: "scantly fro the colde I myght me defende," he complains (7). "The northern wynde," he adds, had "shedde hys mysty cloudes fro the skye"; "The frost fresed / the blastes bytterly.../ And caused me remoue ayenst my wyl" (17–19, 21). The cold, bleak landscape is, of course, a metaphor of the speaker's physical infirmity, but it is also a prolepsis of Creseyde's punishment. Moreover, as Jana Mathews notes apropos the opening stanzas, such dismal, inclement weather during what is likely to be the planting season in Scotland signifies "imminent material loss."[99] Not only is he in pain, he is bound to descend into penury, just like Creseyde does when the gods' sentence takes effect. (In this, both are opposed to the wealthy Troylus, who gives Creseyde "a purse of gold / and many a gay iewel" [521] and potentially promises to redeem the narrator's poverty, which anticipates the role

Shakespeare's rich patron plays in articulating masculine ideality for the poor and sick lover in the sequence.) Henryson's poem, in other words, imagines an uncanny degree of sameness between the narrator's physically ailing and financially unsound body and that of Creseyde, similar to how in sonnet 150 the Shakespearean lover's passion for "what others doe abhor" makes himself abhorred by others. There is perhaps not enough evidence in the poem to categorize Creseyde's infected body as the infecting one in this case and to posit it as the source of the narrator's malady.[100] But there is a distinct possibility that the speaker's metaphorical disease functions as an implicit commentary on his aberrant attraction to Creseyde. To write a poem about the Chaucerian courtly lady's transformation into an abominable leper, to focus on the minute particulars of her revolting sickness, and yet to inscribe in the text of the poem one's desire for this unapologetically repugnant figure—all these point toward a form of erotic pathology.

Through the figures of Troylus and the narrator, then, *The Testament of Creseyde* prefigures the emergence of Shakespearean masculine subjectivity out of a sick desire for abject femininity that threatens to contaminate the lover(s) with physical and economic disease. Henryson's double vision of disease—as both corporeal contagion and pathological appetite—anticipates the tortuous world of Shakespeare's dark lady sonnets. The oxymoronic mechanism of abomination and attraction toward a revoltingly diseased female body and the ensuing possibility of contamination are the aspects of Shakespeare's art that reveal their debt to the memory of poetic discourse, specifically to *The Testament of Creseyde*. Dubrow, in her discussion of the ugly beauty tradition in early modern poetry, usefully links it with the medical realities of Tudor and Stuart England, where women were more susceptible to illness.[101] What her argument ignores, however, is the work of poetic genealogy in such reactions to Petrarchism. Shakespeare's ruminations about the nature of pathological affect display his imaginative ties with the poetics of disgust articulated in Henryson's text. The very possibility of thinking about the attraction toward an abominable object in Shakespeare's sonnets is predicated upon its preexistence in vernacular poetic discourse. Shakespeare's "invention of poetic subjectivity," then, can be rethought as in some respects anticipated by the radical poetics of pathological self-examination developed by such poets as Hoccleve and Henryson. If we wish to grasp the complexities of Shakespeare's vernacular identity, we need to acknowledge that in some respects the sonnets reenact earlier scenarios of literary subjectivity. Shakespeare's version of Petrarchan poetics is among the most aesthetically innovative and disruptive of the tradition, yet even his sonnets—an epitome of modernity—are not untouched by vernacular memories, for the energies perpetuating Petrarchan desires in Shakespeare's sonnets remain tenaciously medieval.

CONCLUSION

The "English Straine" in Early Modern Petrarchism

Poetry, Genealogy, Hermeneutics

Michael Drayton's sonnet sequence *Idea* was first printed as *Ideas Mirrour* in 1594, but it remained in print for the next 25 years until its final version, *Idea: In Sixty Three Sonnets*—incorporating a host of additions, omissions, and revisions—appeared in Drayton's *Poems* in 1619. Drayton's sequence, despite its origins in the Elizabethan sonnet craze of the 1590s, is thus one of the last examples of early modern English Petrarchism. It is hardly surprising, then, that its prefatory poem, "To the Reader of These Sonnets," which introduces a sequence that all but concludes a literary fashion, sets to delineate the poet's relationship with the past and the present of English amatory verse:

> Into these Loves, who but for Passion lookes,
> At this first sight, here let him lay them by,
> And seeke else-where, in turning other Bookes,
> Which better may his labour satisfie.

> No farre-fetch'd Sigh shall ever wound my Brest,
> Love from mine Eye a Teare shall never wring,
> Nor in *Ah-mees* my whyning Sonnets drest,
> (A Libertine) fantastickly I sing:
> My Verse is the true image of my Mind,
> Ever in motion, still desiring change;
> And as thus to Varietie inclin'd,
> So in all Humors sportively I range:
> My Muse is rightly of the *English* straine,
> That cannot long one Fashion intertaine.[1]

The poem posits a predictable contrast between the speaker's original poetics expressing the "true images of his Mind" and the practice of dressing one's desires in "whyning Sonnets," the latter found in "other Bookes" full of conventional conceits. The poet is clearly concerned with distancing himself from the exhausted custom of Petrarchan writing ("farrefetch'd Sigh[s]...Teare[s]...[and] *Ah-mees*"), arguing that he instead is a "Libertine" who sings "fantastickly," that is, following the rules of imagination rather than the jaded "Fashion" of amatory verse. It is striking, however, that Drayton, railing against Petrarchism, locates the foundations of his "Libertine" poetics in what he himself describes as "the *English* straine." Undoubtedly, he associates this poetic "straine" with liberty, "Varietie," "desiring change," and inability to "long one Fashion intertaine," yet the possible meanings of "strain" in early modern English include not just "thread, line or streak" but, crucially, "pedigree, lineage, ancestry, descent" as well as "constraint, compulsion, or requirement."[2] Drayton's poetic freedom proves to be a form of forcible inclusion in discursive tradition, of involuntary dependence on literary lineage, and indeed of writing under the constraints of the past. His "Libertine" English "Muse" is as relaxed in her variability and shape-shifting as she is inhibitory and stifling in her insistence on adherence to the fundamental principles of vernacular English poetry.

In this sense, Drayton's "To the Reader of These Sonnets" emblematizes the complex entanglements of medieval and early modern desires and subjectivities in English Petrarchan poetry explored in this book. Although barely concealed allusions to Sidney ("Bookes," "Muse") and Spenser ("Loves" seems to be an Anglicized form of the Italianate *Amoretti*) give some hint as to which authors and texts constitute "the *English* straine," this discursive streak that Drayton claims to continue is "notably brief and vague" and its contours "are never made explicit."[3] One can thus just as legitimately read "the *English* straine" as an invocation of the whole institution of pre-modern English writing, from Langland and Chaucer to Shakespeare and Drayton himself. This "straine," to use the language of contemporary aesthetics, operates as "the system of *a priori* forms determining what presents itself to sense experience."[4] "Ever in motion, still desiring change," this system is characterized by "Varietie" and ranging in "all Humors," which makes its influence hard to grasp, yet *Idea* is unequivocally indebted to its past. As Pierre Bourdieu would say, Drayton's original "Loves" are "determined by the past conditions which have produced the principle of their production";[5] they receive their meaning elsewhere, in "the *English* straine" that underwrites his Petrarchan sonnets and envelops their multifarious desires.

This "*English* straine" of English Renaissance Petrarchism has been the object of the preceding chapters. I have attempted to demonstrate that early modern Petrarchan poetry in many instances relies in its expressions of desire and subjectivity on medieval structures of discourse and identity. The latter constitutes an area of the vernacular discursive memory— a repertoire of imaginative, rhetorical, and ideological configurations upon which early modern Petrarchan selves are dependent for their successful articulation. The form this return of the medieval takes in early modern Petrarchan poetry differs from text to text: it can be a "complex word" that survives in discursive memory (e.g., "meed"), a mode of figuration that transcends the boundaries of a literary period (e.g., legal diction), a recurring ideologeme (e.g., sovereign marriage), or a distinct form of self-presentation that continues from medieval to early modern (e.g., the melancholy self or the begging self). Regardless of their specific manifestations, however, fragments of medieval discourses and selves pulsate within early modern poetry, at once legitimizing and questioning the originality and authority of Petrarchan writing.

One of the central inferences of this book is that Petrarchan subjectivity is not an exclusively Renaissance phenomenon—rather, it is a palimpsestic layering of imaginative currents in which the past (the Middle Ages) is interlaced with the present (the Renaissance). Each form of Petrarchan selfhood considered in these pages is haunted by a dual temporality: at once medieval and early modern, it belongs to two poetic paradigms that nonetheless are part of the same vernacular continuum. In each case I have made an effort to identify the medieval languages that underwrite the articulations of Petrarchan subjectivity in early modern English poetry and describe the specific relationship that exists between these languages and the vocabularies of Petrarchan desire. My aim has been to present Petrarchan selfhood as at least in part assembled out of medieval fragments of discourse, as a literary construct dislocated from the position of temporal and aesthetic intactness and self-sufficiency.

The book's methodological approach thus shares common ground with Foucauldian genealogy, a theoretical model that I so far have not engaged directly in these pages. Foucault defines genealogy as "studying the constitution of the subject across history which has led us up to the modern concept of the self."[6] It is an investigation into the multilayered constructedness of modern subjectivity, a process of chipping away at its seeming transhistoricity and wholeness and uncovering within the concept of the subject traces of various historically contingent powers. Genealogy is not, however, a teleological enterprise: it refuses to seek for origins and focuses instead on deviations, errors, and inconsistencies in the realm of historical change. As Foucault writes, it "disturbs what was previously considered immobile; it fragments what was thought unified; it shows the heterogeneity of what was imagined consistent with itself...[genealogy's] intention is to reveal the heterogenous systems which, masked by the self, inhibit the formation of any form of identity."[7] Genealogy seeks to disrupt rather than consolidate: by discovering a history behind a concept or institution that previously appeared to have none, it destabilizes and complicates by introducing a historical dimension that subverts any notion of natural cohesion. The present study is genealogical in the sense that it investigates the discursive forces that participated in the production of early modern English Petrarchan subjects by uncovering their possible vernacular pasts: it dismantles the idea of Petrarchan selfhood as an exclusively modern invention and emphasizes the medieval elements that were involved in its construction. Unraveling these discursive agglomerations and tracing medieval histories operating behind the articulations of Petrarchan selfhood in the early modern period, this book demonstrates that English Petrarchan vocabularies of the self are interwoven in early modern sonnets with medieval lexicons of subjectivity.

At the same time, the project of *Renaissance Texts, Medieval Subjectivities* cannot be described as genealogical in the full sense of the word—at least not in the way Foucault understood genealogy. For him, the aim of genealogy was "not to demonstrate that the past actively exists in the present, that it continues secretly to animate the present, having imposed a predetermined form to all its vicissitudes."[8]

Yet this position is unnecessarily restrictive and even counterproductive. As Jacqueline Stevens writes in her critique of Foucault's use of the term—which she shows to be a violent misreading of Nietzsche—the idea of genealogy implies that "one traces out a present connection to ancestors because one thinks that this reveals something essential about who one is now, that this past has a value, and that there is something about one's being now that can be ascertained by knowing one's origins."[9] In this book I have similarly suggested a form of literary history that looks at how various strata of poetic form and meaning are connected in English poetry, how the medieval past does "actively exist" and "secretly animate" the early modern present. I have argued that not only vernacular medieval poetry and poetics remained a meaningful part of the English literary imagination well into the sixteenth and even seventeenth centuries, but also that they are essential to our understanding of English Renaissance poetry, including Petrarchan verse, in our time.

To put it in the more familiar terms of literary criticism, while Foucault denies the hermeneutic aspect of the genealogical framework, for me it is the interpretive potential of investigating the prehistories of Petrarchan subjectivity that justifies reading across the lines of periodization. In my analyses I thus followed Giorgio Agamben's reinterpretation of Foucauldian genealogy as a method of reading signatures—making "intelligible series of phenomena whose kinship had eluded or could elude the historian's gaze," where a signature is a fleeting inscription within another sign that nonetheless "necessarily predetermines [the sign's] interpretation and distributes its use and efficacy according to rules, practices, and precepts that it is our task to recognize."[10] Signatures are residual traces of the prior iterations and uses of a complex sign that are indispensible to the sign's constitution and proper functioning—including interpretation—in the present. By preserving signatures of the past technologies of subjectivity, poetic discourse operates as a site where historical difference can be appreciated and put to interpretive use.

Consequently, my engagement with poetic texts across the temporal divide in this book has been not—or not only—genealogical but hermeneutic as well, inasmuch as I have been concerned with discovering new ways of reading canonical texts through a dialogue between medieval and early modern poetry. As Bruce Holsinger writes, "medieval fragments" unearthed in the structures of modernity function as "productive sacraments of creative ingenuity, partial remains from an unknowable past invested nevertheless with a transformative capacity in the critical present."[11] From a literary perspective, converging within the patchwork of the same verbal text, discursive fragments from different temporalities act upon and transform one another. Conjured as part of the early modern present, the medieval past becomes a crucial element of our critical experience of Renaissance literature. As Hans-Georg Gadamer avers in *Truth and Method*, through a conversation between the past and the present, "written tradition is brought back out of the alienation in which it finds itself and into the living present of conversation."[12] Imbricated within Petrarchan texts, medieval poetics constitute a powerful interpretive code that affects our understanding of Renaissance literature; however, conversely, the latter conditions our relationship with medieval texts. As this book suggests, such reciprocally informed readings have the potential to alter our ways of thinking about the early modern and simultaneously offer an unorthodox view of the medieval through the prism of Renaissance literary culture.

Thus, while the main argument of this book is quite straightforward—that medieval poetry inscribes in the vernacular literary imagination a web of rhetorical structures and associated subject positions and that articulations of subjectivity in early modern English Petrarchan poetry depend upon those medieval structures of discourse—local ramifications of this thesis are more nuanced and complex as far as readings of specific texts are concerned. Chapter 1 suggested that the poetics of meed that Langland articulates in the opening passūs of *Piers Plowman* continues to invest with anxiety the Petrarchan texts of Wyatt and Spenser, poets who place different kinds of reward at the center of their poetic worlds. I argued that the Langlandian notion of meed is indispensible for our understanding of Wyatt's struggles with the limitations of erotic and pecuniary desire and his attempts to reach the meed of divine grace; and further, that Spenser's project of redemptive Petrarchism in the *Amoretti* (in which sexuality, economy, poetic glory, and salvation are intertwined in one imaginative nodule) unfolds in conversation with Langland's vision of meed. Chapter 2 argued that the anti-Petrarchan experiments of Surrey and Sidney, as well as their fragmented selves, are anticipated by Chaucer's poetics of melancholy (articulated most eloquently in the *Book of the Duchess*), a form of subjectivity founded on an indefinite splintering of the "I" and a type of writing that at once engenders and sabotages the production of amatory verse. In chapter 3, I demonstrated that the political and poetic resonances of Mary Stuart's radical rewriting of Petrarchism in the casket sonnets—as a language of sexual gratification and as a discourse of matrimonial desire—can be grasped only when read in an expansive temporal context, not exclusively as an antithesis to the Elizabethan configuration of royal marriage, both literal and figurative, but as part of a pre-modern Anglo-Scots tradition of sovereign love that stretches back into the fifteenth century. It is through the contrast between the casket sonnets and the late medieval poem *Kingis Quair* that Mary's violation of both Petrarchan chastity and of the taboo on consummation in symbolic sovereign marriage reveals its full significance. Similarly, chapter 4 showed that the pervasive uses of legal subjectivity in English Petrarchism were not exclusively a product of Elizabethan legal and literary culture. Rather, they were a late manifestation of the medieval tradition of the laws of love. Underneath the changes in the status and nature of erotic legality, such as its displacement from the position of jurisdictional autonomy to a subspecies of criminal law, the appetite for a law that can redress imperfections in the relationships between the sexes in the sonnets of Daniel and Drayton remains medieval in its essence. Last, in chapter 5, I problematized the idea of modernity associated with the subject of Shakespeare's sonnets. In the young man sonnets, I suggested, the Petrarchan figures of desire, disease, and poverty are underwritten by a medieval tradition of begging poetry, most eloquently exemplified by Hoccleve's "La male regle," in which the poet, like the subject of Shakespeare's sonnets, often assumes the position of economic, medical, and erotic deficiency and writes in the hope of recuperation promised by the wealthy and healthy patron. Further, I demonstrated that the pathological aesthetics of disgust in the dark lady sonnets—the idea that figurative poetic discourse that facilitates the lover's desire for an abominable feminine object is complicit in the lover's sickness—is not merely a late Elizabethan reaction to the Petrarchan model of erotic idealization but a continuation of a vernacular English discursive framework articulated in Henryson's *Testament of Cresseid*.

Each of these chapters is a stand-alone case study of a distinct form of poetic selfhood that was formulated in medieval poetry and later reemerged in early modern Petrarchan writing, working both as a genealogical past and a hermeneutic present. Read together, however, these studies speak to the significance of medieval forms of discourse and identity to a broad range of early modern Petrarchan texts. As such, the chapters of this book present a rethinking of the medieval/ early modern divide along the lines of subjectivity: as they demonstrate, not only are many forms of selfhood in English Renaissance Petrarchism reliant on medieval structures of discourse and identity but many medieval selves display proleptically Renaissance qualities as well. Pre-modern textual subjectivity, in other words, is simultaneously medieval and early modern; it is a palimpsest traversed by multivectorial currents of energy that circumvent the traditional lines of periodic division and, quietly obliterating the criteria for contrast, make the distinction impracticable. But the preceding chapters also reaffirm the intrinsic value of poetry as an object of study and a mode of thought. One of the key functions of literary scholarship is to articulate new readings of old texts, and during the past three decades it has been achieved predominantly through reading literary texts in conjunction with wider extraliterary discursive configurations. As this book suggests, however, much can be gained by opening poetry up to a dialogue with poetry itself—by engaging early modern poetic voices in a hermeneutic conversation with their medieval predecessors. Out of this conversation—which avoids the politics of influence and borrowing, of hierarchy and precedence—poetry emerges as a discursive continuum where past and present forms of poetic imagination interpenetrate and interanimate each other and ultimately assert their own authority.

Of course one book cannot even attempt to exhaust the whole spectrum of potential forms of poetic continuity between medieval and early modern poetry. *Renaissance Texts, Medieval Subjectivities* has probed a very specific segment of this continuum: by focusing on medieval genealogies of the technologies of selfhood in English Petrarchism, it has demonstrated that medieval imaginative energies are found even at the heart of Renaissance literary culture, even within the core of poetic modernity. The modern subject of Petrarchism has been shown to be quite medieval in its desires and formulations. Many other forms of medieval continuance in the memory of discourse into the early modern period have yet to be written. What this book does achieve, I hope, is suggest that learning to discern the medieval voices within Renaissance poetic utterances enriches our understanding of pre-modern poetry. By investigating vernacular genealogies of Renaissance configurations of discourse and subjectivity, we can discover new meanings of the canonical texts and thus achieve a clearer view of the literary practices of the past.

NOTES

Notes to Introduction

1. George Puttenham, *The Arte of English Poesie*, ed. Gladys Doige Wilcock and Alice Walker (Cambridge: Cambridge University Press, 1936), 60; hereafter cited in the text as *Arte*.
2. William Kerrigan and Gordon Braden, *The Idea of the Renaissance* (Baltimore: Johns Hopkins University Press, 1989), 158–59. See also Gordon Braden, *Petrarchan Love and the Continental Renaissance* (New Haven, CT: Yale University Press, 1994), 60–61.
3. A. C. Spearing, *Medieval to Renaissance in English Poetry* (Cambridge: Cambridge University Press, 1985), 5–14, 278–326; Thomas Greene, *The Light in Troy: Imitation and Discovery in Renaissance Poetry* (New Haven, CT: Yale University Press, 1982), 242–47.
4. William Webbe, *A Discourse of English Poetrie*, in *Elizabethan Critical Essays*, 2 vols., ed. G. Gregory Smith (Oxford: Oxford University Press, 1904), 1:240–45.
5. Cathy Shrank, "'Matters of Love as of Discourse': The English Sonnet, 1560–1580," *Studies in Philology* 105, no. 1 (2008): 48.
6. Richard Barnfield, *Poems, 1594–1598*, ed. Edward Arber (Westminster: Archibald Constable, 1896), 119.
7. Andrew Cole and D. Vance Smith, eds., "Outside Modernity," introduction to *The Legitimacy of the Middle Ages: On the Unwritten History of Theory*, 1–36 (Durham, NC: Duke University Press, 2010), 28.
8. Gordon McMullan and David Mathews, eds., "Reading the Medieval in Early Modern England," introduction to *Reading the*

Medieval in Early Modern England, 1–14 (Cambridge: Cambridge University Press, 2008), 6.

9. See, for example, Helen Cooper, *The English Romance in Time: Transforming Motifs from Geoffrey of Monmouth to the Death of Shakespeare* (Oxford: Oxford University Press, 2004); Katherine C. Little, *Transforming Work: Early Modern Pastoral and Late Medieval Poetry* (Notre Dame, IN: University of Notre Dame Press, 2013); Robert J. Meyer-Lee, *Poets and Power form Chaucer to Wyatt* (Cambridge: Cambridge University Press, 2007); Marco Nievergelt, *Allegorical Quests from Deguileville to Spenser* (Cambridge: D. S. Brewer, 2012); James Simpson, *Reform and Cultural Revolution, 1350–1547* (New York: Oxford University Press, 2002); Lynn Staley, *The Island Garden: England's Language of Nation from Gildas to Marvell* (Notre Dame, IN: University of Notre Dame Press, 2012); Paul Strohm, *Politique: Languages of Statecraft between Chaucer and Shakespeare* (Notre Dame, IN: University of Notre Dame Press, 2005); Jennifer Summit, *Lost Property: The Woman Writer and English Literary History, 1380–1589* (Chicago: University of Chicago Press, 2000); David Wallace, *Premodern Places: Calais to Surinam, Chaucer to Aphra Behn* (Oxford: Blackwell, 2004); and Deane Williams, *The French Fetish from Chaucer to Shakespeare* (Cambridge: Cambridge University Press, 2004).

10. See Arthur F. Marotti, "'Love Is Not Love': Elizabethan Sonnet Sequences and the Social Order," *English Literary History* 49, no. 2 (1982): 396–428; Anthony Low, *The Reinvention of Love: Poetry, Politics and Culture from Sidney to Milton* (Cambridge: Cambridge University Press, 1993), 12–30; Ann Rosalind Jones and Peter Stallybrass, "The Politics of *Astrophil and Stella*," *SEL: Studies in English Literature, 1500–1900* 24 (1984): 53–68; Thomas P. Roche Jr., *Petrarch and the English Sonnet Sequence* (New York: AMS, 1989); Heather Dubrow, *Echoes of Desire: English Petrarchism and Its Counterdiscourses* (Ithaca, NY: Cornell University Press, 1995); Barbara L. Estrin, *Laura: Uncovering Gender and Genre in Wyatt, Donne, and Marvell* (Durham, NC: Duke University Press, 1994); Carla Freccero, *Queer/Early/Modern* (Durham, NC: Duke University Press, 2006), 13–25; William J. Kennedy, *The Site of Petrarchism: Early Modern National Sentiment in Italy, France, and England* (Baltimore: Johns Hopkins University Press, 2003); Roland Greene, *Unrequited Conquests: Love and Empire in the Colonial Americas* (Chicago: University of Chicago Press, 1999); Christopher Warley, *Sonnet Sequences and Social Distinction in Renaissance England* (Cambridge: Cambridge University Press, 2005).

11. See Theodor E. Mommsen, "Petrarch's Conception of the 'Dark Ages,'" *Speculum* 17, no. 2 (1942): 226–42.

12. The classical instance of this argument is John Freccero, "The Fig Tree and the Laurels: Petrarch's Poetics," *Diacritics* 5 (1975): 34–40. See also Giuseppe Mazotta, *The Worlds of Petrarch* (Durham, NC: Duke University Press, 1993), 58–79, although Mazotta's position is more tempered. Also see Joel Fineman, *Shakespeare's Perjured Eye: The Invention of Poetic Subjectivity in the Sonnets* (Berkeley: University of California Press, 1986). Fineman, despite contrasting Shakespeare's sonnet sequence with the previous poetic tradition (including Petrarch), still implies (esp. 193) that the Shakespearean "invention" of modern selfhood is indebted to Petrarch.

13. Quotes from, respectively, David Wallace, *Chaucerian Polity: Absolutist Lineages and Associational Forms in England and Italy* (Stanford, CA: Stanford University Press, 1997), 53; Thomas Greene, "The Flexibility of the Self in Renaissance Literature," in *The Disciplines of Criticism: Essays in Literary Theory, Interpretation, and History*, ed. Peter Demetz, Thomas Greene, and Lowry Nelson Jr., 241–64 (New Haven, CT: Yale University Press, 1968), 246.

14. See, for example, Timothy J. Reiss, *Mirages of the Selfe: Patterns of Personhood in Ancient and Early Modern Europe* (Stanford, CA: Stanford University Press, 2003), 303–52.

15. Gary Waller, *English Poetry of the Sixteenth Century* (London: Longman, 1986), 80.

16. *The Riverside Chaucer*, 3rd ed., ed. Larry Benson (Boston: Houghton Mifflin, 1987); *Petrarch's Lyric Poems: The "Rime sparse" and Other Lyrics*, ed. and trans. Robert M. Durling (Cambridge, MA: Harvard University Press, 1976).

17. Piero Boitani, *The Tragic and the Sublime in Medieval Literature* (Cambridge: Cambridge University Press, 1989), 56–74, considers Sonnets 132–34 and their diction to be central to the *Canzoniere*, largely typifying the Petrarchan style.

18. See C. S. Lewis, "What Chaucer Really Did to *Il Filostrato*," in Lewis, *Selected Literary Essays*, ed. Walter Hooper, 27–44 (Cambridge: Cambridge University Press, 1979); Michael R. G. Spiller, *The Development of the Sonnet: An Introduction* (New York: Routledge, 1992), 64–67; Spearing, *Medieval to Renaissance*, 120.

19. William T. Rossiter, *Chaucer and Petrarch* (Cambridge: D. S. Brewer, 2010), 130–31. See also Robin Kirkpatrick, *English and Italian Literature from Dante to Shakespeare* (New York: Longman, 1995), 116. In "English Anti-Petrarchism: Imbalance and

Excess in 'the Englishe straine' of the Sonnet," *Studies in Philology* 109, no. 5 (2012): 552–80, Christine E. Hutchins also argues that Chaucer's translation of the sonnet shaped some of the attitudes toward Petrarchan love among Elizabethan sonneteers.

20. For example, Patricia Thomson, who writes in "The 'Canticus Troili': Chaucer and Petrarch," *Comparative Literature* 11, no. 4 (1959), that Chaucer's translation of the Italian sonnet "marks the beginning of English Petrarchan love poetry," nonetheless concedes that it "is an isolated landmark in literary history" (313–14). Wallace, while arguing that there is "nothing going on in Petrarch and Bocaccio that cannot, with profit, be brought into intelligible relation with Chaucer," points out that Chaucer's "Canticus" is the sole specimen of Petrarchism anywhere outside of Italy prior to 1500 (*Chaucerian Polity*, 7, 263).

21. Thomas Watson, Ἑκατομπαθία; or, *Passionate Centurie of Love* (London, 1582), A3ʳ.

22. See the text of the sonnet in Anthony Mortimer, *Petrarch's Canzoniere in the English Renaissance*, rev. ed. (Amsterdam: Rodopi, 2005), 41. On Chaucer's deviations from the Italian original, see Thomson, "Canticus Troili," 317–20; Ernst H. Wilkins, "Cantus Troili," *English Literary History* 16, no. 3 (1949): 169–70.

23. Roger Ascham, *The Schoolmaster*, ed. Lawrence V. Ryan (Ithaca, NY: Cornell University Press, 1967), 146–47; Samuel Daniel, *A Defence of Rhyme*, in Smith, *Elizabethan Critical Essays*, 2:370.

24. Sir Philip Sidney, *An Apologie for Poetrie*, in ibid., 1:152.

25. David Aers, "A Whisper in the Ear of Early Modernists; or, Reflections on Literary Critics Writing the 'History of the Subject,'" in *Culture and History, 1350–1600: Essays on English Communities, Identities, and Writing*, ed. David Aers, 177–202 (Detroit: Wayne State University Press, 1992), 186. See also Douglas Gray, "Finding Identity in the Middle Ages," in *Sixteenth-Century Identities*, ed. A. J. Piesse, 9–33 (Manchester: Manchester University Press, 2000); Lee Patterson, "On the Margin: Postmodernism, Ironic History, and Medieval Studies," *Speculum* 65, no. 1 (1990): 87–108, esp. 95–101. For useful overviews of the question, see A. C. Spearing, *Textual Subjectivity: The Encoding of Subjectivity in Medieval Narratives and Lyrics* (Oxford: Oxford University Press, 2005), 31–34; Isabel Davis, "Expressing the Middle English I," *Literature Compass* 6, no. 4 (2009): 842–63, esp. 842–45.

26. Helen Cooper, introduction to *The Long Fifteenth Century: Essays for Douglas Gray*, ed. Helen Cooper and Sally Mapstone, 1–14 (Oxford: Clarendon, 1997), 11. For studies of medieval subjectivity, see Sarah Kay, *Subjectivity in Troubadour Poetry*

(Cambridge: Cambridge University Press, 1990); Sarah Spence, *Texts and the Self in the Twelfth Century* (Cambridge: Cambridge University Press, 1996); Gerald A. Bond, *The Loving Subject: Desire, Eloquence and Power in Romanesque France* (Philadelphia: University of Pennsylvania Press, 1995); Michael Zink, *The Invention of Literary Subjectivity*, trans. David Sices (Baltimore: Johns Hopkins University Press, 1999); Peter Haidu, *The Subject Medieval/Modern: Text and Governance in the Middle Ages* (Stanford, CA: Stanford University Press, 2004); Jennifer Bryan, *Looking Inward: Devotional Reading and the Private Self in Late Medieval England* (Philadelphia: University of Pennsylvania Press, 2008).

27. David Schalkwyk, *Speech and Performance in Shakespeare's Sonnets and Plays* (Cambridge: Cambridge University Press, 2002), 107. Cf. "Subjectivity and individuality—the sense that an individual human being has his own 'insides,' feelings, and identity—go back a long way into the past." Anthony Low, *Aspects of Subjectivity: Society and Individuality from the Middle Ages to Shakespeare and Milton* (Pittsburgh: Duquesne University Press, 2003), 184.

28. Jason Scott-Warren, *Early Modern English Literature* (Cambridge: Polity, 2005), 223–26; see also Peter Burke, "Representations of the Self from Petrarch to Descartes," in *Rewriting the Self: Histories from the Renaissance to the Present*, ed. Roy Porter, 17–28 (London: Routledge, 1997).

29. Elizabeth Hanson, *Discovering the Subject in Renaissance England* (Cambridge: Cambridge University Press, 1998), 12.

30. Frederic Jameson, *A Singular Modernity: Essay on the Ontology of the Present* (London: Verso, 2002), 55.

31. For an incisive and provocative reading of the divide between the medieval and the modern as a foundation of our modern concepts of periodization and history, see Kathleen Davis, *Periodization and Sovereignty: How Ideas of Feudalism and Secularization Govern the Politics of Time* (Philadelphia: University of Pennsylvania Press, 2008). Margreta de Grazia also addresses the "irrelevance" of the Middle Ages as a by-product of the medieval/early modern periodization in "The Modern Divide: From Either Side," in *Medieval/Renaissance: After Periodization*, a special issue of *Journal of Medieval and Early Modern Studies* 37, no. 3 (2007): 453–67.

32. Bruce Holsinger, *The Premodern Condition: Medievalism and the Making of Theory* (Chicago: University of Chicago Press, 2005), 6. Holsinger's book investigates the persistence of medieval structures in twentieth century French theory, but I believe his argument comfortably lends itself to a reading of literary texts as well.

33. See, for example, Carolyn Dinshaw, *Getting Medieval: Sexualities and Communities, Pre- and Postmodern* (Durham, NC: Duke University Press, 1999).
34. John Watkins, "Recent Studies in the English Renaissance," *SEL: Studies in English Literature, 1500–1900* 52, no. 1 (2012): 249.
35. On early modern medievalism that "seeks to reproduce, recover, or emulate the quality of a medieval text" or "uses or adapts medieval material with the intention of making it new," see Deanne Williams, "Medievalism in English Renaissance Literature," in *A Companion to Tudor Literature*, ed. Kent Cartwright, 213–27 (Oxford: Blackwell, 2010), 226. On archaic style, see Lucy Munro, *Archaic Style in English Literature, 1590–1674* (Cambridge: Cambridge University Press, 2013).
36. Mikhail M. Bakhtin, *Speech Genres and Other Late Essays*, ed. Caryl Emerson and Michael Holquist, trans. Vern W. McGee (Austin: University of Texas Press, 1986), 93.
37. Mikhail M. Bakhtin, *Problems of Dostoevsky's Poetics*, ed. and trans. Caryl Emerson (Minneapolis: University of Minnesota Press, 1984), 106. My substitution of "discourse" for "genre" is dictated by a desire to overcome the formal difference between Petrarchan sonnets and generically diverse medieval texts. Broadly speaking, I understand poetic discourse as an intersection of rhetorical form, culture, and subjectivity.
38. Nancy Selleck, *The Interpersonal Idiom in Shakespeare, Donne, and Early Modern Culture* (New York: Palgrave, 2008), 1.
39. See Bruno Latour, *We Have Never Been Modern*, trans. Catherine Porter (Cambridge, MA: Harvard University Press, 1993), esp. 67–79; Michel Serres and Bruno Latour, *Conversations on Science, Culture, and Time*, trans. Roxanne Lapidus (Ann Arbor: University of Michigan Press, 1995).
40. Alexander Nagel and Christopher S. Wood, *Anachronic Renaissance* (New York: Zone Books, 2010).
41. Jonathan Gil Harris, *Untimely Matter in the Time of Shakespeare* (Philadelphia: University of Pennsylvania Press, 2008), 7.
42. Sarah Dillon, *The Palimpsest: Literature, Criticism, Theory* (London: Continuum, 2007), 12, 37.
43. Mikhail Bakhtin, *The Dialogic Imagination*, ed. and trans. Michael Holquist, trans. Caryl Emerson (Austin: University of Texas Press, 1981), 293.
44. Daniel Heller-Roazen, *Echolalias: On the Forgetting of Language* (New York: Zone Books, 2005), 77.
45. T. Greene, *Light in Troy*, 20.

46. Brian Cummings and James Simpson, eds., introduction to *Cultural Reformations: Medieval and Renaissance in Literary History*, 1–9 (Oxford: Oxford University Press, 2010), 6.

47. Elizabeth L. Eisenstein, *The Printing Revolution in Early Modern Europe*, 2nd ed. (Cambridge: Cambridge University Press, 2005), 54.

48. On "writing the nation" in post-Reformation England, see Richard Helgerson, *Forms of Nationhood: The Elizabethan Writing of England* (Chicago: University of Chicago Press, 1992); Andrew Hadfield, *Literature, Politics, and National Identity: Reformation to Renaissance* (Cambridge: Cambridge University Press, 1994); Claire McEachern, *The Poetics of English Nationhood, 1590–1612* (Cambridge: Cambridge University Press, 1996); Daniel Woolf, *The Social Circulation of the Past: English Historical Culture 1500–1730* (Oxford: Oxford University Press, 2003); Cathy Shrank, *Writing the Nation in Reformation England* (Oxford: Oxford University Press, 2004).

49. On canon formation in early modern England, see Trevor Ross, *The Making of the English Literary Canon: From the Middle Ages to the Late Eighteenth Century* (Montreal: McGill-Queen's University Press, 1998), 51–64; Philip Schwyzer, *Literature, Nationalism, and Memory in Early Modern England and Wales* (Cambridge: Cambridge University Press, 2004), 60–75.

50. There is vast scholarship on the practices and ideologies of the printing of medieval authors in early modern England. On Chaucer, see Alexandra Gillespie, *Print Culture and the Medieval Author: Chaucer, Lydgate, and Their Books, 1473–1557* (New York: Oxford University Press, 2006); *Rewriting Chaucer: Culture, Authority, and the Idea of the Authentic Text, 1400–1602*, ed. Thomas A. Prendergast and Barbara Kline (Columbus: Ohio State University Press, 1999); Kevin Pask, *The Emergence of the English Author: Scripting the Life of the Poet in Early Modern England* (Cambridge: Cambridge University Press, 1996), 9–52. On the printing of Gower, see N. F. Blake, "Early Printed Editions of *Confessio Amantis*," *Mediaevalia* 16, no. 1 (1993): 289–306. For Lydgate, in addition to Gillespie, *Print Culture*, see Simpson, *Reform and Cultural Revolution*, 38–44. On Crowley's editions of Langland, see R. Carter Hailey, "'Geuyng Light to the Reader': Robert Crowley's Editions of *Piers Plowman* (1550)," *Papers of the Bibliographical Society of America* 95 (2001): 483–502; Larry Scanlon, "Langland, Apocalypse and the Early Modern Editor," in McMullan and Mathews, *Reading the Medieval*, 51–73; J. R. Thorne and Marie-Claire Urhart, "Robert Crowley's *Piers Plowman*," *Medium Aevum* 55 (1986): 248–54.

51. A. S. G. Edwards, "John Stow and Middle English Literature," in *John Stow (1525–1605) and the Making of the English Past: Studies in Early Modern Culture and the History of the Book*, ed. Ian Gadd and Alexandra Gillespie, 109–18 (London: British Library, 2004).

52. William Kuskin, *Recursive Origins: Writing at the Transition to Modernity* (Notre Dame, IN: University of Notre Dame Press, 2013), 20.

53. Anne E. B. Coldiron, "The Mediated 'Medieval' and Shakespeare," in *Medieval Shakespeare: Pasts and Presents*, ed. Ruth Morse, Helen Cooper, and Peter Holland, 55–77 (Cambridge: Cambridge University Press, 2013), esp. 55–58. Classical philology, of course, considered textual transmission a *sine qua non* of literary continuity. For example, see Ernst Robert Curtius, *European Literature and the Latin Middle Ages*, trans. Willard R. Trask (New York: Harper and Row, 1953), 391–97.

54. Munro, *Archaic Style*, 69–104.

55. See, for example, Peggy A. Knapp, *Time-Bound Words: Semantic and Social Economies from Chaucer's England to Shakespeare's* (Basingstoke: Macmillan, 2000).

56. Jacques Derrida, "This Strange Institution Called Literature: An Interview with Jacques Derrida," in his *Acts of Literature*, ed. Derek Attridge, 33–75 (New York: Routledge, 1992), 55.

57. Pierre Macherey, *A Theory of Literary Production*, trans. Geoffrey Wall (London: Routledge, 2006), 106.

58. Michael Grossman, *The Story of All Things: Writing the Self in English Renaissance Narrative Poetry* (Durham, NC: Duke University Press, 1998), 16.

59. Paul Strohm, *England's Empty Throne: Usurpation and the Language of Legitimation, 1399–1422* (New Haven, CT: Yale University Press, 1998), 143.

Notes to Chapter 1

1. On the reception of Langland's poem in early modern England, see Mike Rodman Jones, *Radical Pastoral, 1381–1594: Appropriation and the Writing of Religious Controversy* (Aldershot: Ashgate, 2011), 85–170; Sarah A. Kelen, *Langland's Early Modern Identities* (New York: Palgrave, 2007); and John N. King, *English Reformation Literature* (Princeton, NJ: Princeton University Press, 1982), 319–39.

2. *The Vision of Pierce Plowman, nowe the seconde time imprinted by Roberte Crowlye* (London, 1550), *ii.

3. George Puttenham, *The Arte of English Poesie*, ed. Gladys Doidge Willcock and Alice Walker (Cambridge: Cambridge University Press, 1936), 62.

4. Samantha J. Rayner, *Images of Kingship in Chaucer and His Ricardian Contemporaries* (Cambridge: D. S. Brewer, 2008), 4.

5. On Langland's interest in courtly literature, see Anne Middleton, "The Audience and Public of *Piers Plowman*," in *Middle English Alliterative Poetry and Its Literary Background: Seven Essays*, ed. David Lawton, 101–23 (Cambridge: D. S. Brewer, 1982), 114–20; H. A. Shepherd, "Langland's Romances," in *William Langland's "Piers Plowman": A Book of Essays*, ed. Kathleen M. Hewett-Smith, 69–81 (New York: Routledge, 2001); and Nicolette Zeeman, "Tales of Piers and Perceval: *Piers Plowman* and the Grail Romances," *Yearbook of Langland Studies* 22 (2008): 199–236.

6. James F. G. Weldon, "The Structure of Dream Visions in *Piers Plowman*," *Medieval Studies* 49 (1987): 254.

7. On nonreciprocity in Petrarchism as an economic idea, see Alison V. Scott, *Selfish Gifts: The Politics of Exchange and English Courtly Literature, 1580–1628* (Madison, NJ: Fairleigh Dickinson University Press, 2005), 49.

8. Gilles Deleuze and Félix Guattari, *Anti-Oedipus: Capitalism and Schizophrenia*, trans. Robert Hurley, Mark Seem, and Helen R. Lane (Minneapolis: University of Minnesota Press, 1983), 12.

9. Jacques Derrida, "White Mythology," in *Margins of Philosophy*, trans. Alan Bass, 207–71 (Chicago: University of Chicago Press, 1982), 254: "Doubtless, Hegel's Idea, for example, is not Plato's Idea; doubtless the effects of the system are irreducible and must be read as such. But the word *Idea* is not an arbitrary X, and it bears a traditional burden that continues Plato's system in Hegel's system."

10. All quotations are from *William Langland: The Vision of Piers Plowman*, 2nd ed., ed. A. V. C. Schmidt (London: Dent, 1995); hereafter cited parenthetically in the text by passus and line number.

11. The classic discussion is John A. Yunck, *The Lineage of Lady Meed: The Development of Mediaeval Venality Satire* (Notre Dame, IN: University of Notre Dame Press, 1963), esp. 1–13, 284–306. John A. Burrow, "Lady Meed and the Power of Money," *Medium Aevum* 74, no. 1 (2005): 113–18, points out that she hardly represents a specific threat of money but, rather, betrays an anxiety about worldly wealth in general.

12. *Middle English Dictionary*, ed. Hans Kurath et al. (London: Oxford University Press 1965–2001), "meed," 1a (a), (b), (c). See

also the fascinating account of the semantic pliability of "meed" in Middle English in David Burnley, *A Guide to Chaucer's Language* (New York: Macmillan, 1983), 203–10.

13. James Simpson, *"Piers Plowman": An Introduction to the B-Text* (London: Pearson, 1990), 44. On meed's semantic contestability, also see James Hala, "'For She Is Tikel of Hire Tale': Word-Play in the Lady Mede Episode of *Piers Plowman* B," *Proceedings of the PMR Conference* 14 (1989): 105.

14. The theory of "complex words" that combine conflicting meanings and are thus difficult to read is developed in William Empson, *The Structure of Complex Words* (London: Chatto and Windus, 1951).

15. Helen Cooper, "Gender and Personification in *Piers Plowman*," *Yearbook of Langland Studies* 5 (1991): 36.

16. Eve Kosofsky Sedgwick, *Between Men: English Literature and Male Homosocial Desire* (New York: Columbia University Press, 1985), 25–26. For studies of the traffic in women in the Mede episode, see Clare A. Lees, "Gender and Exchange in *Piers Plowman*," in *Class and Gender in Early English Literature: Intersections*, ed. Britton J. Harwood and Gillian R. Overing, 112–30 (Bloomington: Indiana University Press, 1994); David Aers, "Class, Gender, Medieval Criticism, and *Piers Plowman*," in Harwood and Overing, *Class and Gender*, 59–75; Colette Murphy, "Lady Holy Church and Meed the Maid: Re-Envisioning Female Personifications in *Piers Plowman*," in *Feminist Readings in Middle English Literature: The Wife of Bath and All Her Sect*, ed. Ruth Evans and Lesley Johnson, 140–64 (New York: Routledge, 1994).

17. A. G. Mitchell, "Lady Meed and the Art of *Piers Plowman*," in *Style and Symbolism in Piers Plowman: A Modern Critical Anthology*, ed. Robert J. Blanch, 174–93 (Knoxville: University of Tennessee Press, 1969), 183.

18. As Jean-Joseph Goux notes in *Symbolic Economies: After Marx and Freud*, trans. Jennifer Gage (Ithaca, NY: Cornell University Press, 1990), 27, both "natural exchange" of an equal commodity for another and, especially, exchange involving a general equivalent (such as gold or money) presuppose an excess of valuation (surplus value) above immediate use value. Medieval economic theory also realized that even the so-called just price involved an element of contingency. See D. Vance Smith, *Arts of Possession: The Middle English Household Imaginary* (Minneapolis: University of Minnesota Press, 2003), 113–16. Despite Conscience's insistence that fair market exchange and fair wages are measured, both may be construed as "mesurelees." Symptomatically, in passus V Coveitise

is personified as an unscrupulous merchant selling his wares for exorbitant prices, and as a usurer and thief (V.196–258)—one who desires "mede mesurelees." See Roger Ladd, *Antimercantilism in Late Medieval English Literature* (New York: Palgrave, 2010), 36–37.

19. Robert Adams, "Mede and Mercede: the Evolution of the Economics of Grace in the *Piers Plowman* B and C Versions," in *Medieval English Studies Presented to George Kane*, ed. Edward D. Kennedy, Ronald Waldron, and Joseph S. Wittig, 217–32 (Cambridge: D. S. Brewer, 1988), 219–20.

20. James Simpson, "Spirituality and Economics in Passus 1–7 of the B-Text," *Yearbook of Langland Studies* 1 (1987): 83–103, esp. 93–95, 101.

21. Samuel A. Overstreet, "'Grammaticus Ludens': Theological Aspects of Langland's Grammatical Allegory," *Traditio* 40 (1984): 286.

22. See Marcel Mauss, *The Gift: The Form and Reason for Exchange in Archaic Societies*, trans. W. D. Halls (New York: Norton, 1990). On gift-giving as "an expression of the desire to honor the existence and status of the other," see Marcel Hénaff, *The Price of Truth: Gift, Money, and Philosophy*, trans. Jean-Louis Morhange (Stanford, CA: Stanford University Press, 2010), 153.

23. Georges Bataille, *The Accursed Share*, 2 vols., trans. Robert Hurley (New York: Zone Books, 1989), 1:19–41.

24. Ibid., 1:121.

25. Mauss, *Gift*, 3.

26. Bataille, *Accursed Share*, 1:38.

27. Jacques Derrida, *Given Time: I. Counterfeit Money*, trans. Peggy Kamuf (Chicago: University of Chicago Press, 1992), 12, 23, 76.

28. William Flesch, *Generosity and the Limits of Authority* (Ithaca, NY: Cornell University Press, 1992), 8.

29. Derrida, *Given Time*, 102. Cf. Jacques Derrida, *The Gift of Death*, trans. David Wills (Chicago: University of Chicago Press, 1995), 44: "it is only on the basis of death, and in its name, that *giving* and *taking* become possible."

30. Ken Jackson, "'One Wish' or the Possibility of the Impossible: Derrida, the Gift, and God in *Timon of Athens*," *Shakespeare Quarterly* 52, no. 1 (2001): 40–41.

31. Scott Cutler Shershow, *The Work and the Gift* (Chicago: University of Chicago Press, 2005), 1–2, 81–95, 107–14.

32. Ibid., 85. As Derrida notes, gift is "the very figure of the impossible" (*Given Time*, 7).

33. Aers, "Class, Gender, Medieval Criticism," 67, 69; Lees, "Gender and Exchange," 119, 123; Murphy, "Lady Holy Church," 149.

34. Andrew Galloway, *The Penn Commentary on "Piers Plowman,"* vol. 1 (Philadelphia: University of Pennsylvania Press, 2006), 232.

35. A. C. Spearing, *The Medieval Poet as Voyeur: Looking and Listening in Medieval Love-Narrative* (Cambridge: Cambridge University Press, 1993), 6. On the role of gazing in the genesis of desire in medieval culture, see Dana E. Stewart, *Arrow of Love: Optics, Gender, and Subjectivity in Medieval Love Poetry* (Lewisburg, PA: Bucknell University Press, 2003).

36. John A. Burrow, "The Audience of *Piers Plowman*," *Anglia* 75 (1957): 381.

37. Nancy Vickers, "Diana Described: Scattered Woman and Scattered Rhyme," in *Writing and Sexual Difference*, ed. Elizabeth Abel, 95–109 (Chicago: University of Chicago Press, 1982), 96.

38. On the erotic charge of clothes in medieval courtly writing, see E. Jane Burns, *Courtly Love Undressed: Reading through Clothes in Medieval French Culture* (Philadelphia: University of Pennsylvania Press, 2002); Kathy M. Krause, "The Material Erotic: The Clothed and Unclothed Female Body in the *Roman de la violette*," in *Material Culture and Cultural Materialism*, ed. Curtis Perry, 17–39 (Turnhout, Belgium: Brepolis, 2001); James I. Miller, "How to See through Women: Medieval Blazons and the Male Gaze," in *The Centre and Its Compass: Studies in Medieval Literature in Honor of Professor John Leyerle*, ed. Robert Taylor et al., 267–88 (Kalamazoo, MI: Western Michigan University Press, 1993). The association of female nudity with sin in Christianity is discussed in Margaret R. Miles, *Carnal Knowing: Female Nakedness and Religious Meaning in the Christian West* (Boston: Beacon Press, 1989).

39. James Schultz, *Courtly Love, the Love of Courtliness, and the History of Sexuality* (Chicago: University of Chicago Press, 2006), 17–28, 80–83.

40. Bataille, *Accursed Share*, 2:141–42.

41. D. W. Robertson Jr. and Bernard F. Huppé, *"Piers Plowman" and the Scriptural Tradition* (Princeton, NJ: Princeton University Press, 1951), 51–52.

42. Derrida, *Given Time*, 79–80, 62.

43. See Kellie Robertson, *The Laborer's Two Bodies: Literary and Legal Production in Britain, 1350–1500* (New York: Palgrave, 2006), 45–50.

44. See Eric Jager, *The Tempter's Voice: Language and the Fall in Medieval Literature* (Ithaca, NY: Cornell University Press, 1993).

45. For example, H. A. Mason, *Humanism and Poetry in the Early Tudor Period* (London: Routledge and Kegan Paul, 1959), 171; Raymond Southall, *The Courtly Maker: An Essay on the Poetry of Wyatt and His Contemporaries* (Oxford: Blackwell, 1964), 39–53; Steven Greenblatt, *Renaissance Self-Fashioning: From More to Shakespeare* (Chicago: University of Chicago Press, 1980), 115–56; Elizabeth Heale, *Wyatt, Surrey and Early Tudor Poetry* (London: Longman, 1998), 7–69; Greg Walker, *Writing under Tyranny: English Literature and the Henrician Reformation* (New York: Oxford University Press, 2005), 279–376; Jon Robinson, *Court Politics, Culture and Literature in Scotland and England, 1500–1540* (Aldershot: Ashgate, 2008), 105–40.

46. For overviews of Wyatt's career, see Stephen Merriam Foley, *Sir Thomas Wyatt* (Boston: Twayne, 1990), 4–33; Heale, *Wyatt, Surrey,* 11–19; Walker, *Writing under Tyranny,* 282–86.

47. Reed Way Dasenbrock, *Imitating the Italians: Wyatt, Spenser, Synge, Pound, Joyce* (Baltimore: Johns Hopkins University Press, 1991), 19.

48. Thomas Wyatt, "What vaileth trouth?," in *The Collected Poems of Sir Thomas Wyatt,* ed. Kenneth Muir and Patricia Thomson (Liverpool: Liverpool University Press, 1969); hereafter cited in the text.

49. Greenblatt, *Renaissance Self-Fashioning,* 144.

50. Kenneth Graham, *The Performance of Conviction: Plainness and Rhetoric in the Early English Renaissance* (Ithaca, NY: Cornell University Press, 1994), 25–49.

51. Thomas A. Hannen stresses the speaker's insistence on remaining part of the world the poem constructs in "Humanism of Sir Thomas Wyatt," in *The Rhetoric of Renaissance Poetry, Wyatt to Milton,* ed. Thomas O. Sloan and Raymond B. Waddington, 37–57 (Berkeley: University of California Press, 1974), 40.

52. Jonathan Crewe, *Trials of Authorship: Anterior Forms and Poetic Reconstruction from Wyatt to Shakespeare* (Berkeley: University of California Press, 1990), 26–27.

53. Georges Bataille, "The Notion of Expenditure," in *Visions of Excess: Selected Writings, 1927–1932,* ed. and trans. Allan Stoekl, 116–29 (Minneapolis: University of Minnesota Press, 1985), 120.

54. On giving as an endangering of the self, see Hénaff, *Price of Truth,* 126–29.

55. On linguistic failure in Wyatt, see Thomas Greene, *The Light in Troy: Imitation and Discovery in Renaissance Poetry* (New Haven, CT: Yale University Press, 1982), 242–63; Anne Ferry, *The "Inward" Language: Sonnets of Wyatt, Sidney, Shakespeare, Donne* (Chicago: University of Chicago Press, 1983), 71–118;

Diane M. Ross, *Self-Revelation and Self-Protection in Wyatt's Lyric Poetry* (New York: Garland, 1988), 118–68.

56. Throughout the chapter I quote from *Petrarch's Lyric Poems: The "Rime sparse" and Other Lyrics*, ed. and trans. Robert M. Durling (Cambridge, MA: Harvard University Press, 1976).

57. Although in early modern English "wild" was connoted as both "unrestrained" (i.e., promiscuous) and "shy" (i.e., chaste), its opposition to "tame" would appear to tip the semantic balance toward the former. See Heather Dubrow, *Echoes of Desire: English Petrarchism and Its Counterdiscourses* (Ithaca, NY: Cornell University Press, 1995), 97; Barbara L. Estrin, *Laura: Uncovering Gender and Genre in Wyatt, Donne, and Marvell* (Durham, NC: Duke University Press, 1994), 142; Foley, *Sir Thomas Wyatt*, 99; Greenblatt, *Renaissance Self-Fashioning*, 147–48.

58. Ferry, *"Inward" Language*, 112.

59. I quote from *The Byble in Englishe* (London, 1539).

60. Marguerite Waller, "The Empire's New Clothes: Refashioning the Renaissance," in *Seeking the Woman in Late Medieval and Renaissance Writings: Essays in Feminist Contextual Criticism*, ed. Sheila Fisher and Janet E. Halley, 160–83 (Knoxville: University of Tennessee Press, 1989), 170–72.

61. Ibid., 172.

62. Bradin Cormack, *A Power to Do Justice: Jurisdiction, English Literature, and the Rise of Common Law, 1509–1625* (Chicago: University of Chicago Press, 2007), 91.

63. G. R. Elton, ed., *The Tudor Constitution: Documents and Commentary* (Cambridge: Cambridge University Press, 1982), 364.

64. On the Great Debasement, see John F. Chown, *A History of Money: From 800 AD* (London: Routledge, 1994), 41–59; J. D. Gould, *The Great Debasement: Currency and the Economy in Mid-Tudor England* (Oxford: Clarendon, 1970). On its impact on English literature, see Stephen Deng, *Coinage and State Formation in Early Modern English Literature* (New York: Palgrave, 2011), 87–102; David Landreth, *The Face of Mammon: The Matter of Money in English Renaissance Literature* (Oxford: Oxford University Press, 2012), 15–33.

65. On the post-Henrician history of the Egerton MS containing the poem, see Richard Harrier, *The Canon of Sir Thomas Wyatt's Poetry* (Cambridge, MA: Harvard University Press, 1975), 3–7; Jason Powell, "Marginalia, Authorship, and Editing in Thomas Wyatt's Verse," in *Tudor Manuscripts, 1485–1603*, ed. A. S. G. Edwards, 1–40 (Chicago: University of Chicago Press, 2010).

66. Catherine Bates makes a similar argument in *Masculinity and the Hunt: Wyatt to Spenser* (Oxford: Oxford University Press, 2013), 84, although she reads these elements as the subject's "powerlessness and failure" rather than his economic deficiency.

67. Although spoken by the hind in the first person, the inscription on the hind's collar "betray [her] language as that of another, written by or on behalf of 'Caesar,'" according to Jason Powell, "'For Caesar's I am': Henrician Diplomacy and Representations of King and Country in Thomas Wyatt's Poetry," *Sixteenth Century Journal* 36, no. 2 (2005): 429.

68. Joe Glaser, "Wyatt, Petrarch, and the Uses of Mistranslation," *College Literature* 11, no. 3 (1984): 216.

69. See Alistair Fox, *Politics and Literature in the Reigns of Henry VII and Henry VIII* (Oxford: Blackwell, 1989), 258–64; Walker, *Writing under Tyranny*, 287.

70. Daniel Juan Gil, *Before Intimacy: Asocial Sexuality in Early Modern England* (Minneapolis: University of Minnesota Press, 2006), 17.

71. William P. Marvin, *Hunting Law and Ritual in Medieval English Literature* (Cambridge: D. S. Brewer, 2006), 53.

72. Heale, *Wyatt, Surrey*, 58.

73. Greenblatt, *Renaissance Self-Fashioning*, 148.

74. See Dasenbrock, *Imitating the Italians*, 43, and in more general terms, Jane Hedley, *Power in Verse: Metaphor and Metonymy in the Renaissance Lyric* (Philadelphia: University of Pennsylvania Press, 1990), 115.

75. Crewe, *Trials of Authorship*, 41.

76. See Bates, *Masculinity and the Hunt*, 91, who draws on Michael Bath, "The Legend of Caesar's Deer," *Medievalia and Humanistica* n.s. 9 (1979): 53–66.

77. Foley, *Sir Thomas Wyatt*, 99.

78. See J. W. Lever, *The Elizabethan Love Sonnet* (London: Methuen, 1956), 26; Greene, *Light in Troy*, 261; Greenblatt, *Renaissance Self-Fashioning*, 146; Glaser, "Wyatt, Petrarch, and Mistranslation," 215; Crewe, *Trials of Authorship*, 38; and Robinson, *Court Politics*, 135.

79. Jean-Luc Nancy, *Noli Me Tangere: On the Raising of the Body*, trans. Sarah Clift, Pascale-Anne Brault, and Michael Naas (New York: Fordham University Press, 2008), 52.

80. See Marc Shell, *The Economy of Literature* (Baltimore: Johns Hopkins University Press, 1978).

81. Cf. Roland Barthes, *The Pleasure of the Text*, trans. Richard Miller (New York: Hill and Wang, 1975): "For the text, nothing is

gratuitous except its own destruction: not to write, not to write again, except to be eternally recuperated" (24).

82. Unless otherwise indicated, all quotations from Spenser's poems are from Edmund Spenser, *The Shorter Poems*, ed. Richard A. McCabe (London: Penguin, 1999); hereafter cited parenthetically in the text by poem and line number.

83. Dubrow, *Echoes of Desire*, 80.

84. Roland Greene, "Spenser and Contemporary Vernacular Poetry," in *The Cambridge Companion to Spenser*, ed. Andrew Hadfield, 237–51 (Cambridge: Cambridge University Press, 2001), 237.

85. To my knowledge, outside of the *Amoretti*, the word "meed" occurs in only three other sonnet sequences: Barnes's *Parthenophil and Parthenophe*, E. C.'s *Emaricdulfe*, and Richard Barnfield's *Cynthia* (1595).

86. Richard Helgerson, *Self-Crowned Laureates: Spenser, Johnson, Milton, and the Literary System* (Berkeley: University of California Press, 1983), 29.

87. Robert J. Meyer-Lee, *Poets and Power from Chaucer to Wyatt* (Cambridge: Cambridge University Press, 2007), 20.

88. Richard Rambuss, "Spenser's Lives, Spenser's Careers," in *Spenser's Life and the Subject of Biography*, ed. Judith H. Anderson, Donald Cheney, and David A. Richardson, 1–17 (Amherst: University of Massachusetts Press, 1996), 14.

89. Herbert Berry and E. K. Timings, "Spenser's Pension," *Review of English Studies* 11, no. 43 (1960): 254–59.

90. On the biographical aspect of the sequence, see Fred Blick, "Spenser's *Amoretti* and Elizabeth Boyle: Her Names Immortalized," *Spenser Studies* 23 (2008): 309–15; Ilona Bell, *Elizabethan Women and the Poetry of Courtship* (Cambridge: Cambridge University Press, 1998), 152–84; William C. Johnson, "Gender Fashioning and the Dynamics of Mutuality in Spenser's *Amoretti*," *English Studies* 74 (1993): 503–19.

91. Arthur F. Marotti, "'Love Is Not Love': Elizabethan Sonnet Sequences and the Social Order," *English Literary History* 49, no. 2 (1982): 396–428; on the *Amoretti*, see 413–19.

92. *Zepheria* (London, 1594), B1^r.

93. On the eroticism of Elizabeth's imagery in early modern culture, see, for example, Philippa Berry, *Of Chastity and Power: Elizabethan Literature and the Unmarried Queen* (London: Routledge, 1989), 134–65; Mary R. Bowman, "'She there as Princess rained': Spenser's Figure of Elizabeth," *Renaissance Quarterly* 43, no. 4 (1990): 509–28; Susan Frye, *Elizabeth I: The Competition for Representation* (Oxford: Oxford University Press, 1993), 97–143;

Robin Headlam Wells, *Spenser's "Faerie Queene" and the Cult of Elizabeth* (London: Crook Helm, 1983). On the queen's presence in the *Amoretti* and on the politics of the collection, see Catherine Bates, *The Rhetoric of Courtship in Elizabethan Language and Literature* (Cambridge: Cambridge University Press, 1992), 136–51, esp. 138–40; James Fleming, "A View from the Bridge: Ireland and Violence in Spenser's *Amoretti,*" *Spenser Studies* 15 (2001): 135–64; William J. Kennedy, *Authorizing Petrarch* (Ithaca, NY: Cornell University Press, 1994), 201–35.

94. Patrick Cheney, *Spenser's Famous Flight: A Renaissance Idea of a Literary Career* (Toronto: University of Toronto Press, 1993), 152.

95. Kennedy, *Authorizing Petrarch*, 219. On Spenser's Protestantism in the *Amoretti,* see also John King, *Spenser's Poetry and the Reformation Tradition* (Princeton, NJ: Princeton University Press, 1990), 160–77; and Lisa M. Klein, *The Exemplary Sidney and the Elizabethan Sonneteer* (Newark: University of Delaware Press, 1998), 188–215.

96. Shershow, *Work and the Gift*, 147. See also Hénaff, *Price of Truth*, 268–76.

97. Max Weber, *The Protestant Ethic and the Spirit of Capitalism*, trans. Talcott Parsons (New York: Charles Scribner's Sons, 1958), 80, 121.

98. R. H. Tawney, *Religion and the Rise of Capitalism* (1926; repr., Gloucester, MA: Peter Smith, 1962), 109, also 240–43.

99. The most sustained analysis of the lady's Christ-like characteristics is William C. Johnson, *Spenser's Amoretti: Analogies of Love* (Lewisburg, PA: Bucknell University Press, 1990). See also Klein, *Exemplary Sidney*, 193–96; and Hallett Smith, *Elizabethan Poetry*, 2nd ed. (Ann Arbor: University of Michigan Press, 1968), 167.

100. Gordon Braden, "Beyond Frustration: Petrarchan Laurels in the Seventeenth Century," *SEL: Studies in English Literature, 1500–1900* 26 (1986): 5–11.

101. As Deleuze and Guattari theorize, the transition from precapitalism to capitalism is characterized by a movement away from "the despotic signifier" crushing the interplay of representation toward "the generalized decoding of flows, the new massive deterritorialization, the conjunction of deterritorialized flows" (*Anti-Oedipus*, 224).

102. For the sources of Spenser's sonnet, see Sidney Lee, *Elizabethan Sonnets*, vol. 1 (Westminster, 1904), xcvi–xcvii.

103. On the poem's lust for colonial wealth imagined in gendered terms, see Kim Hall, *Things of Darkness: Economies of Race and Gender in Early Modern England* (Ithaca, NY: Cornell University Press, 1995), 81–82.

104. Lisa Jardine, *Worldly Goods: A New History of the Renaissance* (London: Nan A. Talese/Doubleday, 1996), 124.

105. David Hawkes, *Idols of the Marketplace: Idolatry and Commodity Fetishism in English Literature, 1580–1680* (New York: Palgrave, 2001), 56.

106. Christopher Warley, *Sonnet Sequences and Social Distinction in Renaissance England* (Cambridge: Cambridge University Press, 2005), 111. Aaron Kitch, *Political Economy and the States of Literature in Early Modern England* (Farnham: Ashgate, 2009), detects in Spenser's sonnet biblical antimercantile language, but he insists that the object of passion is still "measured in terms of mercantile bounty" (22).

107. Roger Kuin, *Chamber Music: Elizabethan Sonnet-Sequences and the Pleasure of Criticism* (Toronto: University of Toronto Press, 1998), 33–37.

108. Theresa M. Krier, "Generations of Blazons: Psychoanalysis and the Song of Songs in the *Amoretti*," *Texas Studies in Language and Literature* 40, no. 3 (1998), identifies in the sonnet a note of bitterness akin to "an infant's psychic attack on the desired object which does not perfectly answer its needs" (308).

109. Warley, *Sonnet Sequences*, 113.

110. See Anne Lake Prescott, "The Thirsty Deer and the Lord of Life: Some Contexts for *Amoretti* 67–70," *Spenser Studies* 6 (1985): 33–76.

111. King, *Spenser's Poetry*, 169.

112. Prescott, "Thirsty Deer," 44, 55; see also Johnson, *Spenser's Amoretti*, 190–91.

113. On sovereign violence in the *Amoretti*, see Fleming, "View from the Bridge," esp. 159–61; Andrew Zurcher, *Spenser's Legal Language: Law and Poetry in Early Modern England* (Cambridge: D. S. Brewer, 2007), 209–10.

114. Kennedy, *Authorizing Petrarch*, 264.

115. Carol Thomas Neely, "The Structure of English Renaissance Sonnet Sequences," *English Literary History* 45, no. 3 (1978): 375–76.

116. Lever took the sonnets to be a printer's error (*Elizabethan Love Sonnet*, 128). For numerological readings that insist on the validity of the numbering and ordering of the sonnets, see Alexander Dunlop, "The Unity of Spenser's *Amoretti*," in *Silent Poetry: Essays in Numerological Analysis*, ed. Alistair Fowler, 153–69 (London: Routledge and Kegan Paul, 1970); A. Kent Hieatt, "A Numerical Key for Spenser's '*Amoretti*' and Guyon in the House of Mammon," *Yearbook of English Studies* 3 (1973): 14–27; and Shohachi Fukuda, "The Numerological Patterning of *Amoretti and Epithalamion*," *Spenser Studies* 9 (1991 for 1988): 33–48. Carol V. Kaske, in

"Spenser's *Amoretti* and *Epithalamion* of 1595: Structure, Genre, and Numerology," *English Literary Renaissance* 8 (1978): 280, suggests that the final sonnets form a prelude to the Anacreontics and the marriage song, and that they merely "dramatize the discomforts of the lover as fiancé," who is languishing between promise and consummation. For the interpretation of the sonnets as a record of the lovers' separation during the wedding preparations, see Bell, *Elizabethan Women*, 181; Cheney, *Spenser's Famous Flight*, 185; and Donna Gibbs, *Spenser's Amoretti: A Critical Study* (Hants, NS: Scolar Press, 1990), 14, 99.

117. Peter M. Cummings, "Spenser's *Amoretti* as an Allegory of Love," *Texas Studies in Language and Literature* 12 (1970): 175. Noam Flinker, *The Song of Songs in English Renaissance Literature* (Cambridge: D. S. Brewer, 2000), 79–80, writes about "religio-spiritual tension" in these blazons.

118. The established view is that Spenser's sequence represents "a turn away from the restlessness of Petrarchan love and toward the peace and rest Spenser finds in the sacred world of marriage" (Dasenbrock, *Imitating the Italians*, 48). However, it has recently been questioned in M. L. Stapleton, "Devoid of Guilty Shame: Ovidian Tendencies in Spenser's Erotic Poetry," *Modern Philology* 105, no. 2 (2008): 271–99; and Melissa E. Sanchez, "'Modesty or Comeliness': The Predicament of Reform Theology in Spenser's *Amoretti* and *Epithalamion*," *Renascence* 65, no. 1 (2012): 5–24, both of whom emphasize the persistence of unchaste eroticism in the later sonnets.

119. Warley, *Sonnet Sequences*, 116.

120. Johnson, *Spenser's Amoretti*, 242–43; Gibbs, *Spenser's Amoretti*, 13; Cheney, *Spenser's Famous Flight*, 185.

121. Edmund Spenser, *The Faerie Queene*, 2nd ed., ed. A. C. Hamilton (London: Longman, 2006), 5.9.25.2–3.

122. Maurice Blanchot, in *The Space of Literature*, trans. Ann Smock (Lincoln: University of Nebraska Press, 1982), deploys the notion of unworking (*désoeuvrement*) to describe a discrepancy between the work and the book, the largely unanswerable demands of literary work that overpower the artist on the one hand, and the prosaic worldly object of a book on the other. "That the work is infinite," he writes, "means...that the artist, though unable to finish it, can nevertheless make it the delimited site of an endless task whose incompleteness develops the mastery of the mind." The book, in contrast, represents but "the approach and the illusion" in relation to work: "The writer belongs to the work, but what belongs to him is only a book, a mute collection of sterile words, the most insignificant thing in the world" (21–23).

123. Maurice Blanchot, *The Book to Come*, trans. Charlotte Mandell (Stanford, CA: Stanford University Press, 2003), 235.
124. *Emaricdulfe: Sonnets written by E. C. Esquire* (London, 1595), unlineated; hereafter cited in the text by sonnet number. The available information about the sonnet sequence can be found in Georgia Chapman Caver, "*Emaricdulfe by E. C. Esquier* (1595): Materials toward a Critical Edition" (PhD diss., University of Tennessee—Knoxville, 2007).
125. Barnabe Barnes, *Parthenophil and Parthenophe*, ed. Victor A. Doyno (Carbondale: Southern Illinois University Press, 1971); hereafter cited in the text by poem and line number.
126. Jeffrey N. Nelson, "Lust and Black Magic in Barnabe Barnes's *Parthenophil and Parthenophe*," *Sixteenth Century Journal* 25, no. 3 (1994): 605.
127. Thomas P. Roche Jr., *Petrarch and the English Sonnet Sequence* (New York: AMS, 1989), 247.
128. Neely, "Structure," 382.
129. Bataille, *Accursed Share*, 2:129–36.

Notes to Chapter 2

1. Sir Philip Sidney, *An Apologie for Poetrie*, in *Elizabethan Critical Essays*, 2 vols., ed. G. Gregory Smith (Oxford, 1904), 1:193–94.
2. Ibid., 1:196.
3. Thomas A. Prendergast, *Chaucer's Dead Body: From Corpse to Corpus* (New York: Routledge, 2004), 17–70.
4. See Carol Martin, "Authority and the Defense of Fiction: Renaissance Poetics and Chaucer's *House of Fame*," in *Refiguring Chaucer in the Renaissance*, ed. Theresa M. Krier, 40–65 (Gainesville: University Press of Florida, 1998), 40–41.
5. Stephanie Trigg, *Congenial Souls: Reading Chaucer from Medieval to Postmodern* (Minneapolis: University of Minnesota Press, 2002), 111. On the changing attitudes to Chaucer among writers, see also Seth Lerer, *Chaucer and His Readers: Imagining the Author in Late Medieval England* (Princeton, NJ: Princeton University Press, 1993), 147–208.
6. Richard Firth Greene, *Poets and Princepleasers: Literature and the English Court in the Late Middle Ages* (Toronto: University of Toronto Press, 1980), 12.
7. Originally published by the London printer Richard Tottel in June 1557, Tottel's *Miscellany* (as it is commonly known) was reprinted in July 1557, in 1559 (twice), in 1565 (twice), in 1567, 1574, and 1585. For publication history, see Paul A. Marquis,

"Printing History and Editorial Design in the Elizabethan Version of Tottel's *Songes and Sonettes*," in *Tottel's "Songes and Sonettes" in Context*, ed. Stephen Hamrick, 13–36 (Farnham: Ashgate, 2013); Arthur Marotti, *Manuscript, Print, and the English Renaissance Lyric* (Ithaca, NY: Cornell University Press, 1995), 212–19; and Wendy Wall, *The Imprint of Gender: Authorship and Publication in the English Renaissance* (Ithaca, NY: Cornell University Press, 1993), 23–30.

8. Germaine Warkentin, "Sidney's Authors," in *Sir Philip Sidney's Achievements*, ed. M. J. B. Allen et al., 68–90 (New York: AMS, 1990), 75, 85.

9. C. S. Lewis, *English Literature in the Sixteenth Century Excluding Drama* (Oxford: Clarendon, 1962), 236–38; Leonard Forster, *The Icy Fire: Five Studies in European Petrarchism* (Cambridge: Cambridge University Press, 1969), 133.

10. Anne Ferry, *The "Inward" Language: Sonnets of Wyatt, Sidney, Shakespeare, Donne* (Chicago: University of Chicago Press, 1983), 119.

11. William J. Kennedy, *The Site of Petrarchism: Early Modern National Sentiment in Italy, France, and England* (Baltimore: Johns Hopkins University Press, 2003), 203. For similar arguments, see Elizabeth Heale, *Wyatt, Surrey and Early Tudor Poetry* (London: Longman, 1998), 194; William A. Sessions, "Surrey's Wyatt: Autumn 1542 and the New Poet," in *Rethinking the Henrician Era: Essays on Early Tudor Texts and Contexts*, ed. Peter C. Herman, 168–92 (Urbana: University of Illinois Press, 1994), 179–80.

12. Andrew Hadfield, *Literature, Politics and National Identity: Reformation to Renaissance* (Cambridge: Cambridge University Press, 1994), 143–48. See also Stephen Hamrick, "'Their Gods in Verses': Popular Reception of *Songes and Sonettes* 1557–1674," in Hamrick, *Tottel's "Songes and Sonettes*," 183–86.

13. Wall, *Imprint of Gender*, 24. See also Germaine Warkentin, "The Meeting of the Muses: Sidney and the Mid-Tudor Poets," in *Sir Philip Sidney and the Interpretation of Renaissance Culture*, ed. Gary Waller and Michael D. Moore, 17–33 (London: Croom Helm, 1984), who argues that it is mid-Tudor poetic collections like Tottel's that formulated and developed the discursive model of "the poet's public analysis of his own creativity" later adopted by the poets of Sidney's generation (20).

14. Sidney refers to love poetry as "that Lyricall kind of Songs and Sonnets" (*Apologie*, 201), a generic label applied to Sidney's own verse by Abraham Fraunce on the title page of his *Arcadian Rhetorike* (London: Thomas Orwin, 1588), a rhetorical treatise "made plaine by examples...out of...*Sir Philip Sydnieis Arcadia*,

songs and sonets." The modern title of Sidney's sequence first appears in the 1591 pirated edition of Thomas Newman: *Syr P.S. His Astrophel and Stella[,] Wherein the excellence of sweete poesie is concluded* (London: Thomas Newman, 1591).

15. Ardis Butterfield, "Chaucer's French Inheritance," in *The Cambridge Companion to Chaucer*, ed. Piero Boitani and Jill Mann, 20–35 (Cambridge: Cambridge University Press, 2003), 28.

16. *The Workes of Geffray Chaucer Newly Printed, with Dyuers Works Whiche Were Never in Print Before*, ed. William Thynne (London: Thomas Godfray, 1532]), cclxxi^v; *The Workes of Our Antient and Lerned English Poet, Geffrey Chaucer, Newly Printed* (London: Adam Islip for Bonham Norton, 1598), 244.

17. All quotations are from *The Riverside Chaucer*, 3rd ed., ed. Larry Benson (Boston: Houghton Mifflin, 1987), hereafter cited parenthetically in the text by line number.

18. It is generally accepted that the poem was written for John of Gaunt in order to commemorate the death of his first wife, Blanche of Lancaster, of plague in 1368 or 1369.

19. See David Lawton, *Chaucer's Narrators* (Cambridge: D. S. Brewer, 1985), 53.

20. However, Paul Strohm, "Politics and Poetics: Usk and Chaucer in the 1380s," in *Literary Practice and Social Change in Britain, 1380–1530*, ed. Lee Patterson, 83–112 (Berkeley: University of California Press, 1990), 107, suggests that the dominant force in their exchange is civility between two gentlepersons of similar if not equal social rank.

21. For Barbara Nolan, "The Art of Expropriation: Chaucer's Narrator in the *Book of the Duchess*," in *New Perspectives in Chaucer Criticism*, ed. Donald M. Rose, 203–22 (Norman, OK: Pilgrim, 1981), 221–22, the disjunction between the dreamer and the man in black opens up possibilities for a nonaristocratic critique of courtly culture. On Chaucer's metapoetic agenda in the poem, see also Robert R. Edwards, *The Dream of Chaucer: Representation and Reflection in the Early Narratives* (Durham, NC: Duke University Press, 1989), 65–91.

22. L. O. Aranye Fradenburg, *Sacrifice Your Love: Psychoanalysis, Historicism, Chaucer* (Minneapolis: University of Minnesota Press, 2002), 100.

23. See Elaine Tuttle Hansen, *Chaucer and the Fictions of Gender* (Berkeley: University of California Press, 1992), 60–68.

24. See also Steven Kruger, "Medical and Moral Authority in the Late Medieval Dream," in *Reading Dreams: The Interpretation of Dreams from Chaucer to Shakespeare*, ed. Peter Brown, 51–84 (Oxford: Oxford University Press, 1999), 64–69; Cyndy Hendershot,

"Male Subjectivity, Fin Amor, and Melancholia in the *Book of the Duchess,*" *Mediaevalia* 21 (1996): 12–13.

25. John Lawlor, "The Pattern of Consolation in the *Book of the Duchess,*" *Speculum* 31 (1956): 637; A. C. Spearing, *The Medieval Poet as Voyeur: Looking and Listening in Medieval Love-Narratives* (Cambridge: Cambridge University Press, 1993), 219.

26. John M. Hill, "The *Book of the Duchess,* Melancholy, and That Eight-Year Sickness," *Chaucer Review* 9 (1974): 35–50, esp. 38–41; Carol Falvo Heffernan, *The Melancholy Muse: Chaucer, Shakespeare and Early Medicine* (Pittsburgh: Duquesne University Press, 1995), 41.

27. French courtly poetry provides more than half the content and rhetoric of Chaucer's dream vision. Chaucer's principal sources are Guillaume de Lorris's *Roman de la rose,* Jean Froissart's *Le paradis d'Amour,* and Guillaume de Machaut's *Le dit de la fonteinne amoreuse, Remède de fortune,* and *Le jugement du roy de Behaigne.* See James Wimsatt, *Chaucer and the French Love Poets: The Literary Background of the "Book of the Duchess"* (Chapel Hill: University of North Carolina Press, 1968); *Chaucer's Dream Poetry: Sources and Analogues,* ed. B. A. Windeatt (Totowa, NJ: Rowman and Littlefield, 1982), 3–72.

28. On the significance of reading and writing in the poem, see Glenn Burger, "Reading Otherwise: Recovering the Subject in the *Book of the Duchess,*" *Exemplaria* 5, no. 2 (1993): 325–41.

29. Nancy Ciccone, "The Chamber, the Man in Black, and the Structure of Chaucer's *Book of the Duchess,*" *Chaucer Review* 44, no. 2 (2009), argues that these texts represent "a structural analogue to the main scene in the *Book of the Duchess,* providing commentary on the man in black's autobiography and a cultural perspective on the death of White" (206).

30. Quotations from, respectively, Charles Muscatine, *Chaucer and the French Tradition: A Study in Style and Meaning* (Berkeley: University of California Press, 1965), 107; Ian Robinson, *Chaucer and the English Tradition* (Cambridge: Cambridge University Press, 1972), 41; Edward I. Condren, *Chaucer from Prentice to Poet: The Metaphor of Love in Dream Visions and "Troilus and Criseyde"* (Gainesville: University Press of Florida, 2008), 37.

31. See William Calin, *The French Tradition and the Literature of Medieval England* (Toronto: University of Toronto Press, 1994), 269–370, who insists on the continued importance of French poetry for Chaucer. Susan Schibanoff, *Chaucer's Queer Poetics: Rereading the Dream Trio* (Toronto: University of Toronto Press, 2006), 3–23, 29–41, offers a sensitive discussion of the "rhetoric of liberation" in

Chaucer criticism as an expression of certain class and nationalist tendencies in the academy. Also see Ardis Butterfield, *The Familiar Enemy: Chaucer, Language and Nation in the Hundred Years War* (Oxford: Oxford University Press, 2009), 269–91, who notes that contrasting Chaucer's Englishness with the Frenchness of his sources presupposes a well-defined taxonomy of stable national and linguistic identities, which clearly contradicts the cultural realities of late fourteenth century England.

32. Deanne Williams, *The French Fetish from Chaucer to Shakespeare* (Cambridge: Cambridge University Press, 2004), 31. It is hardly accidental that some critics have described Chaucer's role in the poem as a *bricoleur*—a poet "finding his materials as if by chance, piecing them together in astonishing new ways, moving always slightly outside the bounds of accepted roles and established myths" (Nolan, "Art of Expropriation," 206). See also R. Barton Palmer, "Rereading Guillaume de Machaut's *Vision of Love*: Chaucer's *Book of the Duchess* as Bricolage," in *Second Thoughts: A Focus on Rereading*, ed. David Galef, 169–95 (Detroit: Wayne State University Press, 1998).

33. Kathryn L. Lynch, *Chaucer's Philosophical Visions* (Cambridge: D. S. Brewer, 2000), 46.

34. Donald Beecher and Massimo Ciavolella, "Jacques Ferrand and the Tradition of Erotic Melancholy in Western Culture," introduction to Jacques Ferrand, *A Treatise on Lovesickness*, 1–202 (Syracuse, NY: Syracuse University Press, 1990), 41.

35. Aristotle, *Problems*, trans. W. S. Hett, 2 vols. (London: Heineman, 1953–57), 2:155.

36. Aristotle, *Problems*, 2:159.

37. See Mary Frances Wack, *Lovesickness in the Middle Ages: The "Viaticum" and Its Commentaries* (Philadelphia: University of Pennsylvania Press, 1990), 31–108; Beecher and Ciavolella, "Jacques Ferrand," 62–70; Lesel Dawson, *Lovesickness and Gender in Early Modern English Literature* (Oxford: Oxford University Press, 2008), 14–15; and Heffernan, *Melancholy Muse*, 13–21.

38. Marion A. Wells, *The Secret Wound: Love-Melancholy and Early Modern Romance* (Stanford, CA: Stanford University Press, 2007), 35.

39. On early modern medical humoralism, see Owsei Temkin, *Galenism: Rise and Decline of a Medical Philosophy* (Ithaca, NY: Cornell University Press, 1973); Nancy G. Siraisi, *Medieval and Early Renaissance Medicine* (Chicago: University of Chicago Press, 1990), 78–114; Michael Schoenfeldt, *Bodies and Selves in Early Modern England: Physiology and Inwardness in Spenser, Shakespeare, Herbert, and Milton* (Cambridge: Cambridge University

Press, 1999), 1–39; and Gail Kern Paster, *Humoring the Body: Emotions and the Shakespearean Stage* (Chicago: University of Chicago Press, 2004). In *The Unrepentant Renaissance: From Petrarch to Shakespeare to Milton* (Chicago: University of Chicago Press, 2011), 17–21, Richard Strier challenges one aspect of this critical movement (which he calls "the new humoralism"), namely, its insistence on regulation and moderation and its aversion to passion. However, there is no denying that the Galenic system was at the center of medical thought in the English Renaissance.

40. Thomas Walkington, *The optick glasse of humors* (London, 1631), 126.

41. Thomas Elyot, *The Castel of Helthe* (1541) (New York: Scholars Facsimiles, 1937), 9^v, 72^v.

42. Timothy Bright, *A Treatise of Melancholie* (1586) (Amsterdam: Da Capo Press, 1969), 25.

43. James [Jacques] Ferrand, *Erotomania; or, A treatise discoursing of the essence, causes, symptoms, prognosticks, and cure of love, or erotique melancholy* (Oxford, 1640), 10.

44. Donald Beecher, "The Lover's Body: The Somatogenesis of Love in Renaissance Medical Treatises," *Renaissance and Reformation* n.s. 24, no. 1 (1988): 1–12.

45. M. Andreas Laurentius, *A Discourse of the Preseruation of the Sight: Of Melancholike Diseases; of Rheumes, and of Old Age*, trans. Richard Surphlet (1599) (Oxford: Oxford University Press, 1938), 124.

46. The tendency in recent studies of pre-modern melancholy has been to focus on one cultural construction of the affliction at the expense of others. For examples, Adam H. Kitzes, *The Politics of Melancholy from Spenser to Milton* (New York: Routledge, 2006), seeks to contrast melancholy as a medical and social problem to the "genial" and "erotic" melancholy of Aristotle and Ficino. Douglas Trevor, *The Poetics of Melancholy in Early Modern England* (Cambridge: Cambridge University Press, 2004), insists on the contrast between scholarly melancholy, which Trevor considers to be "dispositional" (caused by humoral imbalance), and love melancholy, which he takes to be "objectal" (induced by an object of desire) (14; see also 19–20, 44, 85).

47. Drew Daniel, *The Melancholy Assemblage: Affect and Epistemology in the English Renaissance* (New York: Fordham University Press, 2013), 17. Cf. Carol Thomas Neely, *Distracted Subjects: Madness and Gender in Shakespeare and Early Modern Culture* (Ithaca, NY: Cornell University Press, 2004), 70: "Melancholy is a capacious disease with a flexible taxonomy."

48. Gerard of Berry, *Commentary*, in Wack, *Lovesickness*, 199.

49. Wells, *Secret Wound*, 43–44.
50. Laurentius, *Discourse*, 87, 121.
51. Ficino, *Commentary on Plato's Symposium on Love*, trans. S. Jayne (Dallas: Spring Publications, 1985), 56.
52. This continuity has been pursued from a variety of perspectives. In addition to Stanley W. Jackson's clinical history of the disorder in *Melancholia and Depression: From Hippocratic Times to Modern Times* (New Haven, CT: Yale University Press, 1986), Juliana Schiesari has traced misogyny in the writings on melancholy from Aristotle to the present in *The Gendering of Melancholia: Feminism, Psychoanalysis, and the Symbolics of Loss in Renaissance Literature* (Ithaca, NY: Cornell University Press, 1992); and Giorgio Agamben has investigated the phantasmatic character of desire in Western culture in *Stanzas: Word and Phantasm in Western Culture*, trans. Ronald L. Martinez (Minneapolis: University of Minnesota Press, 1993), 3–28.
53. Franco "Bifo" Berardi, *The Soul at Work: From Alienation to Autonomy*, trans. Franscesca Cadel and Guiseppina Mecchia (Los Angeles: Semiotext[e], 2009), 137.
54. Sigmund Freud, "Mourning and Melancholia," in *The Standard Edition of the Complete Psychological Works of Sigmund Freud*, 24 vols., ed. and trans. James Strachey 243–58 (London: Hogarth, 1953–74), 14:249.
55. Freud, "Mourning and Melancholia," 247.
56. Freud, *The Ego and the Id*, in *Standard Edition*, 19:28, 30–31.
57. Mikkel Borch-Jacobsen, *The Freudian Subject*, trans. Catherine Porter (Stanford, CA: Stanford University Press, 1988), 21; see also 10–52.
58. Levinus Lemnius, *The Touchstone of Complexions*, trans. Thomas Newton (London, 1576), 138^v.
59. Laurentius, *Discourse*, 94, 97.
60. Walkington, *Optick glasse*, 134.
61. Ibid., 135–36.
62. Robert Burton, *The Anatomy of Melancholy*, 3 vols., ed. Thomas C. Faulkner, Nicholas K. Kiessling, and Rhonda L. Blair (Oxford: Clarendon, 1990), 1:252.
63. Freud, *Ego and the Id*, 29.
64. Julia Kristeva, *Black Sun: Depression and Melancholia*, trans. Leon S. Roudiez (New York: Columbia University Press, 1989), 47.
65. Douglas L. Peterson, *The English Lyric from Wyatt to Donne: A History of the Plain and Eloquent Styles* (Princeton, NJ: Princeton University Press, 1967), 39–86; Elizabeth Pomeroy, *The*

Elizabethan Miscellanies, Their Development and Conventions (Berkeley: University of California Press, 1973), 1–16, 31–52.

66. See especially Paul A. Marquis, "Politics and Print: The Curious Revisions to Tottel's *Songes and Sonettes*," *Studies in Philology* 97, no. 2 (2000): 145–64; and his introduction to *Richard Tottel's "Songes and Sonettes": The Elizabethan Version*, ed. Paul A. Marquis (Tempe: Arizona Center for Medieval and Renaissance Studies, 2007). All references to Surrey's poems will be from Marquis's edition, cited by poem and line numbers in the text.

67. For example, Meredith Anne Skura, *Tudor Autobiography: Listening for Inwardness* (Chicago: University of Chicago Press, 2008), writes that Surrey's "sweet" style "does not usually reveal a specific, individual personality" (39).

68. William A. Sessions, *Henry Howard, Earl of Surrey* (Boston: Twayne, 1986).

69. For the importance of the Troy myth for Surrey, including his translation of two books of the *Aeneid*, see Jonathan Crewe, *Trials of Authorship: Anterior Forms and Poetic Reconstruction from Wyatt to Shakespeare* (Berkeley: University of California Press, 1990), 48–78; Stephen Guy-Bray, "Embracing Troy: Surrey's Aeneid," in *Fantasies of Troy: Classical Tales and the Social Imaginary in Medieval and Early Modern Europe*, ed. Alan Shepard and Stephen D. Powell, 177–92 (Toronto: Centre for Reformation and Renaissance Studies, 2004); Andrew Hiscock, *Reading Memory in Early Modern Literature* (Cambridge: Cambridge University Press, 2011), 53–58; Sessions, *Henry Howard*, 134–52. On the matter of Troy in *Songes and Sonettes*, see Alex Davis, "Tottel's Troy," in Hamrick, *Tottel's "Songes and Sonettes*," 63–85. For Chaucer's own relationship with the Trojan myth, see Lee Patterson, *Chaucer and the Subject of History* (Madison: University of Wisconsin Press, 1991), 84–164.

70. Amanda Holton, "Chaucer's Presence in *Songes and Sonettes*," in Hamrick, *Tottel's "Songes and Sonettes*," 89.

71. Roland Greene, *Post-Petrarchism: Origins and Innovations of the Western Lyric Sequence* (Princeton, NJ: Princeton University Press, 1991), 3–5.

72. Barbara Estrin, *Laura: Uncovering Gender and Genre in Wyatt, Donne, and Marvell* (Durham, NC: Duke University Press, 1994), 12; see also Reed Way Dasenbrock, *Imitating the Italians: Wyatt, Spenser, Synge, Pound, Joyce* (Baltimore: Johns Hopkins University Press, 1991), 17.

73. Christopher Warley, *Sonnet Sequences and Social Distinction in Renaissance England* (Cambridge: Cambridge University Press, 2005), 19–44.

74. Heather Dubrow, *Echoes of Desire: English Petrarchism and Its Counterdiscourses* (Ithaca, NY: Cornell University Press, 1995), 6–8.

75. Sessions describes retrospection as "a major device of Surrey's poetic art" (*Henry Howard*, 71); and Hiscock likewise puts emphasis on Surrey's "poetics of memory" within a larger context of early modern humanistic recovery and argues that "Surrey's very poetic œuvre should be construed as a collective act of memorial construction" (*Reading Memory*, 62, also 37–64).

76. Gordon Braden, "Beyond Frustration: Petrarchan Laurels in the Seventeenth Century," *SEL: Studies in English Literature, 1500–1900* 26, no. 1 (1986): 8.

77. On the balance within Petrarchan oxymora, see William J. Kennedy, *Rhetorical Norms in Renaissance Literature* (New Haven, CT: Yale University Press, 1979), 21.

78. Paul de Man, *Allegories of Reading: Figural Language in Rousseau, Nietzsche, Rilke, and Proust* (New Haven, CT: Yale University Press, 1978), 17.

79. Kristeva, *Black Sun*, 53. I am also indebted to Crewe's remarks that Surrey's poetry narrates "a story...of suicide, in which a 'poetics of suicide' is elaborated, and it is therefore irreducibly a story of willfully embraced failure or defeat" (*Trials of Authorship*, 51), even though Crewe does not link Surrey's suicidal poetics to Petrarchism.

80. Sessions, *Henry Howard*, 128–29.

81. See Candace Lines, "The Erotic Politics of Grief in Surrey's 'So Crewell Prison,'" *SEL: Studies in English Literature, 1500–1900* 46, no. 1 (2006): 1–26.

82. Stephen Guy-Bray, *Homoerotic Space: The Poetics of Loss in Renaissance Literature* (Toronto: University of Toronto Press, 2002), 103–17.

83. Peterson, *English Lyric*, 71.

84. Hiscock, *Reading Memory*, 51. However, as Davis notes, "the speaker of the poem is never overtly identified as female" ("Tottel's Troy," 75). It is worth noting that in the Devonshire manuscript, "O happy dames" is transcribed in a female hand. See Helen Baron, "Mary (Howard) Fitzroy's Hand in the Devonshire Manuscript," *Review of English Studies* n.s. 45 (1994): 318–35; Jonathan Goldberg, "The Female Pen: Writing as a Woman," in *Language Machines: Technologies of Literary and Cultural Production*, ed. Jeffrey Masten, Peter Stallybrass, and Nancy J. Vickers, 17–38 (New York: Routledge, 1997); Elizabeth Heale, "Women and the Courtly Love Lyric: The Devonshire MS (BL Additional 17492)," *Modern Language Review* 90, no. 2 (1995): 296–313.

85. Throughout the chapter, I cite *Petrarch's Lyric Poems: The "Rime sparse" and Other Lyrics*, ed. and trans. Robert M. Durling (Cambridge, MA: Harvard University Press, 1976) by poem and line number.

86. Sessions, *Henry Howard*, 77–80.

87. Twenty years ago Gary Waller, "Struggling into Discourse: The Emergence of Renaissance Women's Writing," in *Silent but for the Word: Tudor Women as Patrons, Translators, and Writers of Religious Works*, ed. Margaret Patterson Hannay, 238–56 (Kent, OH: Kent State University Press, 1985), described Petrarchism as "a theater of desire—one in which men have the active roles and the women are assigned silent, iconic functions, and are notable primarily for their absence from the script" (242). Since then, the possibility of female Petrarchism has been rehabilitated in, for example, Ann Rosalind Jones, *The Currency of Eros: Women's Love Lyric in Europe, 1540–1620* (Bloomington: Indiana University Press, 1990); Rosalind Smith, *Sonnets and the English Woman Writer, 1560–1621: The Politics of Absence* (New York: Palgrave, 2005).

88. Jonathan Goldberg, *Sodometries: Renaissance Texts, Modern Sexualities* (Stanford, CA: Stanford University Press, 1992), 53. On textual cross-dressing involving male subjects appropriating a female voice, see Elizabeth D. Harvey, *Ventriloquized Voices: Feminist Theory and English Renaissance Texts* (New York: Routledge, 1992).

89. Carla Freccero, *Queer/Early/Modern* (Durham, NC: Duke University Press, 2006), 24. Cf. Dubrow, *Echoes of Desire*, who argues that Petrarchism "repeatedly challenges the boundaries between characteristics that might be gendered masculine and feminine" (11).

90. As Jonathan Goldberg demonstrates in *Writing Matter: From the Hands of the English Renaissance* (Stanford, CA: Stanford University Press, 1990), 59–107, the production and use of writing instruments (pens, knives, etc.) was associated with death, for example, in the form of violence aimed at the birds whose feathers were used to make quills or in the uses of the knife to correct writing.

91. See Sessions, "Surrey's Wyatt," 168–92.

92. Frederic B. Tromly, "Surrey's Fidelity to Wyatt in 'Wyatt Resteth Here,'" *Studies in Philology* 77 (1980): 377.

93. Laurentius, *Discourse*, 121.

94. Judith Butler, *The Psychic Life of Power: Essays in Subjection* (Stanford, CA: Stanford University Press, 1997), 134.

95. All quotations are from *The Poems of Sir Philip Sidney*, ed. William A. Ringler Jr. (Oxford: Clarendon Press, 1962), hereafter noted parenthetically in the text by poem and line number.

96. Lemnius, *Touchstone of Complexions*, 135ᵛ.
97. Ibid., 143ᵛ.
98. Young Philip was a man of exceptional promise, but his career as an Elizabethan courtier appears to have been paved with frustration: losing out on the Leicester inheritance, failure in the pursuit of a Protestant league, and the backfiring of his opposition to the queen's marriage to the Duke of Alençon. He waited for a meaningful appointment for almost all his life, yet the one he received, that of the governor of Flushing, resulted in his death soon after. See Katherine Duncan-Jones, *Sir Philip Sidney: Courtier Poet* (New Haven, CT: Yale University Press, 1991), esp. 1–62, 194–250; Alan Stewart, *Philip Sidney: A Double Life* (New York: St. Martin's, 2000). On the social and political subtext of *Astrophil and Stella*, see Arthur F. Marotti, "'Love Is Not Love': Elizabethan Sonnet Sequences and the Social Order," *English Literary History* 49, no. 2 (1982): 396–406; Ann Rosalind Jones and Peter Stallybrass, "The Politics of *Astrophil and Stella*," *SEL: Studies in English Literature, 1500–1900* 24, no. 1 (1984): 53–68; Richard McCoy, *Sir Philip Sidney: Rebellion in Arcadia* (New Brunswick, NJ: Rutgers University Press, 1979), 69–109.
99. Bright, *Treatise of Melancholie*, 131. On insomnia as a stock melancholic symptom among Elizabethan Petrarchans, see Lisle Cecil John, *The Elizabethan Sonnet Sequences: Studies in Conventional Conceits* (New York: Russell and Russell, 1964), 87–92.
100. Laurentius, *Discourse*, 118.
101. Ibid., 90; Bright, *Treatise of Melancholie*, 102.
102. Lawrence Babb, *The Elizabethan Malady: A Study of Melancholia in English Literature from 1580 to 1642* (East Lansing: Michigan State University Press, 1951), 168–70, discusses Sidney's *Arcadia* but does not mention *Astrophil and Stella*; see also Robert L. Montgomery, *Symmetry and Sense: The Poetry of Sir Philip Sidney* (Austin: University of Texas Press, 1961), 105n10; 116n20. More recently, in her psychoanalytic reading of Sidney's sonnets, Catherine Bates, "Astrophil and the Manic Wit of the Abject Male," *SEL: Studies in English Literature, 1500–1900* 41, no. 1 (2001): 1–24, mentions melancholy as one of the mechanisms of producing abjection (4–5), but does not consider it in connection with Sidney's sequence.
103. Gary Waller, "The Re-Writing of Petrarch: Sidney and the Languages of Sixteenth-Century Poetry," in Waller and More, *Interpretation of Renaissance Culture*, 78. Cf. Warley's Marxism-inflected reformulation of this argument, as Astrophil's "paradoxical

existence" between different versions of himself: aristocratic "status" and bourgeois "class" (*Sonnet Sequences*, 76).

104. Theodor Spencer, "The Poetry of Sir Philip Sidney," *English Literary History* 12, no. 4 (1945): 251–78, esp. 248–52.

105. S. K. Heninger Jr., "Sequences, Systems, Models: Sidney and the Secularization of the Sonnets," in *Poems in Their Place: The Intertextuality and Order of Poetic Collections*, ed. Neil Fraistat, 66–94 (Chapel Hill: University of North Carolina Press, 1986), 82.

106. See, respectively, Thomas P. Roche Jr., *Petrarch and the English Sonnet Sequence* (New York: AMS, 1989), 193–242; James J. Scanlon, "Sidney's *Astrophil and Stella*: 'See What It Is to Love' Sensually!," *SEL: Studies in English Literature, 1500–1900* 16, no. 1 (1976): 65–74; Alan Sinfield, "Astrophil's Self-Deception," *Essays in Criticism* 28 (1978): 1–18; Sinfield, "Sidney and Astrophil," *SEL: Studies in English Literature, 1500–1900* 20, no. 1 (1980): 25–41.

107. Edward Berry, *The Making of Sir Philip Sidney* (Toronto: University of Toronto Press, 1998), 102.

108. Dubrow, *Echoes of Desire*, 101.

109. Borch-Jacobsen, *Freudian Subject*, 18.

110. Ronald Levao, *Renaissance Minds and Their Fictions: Cusanus, Sidney, Shakespeare* (Berkeley: University of California Press, 1985), 164. Cf. David Kalstone, *Sidney's Poetry: Contexts and Interpretations* (Cambridge, MA: Harvard University Press, 1965), 106–07; Michael R. G. Spiller, *The Development of the Sonnet: An Introduction* (New York: Routledge, 1992), 102–22.

111. For Astrophil's self-presentation as a schoolboy, see Lisa M. Klein, *The Exemplary Sidney and the Elizabethan Sonneteer* (Newark: University of Delaware Press, 1998), 82–86; Joseph Loewenstein, "Sidney's Truant Pen," *Modern Language Quarterly* 46 (1985): 128–42; and Andrew Strycharski, "Literacy, Education, and Affect in *Astrophil and Stella*," *SEL: Studies in English Literature, 1500–1900* 48, no. 1 (2008): 45–63.

112. See Elizabeth M. Hull, "All My Deed but Copying Is: The Erotics of Identity in *Astrophil and Stella*," *Texas Studies in Language and Literature* 38 (1996): 182–89.

113. Sidney, *Apologie*, 150.

114. See Paul Allen Miller, "Sidney, Petrarch, and Ovid, or Imitation as Subversion," *English Literary History* 58 (1991): 516–18.

115. Burton, *Anatomy of Melancholy*, 1:401.

116. Ficino, *Commentary*, 158. On the animality of premodern melancholic patients, see Beecher and Ciavolella, "Jacques Ferrand," 59–60; Jackson, *Melancholia and Depression*, 345–51; and Kitzes, *Politics of Melancholy*, 59–84.

117. The phrase is from Schiesari, *Gendering of Melancholia*, 236. Cf. Bridget Gellert Lyons, *Voices of Melancholy: Studies in Literary Treatments of Melancholy in Renaissance England* (London: Routledge and Kegan Paul, 1971), 94.
118. Kristeva, *Black Sun*, 145.
119. Lemnius, *Touchstone of Complexions*, 149^v.
120. Burton, *Anatomy of Melancholy*, 1:52.
121. Bright, *Treatise of Melancholie*, 164, 111.
122. Burton, *Anatomy of Melancholy*, 3:8.
123. Syr P.S. *His Astrophel and Stella*, A3^r.
124. On the narrative/lyric tension in Petrarchan poetry, see Dubrow, *Echoes*, 28–35.
125. Marion Campbell, "Unending Desire: Sidney's Reinvention of Petrarchan Form in *Astrophil and Stella*," in Waller and Moore, *Interpretation of Renaissance Culture*, 93. Cf. Greene, *Post-Petrarchism*, 102.
126. Berry, *Making*, 136. Cf. Richard B. Young, "English Petrarke: A Study of Sidney's *Astrophil and Stella*," in *Three Studies in the Renaissance: Sidney, Johnson, Milton*, 5–88 (New Haven, CT: Yale University Press, 1958), 88; McCoy, *Rebellion in Arcadia*, 109; Klein, *Exemplary Sidney*, 101.
127. Kennedy, *Site of Petrarchism*, 176–77.
128. John Harington, *Orlando furioso in English heroical verse* (London, 1591), L4^v.
129. Burton, *Anatomy of Melancholy*, 3:190, 193.
130. Attempting to explain Sidney's half-hearted anti-Petrarchism, scholars argue that he only criticizes the abuses of Petrarchism; see Neil L. Rudenstine, *Sidney's Poetic Development* (Cambridge, MA: Harvard University Press, 1967), 197–206. Other critics point out that the sequence is a parody of Petrarchism and therefore has to present both the Petrarchan conventions (to secure readerly recognition) and their antipodes (Young, "English Petrarke," 5–38).
131. Butler, *Psychic Life of Power*, 182.
132. Maria T. M. Prendergast, *Renaissance Fantasies: The Gendering of Aesthetics in Early Modern Fiction* (Kent, OH: Kent State University Press, 1999), 68–69.
133. On mythologizing the life (and death) of Sidney, see the essays in *Sir Philip Sidney: 1586 and the Creation of a Legend*, ed. Jan Van Dorsten, Dominic Baker-Smith, and Arthur Kinney (Leiden: Brill/Leiden University Press, 1986); Raphael Falco, *Conceived Presences: Literary Genealogies in Renaissance England* (Amherst: University of Massachusetts Press, 1994), 1–123; Klein, *Exemplary Sidney*, 13–38, 103–35, 171–87.

134. On the general influence of *Astrophil and Stella* on English Petrarchism, see Spiller, *Development of the Sonnet*, 123–48; Gavin Alexander, *Writing after Sidney: The Literary Response to Sir Philip Sidney, 1586–1640* (Oxford: Oxford University Press, 2006), 149–219, 283–331. Wall, *Imprint of Gender*, 58–95, traces the role the quartos played in shaping the modern categories of book production. Joel B. Davis in *"The Countesse of Pembrokes Arcadia" and the Invention of English Literature* (New York: Palgrave, 2011), 99–117, analyzes the metrical innovations in Sidney's songs and their appropriations by Samuel Daniel, Thomas Lodge, and Giles Fletcher the Elder.

135. For this argument, see Heninger, "Sequences, Systems, Models," 83; Kalstone, *Sidney's Poetry*, 180–81; Ferry, *"Inward" Language*, 128. Prendergast also credits *Astrophil and Stella* with the inauguration of "anxiety of originality" in English poetry (*Renaissance Fantasies*, 69). Gordon Braden, "Unspeakable Love: Petrarch to Herbert," in *Soliciting Interpretation: Literary Theory and Seventeenth-Century English Poetry*, ed. Elizabeth D. Harvey and Katharine Eisaman Maus, 253–72 (Chicago: University of Chicago Press, 1990), 259, argues that Sidney's anti-Petrarchism is the result of his French influences (esp. Joachim du Bellay). See also Anne Lake Prescott, *French Poets and the English Renaissance: Studies in Fame and Transformation* (New Haven, CT: Yale University Press, 1978).

Notes to Chapter 3

1. *Ane Detectioun of the duinges of Marie Quene of Scottes thouchand the murder of hir husband, and hir conspiracie, adulterie, and pretensed mariage with the Erle Bothwell. And ane defence of the trew Lordis, mainteineris of the Kingis graces actioun and authoritie. Translatit out of the Latine quhilke was written by G. B.* [London, 1571]. All further references to *Ane Detectioun*, including the casket sonnets (Rii^v–Si^r, unlineated), will be to this edition, noted parenthetically in the text. The first English edition, printed by John Day, was followed in 1572 by Robert Lekprevik's Edinburgh impression and, further, by a French edition, printed either in London or in La Rochelle. The English edition was reprinted twice, in 1577 and 1578. The murky publication history of *Ane Detectioun* is traced in I. D. McFarlane, *Buchanan* (London: Duckworth, 1981), 348–50; and John D. Staines, *The Tragic Histories of Mary Queen of Scots, 1560–1690: Rhetoric, Passions, and Political Literature* (Aldershot: Ashgate, 2009), 27–39.

2. Rosalind Smith, *Sonnets and the English Woman Writer, 1560–1621: The Politics of Absence* (New York: Palgrave, 2005), 41.

3. Cathy Shrank, "Manuscript, Authenticity and 'Evident Proofs' against the Scottish Queen," in *Tudor Manuscripts, 1485–1603*, ed. A. S. G. Edwards, 198–218 (Chicago: University of Chicago Press, 2010), 203.

4. Mary's literary taste was to a significant degree shaped by French Petrarchism. As Lisa Hopkins writes, "As first 'reine-dauphine' and later queen of France, [Mary Stuart] became thoroughly steeped in French court culture, and it is against this background, and in particular the tuition she received from Ronsard and the other members of the Pléiade, that her use and development of a poetic voice and persona must be understood." Lisa Hopkins, *Writing Renaissance Queens: Texts by and about Elizabeth I and Mary, Queen of Scots* (Newark: University of Delaware Press, 2002), 72; see also 81–85.

5. On the political uses of Petrarchism in Elizabethan England, see Leonard Forster, *The Icy Fire: Five Studies in European Petrarchism* (Cambridge: Cambridge University Press, 1969), 122–47; Arthur F. Marotti, "'Love Is Not Love': Elizabethan Sonnet Sequences and the Social Order," *English Literary History* 49, no. 2 (1982): 396–428; Ann Rosalind Jones and Peter Stallybrass, "The Politics of Astrophil and Stella," *SEL: Studies in English Literature, 1500–1900* 24 (1984): 53–68; Anthony Low, *The Reinvention of Love: Poetry, Politics and Culture from Sidney to Milton* (Cambridge: Cambridge University Press, 1993), 12–30; and Andrew Zurcher, *Shakespeare and Law* (London: Methuen, 2010), 65–71.

6. See Peter C. Herman, *Royal Poetrie: Monarchic Verse and the Political Imaginary of Early Modern England* (Ithaca, NY: Cornell University Press, 2010). I am indebted to Herman's analysis of monarchical writing throughout this chapter.

7. On Buchanan's life and his relationship with Mary Stuart, see Philip J. Ford, *George Buchanan: Prince of Poets* (Aberdeen: Aberdeen University Press, 1982); and Roger A. Mason, "George Buchanan and Mary Queen of Scots," *Records of the Scottish Church History Society* 30 (2000): 1–27.

8. My brief recapitulation of Mary's last years in Scotland is based on a number of excellent historical studies. See Antonia Fraser, *Mary, Queen of Scots* (London: Weidenfeld and Nicolson, 1969); John A. Guy, *Queen of Scots: The True Life of Mary Stuart* (Boston: Houghton Mifflin, 2004); Retha M. Warnicke, *Mary Queen of Scots* (London: Routledge, 2006); and Jenny Wormald, *Mary Queen of Scots: A Study in Failure* (London: George Philip, 1988).

9. The pamphlet's not-so-covert goal is surmised from a series of exclamations with which it concludes. These identify Mary as a foreign body dangerous to England's political health: "Now iudge Englischmen if it be gud to change Quenis. / O vniting confounding. / Quhen rude Scotland hes vomited vp ane poison, must fine England lick it vp for a restorative? / O vile indignitie. / Quhile your Quenis enemy liueth, hir dangir continueth" (Yiij^r).

10. James E. Phillips, *Images of a Queen: Mary Stuart in Sixteenth-Century Literature* (Berkeley: University of California Press, 1964), 61; Staines, *Tragic Histories*, 35.

11. According to *Ane Detectioun*, "in the castel of Edenburgh there was left by the Erle Bothwell befoir his fleing away, and was sent for by one George Daglish his seruant, quho was taken by the Erle Moreton, one small gilt cofer nat fully ane fwte lang, beying garnishit in sondry places with the Romaine letter *F* vnder ane kyngis crowne, quairin were certaine letters and writynges well knawin, and by othes to be affirmit, to haue been written with the queen of Scottes awne hand to the Erle Bothwell" (Oii^r).

12. Gordon Donaldson, *The First Trial of Mary, Queen of Scots* (London: B. T. Batsford, 1969), 115–16.

13. Guy, *Queen of Scots*, 384–423. Fraser, *Mary, Queen of Scots*, 463–77, likewise questions their authenticity, as does Warnicke, *Mary Queen of Scots*, 176–78. On the contrary, Wormald, *Mary Queen of Scots*, 177–78, leans toward believing them to be genuine. Hans Villius, "The Casket Letters: A Famous Case Reopened," *Historical Journal* 28 (1985): 517–34, argues for their authenticity.

14. Helen Hackett, "Dreams of Designs, Cults of Constructions?: The Study of Images of Monarchs," *Historical Journal* 44 (2001): 814. This creates what Susan Frye aptly terms "competition for representation" in *Elizabeth I: The Competition for Representation* (Oxford: Oxford University Press, 1993), esp. 3–21. This is also the underlying thesis of Louis A. Montrose's *The Subject of Elizabeth: Authority, Gender, and Representation* (Chicago: University of Chicago Press, 2006), and Kevin Sharpe's monumental *Selling the Tudor Monarchy: Authority and Image in Sixteenth-Century England* (New Haven, CT: Yale University Press, 2009).

15. For the significance of writing and reading for both anti- and pro-Marian campaigns in England and Scotland, in addition to Phillips *(Images of a Queen)* and Staines *(Tragic Histories)*, see Jayne E. Lewis, *Mary Queen of Scots: Romance and Nation* (London: Routledge, 1998); and Cathy Shrank, "'This fatall Medea,' 'this Clytemnestra': Reading and the Detection of Mary Queen of Scots," *Huntington Library Quarterly* 73, no. 3 (2010): 523–41.

16. For an analysis of the notion of constancy in Mary's sonnets and its impact on Mary Wroth's *Pamphilia and Amphilanthus*, see Marianne Micros, "'For him what countless tears I must have shed': Identity, Subjection, and Subjectivity in the Sonnets of Mary Stuart and Mary Wroth," *Sidney Journal* 27, no. 2 (2009): 53–70.

17. Sarah M. Dunnigan, *Eros and Poetry at the Courts of Mary Queen of Scots and James VI* (New York: Palgrave Macmillan, 2002), 30, cites an early modern Scots manuscript of the sonnets, most likely copied from *Ane Detectioun*, in which each sonnet is tied to a historic or biographical event in Mary's life. The gloss to the ninth sonnet "declares yt he [Bothwell] had abusit her [Mary's] bodie." On the manuscript, see Peter Davidson, "New Evidence concerning Mary Queen of Scots," *History Scotland* 1 (2001): 28–34. On Mary's rape by Bothwell, see also Jocelyn Catty, *Writing Women, Writing Rape in Early Modern England: Unbridled Speech* (New York: Palgrave, 2010), 124.

18. See Dunnigan, *Eros and Poetry*, 32. *Ane Detectioun* also mentions the wound (Biij^v–Biiij^r).

19. The notion of consent features explicitly in the Elizabethan marriage service (as formulated in the 1559 *Book of Common Prayer*), with newlyweds described by the minister as having "consented together in holy matrimony." *The Book of Common Prayer: The Texts of 1549, 1559, and 1662*, ed. Brian Cummings (Oxford: Oxford University Press, 2011), 159.

20. Dunnigan, *Eros and Poetry*, 33.

21. On the widespread resentment toward the Darnley marriage in Scotland, see Kristen Post Walton, *Catholic Queen, Protestant Patriarchy: Mary Queen of Scots and the Politics of Gender and Religion* (New York: Palgrave, 2007), 116–26.

22. Dunnigan, *Eros and Poetry*, 21.

23. Staines, *Tragic Histories*, 43. On the uses of Mary's "immorality" in the political struggle between the queen and the Confederate lords, see Tricia A. McElroy, "Imagining the 'Scottis Natioun': Populism and Propaganda in Scottish Satirical Broadsides," *Texas Studies in Language and Literature* 49, no. 4 (2007): 319–39.

24. Michel Foucault, *The Use of Pleasure*, vol. 2 of *The History of Sexuality*, trans. Robert Hurley (New York: Vintage, 1990), 173.

25. Sir John Fortescue, *A learned commendation of the politique lawes of Englande* (London, 1567), 88^r.

26. As Richard Strier notes in *The Unrepentant Renaissance: From Petrarch to Shakespeare to Milton* (Chicago: University of

Chicago Press, 2011), a revival of Stoicism in the Renaissance was paralleled by a revival of anti-Stoicism, and "both the humanist and the Reformation traditions provided powerful defenses of the validity and even the desirability of ordinary human emotions and passions" (42). See also Christopher Tilmouth, *Passion's Triumph over Reason: A History of the Moral Imagination from Spenser to Rochester* (Oxford: Oxford University Press, 2007), 1–36.

27. John Knox, *The First Blast of the Trumpet against Monstrous Regiment of Women*, in *The Works of John Knox*, 4 vols., ed. David Laing (Edinburgh, 1864), 4:376.

28. John Ponet, *Shorte Treatise of Politike Power, and of the true Obedience which subiectes owe to kynges and other ciuile Gouernours, with an Exhortacion to all true naturall Englishe men* ([Strasbourg?], 1556), Iij^{r-v}.

29. I thus disagree with Mary E. Burke, who claims that in the casket sonnets a desiring woman "adopts a dominant role, constructing her (silent) male beloved and their relationship as the inverse of traditional gender roles in the sonnet." Mary E. Burke, "Queen, Lover, Poet: A Question of Balance in the Sonnets of Mary, Queen of Scots," in *Women, Writing, and the Reproduction of Culture in Tudor and Stuart Britain*, ed. Mary E. Burke, Jane Donawerth, Linda L. Dove, and Karen Nelson, 101–18 (Syracuse: Syracuse University Press, 2000), 102.

30. Petrarch, *Canzoniere*, 235.3, from *Petrarch's Lyric Poems: The "Rime sparse" and Other Lyrics*, ed. and trans. Robert M. Durling (Cambridge, MA: Harvard University Press, 1976).

31. Herman, *Royal Poetrie*, 97–98; Dunnigan, *Eros and Poetry*, 27; Staines, *Tragic Histories*, 48.

32. Norman Jones, *The Birth of the Elizabethan Age: England in the 1560s* (Oxford: Blackwell, 1993), 118; see also Mortimer Levine, *The Early Elizabethan Succession Question, 1558–1568* (Stanford, CA: Stanford University Press, 1966).

33. Dunnigan, *Eros and Poetry*, 29. On the religious and political contrasts between Elizabeth and Mary, see also Helen Hackett, *Virgin Mother, Maiden Queen: Elizabeth I and the Cult of the Virgin Mary* (New York: St. Martin's, 1995), 74–77; Phillips, *Images of a Queen*, 52–84.

34. *Correspondence of Matthew Parker: Comprising Letters Written by and to Him, from A.D. 1535 to His Death, A.D. 1575*, ed. John Bruce (New York: Johnson Reprint, 1968), 131.

35. See J. E. Neale, *Elizabeth I and Her Parliaments, 1559–1581* (New York: St. Martin's, 1958), 47–50, 101–13, 129–64, 353–54.

36. Elizabeth I, *Collected Works*, ed. Leah S. Marcus, Janel Mueller, and Mary Beth Rose (Chicago: University of Chicago Press, 2000), 58, 79, 95.

37. For detailed accounts of these marriage negotiations, see Susan Doran, *Monarchy and Matrimony: The Courtships of Elizabeth I* (London: Routledge, 1996), esp. 13–153; Jones, *Birth of the Elizabethan Age*, 119–55; Carol Levine, *The Heart and Stomach of a King: Elizabeth I and the Politics of Sex and Power* (Philadelphia: University of Pennsylvania Press, 1994), 39–64. For a useful overview of theories explaining Elizabeth's eventual singleness, see Susan Doran, "Why Did Elizabeth Not Marry?," in *Dissing Elizabeth: Negative Representations of Gloriana*, ed. Julia M. Walker, 30–59 (Durham, NC: Duke University Press, 1998); Hackett, *Virgin Mother, Maiden Queen*, 72–74.

38. This (predominantly dramatic) literature is discussed in Marie Axton, *The Queen's Two Bodies: Drama and the Elizabethan Succession* (London: Swift Printers Ltd. for Royal Historical Society, 1977); Susan Doran, "Juno versus Diana: The Treatment of Elizabeth I's Marriage in Plays and Entertainments," *Historical Journal* 38 (1995): 257–74; Michael A. Winkelman, *Marriage Relationships in Tudor Political Drama* (Aldershot: Ashgate, 2005), esp. 113–68. Stephen Hamrick, *The Catholic Imaginary and the Cults of Elizabeth* (Farnham: Ashgate, 2009), 62–69, touches upon echoes of the debates on Elizabeth's marriage in nondramatic poetry.

39. See Stephen Alford, *The Early Elizabethan Polity: William Cecil and the British Succession Crisis, 1558–1569* (Cambridge: Cambridge University Press, 1998).

40. Smith, *Sonnets*, 55.

41. Elizabeth I, *Collected Works*, 302–03.

42. See discussion in Frances Teague, "Elizabeth I: Queen of England," in *Women Writers of the Renaissance and Reformation*, ed. Katharina M. Wilson, 522–47 (Athens: University of Georgia Press, 1987), 529–30; Helen Hackett, "Courtly Writing by Women," in *Women and Literature in Britain, 1500–1700*, ed. Helen Wilcox, 169–89 (Cambridge: Cambridge University Press, 1996), 175.

43. See Herman, *Royal Poetrie*, 126–27; Ilona Bell, *Elizabeth I: The Voice of a Monarch* (New York: Palgrave, 2010), 151–53.

44. For a detailed analysis of the Petrarchan clichés in the poem, see György E. Szönyi, "Cross-Dressing the Tongue: Petrarchist Discourse and Female Voice in Queen Elizabeth's 'Sonetto,'" *Hungarian Journal of English and American Studies* 11, no. 1 (2005): 78–80.

45. Ilona Bell, *Elizabethan Women and the Poetry of Courtship* (Cambridge: Cambridge University Press, 1998), 108.

46. See Nancy Selleck, *The Interpersonal Idiom in Shakespeare, Donne, and Early Modern Culture* (New York: Palgrave, 2008), 35. Although Selleck argues that Elizabeth's poem is addressed "not to a spouse but to a Petrarchan beloved," she does not appear to consider the possible context of the poem.

47. Herman writes that the poem "contravenes the expectations of monarchic verse by portraying the queen as passive and powerless, a subject rather than monarch" (*Royal Poetrie*, 131). By contrast, Bell argues that "On Monsieur's Departure" "represents Elizabeth I's efforts to break away from the passivity and stasis imposed by the Petrarchan sonnet" (*Elizabethan Women*, 113).

48. Rosalind Smith, "Reading Mary Stuart's Casket Sonnets: Reception, Authorship, and Early Modern Women's Writing," *Parergon* 29, no. 2 (2012): 149.

49. See Louise Olga Fradenburg, *City, Marriage, Tournament: Arts of Rule in Late Medieval Scotland* (Madison: University of Wisconsin Press, 1991), 67–90.

50. See Ann W. Astell, *The Song of Songs in the Middle Ages* (Ithaca, NY: Cornell University Press, 1990), 25–104; J. Christopher King, *Origen on the Song of Songs as the Spirit of Scripture: The Bridegroom's Perfect Marriage Song* (Oxford: Oxford University Press, 2005); and E. Ann Matter, *The Voice of the Beloved: The Song of Songs in Western Medieval Christianity* (Philadelphia: University of Pennsylvania Press, 1990).

51. On the allegorical treatments of the Song of Songs in early modern England, see George L. Scheper, "Reformation Attitudes towards Allegory and the Song of Songs," *PMLA* 89 (1974): 551–62; Max Engammare, *Qu'il me baise des baisiers de sa bouche: La Cantique des Cantiques à la Renaissance* (Geneva: Libraire Droz, 1993), 144–77; and Noam Flinker, *The Song of Songs in English Renaissance Literature: Kisses of Their Mouths* (Cambridge: D. S. Brewer, 2000), esp. 31–65.

52. Ernst H. Kantorowicz, *The King's Two Bodies: A Study in Mediaeval Political Theology* (Princeton, NJ: Princeton University Press, 1997), 221–23; and J. H. Burns, *Lordship, Kingship, and Empire: The Idea of Monarchy, 1400–1525* (Oxford: Clarendon, 1992), 52.

53. Tigurinus Chelidonius, *Most Excellent Hystorie of the Institution and Firste Beginning of Christian Princes* (London, 1571). All further references are noted parenthetically in the text.

54. Michel Foucault, *The Order of Things: An Archaeology of the Human Sciences* (New York: Routledge, 2001), 24.

55. On discursive parallels between the early modern constructions of marriage and monarchy, also see Sid Ray, *Holy Estates: Marriage and Monarchy in Shakespeare and His Contemporaries* (Selinsgrove, PA: Susquehanna University Press, 2004), 26–52.
56. Kantorowicz, *King's Two Bodies*, 223.
57. Philippa Berry, *Of Chastity and Power: Elizabethan Literature and the Unmarried Queen* (London: Routledge, 1989), 61–67; Hackett, *Virgin Mother*, 56–60.
58. Edward Hall, *Vnion of the Two Noble and Illustre Famelies of Lancastre and Yorke* (London, 1548), *ii^v.
59. Sir Richard Morison, *An Exhortation to Styrre all Englyshe Men to the Defence of Theyr Countreye, made by Richarde Morysine* (London, 1539), Bi^v–Bii^r.
60. John Proctor, *The Historie of Wyates Rebellion* (London, 1554), 53^v–54^r.
61. Elizabeth I, *Collected Works*, 59. This account is derived from William Camden's early seventeenth century Latin translation of her speech; the English version appeared in Camden, *Annales the true and royall history of the famous empresse Elizabeth Queene of England France and Ireland* (London, 1625), book 1, 27–29.
62. John N. King, "Queen Elizabeth I: Representations of the Virgin Queen," *Renaissance Quarterly* 43 (1990): 33–36. See also Bell, *Elizabeth I*, 62–63.
63. William Birch, "A songe betwene the Quenes majestie and Englande," in *The Penguin Book of Renaissance Verse, 1509–1659*, ed. David Norbrook and H. R. Woudhuysen (Harmondsworth: Penguin, 1992), 92–94, lines 19–24. See Kevin Curran, *Marriage, Performance, and Politics at the Jacobean Court* (Aldershot: Ashgate, 2009), 24–25.
64. Bell, *Elizabeth I*, 158.
65. K. J. Kesselring, *The Northern Rebellion of 1569: Faith, Politics, and Protest in Elizabethan England* (New York: Palgrave, 2010), 35–38.
66. Thomas Norton, *To the Quenes Maiesties poore deceyued subiectes of the north countrey, drawen into rebellion by the Earles of Northumberland and Westmerland* (London, 1569), Biiij^v.
67. *James I of Scotland: The Kingis Quair*, ed. John Norton-Smith (Oxford: Clarendon, 1971). All subsequent quotations will be from this edition, with line numbers noted parenthetically.
68. A. C. Spearing, "Dreams in *The Kingis Quair* and the Duke's Book," in *Charles d'Orleans in England (1415–1440)*, ed. Mary-Jo Arn, 123–44 (Cambridge: D. S. Brewer, 2000), 124.
69. *The Works of Geoffrey Chaucer and "The Kingis Quair": A Facsimile of Bodleian Library, Oxford, MS Arch. Selden. B.24*,

ed. Julia Boffey and A. S. G. Edwards (Cambridge: D. S. Brewer, 1997), fols. 211ʳ and 911ᵛ.

70. Walter Bower, *Scotichronicon*, in 9 vols., ed. D. E. R. Watt (Aberdeen: Aberdeen University Press, 1987–98), 9:305, 309; John Mair [Major], *A History of Greater Britain as well England as Scotland Compiled from the Ancient Authorities*, ed. and trans. A. Constable (Edinburgh: Scottish Historical Society, 1892), 366.

71. Louise O. Fradenburg, "The Scottish Chaucer," in *Writing after Chaucer: Essential Readings in Chaucer and the Fifteenth Century*, ed. Daniel J. Pinti, 167–76 (New York: Garland, 1998), 171.

72. See E. W. M. Balfour-Melville, *James I, King of Scots, 1406–1437* (London: Methuen, 1936); and Michael Brown, *James I* (Edinburgh: Canongate Academic, 1994).

73. Joanna Martin, *Kingship and Love in Scottish Poetry, 1424–1540* (Aldershot: Ashgate, 2008), 21.

74. The most sustained exploration of the poem's concerns with kingship is Sally Mapstone, "Kingship and the *Kingis Quair*," in *The Long Fifteenth Century: Essays for Douglas Gray*, ed. Helen Cooper and Sally Mapstone, 51–69 (Oxford: Clarendon Press, 1997). For studies that approach the poem through the prism of royal identity, see, for example, Elizabeth Elliott, *Remembering Boethius: Writing Aristocratic Identity in Late Medieval French and English Literatures* (Farnham: Ashgate, 2012), 123–43; Robert Epstein, "Prisoners of Reflection: The Fifteenth-Century Poetry of Exile and Imprisonment," *Exemplaria* 15, no. 1 (2003): 162–70; Martin, *Kingship and Love*, 21–23; Joanna Summers, *Late-Medieval Prison Writing and the Politics of Autobiography* (Oxford: Clarendon Press, 2004), 62–64.

75. Written either in England or in Scotland in a Scots dialect bearing distinct signs of English (and Chaucerian) influence, *The Kingis Quair* is often associated with the Scots prince held in captivity at the English court for 17 years. See Gregory C. Kratzmann, *Anglo-Scottish Literary Relations, 1430–1550* (Cambridge: Cambridge University Press, 1980), 36; John M. Bowers, "Three Readings of *The Knight's Tale*: Sir John Clanvowe, Geoffrey Chaucer, and James I of Scotland," *Journal of Medieval and Early Modern Studies* 34 (2004): 291. Likewise, Mary's "French Sonnettes" are forcibly Anglicized (or Anglo-Scotticized) by the authors of *Ane Detectioun*; they are thus "a 'ghostly' text, caught on the threshold of two versions" (Dunnigan, *Eros and Poetry*, 16).

76. The casket sonnets were not written in prison, yet royal imprisonment, both historical and figurative, is featured prominently in *Ane Detectioun*. I consider the continuities in the

rhetoric of royal imprisonment in the constructions of monarchical subjectivity in *The Kingis Quair* and in *Ane Detectioun* in Danila Sokolov, "*Ane Detectioun* of Mary Stewart, Queen of Scots, and the Languages of Royal Imprisonment in Medieval and Early Modern England and Scotland," *Journal of Medieval and Early Modern Studies* 44 (2014): 321–44, esp. 330–33.

77. A. C. Spearing, *Medieval Autographies: The "I" of the Text* (Notre Dame, IN: University of Notre Dame Press, 2012), 100.

78. Bowers, "Three Readings," 294.

79. Fradenburg, *City, Marriage, Tournament*, 84–90.

80. Martin, *Kingship and Love*, 24; see also Mapstone, "Kingship," 53, as well as Fradenburg, *City, Marriage, Tournament*, 131–34. For a critique of this argument and claims that purification and liberation are in fact a sham, see Vincent Carretta, "*The Kingis Quair* and *The Consolation of Philosophy*," *Studies in Scottish Literature* 16 (1981): 14–28; and Clare F. James, "*The Kingis Quair*: The Plight of the Courtly Lover," in *New Readings of Late Medieval Love Poems*, ed. David Chamberlain, 96–118 (Lanham, MD: University Press of America, 1993).

81. Julia Kristeva, *Tales of Love*, trans. Leon S. Roudiez (New York: Columbia University Press, 1987), 90, 97. Barbara Kiefer Lewalski, in *Protestant Poetics and the Seventeenth-Century Religious Lyric* (Princeton, NJ: Princeton University Press, 1979), similarly notes that the biblical metaphor of marriage does not exploit its sexual connotations, presenting the union as "solemnized but not yet consummated" (99).

82. Denys Turner, *Eros and Allegory: Medieval Exegesis of the Song of Songs* (Kalamazoo, MI: Cistercian Publications, 1995), 84. There appears to be a possibility of consummation at 5:1: "I am come into my garden, my sister, my spouse: I gathered my myrrhe with my spice: I ate mine honie co[m]be with mine honie, I drank my wine with my milke." *The Bible and Holy Scriptures conteyned in the Olde and Newe Testament* (Geneva, 1560). However, Fiona C. Black, *The Artifice of Love: Grotesque Bodies and the Song of Songs* (London: T & T Clark, 2009), 147–53, upon reviewing the available evidence and critical arguments, concludes that the woman's body, even though ready for intercourse, is still protected by prohibition.

83. C. S. Lewis, *The Allegory of Love: A Study in Medieval Tradition* (Oxford: Clarendon, 1953), 237.

84. Erich Auerbach, "Figura," in his *Scenes from the Drama of European Literature*, trans. Ralph Manheim, 11–76 (Minneapolis: University of Minnesota Press, 1984), 58.

Notes to Chapter 4

1. For examples of such synchronic historicism in the study of legal language in Elizabethan sonnets, see Scott Wilson, "Racked on the Tyrant's Bed: The Politics of Pleasure and Pain and the Elizabethan Sonnet Sequences," *Textual Practice* 3, no. 2 (1989): 234–49; Andrew Stott, "From *Voi Che* to *Che Vuoi?*: The Gaze, Desire, and the Law in the 'Zepheria' Sonnet Sequence," *Criticism* 36, no. 3 (1994): 329–58; Andrew Zurcher, *Spenser's Legal Language: Law and Poetry in Early Modern England* (Cambridge: D. S. Brewer, 2007), 203–37; and Bradin Cormack, "Strange Love: Or, Holding Lands," *Law and Humanities* 1 (2007): 221–38.

2. *Petrarch's Lyric Poems: The "Rime sparse" and Other Lyrics*, ed. and trans. Robert M. Durling (Cambridge, MA: Harvard University Press, 1976). Further references are to this translation, hereafter noted parenthetically in the text.

3. *The Collected Poems of Sir Thomas Wyatt*, ed. Kenneth Muir and Patricia Thomson (Liverpool: Liverpool University Press, 1969), 5–9; I. C., *Alcilia: Philoparthens louing folly. Whereunto is added, Pigmalions image: with The loue of Amos and Laura* (London, 1613), E^r–F^r.

4. For the history of the early circulation and publication of *Astrophil and Stella*, see H. R. Woudhuysen, *Sir Philip Sidney and the Circulation of Manuscripts, 1558–1640* (Oxford: Clarendon Press, 1996), 356–84; Joel B. Davis, *"The Countesse of Pembrokes Arcadia" and the Invention of English Literature* (Basingstoke: Palgrave, 2011), 81–85.

5. *Syr P. S. His Astrophel and Stella[,] Wherein the excellence of sweete poesie is concluded. To the end of which are added, sundry other rare sonnets of diuers noble men and gentlemen* (London: [John Charlewood] for Thomas Newman, 1591), 70. For the attribution of the sonnet to Daniel, see *The Complete Works in Verse and Prose of Samuel Daniel*, 4 vols., ed. Alexander Grossart (London: Hazell, Watson and Viney, 1885), 1:28; Samuel Daniel, *Poems and "A Defence of Rhyme,"* ed. Arthur Colby Sprague (Chicago: University of Chicago Press, 1965), 192–93. With the exception of this sonnet, I have used the 1594 version of Samuel Daniel's sequence, *Delia and Rosamond Augmented* (London, 1594). All further quotations are from this edition.

6. Consider, for example, the sensuous language in the following passage: "Property, in chattels personal, may be either in possession; which is where a man hath not only the right to enjoy, but hath the actual enjoyment of the thing: or else it is in action; where a

man hath only a bare right, without any occupation or enjoyment." Sir William Blackstone, *Commentaries on the Laws of England*, 4 vols. (Oxford, 1765–69), 2:309.

7. Thomas Wilson, *The Arte of Rhetorique* (London, 1585), 25.

8. On feminine endings in early modern English poetry as a challenge to patriarchal authority, see Maureen Quilligan, "Feminine Endings: The Sexual Politics of Sidney's and Spenser's Rhyming," in *The Renaissance Englishwoman in Print: Counterbalancing the Canon*, ed. Anne M. Haselkorn and Betty S. Travitsky, 311–26 (Amherst: University of Massachusetts Press, 1990).

9. On parallels between poetic fiction and legal argumentation, see Wesley Trimpi, *Muses of One Mind: The Literary Analysis of Experience and Its Continuity* (Princeton, NJ: Princeton University Press, 1983), 25–72; and Kathy Eden, *Poetic and Legal Fiction in the Aristotelian Tradition* (Princeton, NJ: Princeton University Press, 1986). On *actio* as a rhetorical technique, see Cicero, *Orator*, 55–60, in *Brutus: Orator*, trans. G. L. Hendrickson and H. M. Hubbell (Cambridge, MA: Harvard University Press, 1939); and book 11 of Quintilian's *Institutio Oratoria*, in *The Orator's Education*, vol. 5, books 11 and 12 (Cambridge, MA: Harvard University Press, 2002).

10. *Les termes de la ley; or, Certaine difficult and obscure vvords and termes of the common lawes of this realme expounded* (London, 1624), 67^v.

11. See J. H. Baker, *An Introduction to English Legal History*, 3rd ed. (London: Butterworths, 1990), 365, 614.

12. Ibid., 366.

13. B. J. Sokol and Mary Sokol, *Shakespeare, Law, and Marriage* (Cambridge: Cambridge University Press, 2003), 5.

14. Koen Rase, "On Love and Other Injustices," in *Love and Law in Europe*, ed. Hanne Petersen, 27–51 (Aldershot: Ashgate, 1998), 29.

15. Owen Barfield, "Poetic Diction and Legal Fiction," in *A Barfield Reader: Selections from the Writings of Owen Barfield*, ed. G. B. Tennyson, 56–75 (Middletown, CT: Wesleyan University Press, 1999), 65, 69.

16. Fredric Jameson, *The Political Unconscious: Narrative as a Socially Symbolic Act* (Ithaca, NY: Cornell University Press, 1981), 98.

17. See J. C. Cox, *The Sanctuaries and Sanctuary Seekers of Medieval England* (London: George Allen and Sons, 1911); Gervase Rosser, "Sanctuary and Social Negotiation in Medieval England," in *The Cloister and the World: Essays in Medieval History in Honour of Barbara Harvey*, ed. John Blair and Brian Golding, 57–79 (Oxford: Oxford University Press, 1996).

18. Isobel Thornley, "The Destruction of Sanctuary," in *Tudor Studies Presented to Albert Frederick Pollard*, ed. R. W. Seton-Watson, 182–207 (London: University of London Board of Studies in History, 1924); E. W. Ives, "Crime, Sanctuary, and Royal Authority under Henry VIII: The Exemplary Sufferings of the Savage Family," in *On the Laws and Customs of England: Essays in Honor of Samuel E. Thorne*, ed. Morris S. Arnold, Thomas A. Green, Sally A. Scully, and Stephen D. White, 296–320 (Chapel Hill: University of North Carolina Press, 1981); Iver Kaufman, "Henry VII and Sanctuary," *Church History* 53 (1984): 465–76.

19. See, however, William C. Ryan, "The Historical Case for the Right of Sanctuary," *Journal of Church and State* 29 (1987): 209–32, who argues that what was abolished was the procedural rather than the substantive right (229).

20. Zurcher, *Spenser's Legal Language*, 211. Zurcher restates the case more forcibly in *Shakespeare and Law* (London: Methuen, 2010), 57–102, where he contrasts Shakespeare's use in the sonnets of common-law vocabulary and imagery, particularly those derived from land law and the law of tort, with the poetry of earlier Elizabethan sonneteers, including Sidney and Daniel. He argues that Shakespeare's sonnets "make sense as a concerted, oppositional response to the increasingly centralized and absolutist literary and political tradition in which Shakespeare was working" (64).

21. For one, reading the sonnets of Sidney, Spenser, and Daniel as products of the court preoccupied exclusively with consitutional concerns is a slightly outdated approach. For a critique, see Christopher Warley, *Sonnet Sequences and Social Distinction in Renaissance England* (Cambridge: Cambridge University Press, 2005). Besides, the Inns of Court, whose rise Zurcher links to the domination of the common law, were themselves involved in a great deal of legal theorizing about sovereignty and politics. See Paul Raffield, *Images and Cultures of Law in Early Modern England: Justice and Political Power, 1558–1660* (Cambridge: Cambridge University Press, 2004). On the Inns of Court as an vibrant center of production and consumption of erotic verse, see Jim Ellis, *Sexuality and Citizenship: Metamorphosis and Elizabethan Erotic Verse* (Toronto: University of Toronto Press, 2003), esp. 17–39.

22. See Richard Helmholz, *The Ius Commune in England: Four Studies* (Oxford: Oxford University Press, 2001), 16–81, esp. 56–81; Karl Shoemaker, *Sanctuary and Crime in the Middle Ages, 400–1500* (New York: Fordham University Press, 2011), 167–73.

23. Peter Goodrich, *Law in the Courts of Love: Literature and Other Minor Jurisprudences* (London: Routledge, 1996), 30.

24. See Andreas Capellanus, *The Art of Courtly Love*, trans. John Jay Parry (New York: Frederick Ungar, 1959), 167–86.

25. See W. A. Neilson, *The Origins and Sources of the Court of Love* (Cambridge, MA: Harvard University Press, 1899), 23–168, 240–56; Peter Goodrich, *The Laws of Love: A Brief Historical and Practical Manual* (New York: Palgrave, 2007), 16–29.

26. C. S. Lewis, *English Literature in the Sixteenth Century Excluding Drama* (Oxford: Clarendon, 1962), 223.

27. R. Howard Bloch, *Medieval French Literature and Law* (Berkeley: University of California Press, 1977), 214. Neilson is likewise skeptical about the historical claims of the courts of love, calling them *"jeux d'esprit"* (*Origins and Sources*, 248).

28. Richard Firth Greene, *Poets and Princepleasers: Literature and the English Court in the Late Middle Ages* (Toronto: University of Toronto Press, 1980), 121.

29. Goodrich, *Law in the Courts*, 70–71.

30. Bruce Holsinger, "Vernacular Legality: The English Jurisdictions of *The Owl and the Nightingale*," in *The Letter of the Law: Legal Practice and Literary Production in Medieval England*, ed. Emily Steiner and Candace Barrington, 54–84 (Ithaca, NY: Cornell University Press, 2002), 155.

31. Jean Baudrillard, *Selected Writings*, ed. Mark Poster (Stanford, CA: Stanford University Press, 2001), 109.

32. Goodrich, *Law in the Courts*, 6–7; see also his "Gay Science and Law," in *Rhetoric and Law in Early Modern Europe*, ed. Victoria Kahn and Lorna Hutson, 95–124 (New Haven, CT: Yale University Press, 2001).

33. Subha Mukherji, "Jonson's *The New Inn* and a Revisiting of the 'Amorous Jurisdiction,'" *Law and Literature* 18, no. 2 (2006): 149–69, esp. 153–56, argues for a tempering qualification of Goodrich's celebration of the dissident nature of the laws of love with "historical specificity" (154)—that is, reading these imaginative alternatives to actual legal practice within their specific historical and legal contexts.

34. Peter Goodrich, *Oedipus Lex: Psychoanalysis, History, Law* (Berkeley: University of California Press, 1995), 11.

35. Green, *Poets and Princepleasers*, 122–23.

36. I quote from *Lydgate's Temple of Glas*, ed. J. Schick (London, 1924). All references will appear parenthetically in the text by line number.

37. Wendy Scase, *Literature and Complaint in England, 1272–1553* (Oxford: Oxford University Press, 2007), 185. John Kerrigan also stresses the prominence of the legal aspects of Lydgate's complaints. See his introduction to *Motives of Woe: Shakespeare and*

the *"Female Complaint": A Critical Anthology* (Oxford: Clarendon Press, 1991), 28.

38. C. S. Lewis, *The Allegory of Love: A Study in Medieval Tradition* (Oxford: Clarendon, 1953), 241; A. C. Spearing, *Medieval Dream-Poetry* (Cambridge: Cambridge University Press, 1976), 176; Derek Pearsall, *John Lydgate* (Charlottesville: University Press of Virginia, 1970), 107; and Anna Torti, *The Glass of Form: Mirroring Structures from Chaucer to Skelton* (Cambridge: D. S. Brewer, 1991), 70, 74. Larry Scanlon, "Lydgate's Poetics: Laureation and Domesticity in *The Temple of Glass*," in *John Lydgate: Poetry, Culture, and Lancastrian England*, ed. Larry Scanlon and James Simpson, 61–97 (Notre Dame, IN: University of Notre Dame Press, 2006), 87, notes, however, that the reference is too vague to be interpreted unequivocally.

39. Capellanus, *Art of Courtly Love*, 156, 184.

40. Baker, *Introduction*, 47–49, 117–20. For a more detailed analysis, see Alan Harding, "Plaints and Bills in the History of English Law," in *Legal History Studies 1972*, ed. Dafydd Jenkins, 65–86 (Cardiff: University of Wales Press, 1972).

41. Bradin Cormack, *A Power to Do Justice: Jurisdiction, English Literature, and the Rise of Common Law* (Chicago: University of Chicago, 2007), 3.

42. Thomas Hoccleve, "L'epistre de Cupide," in *"My Compleinte" and Other Poems*, ed. Roger Ellis (Exeter: University of Exeter Press, 2001), 93–11, lines 230–31; italics mine.

43. Torti, *Glass of Form*, 76–80, considers the dichotomy of the female protagonist's individual desire and the constraints of patriarchal society and stresses Lydgate's articulation of a female point of view. Larry Scanlon, "Lydgate's Poetics," esp. 86–89, reads the events of the poem as a sign of the lady's empowerment. Tara Williams, *Inventing Womanhood: Gender and Language in Later Middle English Writing* (Columbus: Ohio State University Press, 2011), 88–100, credits Lydgate with introducing the questions about the nature, agency, and effect of womanhood into English poetry, but insists that he portrays womanhood itself as a constraint.

44. *The Floure and the Leafe and the Assembly of Ladies*, ed. Derek Pearsall (London: Thomas Nelson and Sons, 1962). All subsequent quotations are from this edition. Pearsall dates the poem between 1450 and 1485.

45. Wendy A. Matlock, "'And long to sue it is a wery thing': Legal Commentary in *The Assembly of Ladies*," *Studies in Philology* 101, no. 1 (2004): 20–37.

46. Julia Boffey, "'Forto Compleyne She Had Gret Desire': The Grievances Expressed in Two Fifteenth-Century Dream-Visions,"

in *Nation, Court and Culture: New Essays on Fifteenth-Century English Poetry*, ed. Helen Cooney, 116–28 (Dublin: Four Courts Press, 2001), 122, 128.

47. Piyel Haldar, "The Function of the Ornament in Quintilian, Alberti, and Court Architecture," in *Law and the Image: The Authority of Art and the Aesthetics of Law*, ed. Costas Douzinas and Lynda Nead, 117–36 (Chicago: University of Chicago Press, 1999), 135.

48. Michel Foucault, "Of Other Spaces," *Diacritics* 16, no. 1 (1986): 24.

49. As a markedly gendered text, the poem has elicited a number of feminist readings. See, for example, Jane Chance, "Christine de Pizan as Literary Mother: Women's Authority and Subjectivity in 'The Floure and the Leafe' and 'The Assembly of Ladies,'" in *The City of Scholars: New Approaches to Christine de Pizan*, ed. Margarete Zimmermann and Dina De Rentiis, 245–59 (Berlin: Walter de Gruyter, 1994); Alexandra A. T. Barratt, "'The Flower and the Leaf' and 'The Assembly of Ladies': Is There a (Sexual) Difference?" *Philological Quarterly* 66 (1987): 1–24; Ann McMillan, "'Fayre Sisters Al': The Flower and the Leaf and the Assembly of Ladies," *Tulsa Studies in Women's Literature* 1 (1982): 27–42.

50. Simone Marshall, "Interiors, Exteriors, and the Veiling of Cupid's Martyrs: Gendered Space in *The Assembly of Ladies*," *Philological Quarterly* 84, no. 2 (2005): 161–87.

51. Michael Drayton, *Idea: In Sixty Three Sonnets*, in *The Works of Michael Drayton*, 5 vols., ed. J. William Hebel (Oxford: Basil Blackwell, 1961), vol. 2. All further quotations are from this edition, hereafter cited in the text.

52. *The Poems of Sir Philip Sidney*, ed. William A. Ringler Jr. (Oxford: Clarendon Press, 1962), sonnet 48, line 3, and song 5, line 85; Henry Constable, *Diana: The praises of his mistres, in certaine sweete sonnets* (London, 1592), sonnet 12; William Smith, *Chloris; or, The complaint of the passionate despised shepheard* (London, 1596), sonnet 24; Bartholomew Griffin, *Fidessa, more chaste then kinde* (London, 1596), sonnet 48; Robert Toft, *Laura: The toyes of a traueller* (London, 1597), part 2, sonnet 27.

53. On early modern accusation and investigation, see John G. Bellamy, *The Criminal Trial in Later Medieval England: Felony before the Courts from Edward I to the Sixteenth Century* (Stroud: Sutton, 1998), 19–56; Sir John Baker, *The Oxford History of the Laws of England*, vol. 6, *1483–1558* (Oxford: Oxford University Press, 2003), 512–20.

54. Thomas A. Green, "The Jury and the English Law of Homicide, 1200–1600," *Michigan Law Review* 74, no. 3 (1976): 490. On the increasing role of scientific evidence and the jury's growing responsibility to evaluate it, see the work of Barbara J. Shapiro, for example, *Probability and Certainty in Seventeenth-Century England: A Study of the Relationships between National Science, Religion, History, Law, and Literature* (Princeton, NJ: Princeton University Press, 1983), 167–93; and, more recently, *A Culture of Fact: England, 1550–1720* (Ithaca, NY: Cornell University Press, 2003). The relationship of these changes to English Renaissance literature is explored by Lorna Hutson in *The Invention of Suspicion: Law and Mimesis in Shakespeare and Renaissance Drama* (Oxford: Oxford University Press, 2007).

55. I am referring to a 1575 case, in which a John Saunders was found guilty of murder in causing the death of his three-year-old daughter while attempting to kill his wife by way of a poisoned apple, which his daughter ate by accident. On the legal reasoning in this case of transferred malice, see Luke Wilson, *Theaters of Intention: Drama and the Law in Early Modern England* (Stanford, CA: Stanford University Press, 2000), 43–47.

56. Capellanus, *Art of Courtly Love*, 67.

57. See Keith Thomas, *Religion and the Decline of Magic* (New York: Charles Scribner's Sons, 1971), 220; Hilary M. Nunn, *Staging Anatomies: Dissection and Spectacle in Early Stuart Tragedy* (Aldershot: Ashgate, 2005), 68; Mary Floyd-Wilson, *Occult Knowledge, Science, and Gender on the Shakespearean Stage* (Cambridge: Cambridge University Press, 2013), 58–60.

58. Robert P. Brittain, "Cruentation: In Legal Medicine and in Literature," *Medical History* 9, no. 1 (1965): 82–88; Malcolm Gaskill, "Reporting Murder: Fiction in the Archives in Early Modern England," *Social History* 23, no. 1 (1998): 8–13; Sara M. Butler, *Forensic Medicine and Death Investigation in Medieval England* (New York: Routledge, 2015), 140–42.

59. Malcolm Gaskill, *Crime and Mentalities in Early Modern England* (Cambridge: Cambridge University Press, 2000), 227. On the curious symbiosis between criminal justice and Protestant providentialism, see also Peter Lake, "Deeds against Nature: Cheap Print, Protestantism and Murder in Early Seventeenth-Century England," in *Culture and Politics in Early Stuart England*, ed. Kevin Sharpe and Peter Lake, 257–84 (Stanford, CA: Stanford University Press, 1993), 269–74.

60. See P. G. Lawson, "Lawless Juries?: The Composition and Behavior of Hertfordshire Juries, 1573–1624," in *Twelve Good*

Men and True: The Criminal Trial Jury in England, 1200–1800, ed. J. S. Cockburn and Thomas A. Green, 117–57 (Princeton, NJ: Princeton University Press, 1988).
61. Goodrich, *Laws of Love,* 199.
62. James Simpson, *Reform and Cultural Revolution: 1350–1547* (New York: Oxford University Press, 2002), 558, 122.
63. Cormack, *Power to Do Justice,* 27; see also 24–38.
64. Christopher W. Brooks, "The Common Lawyers in England, c. 1558–1642," in *Lawyers in Early Modern Europe and America,* ed. Wilfred R. Prest, 42–64 (New York: Holmes and Meier, 1981), 42.
65. For the diminishing of ecclesiastical jurisdiction in early modern England, see Christopher W. Brooks, *Law, Politics and Society in Early Modern England* (Cambridge: Cambridge University Press, 2008), 93–122. For the encroachment of the common law over the territory of the canon law, see R. H. Helmholz, *Roman Canon Law in Reformation England* (Cambridge: Cambridge University Press, 1990). While Martin Ingram, *Church Courts, Sex, and Marriage in England, 1570–1640* (Cambridge: Cambridge University Press, 1988), claims that the church courts in fact did not suffer any significant damage to their status, his argument has been recently questioned by Christopher Haigh in *The Plain Man's Pathways to Heaven* (Oxford: Oxford University Press, 2007), 153–57.
66. See Charles M. Gray, *The Writ of Prohibition: Jurisdiction in Early Modern English Laws,* 2 vols. (New York: Oceana Publications, 1994); Brooks, *Law, Politics and Society,* 109–18.
67. Goodrich, *Oedipus Lex,* 12; see also 144–80.
68. See discussions in Tim Stretton, *Women Waging Law in Elizabethan England* (Cambridge: Cambridge University Press, 1998), 1–69; Maria L. Cioni, *Women and Law in Elizabethan England, with Particular Reference to the Court of Chancery* (New York: Garland, 1985).
69. See Garthine Walker, *Crime, Gender and Social Order in Early Modern England* (Cambridge: Cambridge University Press, 2003), 113–58; Peter Lawson, "Patriarchy, Crime, and the Courts: The Criminality of Women in Late Tudor and Early Stuart England," in *Criminal Justice in the Old World and New,* ed. Greg T. Smith, Allyson N. May, and Simon Devereaux, 16–57 (Toronto: Centre of Criminology, University of Toronto, 1998). As Randall Martin suggests in *Women, Murder, and Equity in Early Modern England* (New York: Routledge, 2008), while the authority in the official discourses about murders commited by women (trial records, law reports) is unmistakably masculine, over the course of the sixteenth

and seventeenth centuries other sources of information (ballads, pamphlets, news reports) adopted a more sympathetic and equitable point of view.

70. Mukherji, "Jonson's *The New Inn*," 150.

71. John Lydgate, "The Complaint of the Black Knight," in *The Minor Poems of John Lydgate, Part II: Secular Poems*, ed. Henry Noble MacCracken, 382–410 (London: Oxford University Press for the Early English Text Society, 1934). All further references are to this edition, cited parenthetically by line number.

72. While cases of slander originally fell within ecclesiastical jurisdiction, already in the thirteenth century the royal courts began to claim a number of litigations, especially where real estate was involved. See Theodor F. T. Plucknett, *A Concise History of the Common Law*, 5th ed. (Boston: Little, Brown, 1956), 484–87.

73. Sue Bianco, "New Perspectives on Lydgate's Courtly Verse," in Cooney, *Nation, Court and Culture*, 98.

74. See John A. Alford, "Literature and Law in Medieval England," *PMLA* 92 (1977): 941–51.

75. Cf., "The courts of love have to be understood within the plurality of jurisdictions that preceded the unitary agglomeration and methodological diminution of modern law" (Goodrich, *Laws of Love*, 11).

76. Richard Firth Green, *A Crisis of Truth: Literature and Law in Ricardian England* (Philadelphia: University of Pennsylvania Press, 1999).

77. James J. Paxson, *The Poetics of Personification* (Cambridge: Cambridge University Press, 1994), 21.

78. Roland Barthes, *The Pleasure of the Text*, trans. Richard Miller (New York: Hill and Wang, 1975), 26.

79. Henry Peacham, *The Garden of Eloquence* (London, 1593), 136.

80. Gaskill, "Reporting Murder," 25.

81. Gaskill, *Crime and Mentalities*, 231–38.

82. Diana Fuss, *Dying Modern: A Meditation on Elegy* (Durham, NC: Duke University Press, 2013), 44.

83. Gavin Alexander, "Prosopopeia: The Speaking Figure," in *Renaissance Figures of Speech*, ed. Sylvia Adamson, Gavin Alexander, and Katrin Ettenhuber, 97–112 (Cambridge: Cambridge University Press, 2007), 105.

84. Jacques Derrida, "Before the Law," in Derrida, *Acts of Literature*, ed. Derek Attridge, 181–220 (New York: Routledge, 1992), 192.

Notes to Chapter 5

1. Joel Fineman, *Shakespeare's Perjured Eye: The Invention of Poetic Subjectivity in the Sonnets* (Berkeley: University of California Press, 1986), 2, and throughout.
2. Gordon Braden, "Shakespeare's Petrarchism," in *Shakespeare's Sonnets: Critical Essays*, ed. James Schiffer, 163–83 (New York: Garland, 1999), describes Fineman's knowledge of Petrarchism as "skimpy and secondhand" and argues that Shakespeare's poems are "not mockeries or refutations of Petrarchism, but fulfillments of some of the movement's original potentialities" (166, 171). A number of excellent studies detail Shakespeare's numerous debts to Petrarch and argue for the centrality of the Petrarchan framework to our appreciation of Shakespeare's sonnet sequence. For Thomas P. Roche Jr., *Petrarch and the English Sonnet Sequence* (New York: AMS, 1989), 380–461, Shakespeare inherits the numerological and providential patterns of the *Canzoniere*. Heather Dubrow, *Echoes of Desire: English Petrarchism and Its Counterdiscourses* (Ithaca, NY: Cornell University Press, 1995), 119–34, argues that the instability of the gender poles and the rhetorical ambiguities of Petrarchism inform the problematic of Shakespeare's sonnets. Richard Strier, *The Unrepentant Renaissance: From Petrarch to Shakespeare to Milton* (Chicago: University of Chicago Press, 2011), 59–97, connects to Petrarchism the sonnets' preoccupation with questions of the flesh and the spirit. Suzanne M. Tartamella, *Rethinking Shakespeare's Skepticism: The Aesthetics of Doubt in the Sonnets and Plays* (Pittsburgh: Duquesne University Press, 2014), 19–39, reads the skepticism regarding the poetry of praise in Shakespeare's sonnets as a reconsideration of Petrarch's poetic strategies. Emily Vasiliauskas's "The Outmodedness of Shakespeare's Sonnets" *English Literary History* 82, no. 3 (2015): 759–87, argues that the belated deployment of Petrarchism—a markedly obsolete and "outmoded" form in Jacobean England—in Shakespeare's collection is a calculated move aimed at creating an oppositional erotic and political aesthetic.
3. See *Shakespeare and the Middle Ages*, ed. Curtis Perry and John Watkins (Oxford: Oxford University Press, 2009); *Premodern Shakespeare*, ed. Sarah Beckwith and James Simpson, special issue of *Journal of Medieval and Early Modern Studies* 40, no. 1 (2010); Helen Cooper, *Shakespeare and the Medieval World* (London: Bloomsberry, 2010); *Medieval Shakespeare*, ed. Christina Wald, special issue of *Shakespeare* 8, no. 4 (2012); and *Medieval Shakespeare: Pasts and Presents*, ed. Ruth Morse, Helen Cooper, and Peter Holland (Cambridge: Cambridge University Press, 2013).

4. Cooper, introduction to Morse, Cooper, and Holland, *Medieval Shakespeare*, 2.

5. The only exceptions are two essays from Perry and Watkins, *Shakespeare and the Middle Ages*: Christopher Warley's "Shakespeare's Fickle Fee-Simple: A Lover's Complaint, Nostalgia, and the Transition from Feudalism to Capitalism" (21–44), and Patrick Cheney's "The Voice of the Author in 'The Phoenix and the Turtle': Chaucer, Shakespeare, Spenser" (103–25). Neither, however, deals with the sonnets.

6. Michael R. G. Spiller, *The Development of the Sonnet: An Introduction* (New York: Routledge, 1992), 154.

7. Helen Vendler, *The Art of Shakespeare's Sonnets* (Cambridge, MA: Harvard University Press, 1997), 17.

8. *Shakespeare's Sonnets*, ed. Stephen Booth (New Haven, CT: Yale University Press, 1977). Throughout the chapter, I quote from the unmodernized 1609 quarto text printed in Booth's edition. All subsequent references will appear in the text by sonnet and line number.

9. *Shakespeare's Sonnets: The Arden Shakespeare*, ed. Katherine Duncan-Jones (London: Thomas Nelson, 1997), 322.

10. Quotations from, respectively, Gerald Hammond, *The Reader and Shakespeare's Young Man Sonnets* (Totowa, NJ: Barnes and Noble, 1981), 166; and Paul Ramsey, *The Fickle Glass: A Study of Shakespeare's Sonnets* (New York: AMS, 1979), 44.

11. See, respectively, *"The Sonnets" and "A Lover's Complaint,"* ed. John Kerrigan (New York: Penguin, 1995), 8; Duncan-Jones, *Shakespeare's Sonnets*, 322; and Vendler, *Art of Shakespeare's Sonnets*, 442.

12. On Chaucer, see *Shakespeare's Sonnets: A Modern Edition, with Prose Versions, Introduction and Notes*, 3rd ed., ed. A. L. Rowse (London: Macmillan, 1984), 215; on *Faerie Queene*, see Patrick Cheney, "Shakespeare: Sonnet 106, Spenser's National Epic, and Counter-Petrarchism," *English Literary Renaissance* 31, no. 2 (2001): 331–64, esp. 340–64; and on Petrarchan tradition, see Vasiliauskas, "Outmodedness," 679–770, and Tartamella, *Rethinking Shakespeare's Skepticism*, 19.

13. Frederic Jameson, *A Singular Modernity: Essay on the Ontology of the Present* (London: Verso, 2002), 24.

14. On the association of blazon with Petrarchism, see Nancy Vickers, "'The blazon of sweet beauty's best': Shakespeare's *Lucrece*," in *Shakespeare and the Question of Theory*, ed. Patricia Parker and Geoffrey Hartman, 95–115 (New York: Methuen, 1985), 95–96.

15. Vendler, *Art of Shakespeare's Sonnets*, 450.

16. Fineman, *Shakespeare's Perjured Eye*, 50.

17. Bruce R. Smith, *Homosexual Desire in Shakespeare's England: A Cultural Poetics* (Chicago: University of Chicago Press, 1991), 258.
18. Fineman, *Shakespeare's Perjured Eye*, 15.
19. Petrarch, *Canzoniere*, 233.11, from *Petrarch's Lyric Poems: The "Rime sparse" and Other Lyrics*, ed. and trans. Robert M. Durling (Cambridge, MA: Harvard University Press, 1976); hereafter cited in the text.
20. It is reasonable to assume that Shakespeare was familiar with Henryson's poem simply because it appeared among Chaucer's works in all early modern editions from William Thynne's (1532) to Thomas Speght's (1598). Critics attribute Shakespeare's negative attitude to Cressida in *Troilus and Cressida* absent in Chaucer's poem to the influence of Henryson's text. See E. T. Donaldson, *The Swan at the Well: Shakespeare Reading Chaucer* (New Haven, CT: Yale University Press, 1985), 76–78; Valerie Smith, "The History of Cressida," in *Self and Society in Shakespeare's "Troilus and Cressida" and "Measure for Measure,"* ed. J. A. Jowitt and R. K. S. Taylor, 61–79 (Bradford, UK: University of Leeds Centre for Adult Education, 1982); and Ann Thompson, *Shakespeare's Chaucer: A Study in Literary Origins* (New York: Barnes and Noble, 1978), 121.
21. See Margreta de Grazia, "The Scandal of Shakespeare's Sonnets," in Schiffer, *Shakespeare's Sonnets*, 92–93.
22. Heather Dubrow, "'Incertainties Now Crown Themselves Assur'd': The Politics of Plotting Shakespeare's *Sonnets*," in Schiffer, *Shakespeare's Sonnets*, 113–33, stresses the gender uncertainty of the first- and second-person pronouns in the sonnets, arguing that "often there is no way of being reasonably confident whether a given poem involves the Friend, the Dark Lady, or some third party" (116); also see Dubrow, *Echoes of Desire*, 122–23; and Robert Matz, *The World of Shakespeare's Sonnets: An Introduction* (Jefferson, NC: McFarland, 2008), 14–15. Along the same lines, Douglas Trevor, "Shakespeare's Love Objects," in *A Companion to Shakespeare's Sonnets*, ed. Michael Schoenfeldt, 225–41 (Oxford: Blackwell, 2007), argues that the sonnets' preoccupation with poetry undermines the sharp gender binarism of the two objects of desire, whereas Michael Stapleton, "Making the Woman of Him: Shakespeare's Man Right Fair as Sonnet Lady," *Texas Studies in Language and Literature* 46, no. 3 (2004): 271–95, suggests that both objects of Shakespeare's love are feminine, one (the dark lady) grammatically and the other (the young man) rhetorically, the latter constructed to parody the Petrarchan lady.

23. Valerie Traub, "Sex without Issue: Sodomy, Reproduction, and Signification in Shakespeare's Sonnets," in Schiffer, *Shakespeare's Sonnets*, 442.

24. Fineman, *Shakespeare's Perjured Eye*, 52, 18.

25. Christopher Warley, *Sonnet Sequences and Social Distinction in Renaissance England* (Cambridge: Cambridge University Press, 2005), 124.

26. On the discourse of patronage in Shakespeare's sonnets, see Arthur F. Marotti, "'Love Is Not Love': Elizabethan Sonnet Sequences and the Social Order," *English Literary History* 49, no. 2 (1982): 410–13; and Marotti, "Shakespeare's Sonnets as Literary Property," in *Soliciting Interpretation: Literary Theory and Seventeenth-Century English Poetry*, ed. Elizabeth D. Harvey and Katharine Eisaman Maus, 143–73 (Chicago: University of Chicago Press, 1990); Heather Dubrow, *Captive Victors: Shakespeare's Narrative Poems and Sonnets* (Ithaca, NY: Cornell University Press, 1987), 202–06; Dennis Kay, *William Shakespeare: Sonnets and Poems* (New York: Twayne, 1998), 130–33; Lynne Magnusson, "'Power to Hurt': Language and Service in Sidney Household Letters and Shakespeare's Sonnets," *English Literary History* 65, no. 4 (1998): 799–824.

27. Marotti, "'Love Is Not Love,'" 410.

28. David Schalkwyk, *Shakespeare, Love and Service* (Cambridge: Cambridge University Press, 2008), 115, also 115–22, 176–85.

29. Dubrow, *Echoes of Desire*, 55.

30. Keith Wrightson, *Earthly Necessities: Economic Lives in Early Modern Britain* (New Haven, CT: Yale University Press, 2000), 3. For a similar claim, see Jean-Christophe Agnew, *Worlds Apart: The Market and the Theater in Anglo-American Thought, 1550–1750* (Cambridge: Cambridge University Press, 1986), 59, although Agnew admits that the pecuniary complaint genre had powerful medieval precursors. On the economic language of the sonnets, see David Hawkes, *Idols of the Marketplace: Idolatry and Commodity Fetishism in English Literature, 1580–1680* (New York: Palgrave, 2001), 95–114; Peter C. Herman, "What's the Use?; or, The Problematic of Economy in Shakespeare's Procreation Sonnets," in Schiffer, *Shakespeare's Sonnets*, 263–84; John B. Mischo, "'That Use Is Not Forbidden Usury': Shakespeare's Procreation Sonnets and the Problem of Usury," in *Subjects on the World's Stage: Essays on British Literature of the Middle Ages and the Renaissance*, ed. David C. Allen and Robert A. White, 262–79 (Newark: University of Delaware Press, 1995).

31. See John A. Burrow, "Poet as Petitioner," *Studies in the Age of Chaucer* 3 (1981): 61–75; Robert J. Meyer-Lee, *Poets and Power from Chaucer to Wyatt* (Cambridge: Cambridge University Press, 2007), 1–11, 88–132.

32. Antony J. Hasler, *Court Poetry in Late Medieval England and Scotland: Allegories of Authority* (Cambridge: Cambridge University Press, 2011), 14, 8.

33. *The Riverside Chaucer*, 3rd ed., ed. Larry Benson (Boston: Houghton Mifflin, 1987), 656, lines 1–7. All further quotations from Chaucer are from this edition.

34. John Lydgate, "Lydgate's 'Letter to Gloucester,'" in *The Minor Poems of John Lydgate, Part II: Secular Poems*, ed. Henry Noble MacCracken (London: Oxford University Press for the Early English Text Society, 1934), 665–67, lines 1–8.

35. See Lisa H. Cooper, "'His guttys wer out shake': Illness and Indigence in Lydgate's *Letter to Gloucester* and *Fabula duorum mercatorum*," *Studies in the Age of Chaucer* 30 (2008): 303n1.

36. Thomas Hoccleve, "La male regle de T. Hoccleue," in *"My Compleinte" and Other Poems*, ed. Roger Ellis (Exeter: University of Exeter Press, 2001), 64–78. All quotations are from this edition, hereafter cited parenthetically by line number.

37. On Hoccleve's bureaucratic service and the circumstances of the poem's composition, see John A. Burrow, *Thomas Hoccleve* (Aldershot: Variorum, 1994), 11–16; Ethan Knapp, *The Bureaucratic Muse: Thomas Hoccleve and the Literature of Late Medieval England* (University Park: Pennsylvania State University Press, 2001), 36–43.

38. David Mills, "The Voices of Thomas Hoccleve," in *Essays on Thomas Hoccleve*, ed. Catherine Batt, 85–107 (Turnhout, Belgium: Brepolis, 1996), 102.

39. A. C. Spearing, *Medieval to Renaissance in English Poetry* (Cambridge: Cambridge University Press, 1985), 118.

40. Sarah Tolmie, "The Professional: Thomas Hoccleve," *Studies in the Age of Chaucer* 29 (2007): 361–62.

41. I thank Sean Henry and Beth Quitslund for bringing this point to my attention.

42. Fineman, *Shakespeare's Perjured Eye*, 2, 26, and throughout.

43. John Freccero, "The Fig Tree and the Laurels: Petrarch's Poetics," *Diacritics* 5, no. 1 (1975): 34–40.

44. Gordon Braden, "Unspeakable Love: Petrarch to Herbert," in Harvey and Maus, *Soliciting Interpretation*, 258.

45. Giuseppe Mazotta, *The Worlds of Petrarch* (Durham, NC: Duke University Press, 1993), 59. See also Gur Zak, *Petrarch's*

Humanism and the Care of the Self (Cambridge: Cambridge University Press, 2010), 113.

46. Lee Patterson, "On the Margin: Postmodernism, Ironic History, and Medieval Studies," *Speculum* 65, no. 1 (1990): 99–100.

47. Nancy Selleck, *The Interpersonal Idiom in Shakespeare, Donne, and Early Modern Culture* (New York: Palgrave, 2008), 111; see also 97–105, 111–22.

48. Warley, *Sonnet Sequences*, 139.

49. As Thomas M. Greene, "Pitiful Thrivers: Failed Husbandry in the Sonnets," in Parker and Hartman, *Shakespeare and the Question of Theory*, 230–44 notes in connection with this sonnet, "the worth of the friend may reside after all in the poet's own fancy" because "the substance of abundance may actually derive from the shadow of projection" (233).

50. See Martin Green, *The Labyrinth of Shakespeare's Sonnets: An Examination of Sexual Elements in Shakespeare's Language* (London: Charles Skilton, 1974), 16–20.

51. Tartamella, *Rethinking Shakespeare's Skepticism*, 96.

52. Cf. Vendler, *Art of Shakespeare's Sonnets*, who argues that the lover's desire to damage his health is in itself pathological: "How can one tire of well-being and goodness? How can one turn against them and seek out 'diseased' loves?" (501).

53. On *pharmakon*, see Jacques Derrida, *Dissemination*, trans. Barbara Johnson (Chicago: University of Chicago Press, 1981), 63–171, esp. 65–75, 95–105.

54. Robert Meyer–Lee, "Hoccleve and the Apprehension of Money," *Exemplaria* 13, no. 1 (2001): 193.

55. Ficino, *Commentary on Plato's Symposium on Love*, trans. S. Jayne (Dallas: Spring Publications, 1985), 162.

56. Barnabe Googe, "Egloga prima," in *Eclogues, Epitaphs, and Sonnets*, ed. Judith M. Kennedy (Toronto: University of Toronto Press, 1989), lines 75–76; Barnabe Barnes, *Parthenophil and Parthenophe*, ed. Victor A. Doyno (Carbondale: Southern Illinois University Press, 1971), sonnet 38, line 14.

57. On syphilis in Renaissance Europe, see Jon Arrizabalaga, John Henderson, and Roger French, *The Great Pox: The French Disease in Renaissance Europe* (New Haven, CT: Yale University Press, 1997); Anna Foa, "The New and the Old: The Spread of Syphilis (1494–1530)," in *Sex and Gender in Historical Perspective*, ed. Edward Muir and Guido Ruggiero, 26–45 (Baltimore: Johns Hopkins University Press, 1990); Claude Quétel, *History of Syphilis*, trans. Judith Braddock and Brian Pike (Baltimore: Johns Hopkins University Press, 1990), 9–72; Eugenia Tognotti, "The Rise and Fall

of Syphilis in Renaissance Europe," *Journal of Medical Humanities* 30 (2009): 99–113.

58. See Johannes Fabricius, *Syphilis in Shakespeare's England* (London: Jessica Kingsley, 1994), esp. 57–83; Greg W. Bentley, *Shakespeare and the New Disease: The Dramatic Function of Syphilis in "Troilus and Cressida," "Measure for Measure," and "Timon of Athens"* (New York: Peter Lang, 1989).

59. Booth, *Shakespeare's Sonnets*, 533–34; Fabricius, *Syphilis*, 140; Michael Schoenfeldt, *Bodies and Selves in Early Modern England: Physiology and Inwardness in Spenser, Shakespeare, Herbert, and Milton* (Cambridge: Cambridge University Press, 1999), 79.

60. See Margaret Healy, *Fictions of Disease in Early Modern England: Bodies, Plagues, and Politics* (New York: Palgrave, 2001), 124; Jane Kingsley-Smith, *Cupid in Early Modern Literature and Culture* (Cambridge: Cambridge University Press, 2010), 72. However, Rebecca Totaro, *Suffering in Paradise: The Bubonic Plague in English Literature from More to Milton* (Pittsburgh: Duquesne University Press, 2005), esp. 87–108, insists on the referential specificity of "plague" in Shakespeare's culture.

61. Kevin P. Siena, "Pollution, Promiscuity and the Pox: English Venereology and the Early Modern Medical Discourse on Social and Sexual Danger," *Journal of the History of Sexuality* 8, no. 4. (1988): 557; see also Winfred Schleiner, "Infection and Cure through Women: Renaissance Constructions of Syphilis," *Journal of Medieval and Renaissance Studies* 24, no. 3 (1994): 499–517, esp. 502–06.

62. When faced with the problem of syphilis and its contagiousness, early modern medicine (Fracastoro and Paracelsus) was forced to abandon the Galenic model of disease as a humoral imbalance and to develop the notion of contagion that anticipates our microbiological model of the exogenous origins of pathogens. In these new theories, "the body's porousness was being increasingly reconfigured as a disconcerting vulnerability to illicit invasion by venomous pathogens." Jonathan Gil Harris, *Foreign Bodies and the Body Politic: Discourses of Social Pathology in Early Modern England* (Cambridge: Cambridge University Press, 1998), 26. On Fracastoro's theory, see Vivian Nutton, "The Seeds of Disease: An Explanation of Contagion and Infection from the Greeks to the Renaissance," *Medical History* 27 (1983): 1–34, esp. 21–33; on Paracelsus, see Walter Pagel, *Paracelsus: An Introduction to Philosophical Medicine in the Era of the Renaissance* (Basel: Karger, 1958), esp. 134–40. It is unclear, however, to what extent Shakespeare could have been familiar with these new developments. For a discussion,

see David F. Hoeniger, *Medicine and Shakespeare in the English Renaissance* (Newark: University of Delaware Press, 1992), 189–90. Schoenfeldt, *Bodies and Selves*, 94, argues that in Shakespeare's sequence "even venereal disease [is] imagined...not as a contagious disease but rather as a moral and humoral imbalance."

63. On the ugly beauty motif in these poems, see Dubrow, *Captive Victors*, 232–45.

64. Karmen MacKendrick, *Counterpleasures* (New York: State University of New York Press, 1999), 30, 33. While MacKendrick focuses on asceticism, sadism, and masochism, her concept lends itself to an understanding of the intense pleasure that the Shakespearean lover finds in the ugliness of his dark lady.

65. The line may conceal a reference to syphilitic pustules. "The deed euyl," writes Joannes de Vigo in a chapter on pox, "is a maligne, filthy, and corrupt scabbe." See his *The Most Excellent Workes of Chirurgerye* (1543) (New York: Da Capo, 1968), clxiiii^r.

66. As Dubrow notes, "The primary formal and psychological patterns that we will discern in the speaker of the sonnets are versions of paradox" (*Captive Victors*, 170, also 192–202). On the poetic praise of ugliness as an instance of early modern European culture of paradox—the paradoxical encomium—see Henry Knight Miller, "The Paradoxical Encomium, with Special Reference to Its Vogue in England, 1600–1800," *Modern Philology* 53, no. 3 (1956): 145–78; Patrizia Bettella, *The Ugly Woman: Transgressive Aesthetic Models in Italian Poetry from the Middle Ages to the Baroque* (Toronto: University of Toronto Press, 2005), 81–83.

67. Respectively, Aurel Kolnai, *On Disgust*, ed. Barry Smith and Carolyn Korsmeyer (Chicago: Open Court, 2004), 42, 60; Julia Kristeva, *Powers of Horror: An Essay on Abjection*, trans. Leon S. Roudiez (New York: Columbia University Press, 1982), 1; William Ian Miller, *The Anatomy of Disgust* (Cambridge, MA: Harvard University Press, 1997), 109–19; Winfried Menninghaus, *Disgust: Theory and History of a Strong Sensation*, trans. Howard Eiland and Joel Golb (Albany: State University of New York Press, 2003), 36.

68. Benedict Robinson, "Disgust c. 1600," *English Literary History* 81, no. 2 (2014): 555.

69. Carolyn Korsmeyer, *Savoring Disgust: The Foul and the Fair in Aesthetics* (Oxford: Oxford University Press, 2011), 119. Cf.: "It is important to point out that a fascination for and delight in the freakish is, in a significant sense, perverse." Matthew Kieran, "Aesthetic Value: Beauty, Ugliness, and Incoherence," *Philosophy* 72 (1997): 397.

70. The importance of female ugliness to the production of male subjectivity in early modern English culture is the object of

attention in Naomi Baker, *Plain Ugly: The Unattractive Body in Early Modern Culture* (Manchester: Manchester University Press, 2010). As she writes, "representations of ugly women...have as much, if not more, to tell us about the formulation of male subjectivity in this era as they do about available models of female selfhood." However, the ugly woman, she continues, and "her exaggerated, inchoate form perpetually undermines the boundaries of the self which she helps to constitute" (7, 98).

71. Booth, *Shakespeare's Sonnets*, 398.

72. Schoenfeldt, in accord with humoral theory, reads the disease as a consequence of unregulated passion (*Bodies and Selves*, 78–79). Suparna Roychoudhury, "Forswearing Fever: Medicine, Materialism, and Shakespeare's Sonnet 147," *Journal for Early Modern Cultural Studies* 12, no. 1 (2012): 4–25, argues that the "feauer" of sonnet 147 is a separate disease. It may also be another allusion to syphilis. Willyam Bulleyn, in his 1562 *Boke of Compoundes, Bulleins Bulwarke of Defe[n]ce againste all Sicknes Sornes and Woundes* (New York: Da Capo, 1971), claims that by many the disease "would faine bee called, but a feuer" (xlvii^r).

73. See Niklas Luhmann, *Love as Passion: The Codification of Intimacy*, trans. Jeremy Gaines and Doris L. Jones (Stanford, CA: Stanford University Press, 1998), 43–57.

74. Richard Halpern, *Shakespeare's Perfume: Sodomy and Sublimity in the Sonnets, Wilde, Freud, and Lacan* (Philadelphia: University of Pennsylvaina Press, 2002), 2, 21, advances an important thesis that in Shakespeare's sonnets aesthetics operate not as a sublimated form of sexual desire but, rather, as the origin of sexuality.

75. Fineman, *Shakespeare's Perjured Eye*, 179.

76. Cynthia Marshall, *The Shattering of the Self: Violence, Subjectivity, and Early Modern Texts* (Baltimore: Johns Hopkins University Press, 2002), 69.

77. Baker, *Plain Ugly*, 137.

78. The standard text is *The Poems of Robert Henryson*, ed. Denton Fox (Oxford: Clarendon, 1981), 111–31. However, throughout the chapter I quote from the anglicized version of the poem (*The testament of Creseyde*) from Thynne's 1532 edition of Chaucer, *The workes of Geffray Chaucer newly printed, with dyuers workes whiche were neuer in print before* (Lo[n]don: Thomas Godfray, 1532), Qqiii^a–Qqvi^b, as one that would have been more readily available and familiar to early modern English readers, including Shakespeare. All quotations will be from Thynne's unlineated edition, but for convenience I provide parenthetical references to the line numbers adopted in Fox's text.

79. C. David Benson, "Critic and Poet: What Lydgate and Henryson Did to Chaucer's *Troylus and Criseyde*," in *Writing after Chaucer: Essential Readings in Chaucer and the Fifteenth Century*, ed. Daniel J. Pinti, 227–42 (New York: Garland, 1998), goes as far as characterizing the text as a Renaissance poem "based on the poet's own invention rather than the repetition of approved sources" (235).

80. Sir Francis Kinaston, in a note appended to his 1639 translation into Latin of *The Testament*, describes the poem as "this supplement called the Testament of Creseid, which may passe for the sixt & last booke of [Chaucer's] story." Qtd. in Robert L. Kindrick, *Robert Henryson* (Boston: Twayne, 1979), 18.

81. Medieval culture insisted on a direct correlation between physical ugliness and moral depravity. See, for example, Henrik Specht, "The Beautiful, the Handsome and the Ugly: Some Aspects of the Art of Character Portrayal in Medieval Literature," *Studia Neophilologica* 56, no. 2 (1984): 129–46; Jan Ziolkowski, "Avatars of Ugliness in Medieval Literature," *Modern Language Review* 79, no. 1 (1984): 1–20.

82. Susan Zimmerman, "Leprosy in the Medieval Imaginary," *Journal of Medieval and Early Modern Studies* 38, no. 3 (2008): 560.

83. Steven Kruger, "Medical and Moral Authority in the Late Medieval Dream," in *Reading Dreams: The Interpretation of Dreams from Chaucer to Shakespeare*, ed. Peter Brown, 51–83 (Oxford: Oxford University Press, 1999), 53; Tory Vandeventer Pearman, *Women and Disability in Medieval Literature* (New York: Palgrave, 2010), 100–06; Carole Rawcliffe, *Leprosy in Medieval England* (Woodbridge, UK: Boydell, 2006), 75.

84. Sander L. Gilman, *Disease and Representation: Images of Illness from Madness to AIDS* (Ithaca, NY: Cornell University Press, 1988), 252. See also Saul Brody, *Disease of the Soul: Leprosy in Medieval Literature* (Ithaca, NY: Cornell University Press, 1974), 56–58; Fabricius, *Syphilis*, 3–5; Bryon Lee Grigsby, *Pestilence in Medieval and Early Modern Literature* (New York: Routledge, 2004), 42–44, 70–76, 157–77; Healy, *Fictions of Disease*, 133–37; Rawcliffe, *Leprosy*, 87–88.

85. The claim that Creseyde's sickness is syphilis was made by Beryl Rowland, "'The Seiknes Incurabill' in Henryson's *Testament of Cresseid*," *English Language Notes* 1 (1964): 175–77; for critiques of her argument, see Kathryn Hume, "Leprosy or Syphilis in Henrysons's *Testament of Cresseid?*," *English Language Notes* 6 (1969): 242–45; Grigsby, *Pestilence*, 98.

86. Menninghaus, *Disgust*, 229. On the medieval leper as "the most polluting of beings," see also Miller, *Anatomy of Disgust*, 154–55.

87. Kristeva, *Powers of Horror*, 1–2, 3–4.
88. Ibid., 1, 4, 71.
89. Felicity Riddy, "'Abject Odious': Feminine and Masculine in Henryson's *Testament of Cresseid*," in *The Long Fifteenth Century: Essays for Douglas Gray*, ed. Helen Cooper and Sally Mapstone, 229–48 (Oxford: Clarendon, 1997), 244, 248.
90. Riddy, "Feminine and Masculine," 240–41.
91. Ibid., 245.
92. Although, as I indicated, theories of malignant transference were not developed until the late sixteenth century, late medieval understandings of leprosy occasionally implied rudimentary notions of contagion. See Rawcliffe, *Leprosy*, 90–95.
93. Catherine S. Cox, "Froward Language and Wanton Play: The 'Commoun' Text of Henryson's *Testament of Cresseid*," *Studies in Scottish Literature* 29 (1996): 67, 71.
94. On the confusion of the points of view of Troilus and the narrator in Chaucer's poem, see A. C. Spearing, *Textual Subjectivity: The Encoding of Subjectivity in Medieval Narratives and Lyrics* (Oxford: Oxford University Press, 2005), 68–100.
95. On mimetic desire, see Rene Girard, *Deceit, Desire and the Novel: Self and Other in Literary Structure* (Baltimore: Johns Hopkins University Press, 1966). Sandra M. Hordis, "Metatextual Resistance in Henryson's *Testament of Cresseid*," in *Standing in the Shadow of the Master?: Chaucerian Influences and Interpretations*, ed. Kathleen A. Bishop, 46–64 (Newcastle: Cambridge Scholars, 2010), describes Henryson's relationship with Chaucer as a form of rivalry aimed at formulating a distinct Scots literary identity.
96. Fineman, *Shakespeare's Perjured Eye*, 24.
97. Kristeva, *Powers of Horror*, 26.
98. Pearman, *Women and Disability*, 97.
99. Jana Mathews, "Land, Lepers, and the Law in *The Testament of Cresseid*," in *The Letter of the Law: Legal Practice and Literary Production in Medieval England*, ed. Emily Steiner and Candace Barrington, 40–66 (Ithaca, NY: Cornell University Press, 2002), 41.
100. However unlikely this scenario of contagion may sound, it was not inconceivable for early modern readers. Sir Francis Kinaston's gloss on Henryson's biography dwells at length on the circumstances of the poet's death, who "being very old he dyed of a diarrhea or fluxe" (qtd. in Kindrick, *Robert Henryson*, 18). The textual proximity of this description of the poet's failing body to the description of Creseyde's illness suggests, as Healy notes, that "Creseyde is no longer just a danger to herself: Kinaston rather curiously implicates Henryson's depiction of her disease in the poet's own painful demise" (*Fictions of Disease*, 137).

101. Dubrow, *Echoes of Desire*, 163–201; on the ugly female body as a predominantly sick body in Renaissance England, see also Baker, *Plain Ugly*, 98–107.

Notes to Conclusion

1. Michael Drayton, *Idea: In Sixty-Three Sonnets*, in *The Works of Michael Drayton*, ed. J. William Hebel, 5 vols. (Oxford: Basil Blackwell, 1961), 2:310.

2. *OED Online*, 2nd ed. (Oxford University Press, 1989), s.v. "strain," n., 3.1, 1.II.4, 5, 2.II.2, 5c.

3. Christopher Warley, *Sonnet Sequences and Social Distinction in Renaissance England* (Cambridge: Cambridge University Press, 2005), 2.

4. Jacques Rancière, *The Politics of Aesthetics: The Distribution of the Sensible*, trans. Gabriel Rockhill (New York: Continuum, 2004), 13.

5. Pierre Bourdieu, *Outline of a Theory of Practice*, trans. Richard Nice (Cambridge: Cambridge University Press, 1977), 72.

6. Michel Foucault, "About the Beginning of the Hermeneutics of the Self: Two Lectures at Dartmouth," *Political Theory* 21, no. 2 (1993): 202.

7. Michel Foucault, "Nietzsche, Genealogy, History," in *Language, Counter-Memory, Practice: Selected Essays and Interviews*, ed. D. F. Bouchard, 139–64 (Ithaca, NY: Cornell University Press, 1977), 147, 162.

8. Foucault, "Nietzsche, Genealogy, History," 146.

9. Jacqueline Stevens, "On the Morals of Genealogy," *Political Theory* 31, no. 4 (2003): 581.

10. Giorgio Agamben, *The Signature of All Things: On Method*, trans. Luca D'Isanto and Kevin Atell (New York: Zone Books, 2009), 31, 64.

11. Bruce Holsinger, *The Premodern Condition: Medievalism and the Making of Theory* (Chicago: University of Chicago Press, 2005), 5.

12. Hans-Georg Gadamer, *Truth and Method*, 2nd rev. ed., trans. Joel Weinsheimer and Donald G. Marshall (London: Continuum, 2006), 362. For the notions of tradition and hermeneutic conversation, also see 110–30, 268–306, and 385–493. The usefulness of Gadamerian hermeneutics to transperiodic literary history is touched upon by James Simpson in "Diachronic History and the Shortcomings of Medieval Studies," in *Reading the Medieval in Early Modern England*, ed. Gordon McMullan and David Mathews, 17–30 (Cambridge: Cambridge University Press, 2008).

INDEX

'Abdullah Ali Sinā (Avicenna), 94
abjection, 258
Adams, Robert, 33
Aers, David, 10
Agamben, Giorgio, 274
Alençon, Francis, Duke of, 155, 157–58
'Ali ibn al-'Abbās (Haly Abbas), 94
Anjoy, Henry, Duke of, 155
anti-Petrarchism, 104–17, 129–33, 312n130
Aristotle, 94
Arran, James Hamilton, Earl of (and Duke of Châtelherault), 155
Ascham, Roger, 9
The Assembly of Ladies (Anonymous), 177, 191, 196–99, 202, 208
Auerbach, Eric, 173
Augustine, Saint, 10

Bacon, Francis, 205
Baker, Naomi, 253
Bakhtin, Mikhail M., 12–13, 17, 286n37
Bale, John, 15
Barnes, Barnabe, *Parthenophil and Parthenophe*, 19, 26–27, 75–81, 247
Barnfield, Richard, 4
Barthes, Roland, 214, 295n81
Bataille, Georges, 30–36, 39, 45, 80
Bates, Catherine, 295n66, 310n102
Baudrillard, Jean, 189–90

Beaufort, Joan, 169
Beecher, Donald, 94
begging poetry, 21, 226, 231–37
Bell, Ilona, 319n47
Berardi, Franco, 98
Berry, Edward, 123
Berthelette, Thomas, 16
black bile, 95–96
Blanchot, Maurice, 70–71, 299n122
blazons, 38–40, 67
Bloch, R. Howard, 189
Boccaccio, Giovanni, 9
Boffey, Julia, 197
Boitani, Piero, 283n17
Boleyn, Anne, 50
Bolingbroke, Henry, 212
Booth, Stephen, 251
Borch-Jacobsen, Mikkel, 123
Bothwell, James Hepburn, Earl of, 140, 142, 147–49, 151, 156, 171
Bourdieu, Pierre, 271
Bower, Walter, 167
Boyle, Elizabeth, 56, 66–67
Braden, Gordon, 2, 238, 332n2
Bright, Timothie, 95–96
Buchanan, George, 141; *Ane Detectioun of the duinges of Marie Quene of Scottes*, 139–42, 156, 162, 313n1; *Detectio*, 139
Burke, Mary E., 317n29
Burrow, John A., 289n11
Burton, Robert, 100–01, 126, 127, 130–31

Butler, Judith, 131
Butterfield, Ardis, 87, 304n31

Calin, William, 303n31
Calvinism, 57
Campbell, Marion, 128
Campion, Thomas, 178
Capellanus, Andreas, *De amore*, 188–89, 193, 203
Caxton, William, 16
Cecil, William, 141, 150, 156
Champagne, Countess of, 187
Charles, Archduke, 155
Chaucer, Geoffrey, 3, 4, 9, 19, 167; *The Book of the Duchess*, 5, 19, 85–93, 101–03, 112–13, 210, 276, 302n18, 303n27, 304n32; "The Complaint of Chaucer to His Purse," 232–33; complete works of, 16; melancholy in work of, 85, 86, 90, 101–03, 133; *Parliament of Fowls*, 190; subjectivity in work of, 85, 87–93; Surrey and, 103–05, 111–12; *Troilus and Criseyde*, 8–9, 83–84, 103, 254–55, 262
Chelidonius, Tigurinus, *Most Excellent Hystorie of the Institution and Firste Beginning of Christian Princes*, 161–62
Cheney, Patrick, 56
Christine de Pisan: *L'epistre au dieu d'amours*, 195; *Le livre de trois jugemens*, 188
Ciavolella, Massimo, 94
Clanvowe, John, *The Book of Cupid, God of Love*, 190
Coldiron, Anne, 16–17
Cole, Andrew, 6
common law, 182–83, 186–87, 193–94, 205–09, 212, 213–14, 218
complex words, 29, 290n14
Constable, Henry, 137; *Diana*, 201
Constantine of Africa, *Viaticum*, 94
Cooper, Helen, 10
Cormack, Bradin, 195, 207
Cort d'amor (Anonymous), 188
cours amoreuses (courts of love), 187–200
courtly writing: on amorous jurisprudence, 188; Chaucer and, 85–93, 101–03, 303n27; French,

89, 91–93, 101–02, 303n27; *The Kingis Quair* and, 166–67; Langland's *Piers Plowman* and, 26; Spenser's *Amoretti* and, 68; Wyatt's poetry and, 42
The Court of Love (Anonymous), 191
Crewe, Jonathan, 308n79
Crowley, Robert, 16, 25–26
cruentation, 204–05
Cummings, Brian, 15

Daniel, Drew, 96
Daniel, Samuel, 5, 9, 73, 137; *Delia*, 20, 22, 177–87, 199–200
Dante Alighieri, 9
Darnley, Henry Stewart, Lord, 140, 149, 151
death: and concept of the gift, 35–36, 52–53; in Spenser's *Amoretti*, 58, 60; in Wyatt's love lyrics, 46–47, 50, 52–54
debt, love as, 180–82
Deleuze, Gilles, 297n101
De Man, Paul, 107
Derrida, Jacques, 17, 27, 35, 40–41, 218, 289n9, 291n29
desire: in Barnes's *Parthenophil and Parthenophe*, 75–76; disgust and, 248–54, 258–67; economy of, 58, 60, 75–76; meed and, 32, 37–39; in Spenser's *Amoretti*, 58, 60, 67
Desportes, Philippe, 61, 72, 77
De Worde, Wynken, 16
Dillon, Sarah, 14
discursive memory, 12–18, 286n37
disease, in Shakespeare's sonnets, 225–54
disgust, 21, 225–26
Drayton, Michael, 5; *Idea*, 20, 177, 200–10, 214–18, 269–70
Dubrow, Heather, 54, 105, 231, 266, 309n89
Dunnigan, Sarah M., 153, 154

E. C., *Emaricdulfe*, 19, 26–27, 71–75
economics: medieval begging poetry and, 234–37; Petrarch and, 230; Shakespeare's sonnets and, 229–31, 236–37
Edward VI, 163
Eisenstein, Elizabeth L., 15

Eleanor, Queen, 187
Elizabeth, Queen, 20, 55–56, 66–67, 154–66, 186; "On Monsieur's Departure," 157–60, 165, 171–72
Elizabeth of York, 163
Elyot, Thomas, 95
Empson, William, 290n14
English medieval poetry: begging poetry, 21, 226, 231–37; law and, 209–10; literary courts of love in, 188–200; Petrarchism in relation to, 3–5, 7–9, 12–18, 237–45, 271–72, 277–79; recent scholarship on, 5–6; Shakespeare and, 221–54
English modern poetry, 1–5, 207–09
Eric XIV of Sweden, 155
Estrin, Barbara, 105

Ferrand, Jacques, 96
Ferry, Anne, 85
Ficino, Marsilio, 97, 126, 246
fin' amor, 42, 44
Fineman, Joel, 221–22, 224–25, 228, 237–39, 252, 254, 263, 283n12, 332n2
Fortescue, John, 150
Foucault, Michel, 150, 162, 197, 272–74
Fournivall, Thomas Neville, Lord, 233–34
Fradenburg, Louise Olga Aranye, 89, 168, 170
François (Dauphin), 140
Freccero, John, 238
French literature, 89–93, 101–02, 314n4
Freud, Sigmund, 98–102, 121
Froissart, Jean, Le paradis d'Amour, 90
Fuss, Diane, 215

Gadamer, Hans-Georg, 275
Galen, 94–95
Gascoigne, George, 4
Gaskill, Malcolm, 205, 215
gender: law and, 195–96, 198, 208–09, 330n69; meed linked to, 31–32, 39–40; Petrarchism and, 309n87, 309n89; in Shakespeare's sonnets, 226, 230–31, 334n22; in Surrey's Songes and Sonettes, 109–10

genealogy, 272–74
genre criticism, 54–55
Gerard of Berry, 94
gifts, 34–36, 42–54
Giles of Santarem, 94
Gilman, Sander L., 256–57
God, 30–35, 51–53
Goodrich, Peter, 188–90, 206
Googe, Barnabe, 4; Eclogues, 246–47
Gordon, Jean, 142
Goux, Jean-Joseph, 290n18
Gower, John, 3, 4, 9, 16, 167
Green, Richard Firth, 85, 189, 212–13
Greenblatt, Steven, 43–44, 51
Greene, Thomas, 1–2
Greville, Fulke, 178
Griffin, Bartholomew, Fidessa, 201
Guattari, Félix, 297n101
Guy, John, 142
Guy-Bray, Stephen, 109

Hackett, Helen, 142
Hadfield, Andrew, 86
Hall, Edward, 163
Harington, John, 130
Harris, Jonathan Gil, 14
Hasler, Antony, 232
Helgerson, Richard, 55
Heller-Roazen, Daniel, 15
Heninger, S. K., Jr., 121
Henry IV, 233
Henryson, Robert, 5, 16; The Testament of Cresseid, 21, 225–26, 254–66, 277
Henry VI, 169
Henry VII, 163, 185
Henry VIII, 42, 49, 50–51, 53, 109, 163, 185
Herman, Peter, 139, 153, 319n47
heterotopias, 197–98, 217
Hiscock, Andrew, 308n75
Hoccleve, Thomas, 5, 16, 85; Epistle to Cupid, 190, 195; "La male regle," 21, 225, 233–36, 243–45, 277
Holsinger, Bruce, 189, 275, 285n32
Holton, Amanda, 104
Howell, Thomas, 4
humors, 95–96
Hutchins, Christine E., 284n19

I. C., "Loues Accusation at the
  Judgement-seate of Reason," 176
identification, 99–101
Inns of Court, 186, 218, 325n21

James I, *The Kingis Quair*, 20, 138,
  166–74, 276
Jameson, Frederic, 11, 223–25
James V of Scotland, 139
James VI/I, 140, 205
Jardine, Lisa, 62
Ibn al-Jazzār, *Zād al-musāfir*, 94
Jesus, 49, 51–52, 65
John of Gaunt, 302n18
juries, 202, 205–06

Kantorowicz, Ernst, 162
Kaske, Carol V., 298n116
Kennedy, William, 67, 85–86, 130
Kerrigan, John, 326n37
Kerrigan, William, 2
King, John, 65
The Kingis Quair. See James I
Kitch, Aaron, 298n106
Kitzes, Adam H., 305n46
Knox, John, 151
Korsmeyer, Carolyn, 250
Krier, Theresa M., 298n108
Kristeva, Julia, 102, 108, 126, 171,
  258, 264
Kuin, Roger, 63
Kuskin, William, 16

labor, 22
Langland, William, 3, 5, 16, 18–19;
  Piers Plowman, 25–42, 44, 52, 57,
  59–61, 69–70, 276
Latour, Bruno, 13
laureates, 55
Laurentius, Andreas, 96, 97, 100, 116
law, 20, 22, 175–219; common,
  182–83, 186–87, 193–94, 205–09,
  212, 213–14, 218; *cours amoreuses*
  and, 187–200; Daniel's *Delia* and,
  178–87; gender and, 195–96,
  198, 208–09, 330n69; love and,
  177–219, 277; medieval vs.
  modern, 185–87, 199–200, 202–03,
  207–08; poetry in relation to,
  210–19; positive, 177, 183–84,

187–90, 194, 198, 203, 205;
  sanctuary and, 184–85; sovereign
  rule and, 185–86; and subjectivity,
  177
Leland, John, 15
Lemnius, Levinus, 100, 118, 126
leprosy, 255–64
Lewis, C. S., 172–73, 188
Locke, Anne, *Meditation of a
  Penitent Sinner*, 136
love, 20; in Barnes's *Parthenophil
  and Parthenophe*, 75–81; *cours
  amoreuses* and, 187–200; Daniel's
  Delia and, 178–87; as disease,
  225–67; in E. C.'s *Emaricdulfe*,
  71–75; in *The Kingis Quair*, 167,
  169–74; law and, 177–219, 277;
  in Mary Stuart's casket sonnets,
  143–45; Petrarchan, 152–53, 158,
  181, 225, 237; reward and, 43–54;
  in Shakespeare's sonnets, 227–54,
  261–62; in Sidney's *Astrophil and
  Stella*, 119; in Spenser's *Amoretti*,
  68–69; in Surrey's *Songes and
  Sonettes*, 109–14; tropes of, 22
lovesickness, 93–97, 106, 115–16,
  120, 130
Luhmann, Niklas, 252
Luther, Martin, 57
Lydgate, John, 3, 4, 5, 16, 85;
  Complaynte of a Louers Lyfe,
  20, 177, 190, 210–13; "Letter to
  Gloucester," 233; *The Temple of
  Glas*, 20, 177, 190–99, 202, 203, 208

Machaut, Guillaume de: *Le jugement
  dou Roy de Behuinge*, 188;
  Remede de fortune, 188
MacKendrick, Karmen, 248
Mair, John, 167
Malone, Edmond, 227
Marotti, Arthur, 231
Marquis, Paul, 103
marriage, 20, 22, 57, 64; Elizabeth
  and, 154–66; Mary Stuart and, 137,
  144–54, 156, 164–66; sovereign,
  138, 144–66, 171–74
Marshall, Cynthia, 253
Martial d'Auvergne, *Les arrêts d
  amour*, 188

Martin, Joanna, 168
Mary Stuart, Queen of Scots, 139–41, 147, 156, 160; casket sonnets, 5, 19–20, 135–54, 156–58, 164–66, 171–74, 276
Mary Tudor, 163
Mathews, Jana, 265
Matlock, Wendy, 196–97
Mauss, Marcel, 34–35
medieval period: law in, 185–87; modernity in relation to, 6–7, 11–14, 185–87, 199–200, 202–03, 207–08, 218–19, 237–45, 275, 278–79; subjectivity associated with, 9–12. *See also* English medieval poetry
meed, 18; in Barnes's *Parthenophil and Parthenophe*, 76–80; and desire, 32, 37–39; divine, 30–35, 52–53, 56–57, 65; economy of, 30–36, 39–42, 70; in E. C.'s *Emaricdulfe*, 74–75; gender linked to, 31–32, 39–40; in Langland's *Piers Plowman*, 26–27, 60–61, 69–70, 80–81; meanings of, 28–30, 60–61, 70; measureless, 31–36, 39–42, 45, 48–49, 52–54, 56, 59, 62–63, 67, 70–71, 75, 290n18; in medieval and Renaissance poetry, 80–81, 296n85; modern analogs to, 35–36; moral classification of, 30–32; in Spenser's *Amoretti*, 54–71; and subjectivity, 36–42; in Wyatt's love lyrics, 46–49, 52. *See also* gifts; reward
melancholy, 19; in Chaucer's work, 85, 86, 90, 101–03, 133; lovesickness in relation to, 93–97; modern view of, 97–99; pre-modern view of, 93–97, 305n46; subjectivity and, 87, 93, 97–103, 117–33; in Surrey's *Songes and Sonettes*, 105; and writing, 101–02
Meyer-Lee, Robert, 243
The Mirror for Magistrates (Anonymous), 84
modernity: medieval period in relation to, 6–7, 11–14, 185–87, 199–200, 202–03, 207–08, 218–19, 237–45, 275, 278–79; Petrarchism associated with, 2; Shakespeare's, 222–24, 227, 237–45; subjectivity associated with, 9–11
Morrison, Richard, 163
Mukherji, Subha, 209, 326n33
multitemporality, 13
murder, 200–04, 211, 213–17

Nagel, Alexander, 14
Nancy, Jean-Luc, 53
Nashe, Thomas, 127
Neely, Carol, 68
Neoplatonism, 62
Neville, William, *The Castell of Pleasure*, 191
Newman, Thomas, 178
Nietzsche, Friedrich, 274
Nolan, Barbara, 304n32
Norton, Thomas, 165–66

Origen, 161
Overstreet, Samuel A., 33

palimpsests, 14
Parker, Matthew, 154
Patterson, Lee, 238
Paxson, James, 214
Peter of Spain, 94
Petrarch: "Una candida cerva" (190), 48, 50, 52; *Canzoniere*, 114–15, 153, 176, 200; legal references in, 176; literary contribution of, 7; "Passa la nave mia colma d'oblio" (189), 110; "Qual à già i nervi e i polsi e i pensier egri" (328), 230–31; "Quel antiquo mio dolce empio signore" (360), 176, 188; *Rime sparse*, 59
Petrarchism: and anti-Petrarchism, 104–17, 129–33, 312n130; Chaucer's contribution to, 103; French, 314n4; gender and, 309n87, 309n89; genealogy of, 272–73; legal references in, 177; Mary Stuart's casket sonnets and, 137–38, 148–49, 160, 174, 314n4; medieval poetry in relation to, 3–5, 7–9, 12–18, 237–45, 271–72, 277–79; poetic language and subjectivity in, 238–45; role of, in

English poetry, 1–9; sexuality and, 137–38; Shakespeare and, 222–24, 236–37, 332n2; Sidney's *Astrophil and Stella* and, 85, 120–32, 312n130; and sovereign marriage, 157–58; and sovereign rule, 137–38; Spenser and, 55; subjectivity of, 7, 238–45, 272–73; Surrey and, 86, 103–07, 113; temporality in, 14; "Una candida cerva," 64
pharmakon (remedy/poison), 242–44
Philip II of Spain, 155
Philip of Spain, 163
Phillips, James E., 141
poetic craft: in Barnes's *Parthenophil and Parthenophe*, 78–79; in E. C.'s *Emaricdulfe*, 71, 73–74; gender, disgust, and, 253–54, 263–64; in Langland's *Piers Plowman*, 41–42; in Spenser's *Amoretti*, 55–57, 59, 61, 64–67, 69–71; in Wyatt's love lyrics, 47, 53–54
polychronicity, 13
Ponet, John, 151–52
positive law, 177, 183–84, 187–90, 194, 198, 203, 205. *See also* common law
Powell, Jason, 295n67
Prendergast, Maria, 131–32
Prendergast, Thomas A., 84
Prescott, Anne Lake, 65
printing, 15
prosopopeia, 215–16
Protestantism, 57, 161, 205
Pseudo-Aristotle, *Problems*, 94, 204–05
psychoanalysis, 97–98
Puttenham, George, 1–3, 25–26
Pynson, Richard, 16

Raleigh, Walter, 130
Rambuss, Richard, 55
al-Rāsi (Rhazes), 94
Reformation, 57
Revolt of the Northern Earls, 165
reward: economy of, 30–36, 39–42, 45, 48; meed as, 18, 26–27; sex as, 43–44, 47–48, 56; in Wyatt's love lyrics, 43–54. *See also* meed
rhetoric, 179–80

Richard II, 212
Richmond, Henry Fitzroy, Duke of, 109–10
Riddy, Felicity, 258, 260–61
Robinson, Benedict, 250

salvation, 22
Sanchez, Melissa E., 299n118
sanctuary, 184–85
Scanlon, Larry, 327n43
Schalkwyk, David, 10, 285n27
Schibanoff, Susan, 303n31
Scott-Warren, Jason, 10
self. *See* subjectivity
Selleck, Nancy, 13, 239, 319n46
Serres, Michel, 13
Sessions, William, 103, 308n75
sexuality: in Barnes's *Parthenophil and Parthenophe*, 75–80; Elizabeth and, 158–60; in Mary Stuart's casket sonnets, 144–54; meed and, 37–38; and Petrarchism, 137–38; reward and, 43–44, 47–48, 56; in Spenser's *Amoretti*, 56, 62, 68–69
Shakespeare, William, 5, 221–22; dark lady sonnets, 225–27, 245–54, 261–62, 266; Henryson's *Testament* as precursor of, 257, 260–67, 334n20; modernity of, 222–24, 227, 237–45; and Petrarchism, 222–24, 236–37, 332n2; sonnet 37, 229–31, 239; sonnet 118, 241–43; sonnet 141, 246–48; sonnet 147, 251–53; sonnet 150, 248; sonnet 154, 247; sonnets, 21, 22, 221–54, 261–62, 266–67, 277; subjectivity in sonnets of, 225, 227–54, 266–67; young man sonnets, 225, 227–37
Shershow, Scott, 36
Shrank, Cathy, 4, 136
Shultz, James, 38–39
sickness. *See* disease
Sidney, Philip, 4, 5, 9, 137, 276, 310n98; *An Apologie for Poetrie*, 83; *Astrophil and Stella*, 19, 22, 85–86, 117–33, 178, 200–01, 301n14
Siena, Kevin, 247
Simpson, James, 15, 28–29, 33, 207
Smith, D. Vance, 6

Smith, Rosalind, 157
Smith, William, *Chloris*, 201
Song of Songs, 161, 171–72
sonnet sequences, 103, 136, 157, 175–76, 186
sovereign love/marriage, 138, 144–66, 171–74
Spearing, A. C., 1–2, 38, 167
Speght, Thomas, 16, 88
Spencer, Theodor, 121
Spenser, Edmund, 4, 5, 73, 137, 276; *Amoretti*, 18, 22, 26–27, 54–71, 137, 276; *The Faerie Queene*, 56, 69, 223; *Shepheardes Calender*, 84
Staines, John D., 141
Stapleton, M. L., 299n118
Stevens, Jacqueline, 274
Stow, John, 16
Strohm, Paul, 22–23
subjectivity: and abjection, 258–59; in Barnes's *Parthenophil and Parthenophe*, 76; in Chaucer, 85, 87–93, 101–03; economy of, 45–46; Elizabeth's, 160; genealogy of, 272–73; hermeneutic understanding of, 274–75; historical continuity of, 13, 17–18; legal, 177, 182–83, 218; in Mary Stuart's casket sonnets, 137, 142–43, 150–54, 158, 166, 171–74; medieval, 5, 9–12, 236–37, 278; meed and, 36–42; melancholy and, 87, 93, 97–103, 117–33; modernity associated with, 9–11; Petrarchan, 5, 7, 111–14, 131, 238, 272, 278; of the ruler, 150–54; in Shakespeare's sonnets, 225, 227–54, 266–67; in Sidney's *Astrophil and Stella*, 85, 117–32; in Spenser's *Amoretti*, 59, 61–63; in Surrey's *Songes and Sonettes*, 103–17; in Wyatt's love lyrics, 44–46, 51–53, 76
Surrey, Henry Howard, Earl of, 1–4, 5, 19, 84–86, 276; *Songes and Sonettes*, 86, 103–17
syphilis, 22, 247, 256–57, 338n62

Tawney, R. H., 57
temporality, 13–15
Thomson, Patricia, 284n20
Thynne, William, 16, 88
Toft, Robert, *Laura*, 201
Torti, Anna, 327n43
Tottel, Richard, *Miscellany*, 19, 85–86, 103, 106, 108–09, 111–12, 117, 130
Traub, Valerie, 227
Trevor, Douglas, 305n46
Turberville, George, 4

Vendler, Helen, 224
vernacular discourse: Chaucer and, 86; love and law in, 177; medieval period and, 271–72; Shakespeare and, 226–27; Surrey and, 104, 113

Walkington, Thomas, 95, 100
Wall, Wendy, 86
Wallace, David, 284n20
Waller, Gary, 120, 309n87
Waller, Marguerite, 49
Warley, Christopher, 69, 105, 240
Watkins, John, 12
Watson, Thomas, 8, 130
Webbe, William, 3–4
Weldon, James, 26
Wells, Marion A., 94–95
Williams, Deanne, 92
Williams, Tara, 327n43
Wilson, Thomas, 139, 141, 149, 179
Wood, Christopher S., 14
Wyatt, Thomas, 1–3, 5, 8, 18, 85–86, 104, 115, 276; love lyrics of, 26–27, 42–54; "My galley charged with forgetfulnesse," 110; "Myne olde dere enmy," 176, 188; "Who so list to hounte," 48, 64, 76
Wyatt, Thomas, the Younger, 163

Zepheria (Anonymous), 56
Zimmerman, Susan, 256
Zurcher, Andrew, 186, 325n20